XML Design and Implementation

Paul Spencer

Wrox Press Ltd. ®

XML Design and Implementation

Published 1999

Reprinted Febuary 2000

wrox

Published by Wrox Press Ltd.
Arden House, 1102 Warwick Road, Acocks Green, Birmingham, B27 6BH, UK
Printed in USA
ISBN 1-861002-28-9

Trademark Acknowledgements

Credits

Author

Paul Spencer

Additional Material

Alex Homer

Managing Editors

Anthea Elston
Dominic Shakeshaft

Editors

Andy Corsham
Peter Jones

Photo Credit

Raymond Thatcher

Technical Reviewers

Richard Anderson
Michael Corning
Jim Johnson
Richard Harrison
Rick Kingslan
Benoit Marchal
Mark Oswald

Design/Layout

Tony Berry
Frances Olesch

Cover

Andrew Guillaume

Index

Marilyn Rowland
Andrew Criddle

About the Author

Paul Spencer is the founder and managing consultant of Boynings Consulting, where he operates in two main areas. He advises companies on where and how to incorporate XML into their products, reviewing existing product ranges and helping to manage implementations where necessary. He also advises companies on how to use intranets, extranets and the Internet to help manage relationships with staff, customers and suppliers, implementing solutions where appropriate. Many of the solutions developed use XML.

Before starting Boynings Consulting, Paul worked in travel distribution, running development and MIS departments. He has worked with many of the major tour operators, as well as with travel agents, airlines, technology providers and companies outside the travel industry.

Acknowlegements

I would like to thank the following people for their valuable contributions to this book:

Michael Corning, Adam Denning, Jeff Fisher, Darren Gill, David Griffiths (Panorama Holidays), Mathilde Robert (Argo Holidays), Nicola Spencer (I promised a mention in exchange for *lots* of typing price lists into the database), Phil Stradling, David Turner, and Ralf Westphal.

Thank you all.

Table of Contents

Introduction

What is this Book about?

The **Extensible Markup Language (XML)** is the most exciting development on the Internet since the World Wide Web was kicked off by the introduction of the Hypertext Markup Language (HTML). HTML took the Internet from being a text-based medium to an interactive multi-media environment. XML adds flexibility and richness to the world of data exchange on the Net.

XML and its related standards improve the Web's data exchange environment, and are helping to change the Internet into a robust medium for *structured* data transfer. XML lets different systems exchange data through agreed structures and specifications. More than that, XML transcends the world of static, linear documents by introducing an object model that lets you sort, select, and manipulate the data in documents - on the server, or on the client machine.

All this facilitates the Net's incorporation into electronic commerce applications. XML is supported by all the major Internet players, including Microsoft, IBM, Sun and Netscape. In this book, we explore how XML and its related technologies can be incorporated into multi-tier Web applications to make rich data exchange achievable. We do this by looking at the core features of XML and applying them in a realistic case study application. We aim to draw away the veils of mystery and abstraction that surround XML and show how you can use it in the real world.

Who is this Book for?

This book is designed for system developers, and for Website designers and programmers who need to know the structures, tools, and techniques associated with XML. We aim to satisfy these needs by placing XML firmly in the context of implementation of a real-world application.

To make this book accessible to the widest possible audience, I have written the case study application (which is called *Centaur*) without the use of traditional programming languages. You will not find an ActiveX control unless it is part of a standard Microsoft product, and you will not find Java code. Instead, you will find HTML and scripting. So how is this useful to current programmers? I will show you what can be done with XML without telling you how to do what you already know. You can then take away what you learn here and apply your existing knowledge to use XML in your own development environment.

So what do you need to know to get the most out of this book? Firstly, and most importantly, you need some grounding in HTML, DHTML and ASP. It would also help to know some JavaScript and VBScript. The rest is easy. Even if you are unfamiliar with these technologies, most of the code is simple enough to be accessible. All the code in the application, and the example code in the chapters, is downloadable from the Wrox Website (`www.wrox.com`).

There are two main ways that you can use this book. You can follow it from beginning to end, downloading all the code from the Wrox Website and building your own version of Centaur on your own machine. Alternatively, you can dip in to look up the specific bits of information you need. Whichever approach you choose, we aim to give a foundational working knowledge of XML in the dirty world of real-life programming.

How is this Book Structured?

This book is split into two parts. The first part acts as an XML tutorial, taking you through the standards and techniques, using examples to help you learn. We do this in the context of satisfying the requirements of the Centaur system, which we outline in Chapter 1. Many of the examples we use are taken from the case study, so we will have seen all of the important techniques by the time we examine the application in detail in the second part of the book. The second part walks us through the case study, describes the design of the system, and describes how it uses XML to achieve the system requirements.

The following two sections give a sketch of how we'll proceed through the book.

The XML Tutorial Chapters

We start in chapter 1 with a high-level description of Centaur, and sketch its system requirements. This provides the application context for the XML techniques that we'll examine in the tutorial chapters.

In Chapter 2 we put XML in brief historical context before describing its key features, and we then discuss the benefits that it brings. In Chapter 3 we introduce the important **Document Object Model** (**DOM**) concept. It is the DOM that provides us with the power to manipulate data in a consistent but highly flexible manner. In Chapter 4 we start delving into XML in more detail, seeing how to code XML before moving on to three different display techniques that we can use with XML. These three display techniques are: using **Cascading Stylesheets** (**CSS**) with XML; manipulating XML documents using the object model and scripting; and using Microsoft's databinding technology to link and display data via XML code. In Chapter 5, we look at the technology that overcomes the limitations of CSS - the **Extensible Stylesheet Language** (**XSL**). As well as describing the draft recommendation for XSL, we show how these principles are implemented in IE5. We will use several examples to show different ways in which XSL can be used, and how it can be combined with other technologies. Finally in this first section, Chapter 6 examines a number of further XML techniques that we use in the case study.

The Case Study Chapters

The first of these chapters (Chapter 7) gets 'under the hood' of the Centaur application, describing how the system works and detailing how the different code pages in the application fit together and satisfy the system requirements.

In Chapter 8, we discuss how XML combines with other technologies to present the user interface that Centaur shows to the world, and how this interacts with the other parts of the application to present the user with the information that they need.

Finally, in Chapter 9, we examine how the user interface dovetails with the server-side code and external data providers to create the complete Centaur system. In both of these final chapters, we do not look at every line of code, but instead concentrate on the significant XML-related content that binds the application together and allows it to integrate data from a variety of sources and present it to the user in a consistent way. If you want to look in detail at all of the code, you can download it from the Wrox site. Selected code is illustrated in the chapters themselves, and in Appendix B.

About the Case Study

What does the system do? The Centaur user can search descriptions of vacations. These descriptions are derived from tour operator systems, but are stored locally by Centaur. When they search through this information, the user specifies a variety of criteria, and Centaur produces a short-list of vacations that meet their needs. Once they have this information, the user can request more detail on selected vacations and add them to a customized brochure, which they can save and browse off-line. Once a vacation has been chosen, the user will be able to get a price from the tour operator and make a booking.

Centaur is a system for booking packaged vacations (known as package holidays in the UK) over the Internet. There are several such systems around, so what does Centaur bring that is new? Firstly, it combines vacation packages from several operators on a single, searchable system. Secondly, you can see the details of the vacations, then get quotations and book *directly* over the Internet. Both of these features are unusual at the time of writing, but will quickly become more common. It is XML that enables us to implement these novel features.

Centaur drives a Web browser at the client end, and interfaces to tour operator systems which provide information and transactional capabilities. Vacation brochure information is held within Centaur, and can be searched. The transactional aspects of quotation and booking are carried out by the tour operators' own systems. The interface to external tour operator systems will be defined as part of the project, and we will simulate these within Centaur.

What Support Do I Get?

As we've already said, you can download all the sample code for this book, and the complete Centaur application to install on your own server, from the Wrox Website. Details of this process are given in Appendix A.

This book is also covered by the usual Wrox support mechanisms - see Appendix I.

Conventions Used In this Book

We have used a number of different styles of text and layout in the book to help differentiate between the different kinds of information. Here are examples of the styles we use and an explanation of what they mean:

Advice, hints and background information comes in this type of font.

Important pieces of information come in boxes like this.

Bullets appear indented:

- **Important Words** are in a bold type font
- Words that appear on the screen, in menus like the File or Window, are in a similar font to that which you see on screen
- Keys that you press on the keyboard, like *Ctrl* and *Enter*, are in italics

Code has several fonts. If it's a word that we're talking about in the text – for example, when discussing the `For...Next` loop – it's in a bold font. If it's a block of code that you can type in as a program and run, then it's also in a gray box:

```
Response.Write("Hello World")
```

Sometimes you'll see code in a mixture of styles, like this:

```
<%
  Dim strLastName
  strLastName = Request.Form("LastName")
  Response.Write("Your surname is " & strLastName)
%>
```

The code with a white background is code we've already looked at and that we don't wish to examine further.

And Next...

Now that we have sketched the shape of the book, let's begin by taking a look at the requirements of the Centaur system. Once we have established what these are, we can move on and see how XML fits into the picture of how we satisfy them.

1

Introducing the Centaur Case Study

Introduction

In this chapter, we will take a more detailed tour of the Centaur system that is the subject of the application case study. By the end of the chapter, you will:

- understand something about the market that Centaur is addressing
- understand the aims of the system
- understand some ways in which it differs from a commercially viable system
- know the basic structure and functions of the system
- know where XML is used within the system

Capturing Requirements

Some years ago, I heard of a software house developing a large and complex system for a customer. This was the biggest system they had ever undertaken, and they delivered it to the specification, on time and on budget. At the end of the year, they celebrated this as the best project they had undertaken all year. And what happened to the system? The customer decided that the system performance (which had been excluded from the specification to save time in negotiations) was inadequate, threw it away and started again with an in-house development team.

On another occasion, a joint venture was established to develop a new industry-wide system. The project ran for a year, then there were rumours of problems. The consortium comprised industry suppliers and the developers of their technology, but the industry traditionally sold through agents, and the agents had not been involved. When they were asked, the views of the major agents ranged from indifference to the project to antipathy since the system did not meet their needs, and would be more expensive and harder to use than the supposedly outdated technology they already had.

Why do such projects fail? In nearly twenty years of running development teams, I have never known a project to fail because of the incompetence of the developers. Instead, they fail because of poor management, poor requirements, or failure to involve all parties affected by the system.

Why am I telling you this? I have consulted various interested parties while designing and developing Centaur, but since this is not a book about project management or development methodologies, you will only see the results in the product itself, not as documentation in this book. The design method I used is typical of iterative rapid application development, but too many people see this as an excuse not to collect proper requirements and not to define their system. By all means keep your methodology light, but don't ignore it altogether. So I would like to make it clear, that although the case study in this book lacks some features that would be needed in a full commercial implementation, which I will indicate, it nonetheless fulfils a defined set of initial requirements, as we shall see soon.

Background

The diagram below shows the traditional model for buying vacations in the UK:

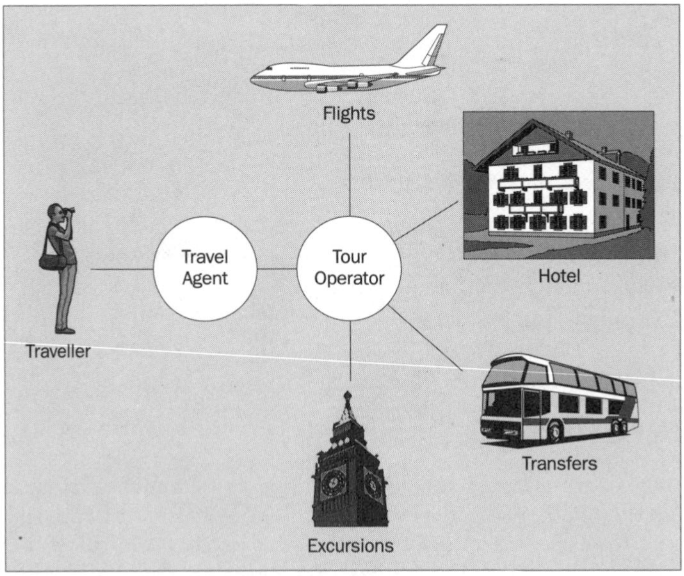

In recent years, this model has been changing, with tour operators buying up travel agents and charter airlines to provide a vertically integrated market. Up until now, these vertically integrated companies have sold seats on their airlines to other tour operators, and provided shelf space for their competitors' brochures in their travel agencies.

Now the market is changing. Investigations by the UK government and consumer organisations have shown that the major companies are starting to use their power to push their own products through their agencies. The smaller tour operators are starting to worry about their seat allocations on the charter airlines. The 1998 survey[1] shown below indicated that twice as many agents think that independent tour operators will be squeezed out by the major tour operator groups as think they won't.

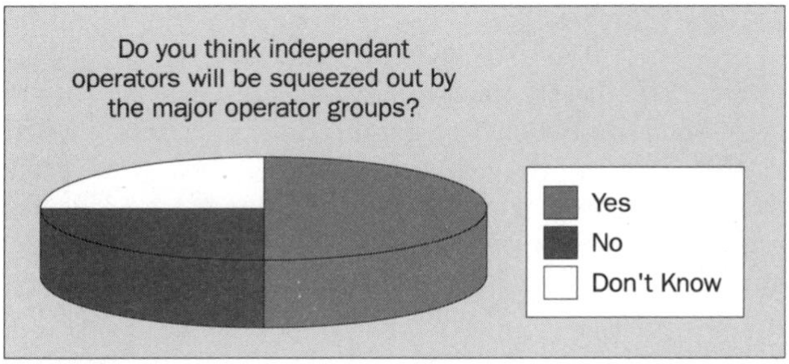

The trend seems set to continue, to the point that the vertically integrated travel agencies are likely to be re-branded under the tour operator name and cease all pretence of being independent. This will divide the market into two – the major tour operators with strong branding and a good high street presence and the smaller, independent, tour operators selling through independent travel agents.

At the same time, we have new distribution channels. Although the complexity of travel products means it has taken some time, the large tour operators are starting to sell through the Internet. Then the likes of Microsoft Expedia (`http://expedia.msn.com/daily/home/default.hts`) are expanding from the scheduled market to packaged vacations. Who will they be talking to – the top few operators or Mom and Pop Tours? You guess. It goes on, with portal sites seeing travel as a major market area.

Oh dear, who would be an independent tour operator? Then it gets worse. In the diagram earlier, there is clearly an intermediary too many in the loop. Why have both a tour operator and a travel agent in the supply chain when selling through the Internet? While the tour operator can sell direct, the independent agents could start putting bespoke tours together using bookable sites available on the Internet. Currently, the commercial model, where tour operators use their buying power to get good discounts, may make this uncompetitive, but I would not want to base my future on this situation lasting.

Once the top few tour operators are selling through the Internet, what chance have the rest got of people even visiting their sites? Unable to compete on advertising expenditure, they will be relying on word of mouth for future business.

But wait! Isn't the Internet meant to make it easy for the small guys to look as impressive as the majors? Well, maybe on static sites, but providing facilities for booking complex products is expensive, and anyway, why should someone visit a site only covering vacations in Corfu when they can go to one covering the world?

[1] Survey by The Network, published in the Travel Trade Gazette 9/9/98.

Enter Centaur. Centaur works on a model where the tour operator stays in the loop, and addresses the issues of cost and visibility by operating with a wide range of tour operators. Whether the vacations are booked directly by the public or through travel agents is a political question which I can conveniently ignore for the sake of this demonstration system. Another major part of the business model is that many of these tour operators are specialists and so are not competing directly with each other. While a Corfu specialist and a Caribbean specialist may both be after the same traveler's wallet, they are likely to see the benefit of co-operating as outweighing the disadvantages.

Let's come back for a moment to the direct vs. travel agent question. When we are talking about the Internet, aren't we meant to be talking about new paradigms? How about a "vacation café" on the model of the Internet café? Or supermarkets building coffee lounges with terminals connected to Centaur and a few experts around to help people book their vacations? Here I am, making a couple of dollars from your buying this book (you *did* buy it, didn't you?), and giving you ideas for making millions. I hope you remember me in your will.

So Centaur allows many tour operators to share a single system while maintaining their own branding. Centaur will cover vacations all over the world for all seasons of the year. Because it will have so many companies using it, it can afford to advertise and will be big enough to compete with the major tour operators' web-based systems. It will provide integrated searching, allowing the traveler or agent to find the perfect vacation, regardless of the tour operator, then book on-line. It will be available from the home, and possibly through a new model for travel booking through supermarkets, cafés, banks and wherever. Suddenly Mom and Pop are competing on equal terms.

Centaur Description

This diagram shows how Centaur fits into the booking environment to allow booking of tour operators.

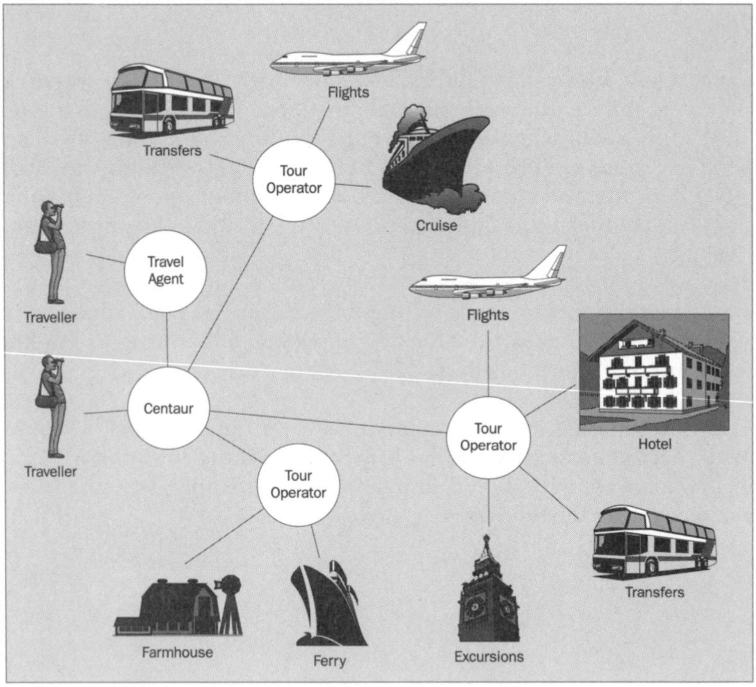

In principle, the system can be used for either direct sales or sales through agents. For direct sales, the system can be financed through a booking fee taken from the revenue that would normally be paid to the agent as commission. For sales through agents, it is less obvious where the funding comes from. The only direct payment saved is the fee paid to the value added networks that currently connect agents to tour operators. In practice, agents may still want the security of such a network. So the revenue for Centaur has to be generated by savings elsewhere or the ability to charge more to the client.

In operation, Centaur collects brochure descriptions of vacations from the tour operators and stores and indexes these. The traveler then conducts a search of this database, and gets a list of vacations meeting his or her needs. It is then possible to refine the search or get more information on selected vacations. Searching is branded as Centaur, but individual vacation descriptions carry the tour operator's branding.

Once a vacation has been selected, Centaur collects information about the number of travelers and opens a conversation with the tour operator system to allow quotation, availability checking and booking. The booking appears as "direct" with the tour operator, Centaur operating as an intelligent gateway rather than a travel agent:

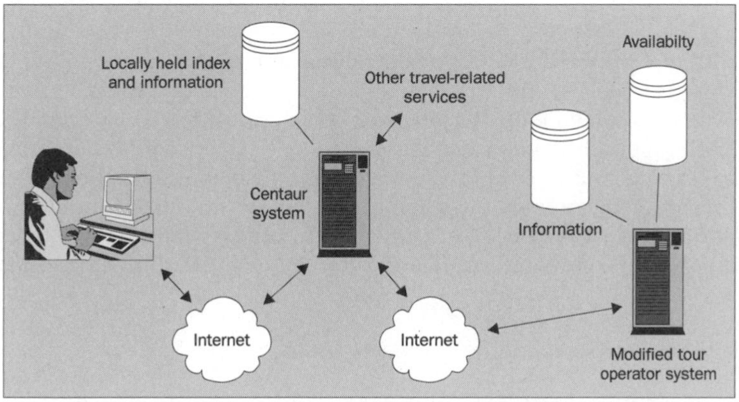

This diagram shows the opportunity for selling additional services, either directly or by linking into other sites. These services would include insurance, guides, maps and other travel accessories. These additional services, along with advertising, would generate additional revenue for a commercial system, but are not relevant to the use of XML and so will not be included in the demonstration system.

The Aims of Centaur

Centaur is being developed for a variety of purposes. Firstly, it is clear from the above that a system like this is needed in the travel industry. The threat from major tour operators is to small companies, and these are often so heads down that they do not address the threat, or they are so unaware of what technology could do for them that they cannot see the solution. As a demonstration system, Centaur is designed to increase awareness of the possibilities for this group by showing them a real working prototype.

Secondly, it is being developed as a prototype for a production system. Most systems users and purchasers cannot easily express what they want until they see something different. In other words, it is easier to say what is wrong with something you can see than it is to specify requirements on a blank sheet of paper. Centaur provides the initial writing on the paper, and, as such, is a system waiting to be shot down as "not what we need".

As a consultant in XML, I spend time developing little prototype systems to help people become aware of the possibilities of the technology. With a new technology that many of those who could benefit have never heard of, this is essential to business development. Centaur is such a system, but on a bigger scale.

The fourth aim is a bit of a personal one. As a contributor to the discussions within the United Nations on using XML as a mechanism for electronic data interchange (EDI), I have come across people who are very good at playing devil's advocate. One point I have heard made is that it is impossible to use XML as a trading language without being a Java programmer. Some books on XML support this view by leaping straight into Java code even to display information. If such programming is necessary, XML becomes unavailable to web site developers and others who do not have a programming background, but have become familiar with scripting languages. The aim of Centaur is to demonstrate that powerful web-based applications can be developed in XML using only standard scripting languages.

And the fifth aim is to provide a case study for this book.

These aims conflict to some degree. The requirement for the book is to maximise the variety of ways in which XML is used, while minimising any parts of the system that do not require XML. Hence the elimination of payment mechanisms, which are complex, well catered for with existing products and would contribute little to this book. I am also restricting myself to scripting languages, which could result in a commercial system hitting performance problems in some areas. Of course, this is one of the benefits of a prototype – Centaur will indicate those areas where a commercial system needs some performance enhancements.

Differences from a Commercial System

I have already said that the case study differs from a commercial system by excluding a payment mechanism. There are other areas where there is little benefit in implementing complex business logic when trying to demonstrate the use of XML.

The first is in the direct sell versus travel agent model. Requirements here are different. A travel agent would need to log in and be recognised so that commission can be paid. The tour operator system itself would track commissions due and make payments, so adding this functionality is purely a matter of one or two additional screens and additional messages between Centaur and the tour operator system.

Centaur will include a search capability as that is a key part of the requirement. However, this can be kept simple, since complex searches merely require more complex logic. For this reason, the range of vacation types is also limited (for example, no account is taken of ferry travel or multi-centre vacations). Most commercial travel systems on the Internet use a keyword search mechanism. I would like to see this supplemented with the sort of free format "I want to go somewhere hot near a golf course in August" searches that are familiar to Microsoft Office users.

The other major area of complexity is when the user wants to cancel or change a vacation booking. In practice, tour operators have different ways of handling these events, and would almost certainly prefer to do this over the phone rather than over the Internet so they can explain the cancellation charges that will be applied and discuss whether insurance covers these.

A commercial system would include not only vacations, but also the travel ancillaries such as the insurance, guide books and maps that I mentioned before. In the UK, tour operators insist that the traveler has adequate insurance taken out at the time of booking. The user will therefore either have to take out a policy through the tour operator, or provide details of existing insurance. This would be an opportunity for the Centaur operator to earn commission by linking through to a preferred insurance supplier.

And finally, remember the system is simplified. There are no queuing mechanisms and no transactional controls – familiar areas of commercial systems and well catered for with existing products. The aim is to expose the XML, not teach you the details of complex transactional systems. Similarly, there are no pretty graphics to get you into the vacation mood. Just one logo and boring text and grey buttons as this simplifies the appearance of the scripts, all of which are included in the downloadable files, and much of which is discussed in more detail in later chapters. Doubtless you will spot some of the other areas where there is a need for more error checking or other enhancements.

Well actually, that wasn't "finally" at all. By far the most important difference is that Centaur relies on the facilities of Microsoft Internet Explorer version 5 – a browser that has only just been released at the time of publication. This would probably limit the system to less that 5% of its available market in the short term. Unfortunately, a real commercial system at the moment would have much of the client-side XML stripped out. It would be replaced by a combination of server-side processing (for example where XSL is used to display vacation details) and more conventional mechanisms in other areas.

Up until now, I have used the term Centaur for both the demonstration and commercial systems. From here on, I am discussing the demonstration system unless I need to point out how a commercial system would differ.

So What Does Centaur Do?

I have already described Centaur as the middle tier of a three tier system for booking package vacations. What is a three tier system? It is usually described as a system that incorporates display logic in one system (the browser), business logic in another (the middle tier) and database services in a third tier (the server tier):

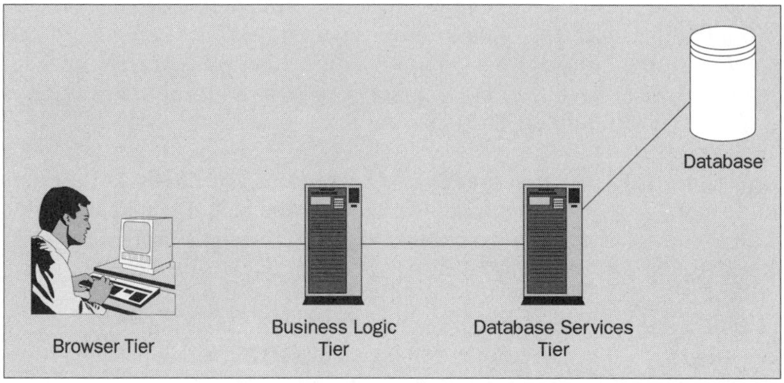

As was shown in the diagram earlier, Centaur uses a slightly different model, combining business logic with a simple database in the middle (Centaur) tier, and using existing tour operator systems, which include both databases and business logic, as the server tier. There are two reasons for this approach. The first is that a vendor-independent search is simpler, quicker, more reliable and uses less network bandwidth if it is conducted on a single server. It's simpler because all the information is held locally in a consistent format, quicker and lower bandwidth because there is no need to interrogate other servers. And it's also more reliable since everything is held on a single server, which could have any degree of fault tolerance required, rather than on multiple remote servers, the failure of any one of which, or the network in between, would limit the value of the search.

The second reason is that, when we look at the functionality of the tour operator systems, they generally do not have the facilities for supplying vacation details. They tend to be old systems that manage only the transactional elements. This is why most multi-vendor on-line booking systems currently operating don't show any detailed information about the vacations. Typically, the information found in the brochure is held in a variety of word processor documents, spreadsheets and databases and only comes together at the publisher. So for Centaur, we will have to collect this information once only and hold it in the local database. This will ease implementation for the tour operator at the expense of increasing the size and complexity of the Centaur database.

So Centaur itself holds a database with information about the tour operators, their vacation destinations and individual vacations. The user can search for a vacation based on information about both the destination and the hotels (or villas or whatever) there. In general, we will use the terms "tour" and "vacation" and there is no reason why Centaur should not be used for cruises and other sorts of vacation as well.

A Brief Tour of Centaur

The diagram that follows shows typical navigation round the system. Of course, being an internet-based system, the user can go backwards and forwards as he or she pleases:

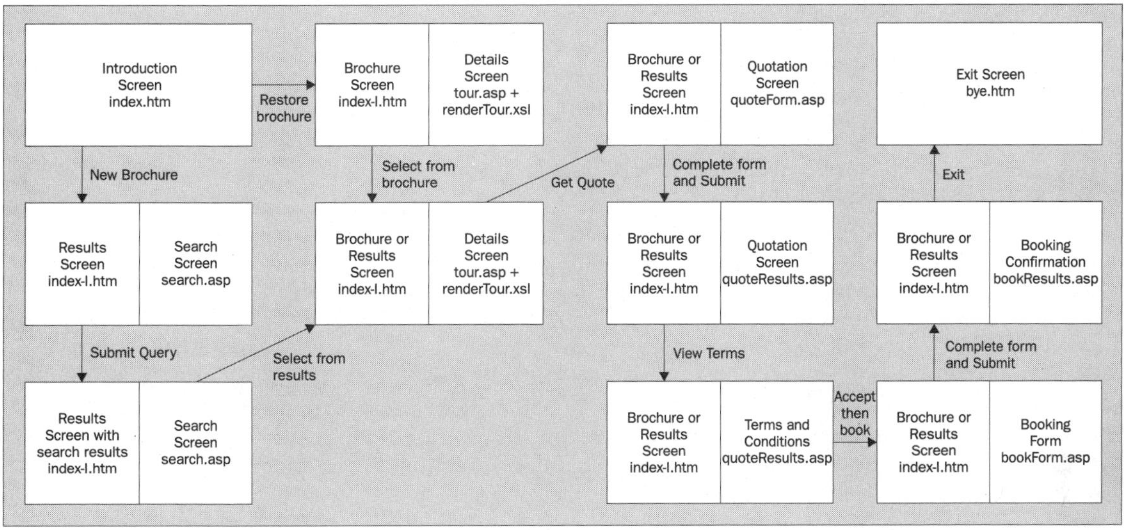

Let's now walk through the process that the diagram illustrates.

Welcome to Centaur!

When you log into the system (remember that you can build a copy of Centaur on your own machine – see Appendix A) you should see this screen:

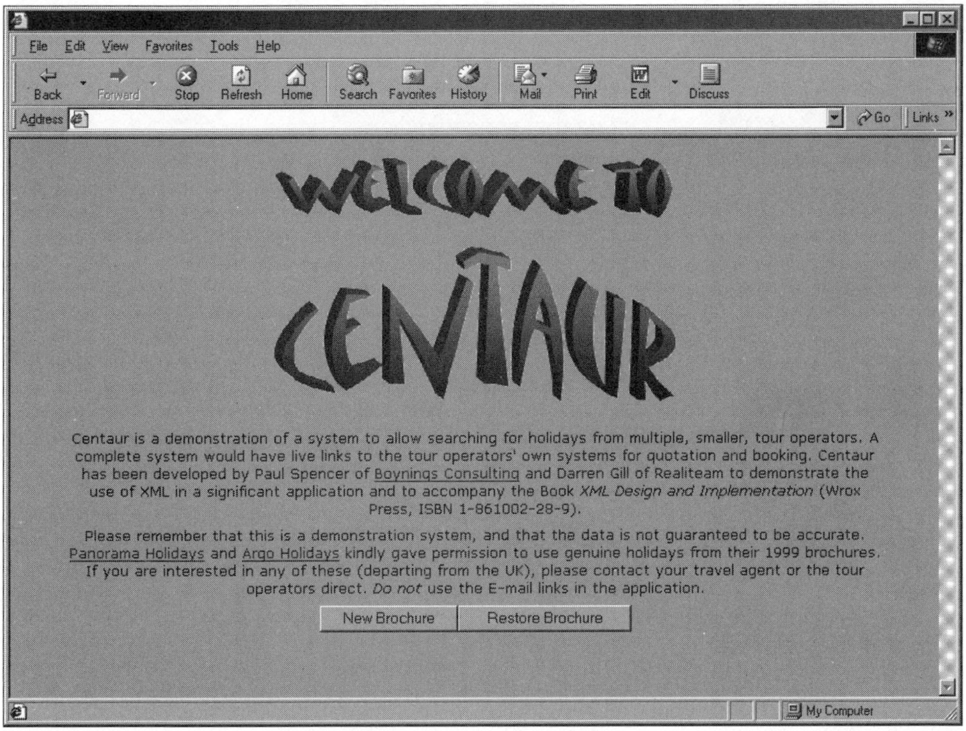

As you can see, this welcome page tells you a little about the system and this book. In a commercial venture, I would expect all pages to make far more use of graphics (especially to get rid of those horrible grey buttons, which are used all over the application simply because using something better would not add anything to the XML aspects). This screen could also include advertising and links to other travel-related products such as insurance and books.

Finding and Displaying the Vacations

Suppose you click on the button to open a new brochure. This will take you to the main search screen, from which you can select vacations based on the type of vacation you want, where you want to go and the facilities you would like either on site or close by. If you select some criteria and submit the search, you will get one of three results. You could get no matches at all, which is quite likely as there are only fifteen vacations in the system database. You could get so many vacations that the search results would be confusing. In this case, you will get a message and the opportunity to see the results anyway or refine your search criteria. Of course, with fifteen vacations, this is not going to be the case, so the limit of the number of vacations to display before sending this message has been set artificially low at ten. You will get this result if you do not set any criteria before searching, or if you search for all Mediterranean vacations.

Of course, the result we want is a limited number of vacations as shown here:

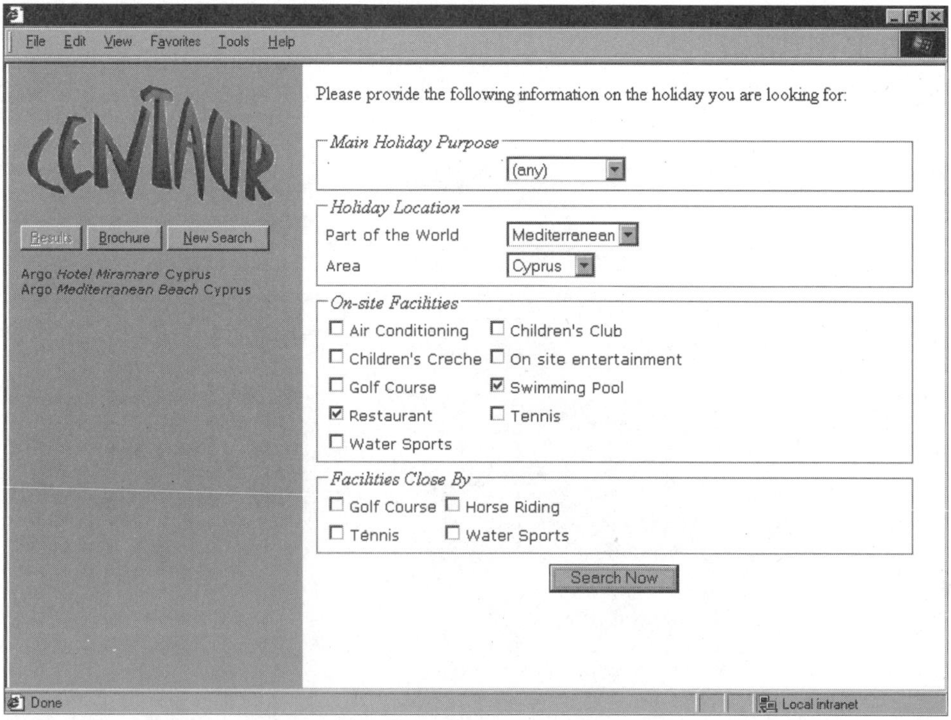

Clicking on either of the vacations listed in the left frame will show its details in the right frame. The information displayed is similar to that available in a tour operator's brochure. However, a brochure gives much more freedom to vary the layout from page to page. I have limited the tour operator to one photo of the resort and one for the individual vacation. If they want more, they have to create a montage. Here is the page for a vacation in Hammamet, Tunisia:

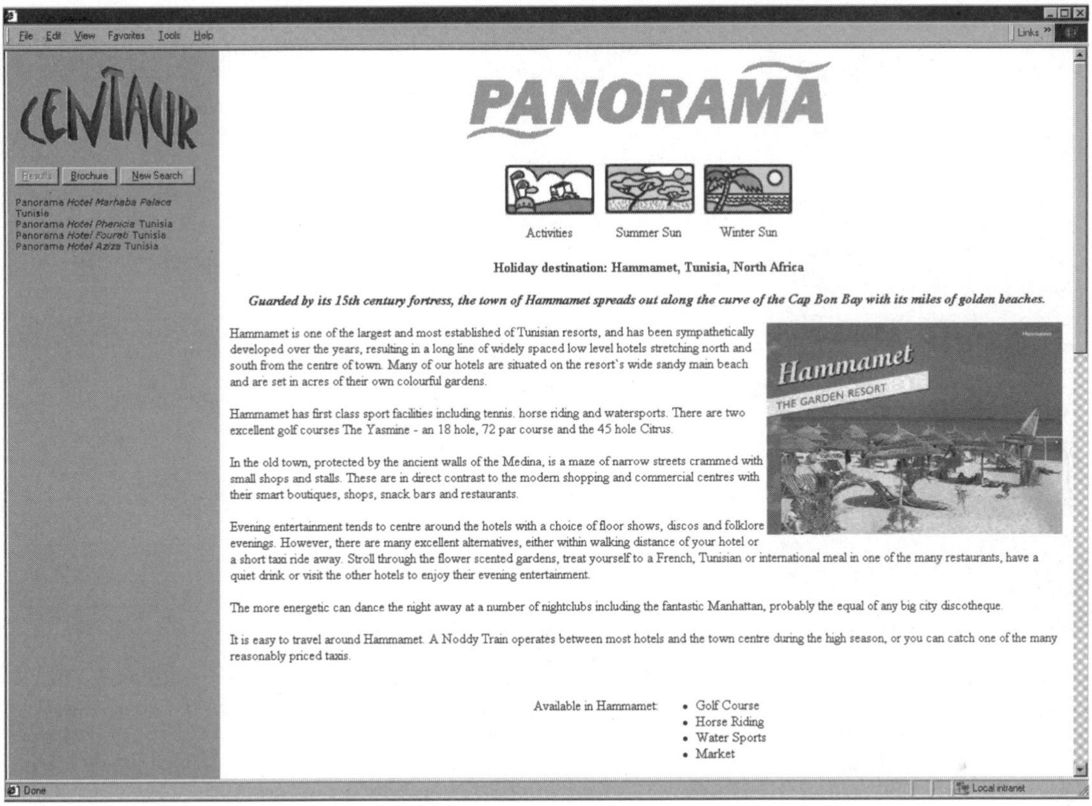

As I have it all resorts will be shown in the same format, but in the real world each tour operator will have a corporate image. One option would be to use my page layout as a standard, but develop individual styles for different companies as an extra-cost option. We will explore the ways that we might achieve this in Chapters 4 and 5.

Using the Brochure

What if you are at home viewing these vacations during the day and you see several you like that you would like to show the rest of your family later? Rather than write them down and search for them again, it would be good if you could save them in your own electronic brochure. Obviously, the brochure needs be saved and restored, so that you do not have to start from scratch if you come back to the system later. In the demonstration, the brochure is saved as a cookie on the client system, which will be wiped after 30 days (so make sure you have cookies enabled when you access the system!). We will see how to do this in Chapter 6.

There are advantages and disadvantages of this approach that will be discussed when we look at the brochure in more detail.

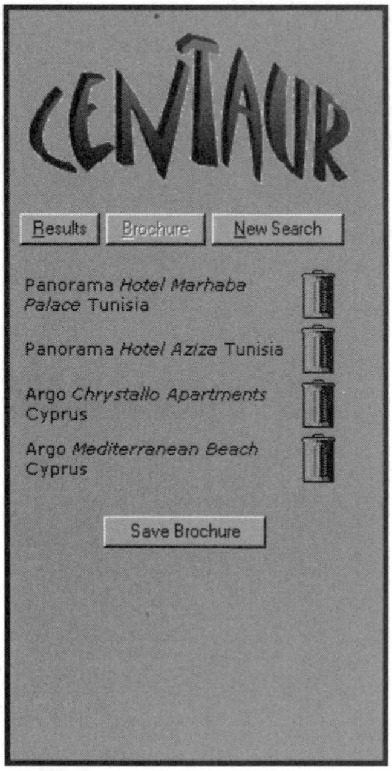

An advantage of the electronic brochure is that you can conduct further searches with different criteria and add more vacations to the brochure. This saves having to provide complex Boolean searching such as looking for a vacation in either Majorca or Cyprus, but nowhere else in the Mediterranean. The user should be able to view this brochure at any time and see the same details of the vacations as they did for the original search.

Care has been taken in the design of Centaur to ensure that the brochure is also accessible off-line. If you switch your browser to off-line mode (File | Work Offline), you will still be able to retrieve the brochure. This is particularly valuable where you are paying for online charges, either through your telecomms company or Internet Service Provider, as it allows you to browse at your leisure without incurring costs. This is more the atmosphere a tour operator would want while you are choosing your vacation.

Getting a Quotation

Once you have found a vacation you are interested in, the next step is to get a quotation. Centaur has a screen that will allow you to complete a form showing the start date and duration of your vacation and the number of adults, children and infants that you are booking for. From here, you can go back to the vacation details, but you are more likely to want to submit the information and get the quotation.

A fully commercial Centaur would, at this point, submit this information to the tour operator system to check availability and get an up to date price. It would be possible to calculate the price from the price tables, but tour operators may change prices without updating Centaur, so it is better to get the information directly from a system that we know will be kept up to date. This gives us both access to current availability and protects us from the situation that an airline got into in the early days of the Internet when it was prosecuted and fined for having out of date prices on its web site.

In the demonstration system, the tour operator system is simulated using a random number generator within Centaur, so the price you get will bear no relation to the brochure price.

Once you have submitted the form, you will see your quotation:

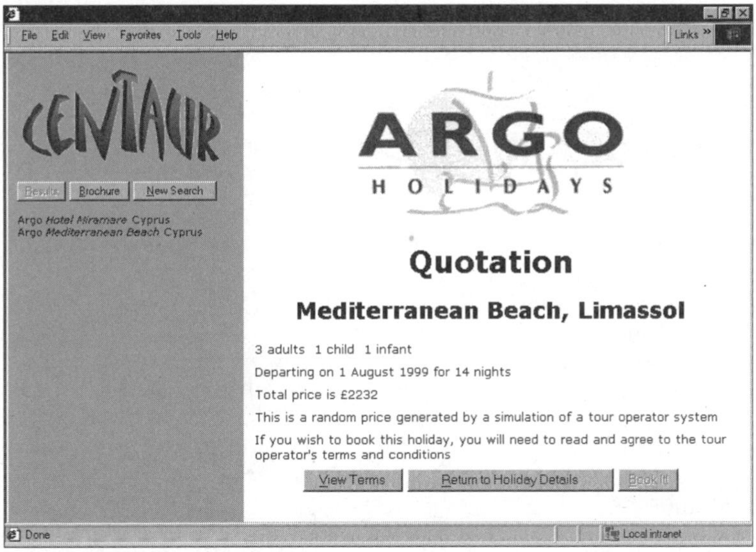

You can see that you have three options from here. Well, actually two, as we are not going to let the user book the vacation until they have accepted the supplier's terms and conditions.

So, assuming you want to go ahead and book, you can click to view the terms, then accept these. This will return you to the screen above, as well as enabling the booking option.

Making the Booking

The booking form is pre-populated with the details of the vacation chosen. There are also fields that can be filled in to specify a contact traveler, and for any others travelling with you.

After submitting the form, the user will get a confirmation screen for the booking:

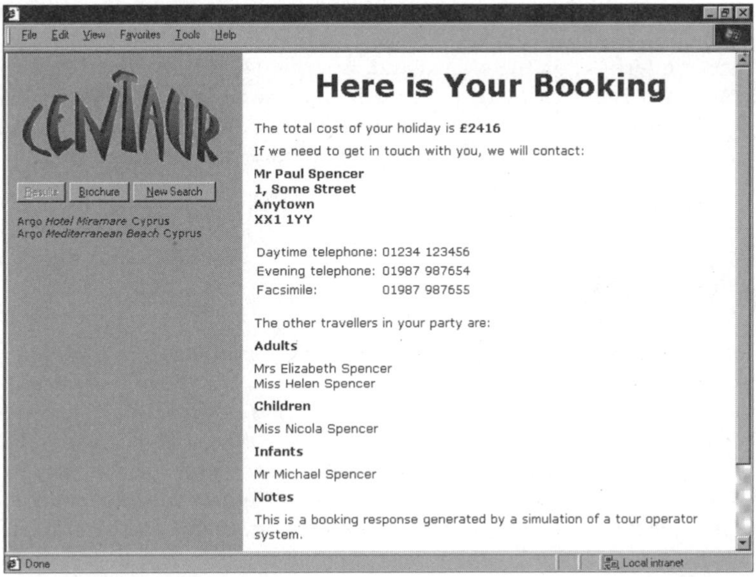

And that is it. At the bottom of the screen (out of shot) is an Exit button. Clicking on this will take the user to an exit screen, from which they can get back into the main Centaur search screen using the startup option (new or existing brochure) used initially.

The Use of XML in Centaur

The two main uses of XML are for data interchange and for separating content from style when rendering pages for display. As a case study, it is clearly important that Centaur demonstrates both. The diagram shows where this is done:

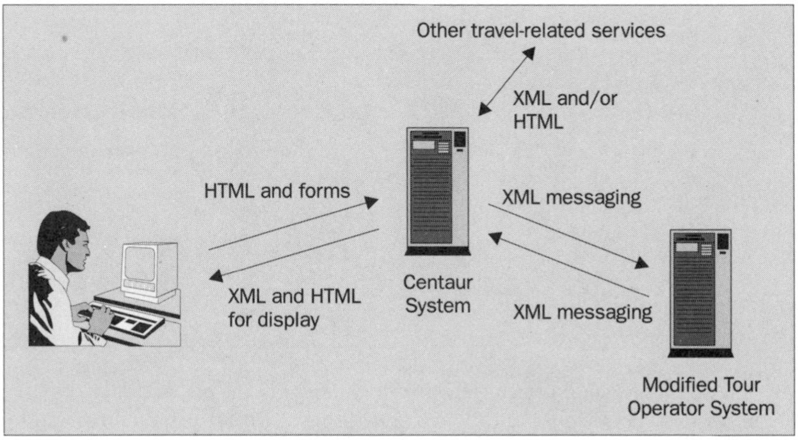

The interface between Centaur and the tour operator system is clearly a messaging interface, and so can benefit from the use of XML as a data interchange technology. As such, it will require a DTD so the parser can be used to validate messages. This is a design decision that has an alternative. By enforcing a standard XML interface on all tour operators, I am forcing them to develop new front-ends to their systems. In a commercial environment, issues such as this generate power plays, with the possibility of some tour operators being able to say that their presence is necessary to the commercial viability of Centaur, and so I should interface to their proprietary interface. Should a particular tour operator wish to stick with their own proprietary DTD if necessary we can accommodate this by converting it using the transformations possible with XSL.

The user interface, on the other hand, is largely a display-based system that could be built quite adequately using HTML. However, XML has some real benefits in this environment, which I shall indicate as I build the interface. There are places where I use XSL to display pages, and places where I use the DOM and JScript. All these techniques are described in subsequent chapters.

The brochure is also stored as an XML text string in a cookie.

The Vacations

Centaur is designed to search for and display vacations from multiple tour operators. It would obviously make the system more realistic if we were to use real vacations rather than make them up. So, many thanks to two UK tour operators – Panorama Holidays and Argo Holidays – that have allowed me to use material from their Winter 1998/99 and Summer 1999 vacation brochures. These tour operators fit the Centaur profile well – Argo specialises in vacations to a single location – Cyprus, while Panorama has a few brochures, both to specific locations such as Tunisia and for specialist vacations such as golfing vacations. So, thanks to them, we can look at real vacations in Centaur.

Summary

This chapter has been very much about the background to the case study, and the process of user interaction with the system. You should now understand:

- some of my views on software development
- a bit about recent changes in the UK leisure travel industry
- the aims of Centaur and the conflicts between those aims
- some of the changes that would be necessary to turn Centaur into a commercial system
- what Centaur does and how it uses XML

We also now have a list of the basic functional requirements for our application. It must:

- be able to interface with, and retrieve up-to-date data from, tour operator information databases based on search criteria the user specifies
- be able to collate that data into an integrated, sorted data set
- allow the user to select a subset of the vacations information from the data set, and persist that on the off-line client machine as a personalized brochure
- allow the user to select a vacation from the brochure, get a quotation, and if they want to, book it

In the next chapter we will take a look at XML and why it provides the means to satisfy these requirements in a comparatively straightforward manner, without the need for complex format conversion components.

2

XML Overview

Imagine a world where all information is stored in a way that enables it to be indexed, found and combined in a common format. Where, when you want to trade electronically with a new company, you can be sure you are using compatible systems. Where links between web sites are never broken. Where complex web sites are easy to maintain. Utopia? Perhaps, but this is the promise of XML. Not because it is necessarily the best technology in all cases, but because there are many applications where its use approaches the ideals above. Owing to this it is rapidly becoming the standard for marking up structured data for use over intranets and the Internet.

In this chapter, we will start to explore how XML fits into the world of the Internet. We will see where it is similar to, and how it differs from, HTML, see some examples of how XML can provide benefits over HTML, and look at the standard itself.

By the end of this chapter, you will understand:

- why XML was developed and its relationship to HTML
- the main classes of application where XML is useful
- the fundamentals of the XML specification, including the use of the Document Type Definition
- what XML namespaces are and why they are needed

What's Wrong with HTML?

The Hypertext Markup Language (HTML) is an example of a **markup language**. Markup is simply a way of adding meaning to data. In the case of HTML (and XML), that data is text. A markup language is a set of rules that defines and limits the markup that can be used. For HTML, these rules indicate that the additional meaning is encompassed in text that is included within tags. The tags themselves are delimited by angle brackets. This is simply a fairly formal description of something you already know.

With HTML, most tags relate to how a document should be laid out on the screen. We all know additional tags, such as the anchor tag, `<A>`, often used to describe a link, and the meta tag `<META>` used to provide extra information. However, the key to HTML is that the tag set is fixed, and this allows people to develop browsers that can interpret the tags and hence lay out a page according to the page designer's wishes.

HTML is a wonderful technology. What else could be so simple, yet so powerfully enable rapid exchange of formatted information over the World Wide Web? But as the Web has grown, it has hit problems of complex page design, broken links, disastrous searching and an inability to support inter-company electronic trading. The technology has tried to keep up by developing JavaScript, Java applets, ActiveX, Active Server Pages, Dynamic HTML and so on, but the result is added complexity, while the problems are still there for all to see.

In this chapter we will see that XML is conceptually simpler than HTML while being more powerful and, with its related standards, resolving many of the problems of data exchange over the Web.

How Does XML Help?

The secret of XML is in the X. The language is extensible in that it does not have a fixed set of tags as HTML does. In fact, it has a misleading name in that XML is not a markup language at all. Technically, it is a **metalanguage**, a language that describes or defines another language. Earlier, we saw that a markup language is a set of rules for how we can use markup. A markup metalanguage is a set of rules for defining markup languages. In the case of XML this means it is a framework for designing markup languages.

This means that we can use XML to develop markup languages that are specific to an application, a technology or an industry. Often, we will not consciously create a language - we can just use any tag names we like ad hoc. However, if we wish to inter-operate with others, we need to create standards across an industry or for use with a specific technology. These standards create a specific markup language by defining the tags and how they can be used.

There are already many examples of languages derived from XML. If you use Internet Explorer, you will be familiar with **channels**. These use a language called the **channel definition format**, or CDF, which is an XML language. In this case, CDF was defined before XML was fully standardized, and so currently is not quite XML compliant. Other languages are being, or have been, developed for specific technologies. The Synchronized Multimedia Integration Language (SMIL - pronounced "smile") is an XML language and is used to synchronize multimedia streams being delivered over the Internet. It will, for example, allow the developer to specify that a certain sound should start ten seconds after the start of a video clip.

So there is one source of the power: XML allows us to define our own tags – it is not limited by a fixed tag set. Therefore, while HTML restricts us to displaying information, XML allows us to mark up information in any way we like to suit whatever data exchange needs we have. An example will help to illustrate this.

An Example of XML in Use

Let me start with a single example of how XML can be used, and why it suits this particular application. As we go through the book, we will introduce others.

My professional background is in travel technology, and we will see examples where I use this background later. However, my true love is dinghy racing, so I will use that for this example.

Here is a web page that describes a dinghy class:

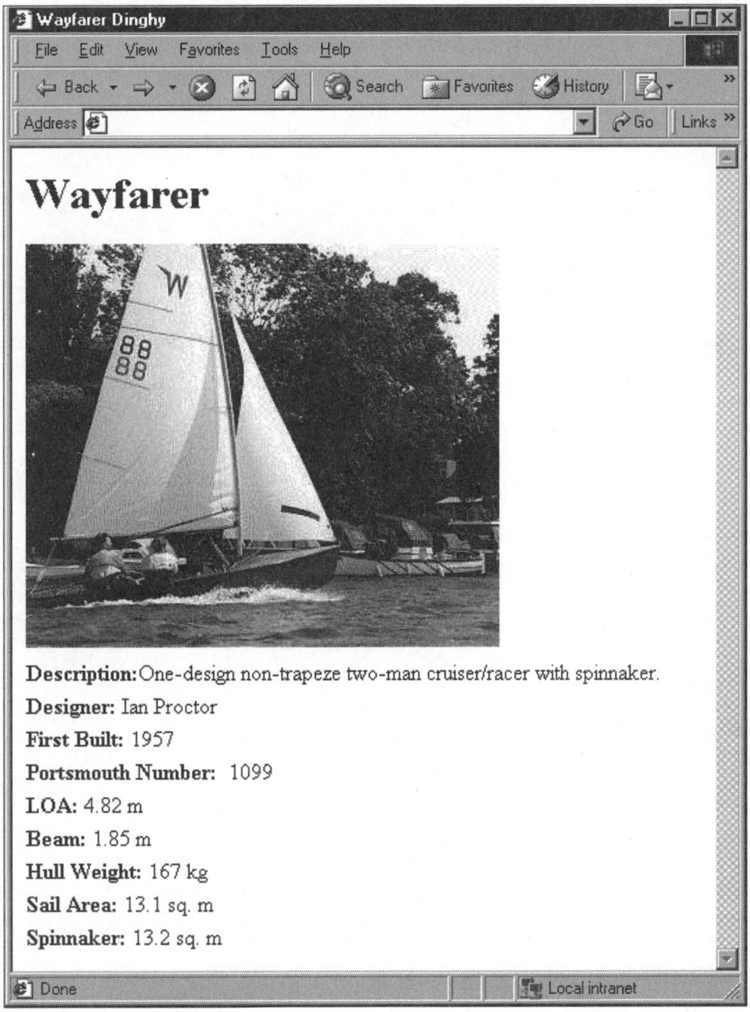

This is the HTML code (`wayfarer.htm`) used to create that page:

```
<HTML>
<HEAD>
<TITLE>Wayfarer Dinghy</TITLE>
<STYLE>
  DIV {margin-top: 4pt}
</STYLE>
</HEAD>

<BODY>
<H1>Wayfarer</H1>
<IMG ALT SRC="w88.jpg" WIDTH="343" HEIGHT="293">
<DIV><STRONG>Description:</STRONG>One-design non-trapeze two-man cruiser/racer
with spinnaker.</DIV>
<DIV><STRONG>Designer: </STRONG>Ian Proctor</DIV>
<DIV><STRONG>First Built: </STRONG>1957</DIV>
<DIV><STRONG>Portsmouth Number:</STRONG>  1099</DIV>
<DIV><STRONG>LOA: </STRONG>4.82 m</DIV>
<DIV><STRONG>Beam: </STRONG>1.85 m</DIV>
<DIV><STRONG>Hull Weight: </STRONG>167 kg</DIV>
<DIV><STRONG>Sail Area: </STRONG>13.1 sq. m</DIV>
<DIV><STRONG>Spinnaker: </STRONG>13.2 sq. m</DIV>
</BODY>
</HTML>
```

This is fine for display, and I can add more dinghy types to the file, but what can I do apart from display the information? Not very much.

Here is the same information marked up in a different way (`wayfarer.xml`):

```
<?xml version="1.0"?>
<dinghy>
  <title id="wayfarer">Wayfarer</title>
  <image src="w88.jpg" />
  <description text="Description">One-design non-trapeze two-man cruiser/racer
    with spinnaker.</description>
  <designer text="Designer">Ian Proctor</designer>
  <first text="First Built">1957</first>
  <pn text="Portsmouth Number">1099</pn>
  <loa text="LOA">4.82 m</loa>
  <beam text="Beam">1.85 m</beam>
  <weight text="Hull Weight">167 kg</weight>
  <sail text="Sail Area">13.1 sq. m</sail>
  <spin text="Spinnaker">13.2 sq. m</spin>
</dinghy>
```

Of course, this is XML. We do not yet need to be concerned with the details of the file, but we can immediately see some key structural similarities and differences from the HTML representation:

- Like HTML, the document comprises tags and data
- Like HTML, the tags can contain attributes
- **Unlike** HTML, the tag names are meaningful in the context of the information
- **Unlike** HTML, the tag names tell us something about the items to which they relate
- **Unlike** HTML, the tags tell us nothing about how to display the item

In later chapters, we will see that there are several ways we can tell an XML-compliant browser how to display this file. We will also see that we can process the XML on the server and send the resulting HTML to a browser. This means we can start to use XML *now*, even if we are dealing with browsers that do not support it. As with anything else in life, you don't get something for nothing, and we will see that doing this not only increases the load on the server, but can also decrease the flexibility of applications compared to processing the XML in the browser.

However, what can we do apart from display the information? We could, if we wanted to, develop a simple application that would allow us to browse through a complete list of dinghies. This could give us a display like this:

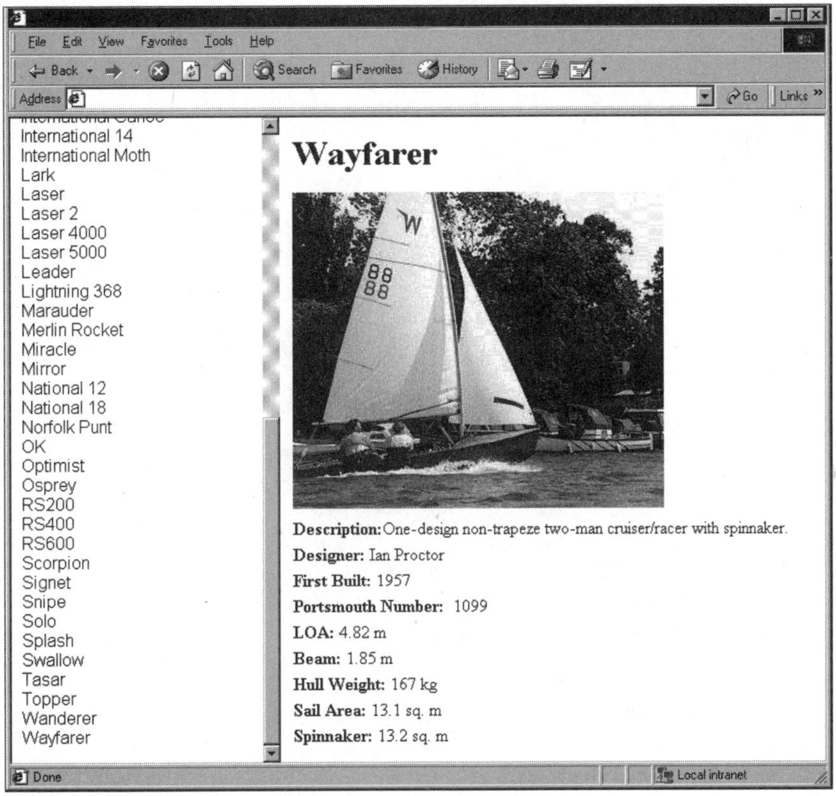

Once we start to use the fact that our tags contain meaningful information, we could search for dinghies within a certain range of Portsmouth Numbers (which indicate the relative performance of the dinghy and are used for handicapping). Or we could submit a document containing dinghy names (perhaps a regatta report) to a web site that would automatically add links to the XML document. Then, when someone clicks on the name of any dinghy, a window could pop up with all the relevant information displayed. The key point is that we can **re-use** the data, and it is describing the data **as data**, not in terms of how to display it, that has allowed us to do this. We don't have to recreate the data every time we want to do something different with it - we just use the same data in a different way.

This immediately opens up the information market place. By describing data such as stock prices, football scores or drug interactions in XML, I could sell this information on to people who could provide direct access to it through custom web applications.

What we have seen is that HTML was developed as a display technology, while XML was not. This is one of the key points – what HTML is to display, XML is to data. In this lies the power of XML. Without the restrictions of a fixed tag set, we can do what we like with the data we receive.

XML in an Information Context

We have seen that XML is an ideal mechanism for information dissemination. Of course, this is already being done with HTML. Let's look at some more ways in which XML brings advantages.

Separation of Content From Style

One of the important by-products of XML being purely a data markup metalanguage (without a fixed tag set) is that the styling that needs to be added for adequate display of the information in certain contexts isn't built in to the meaning of any tags that you define. Though you might not think so at first, this is actually a good thing.

Separating information content from display style is especially relevant when material is being generated from one source for layout by others. Think of this book as an example. I am generating the material, but have no influence over how it is displayed. Those hard-working people at Wrox Press don't want to work excessively hard, so they have provided me with a template to use in my wordprocessor to help make the editorial process more efficient. By doing so, they don't have to spend unnecessary time adding styling to my writings later on – the template means that the various different styles of text in the chapter are marked and can be styled as the publisher sees fit later on.

Now put this in an Internet context. If I were writing for the Internet, and put in HTML tags, I would be controlling the layout. If I were to write using XML markup, the publisher could apply a stylesheet (a set of rules defining the styling) at the publication stage.

Of course, they could use several different stylesheets for different purposes. Perhaps material would be used for a simple Web page and for an online training course. Again, the same material could be used, just different stylesheets. As we will see later, although XML was designed for the Internet, we can use it to generate arbitrary output; for example, using one stylesheet for display and another to format for typesetting. In fact, this is already happening. For an XML conference at which I am speaking, I have been asked to submit my paper in XML. From this, the conference organisers will be able to produce both a paper-based handout and publish papers on the Web without any change to the document I submit.

So far, we have discussed simple hand-crafted documents. XML becomes even more useful when used with database content. Currently, publishing database material over the web involves using a mechanism, such as an Active Server Page, to extract the information and put it into a HTML page. Again, we are mixing content and style. Let's look at two travel industry examples.

Multiple Styles From a Single Source

Consider a company that runs a reservations system as a bureau service through tour operators that sell packaged vacations. There is a standard application that manages the inventory of these operators in a similar way, using similar database structures. However, these tour operators are competing with each other, and each wants to differentiate itself through its web interface to the consumer. As the diagram below shows, a programmer develops a common Active Server Page that extracts the information from the database. Copies of this page are then sent to the graphics designers, who change it for each tour operator.

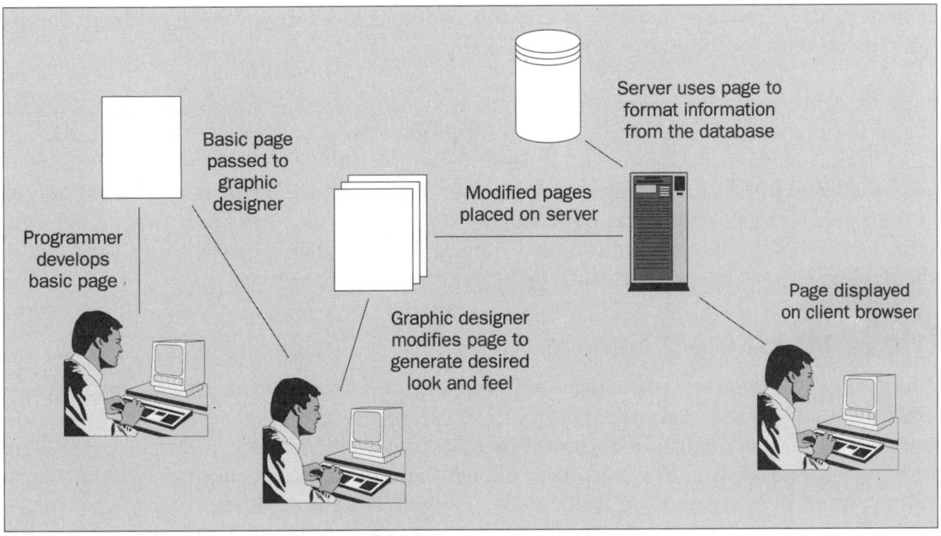

Unfortunately, they are having to work with complex database extraction code about which they know little, and so tend to introduce errors.

Later, the database might be restructured to add a new facility. The code for each tour operator must therefore have the same changes made to it. This is a version control nightmare.

Now consider the same situation with XML. The developer defines an XML format for the data that needs to be extracted from the database. While she is developing the code to do this, the graphic designer is developing a stylesheet based on the XML data format. The two are stored on the server. When the user requests a page, the data is extracted from the database and formatted as XML. This XML is displayed on the client browser using the appropriate stylesheet, depending on the tour operator whose system is being accessed:

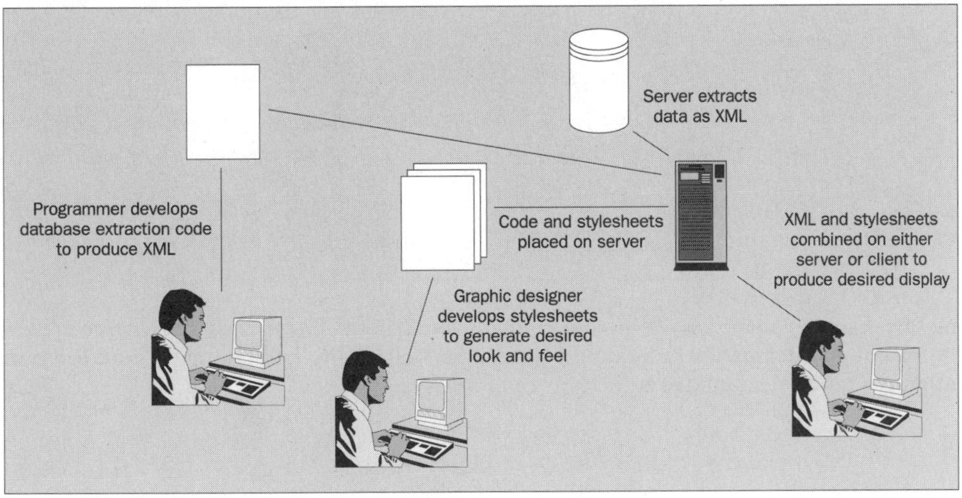

The graphic designer no longer touches the database extraction code, and cannot interfere with it. If the database structure changes, only the extraction code has to change - the stylesheets are not affected. (We'll see more on how this works in Chapter 5.)

In this example, XML provides an intermediate format, allowing the server to produce a structured XML file, and the browser to display it in a fashion defined by a stylesheet. Don't HTML stylesheets achieve this? Well, not quite. Using a cascading stylesheet with HTML allows the format of individual elements to be altered just by changing the stylesheet. However, the basic layout of the page is defined in the HTML page, which also contains the data. The stylesheets used with XML allow both the character styles *and* the basic layout to be changed without changing the more complex code that extracts the data.

Single Style From Multiple Sources

That example showed the benefit of using XML when generating multiple *display* formats from a single *source* format. The case study for this book uses the converse case – getting information from several sources and displaying it in a common format. Information about the vacation packages provided by tour operators is held on a server called Centaur. The information held is the same as that typically printed in brochures, so it does not change frequently. When the browser requests this information, it is retrieved from the Centaur database and formatted for display:

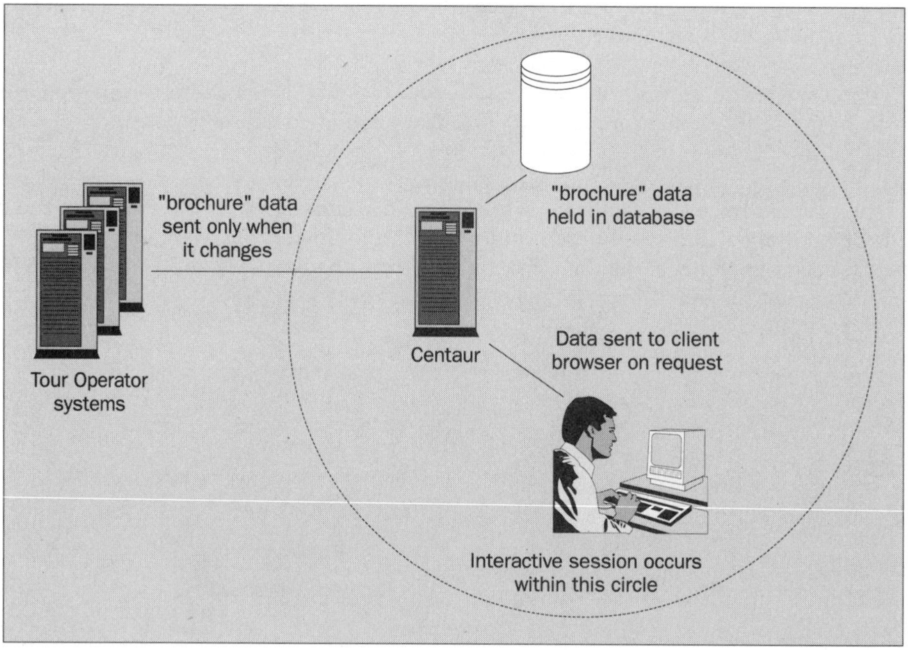

By doing this, Centaur maintains complete control over layout. There is an alternative architecture, in which only enough information is held on Centaur for searches to be conducted, and the remaining information is sent on demand from the tour operator systems:

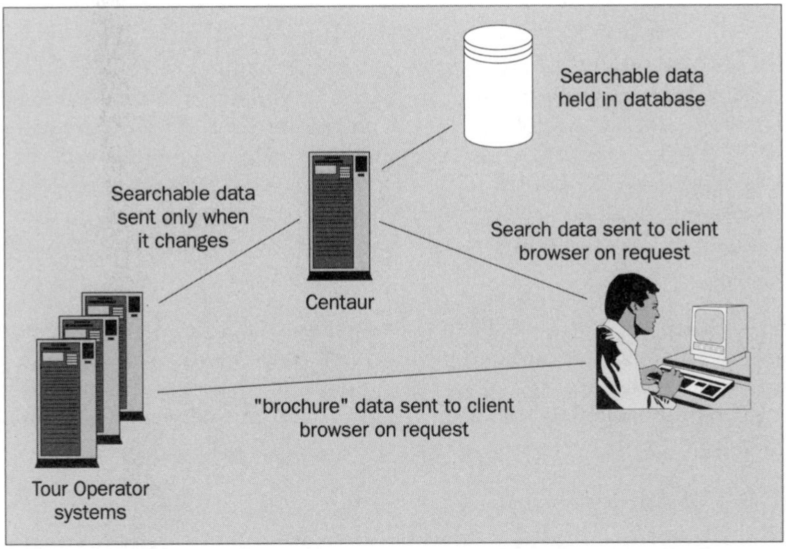

How should the brochure information now be sent? If we allow it to be sent as HTML, the tour operators will not only have to develop the pages, they will have complete control over look and feel. However, I, as the Centaur operator, want to maintain a consistent look and feel throughout the application. I could provide style guidelines and CSS stylesheets, but there will inevitably be errors, and probably some tour operators wanting to stand out from the crowd by filling their pages with animated GIFs and other bandwidth-hungry effects.

Now consider the Centaur application (which can be downloaded from `www.wrox.com`). There is some difference in style between the tour operators, but, using XML, I have been able to control these differences. In the diagram above, where the tour operator sends information directly to the client, we could maintain this control by providing the stylesheet directly from Centaur. We can only do this if the tour operators send their information as XML.

Searching

In the longer term, XML should bring big benefits when searching the Internet. We have all used the search engines such as Hotbot (`http://www.hotbot.com`) and Altavista (`http://www.altavista.digital.com`) and found that we get hundreds of thousands of hits when we try a general search, then none at all when we try to refine our search criteria. Clever though these search engines are, they are fighting an uphill battle because all they have to work on is plain text. A search term such as "galileo" could match a renaissance scientist, a global travel distribution system or a space probe.

Since XML allows us to define our tags, we can use these to help provide context for our search. For example, if searching for the company Galileo, we might reference keywords, such as "travel" and "head office" that would be held within XML elements.

So why do I say that this is in the longer term? Remember that XML does not define these tags for us. If they are to be useful, we need groups of companies to define suitable tags, and then others to start using them. This is already happening in many industries, but it will be some time before they are sufficiently ubiquitous for us to access them as we would like.

Other Benefits

Many web developers were initially skeptical about the linking facilities of HTML. In fact, the simple linking has proved remarkably powerful. However, there are limitations to what can be done. For example, I have wanted to provide a string of links, such that the user of a web site will look at pages in a pre-determined order, the order changing according to some parameter. This is not possible with HTML. There is a working draft, **XLink** (XML Linking Language), which promises to enable this and many other powerful linking facilities. For example, it will allow links to be held in databases, or traversed in either direction. Successful though HTML linking has been, XML and XLink promise to take linking one stage further.

I could keep going. Web site designers will like the ease with which information common to several pages can be written and maintained once and incorporated many times. Web site hosts will like the fact that XML can result in fewer trips to the server as more information is sent at one time. In fact, get to the position where no further trips are required to the server, and you could continue to work offline. We will explore this more in the case study.

So in this context, XML has many benefits:

- Web pages that are more consistent and easier to maintain through separating style from content
- Easier database publishing
- Better searching and linking
- A lower load on the server

It's looking good even before we start to look at the transactional aspects.

XML in a Transactional Context

XML describes data, so why not use it for transactions? I'll send you a message to ask for the availability of a vacation:

```
<?xml version="1.0"?>
<vacation-availability-request>
  <vacation-ref>125</vacation-ref>
  <adults>2</adults>
  <children>1</children>
  <infants>0</infants>
  <departure-date>19990412</departure-date>
  <nights>14</nights>
  <my-ref>paul01</my-ref>
</vacation-availability-request>
```

and you can send me a reply:

```
<?xml version="1.0"?>
<vacation-availability-response>
  <your-ref>paul01</your-ref>
  <availability>true</available>
<vacation-availability-response>
```

It all looks so simple, but it is one of the most controversial aspects of XML. Why controversial? Because many people have invested years of effort in developing Electronic Data Interchange (EDI) protocols to do this. These people think the XML pundits who suggest XML as a replacement for traditional EDI are over-simplifying and that XML neither addresses the weaknesses of traditional EDI, such as the complexity of the messages, nor duplicates strengths such as the ability of transactions to be audited. Meanwhile, those on the XML side (and this is an argument where people take sides) say that EDI is too complex and so has not had the wide acceptance that XML will.

As usual with these arguments, there are strong cases on both sides. Traditional EDI methods such as X12 have evolved to cater for every imaginable variation of the documents being exchanged. They are heavily standardized, and tools are available to use them. X12 syntax is concise compared to XML, and standard tools check both syntax and semantics. XML on the other hand, is designed to be human-readable, and so is verbose (the W3C recommendation contains in the design goals a statement that "terseness in XML markup is of minimal importance"), and parsers currently check only for correct syntax. Also, the mechanisms for ensuring that we are working with trusted partners and that transactions can be audited are not yet in place.

However, XML has one major advantage. In many cases EDI is enforced by major customers on small suppliers. These suppliers sometimes cannot afford the EDI systems to handle documents automatically and so print out the documents they receive and re-key information into their own systems. Since the documents are not designed to be human-readable, this can be a skilled and time-consuming task. XML messages, on the other hand, could be printed in a more friendly fashion with a stylesheet and treated as standard paper documents.

A combination of this advantage, the perceived simplicity of XML, and the huge skills base that will quickly build up will ensure that XML secures its place in electronic document exchange. Initially, this will be in areas where traditional EDI has no presence, especially in the simpler applications. Over time, it is likely to spread to replace the traditional EDI syntaxes.

OK Then, So What (Exactly) is XML?

So that gives a flavour of XML, why it was developed and what can be done with it. This section will tell you more about the standard itself. It is an overview rather than a complete definition, and is intended to help you understand what XML is about and how it can be used. An excellent resource to help with the missing detail is Tim Bray's annotated version of the specification at `http://www.xml.com/axml/testaxml.htm`.

XML is a subset of the **Standard Generalized Markup Language** (SGML) designed to provide most of the power of SGML without as much complexity. SGML is a metalanguage that was designed as a way of defining **markup** for documents of all types. Markup is the addition of 'tags' to data, the tags having some significance for the processing of the data by an application.

An XML document comprises a combination of markup and **character data**. The markup contains the meaning, such as "this is the designer of the dinghy" and is held in tags and other XML elements, while the character data is the content, such as the name of the designer. Here is an example XML element showing the tags, delimited by < and >, either side of the dinghy designer's name.

```
<dinghy-designer>Ian Proctor</dinghy-designer>
```

The XML subset is specifically targeted at the Web. HTML is an implementation of SGML, which explains the similarity in appearance between that and XML. Why do I say that XML is a subset and HTML is an implementation? Now that we know the difference between a markup language and a metalanguage, the explanation is simple. Like XML, SGML is a metalanguage. Since XML is a cut-down version of SGML, we can safely call it a subset. HTML, however, is a language that meets the requirements defined in SGML. It is therefore an implementation. Earlier, we mentioned some implementations of XML, such as CDF and SMIL. There are plenty of others, such as the Chemical Markup Language (CML) for describing chemical formulae and the Mathematical Markup Language (MML) for describing mathematical equations. These are two very good examples of XML in use, in that both allow a textual representation of complex formulae that can then be rendered in a graphical form by a suitable client tool. The relationships between these various languages and metalanguages can be described simply in a diagram:

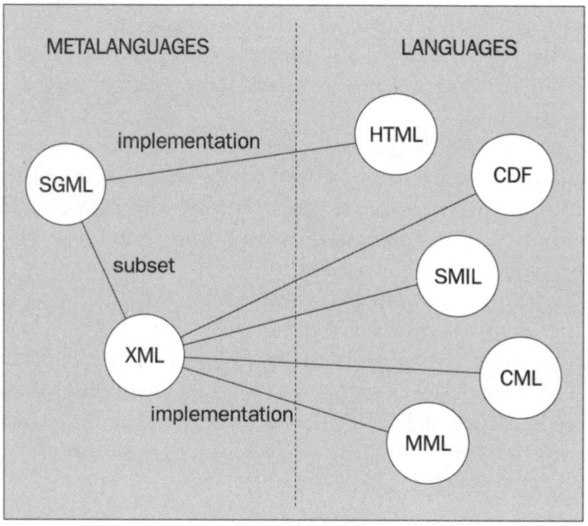

The fact that XML is based on SGML has many good and a few bad points. Since SGML has been around since the 1980s, there are plenty of experts around, and also tools that either support XML already, or can be easily adapted to do so. The existence of these experts has led to a robust standard that is immediately useful. Forget the normal "version 1 is for the pioneers" – XML is ready to use.

The most apparent downside is that the structure of an XML document is described in something known as a **Document Type Definition** (DTD) that has a syntax all of its own. Moves are afoot to improve this position, as we shall see later, but for the moment we are stuck with learning two syntaxes – one for XML tags, and one for the DTD.

Well-Formed Documents

Since XML is a metalanguage, it is up to the user to define a set of tags suitable for the application. A document must contain a single tag pair to define a **root element**. All others must be in pairs nested within this pair, and any sub-elements correctly nested within their parent elements, forming a hierarchical data structure in the document. There is also an empty tag construct, formed by putting an oblique (/) after the tag name, so we have `<tagname />` which saves typing `<tagname></tagname>` with no text enclosed. The space between the tagname and the oblique is optional. Note that the unmatched tags allowed in HTML (for example, the `<P>` paragraph tag can have a `</P>` closing tag, but it is not essential) are not permitted in XML.

Why have a tag if it going to be empty? There are two main reasons. The first is that the tag alone may be sufficient for its purpose. For example, if you wanted to emulate the HTML line break tag `<BR>`, you could use the empty tag `<BR />` in XML. The second reason is that the tag can contain an attribute, and that may be sufficient without any character data.

In XML, all tag and attribute names must start with an alphabetic character, an underscore (_) or colon (:), and not contain any white space (space, tab, line feed or carriage return). Most punctuation characters are allowed within a tag name, although the colon is reserved for **namespace** references, a feature that helps make tag names globally unique if we wish them to be. We will look at namespaces later in the chapter.

Names also cannot start with the characters "xml" in any combination of upper and lower case as this is a reserved name within XML. Unlike HTML, names in XML are case sensitive, so the tag `<dinghy>` is different from the tag `<Dinghy>` or the tag `<DINGHY>`.

A document is described as **well-formed** if it meets the well-formedness constraints of the XML recommendation. Principally, this means it must have a single root element and all other elements must be correctly nested. If a document is well-formed, it can be correctly parsed by a computer program. If it is not, the document is meaningless as XML and any program working with it must report the error and must not continue to process the document except to report further errors.

I say it is meaningless. In most cases, this is true. However, there are times when an XML document could mean something to a human, but still not be well-formed. For example, using the following as part of a document would cause the document not to be well-formed since the tags are incorrectly nested:

```
<para>I am going to put the end of this paragraph <bold>in bold.</para>
<para>And also the start</bold> of the next</para>
```

IE5 will report the error to us like this:

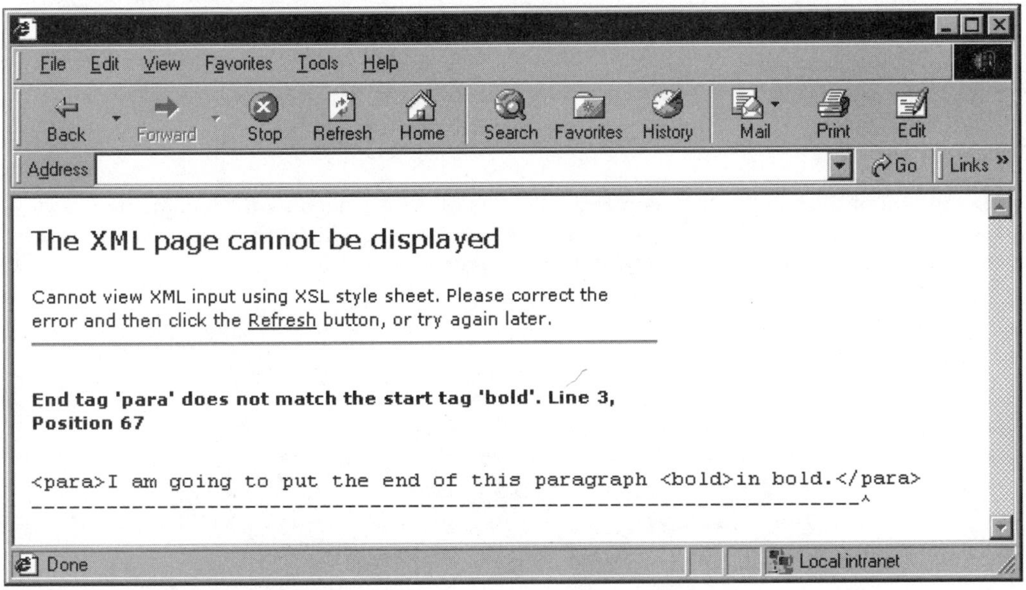

This error is easy to correct by adding a closing `</bold>` tag to the first line and a new opening tag in the second:

```
<para>I am going to put the end of this paragraph <bold>in bold.</bold></para>
<para><bold>And also the start</bold> of the next</para>
```

Valid Documents

So far, we have talked about documents being well-formed, which means that they are legal XML and can be processed by a parser or other XML processor. A document may also contain, or reference, a **Document Type Definition**, or DTD. The DTD performs several functions, one of which is to place constraints on the contents of the document. For example, the DTD defines the tag names that can be used in the document and the order in which the tags occur. We will be looking at the DTD in more detail shortly.

With the DTD comes the concept of a **valid** document. This means that the document contains (or references) a DTD, and that the markup of that document matches the DTD. Valid is a slightly confusing term - there is nothing wrong with a document that does not have a DTD, as long as it is well formed, and often there is no need for one.

Parsing XML

We have talked of processing XML documents, but have not described where to start doing this. The answer is with an XML **parser**. A parser breaks down the structure of an XML document into a tree structure than can be manipulated through programs or scripts.

Just as XML documents fall into two classes - well-formed and valid - so do parsers. A non-validating parser will create the tree structure from an XML document, ignoring the constraints of any DTD. A validating parser, such as the MSXML parser included as part of IE5 is a much more complex animal, and will check that a documents meets the constraints of its DTD if it has one. If there is no DTD, a validating parser will perform as a non-validating parser.

There is a little more to parsing than this, since the DTD does more than provide constraints. We will look at these aspects later.

Tags

With an understanding of the terminology and requirements of well-formed XML documents, we can start looking at the use of tags in XML by considering a book catalog, where, of course, the number of books in the catalog is unlimited. If the catalog were structured like this:

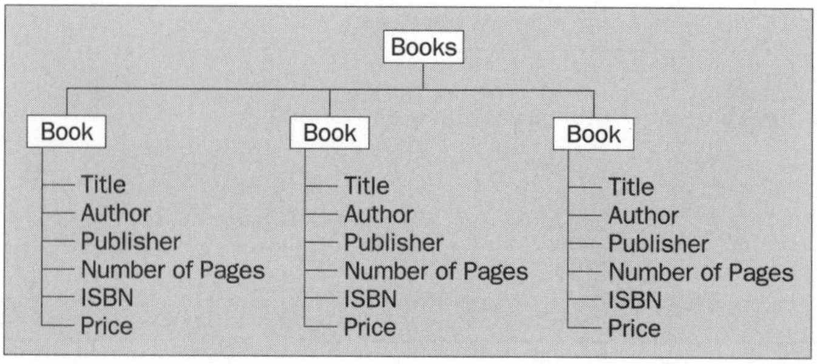

a two book catalog could be expressed in XML as follows:

```
<books>
  <book>
    <title>Clouds to Code</title>
    <author>Jesse Liberty</author>
    <publisher>Wrox Press</publisher>
    <pages>393</pages>
    <isbn>1-861000-95-2</isbn>
    <price>40.00</price>
  </book>
  <book>
    <title>Beginning Active Server Pages 2.0</title>
    <author>Francis, Kauffman, Llibre, Sussman, Ullman</author>
    <publisher>Wrox Press</publisher>
    <pages>653</pages>
    <isbn>1-861001-34-7</isbn>
    <price>39.99</price>
  </book>
</books>
```

There are a few points to note about this. The first line contains the opening tag of the `books` element. This element is known as the **root** element and, as we have seen, there must be one and only one in any XML document. Like all other elements, this must have a matching closing tag, `</books>`, which it does at the end of the document. Next we have an opening tag for the first book, which again has a closing tag later. The element `book` is a **child** of the element `books`, and `books` is a **parent** to both the child `book` elements. This is an important relationship in XML. Every element, other than the root element, must have a single parent element. An element may have one or more children. The element `book` has its own children, `title`, `author`, `publisher`, `pages`, `isbn` and `price`. All the elements are fully nested within each other.

There are two other points to note. The first is that we have a price, but no idea if this is in dollars, pounds sterling, euros, yen or any other currency. We could counteract this by expressing the first price as:

```
<price>$40.00</price>
```

However, this would not easily allow processing such as currency conversion. An alternative would be to add more tags:

```
<price>
  <amount>40.00</amount>
  <currency>USD</currency>
</price>
```

This would meet the need to be able to process the price, but is long-winded. An alternative is to describe the currency using a `currency` **attribute**:

```
<price currency="USD">40.00</price>
```

The attribute is used in much the same way as an HTML attribute, but, just as we can define our own tag names, we can define our own attribute names. One important point is that the value of the attribute **must** be in single or double quotes. While you can get away without this in HTML, you cannot in XML.

The other point is that we have listed the multiple authors of the second book on a single line. It would seem more logical to list them separately as follows:

```
<book>
  <title>Beginning Active Server Pages 2.0</title>
  <authors>
    <author>Francis</author>
    <author>Kauffman</author>
    <author>Llibre</author>
    <author>Sussman</author>
    <author>Ullman</author>
  </authors>
  <publisher>Wrox Press</publisher>
  <pages>653</pages>
  <isbn>1-861001-34-7</isbn>
  <price>39.99</price>
</book>
```

This is perfectly good XML. When I discuss DTDs later, I will describe how it is possible to ensure that a book can only have one title, but may have multiple authors.

Instead of all these elements, we could describe the book using just attributes:

```
<book title = "Clouds to Code" author = "Jesse Liberty" publisher = "Wrox Press"
pages = "393" isbn = "1-861000-95-2" currency = "USD" price = "40.00" />
```

It is one of the challenges of XML design to know when it is most appropriate to use an element and when an attribute. In this case, the use of an attribute for the author was not appropriate. The reason is that you can only have a single attribute of any name, and so describing the second book as:

```
<book title="Beginning Active Server Pages 2.0" author="Francis" author="Kauffman
… />
```

would not be well-formed XML.

Types of XML Tags

To meet its requirements as a metalanguage, XML has a number of different types of constituent parts for use in documents. The tags we have met so far describe XML **elements**. An element is simply an entity starting with a start tag and ending with an end tag. As we have just seen above, an element may also be empty, and can be represented with a shorthand syntax. We have seen elements that contain text and elements that contain other elements.

Other possible parts of an XML document are:

- processing instructions, which pass application-specific instructions to the program using the XML
- CDATA sections, which allow non-XML text content to be contained within an XML document
- entity references, which allow substitutions of the reference with other text or XML information
- character references, which allow any of a wide range of characters to be included in an XML document
- comments, which are, well, comments

Let's look at each in turn.

Processing Instructions

Processing Instructions, or **PIs**, are not part of the character data of the XML document, but instructions to the parser or some other application. The instruction starts with an identifier for the target application and then contains the instructions:

```
<?TargetApplicationName   Instruction set for the application?>
```

You might have noticed that an XML document starts with an instruction that has the same format.

```
<?xml version="1.0" encoding="UTF-8"?>
```

There is some debate about whether this is strictly speaking a PI in the terms of the specification, particularly given its role. So here we will hedge our bets and say that it is a specific PI called the **XML declaration**, and as such is the only one that can start with the characters "xml". They must be in lower case in the XML declaration, and cannot be used in any combination of upper and lower case in other PIs.

This is the second time we have met a restriction on the use of the character string "xml" in names (the first was at the start of an element name). I play safe and avoid the string altogether in documents except where it is mandatory. It is strongly recommended that an XML document starts with an XML declaration to tell the parser which version of XML it is using, and possibly the character set. The character set encoding attribute can be important where XML is to be used for communication between different systems, especially when you are working across international boundaries.

CDATA Sections

Occasionally, there may be a need to pass a whole string of characters to an application without the parser getting involved in the processing. This would be needed, for example, where the content of the data contains **reserved characters** in XML. We have not covered reserved characters yet, and there are very few, fewer than in HTML. In fact, there are two – the < and the `&` characters. The former, being the start of a tag, would indicate to the parser that the next piece of text is a new tag. The latter is used as an **escape** character as we shall see in a moment when we look at entity references. The **CDATA** markup element was designed for this purpose.

For example the text "Ben & Jerry's" could not be marked up as,

```
<icecream>Ben & Jerry's</icecream>
```

as this would cause the document not to be well-formed and the parser would indicate an error. Using a CDATA section, the text could be included as

```
<icecream><![CDATA[Ben & Jerry's]]></icecream>
```

In a moment, we will see alternative ways of handling this case. In practice, the CDATA markup is most useful where text may contain a large, and unknown, number of reserved characters, for example because it is an image that has been binary encoded or some code written in a scripting language.

Entity References

Entity references force the parser to replace the reference with certain data, and are used for two purposes.

The first reason to use an entity reference is to allow reserved and a few other characters to be included in documents. I have already said that & and < are reserved characters. Quotes and apostrophes can also cause problems, and so can be escaped using an entity reference when they are part of the character data. Finally, the > character can be escaped, not because XML technically needs it to be, but for the sake of symmetry. Apart from these built-in entity references, which can be used in any well-formed XML document, you can define your own entity references in the DTD and use these as you like. However, such references are not possible unless the document in question has a DTD.

Entity references can be easily identified as they are preceded by an ampersand and end with a semi-colon. The built-in references are coded as:

Character	Reference
<	<
>	>
&	&
'	'
"	"

The second reason to use an entity reference is to cause a larger substitution to be made within the document. For example, the contents of this book might be coded as:

```
<book>
  <title>XML Design and Implementation</title>
  <author>Paul Spencer</author>
  <creationDate>&createdate;</creationDate>
  <content>
    &contents;
    &chapter1;
    &chapter2;
    &chapter3;
        .
        .
    &appendixA;
        .
        .
    &index;
  </content>
</book>
```

In this case, both the creation date and the content of the book would be produced by substitution from other XML documents. The Uniform Resource Identifiers (URIs) for these external resources are found in the Document Type Definition, which we shall be looking at later in this chapter.

For those not familiar with the term URI, it is used to include both Uniform Resource Locators - the familiar URL - and URNs, or Uniform Resource Names. URNs are currently being developed, and are intended to provide a way of naming a resource in a way that ensures that the name does not change if the location of the resource changes.

The ability to substitute text can also be used to simplify things where the same text is repeated in several places. For example, my web site has a copyright notice at the bottom of every page. In HTML, I have to cut and paste it into every page. Were I to re-write my site in XML, which I am in the process of doing, I could include this statement in an entity reference as `&copyright;`. The DTD would then be used to declare the text that is to be substituted.

Character References

The **character reference** markup type allows any character in the ISO/IEC 10646 character set (a very broad character set, equivalent to Unicode (see `http://www.unicode.org/unicode/uni2book/u2.html` and `ftp://ftp.unicode.org/Public/UNIDATA/UnicodeData-Latest.txt`), designed to include most international characters) to be included in a document, even though it might not be included on the user's keyboard. It can therefore also be used as an alternative (but less obvious to the reader) way of escaping reserved characters. The character is referenced by its position in the character set, preceded by `&#` if specified in decimal or by `&#x` if specified in hexadecimal. We Brits can use `£` to represent £ - our currency symbol, at least for the next few years.

We could also reference the pound sign with an entity reference as `£`. Each representation has advantages and disadvantages. The entity reference is more easily understood by someone reading the document, but it has the disadvantage that it can only be used in documents where its replacement text is defined in a declaration within a DTD. Is this a disadvantage? Well, only if we do not need a DTD for other reasons and only include it for a few entity references. Character references, by contrast, do not need to be declared.

Comments

As some light relief before moving onto the Document Type Definition, you may be relieved to know that the XML **comment** is identical in style to the HTML comment, with `<!--` and `-->` as its start and end delimiters.

For compatibility with SGML, it is not permitted to put two hyphens in a row within a comment as these could be mistaken by a parser as being part of the comment's end delimiter. However, the XML reserved characters are allowed without the need to escape them.

```
<!-- here is a comment -->
<!-- but this -- is not allowed-->
```

Note that if you are used to commenting HTML like this:

```
<!-- ------------------------------------ -->
<!-- this is the start of a block of HTML -->
<!-- ------------------------------------ -->
```

it is not going to work in XML. Instead, I use:

```
<!-- =================================== -->
<!-- this is the start of a block of XML -->
<!-- =================================== -->
```

The Document Type Definition

As we said earlier, one function of the DTD is to constrain the element types that can be included in a document. We also saw that it is necessary if we are to use entity references other than for built-in entities. In this section, we will look at the DTD from the point of view of someone developing data-driven web applications. These applications do not require the more complex aspects of the DTD, and so these will be covered in less detail. So treat this as an introduction to the DTD rather than a reference work. The XML recommendation itself (included in Appendix C) is the reference for the DTD.

It is not necessary for an XML document to contain a DTD, but there are occasions when it is beneficial. For example, the case study in this book is a system that will interface to many tour operators, each with its own reservations system. Enforcing the use of a DTD ensures that we can get the parser in IE5 to check documents and messages for many more errors than we could without one. For example, using a DTD, we can ensure not only that a document (or message) contains all the elements we expect, but we can also check that the elements contain the attributes we need and even that these attributes have the content we expect. And what do we have to do to achieve this? Nothing! The XML parser will do it for us.

I have said that the DTD has a syntax all of its own – a legacy of XML's origin as a subset of SGML. In what follows, I will run through the basic DTD for the book catalog example to show some of the main elements of the DTD, and briefly describe this syntax. Then we will look at other more complex aspects of the DTD that we will need to know for our look at the Centaur application.

Here is the version of book catalog XML file that we will be working with:

```
<books>
  <book>
    <title>Clouds to Code</title>
    <authors>
      <author>Jesse Liberty</author>
    </authors>
    <publisher>Wrox Press</publisher>
    <pages>393</pages>
    <isbn>1-861000-95-2</isbn>
    <price currency = "USD">40.00</price>
  </book>
  <book>
    <title>Beginning Active Server Pages</title>
    <authors>
      <author>Francis</author>
      <author>Kauffman</author>
      <author>Llibre</author>
      <author>Sussman</author>
      <author>Ullman</author>
    </authors>
    <publisher>Wrox Press</publisher>
    <pages>653</pages>
    <isbn>1-861001-34-7</isbn>
    <price currency = "USD">39.99</price>
  </book>
</books>
```

In Appendix D, we discuss proposals for **XML Schemas**, which provide an alternative to the DTD that uses the standard XML element and attribute syntax of the document.

An Example DTD

Let's create a DTD for the book catalog. The DTD goes after the XML declaration, and starts by defining the type of document by referencing its root element:

```
<?xml version = "1.0"?>
<!DOCTYPE books [
...declarations go here ...
]>
```

This DOCTYPE statement is the **Document Type Declaration**. This and the statements between the opening square bracket and the closing square bracket comprise the **Document Type Definition** and define the grammar of the document. Both of these terms tend to be abbreviated to DTD, but it is usually clear from the context which is meant.

One rule of the Document Type Declaration is that the DOCTYPE name, books in our example, must match the root element of the document, in this case, <books>. This root element must also appear in an **element declaration**. This element declaration defines what elements it can in turn contain. In our case, it can only contain book elements:

```
<!ELEMENT books (book)*>
```

The * indicates that it can contain zero or more of these elements. The complete set of declarations relating to any element is known as the **content model** for that element. For the books element, being the root element of the document, the content model is made up of all the declarations for all the elements nested within this root element.

Next we show that a book has a title, an authors element, a publisher, optionally a number of pages and one or more price elements:

```
<!ELEMENT book (title, authors, publisher, pages?, isbn, price+)>
```

This introduces three more special characters - the ? to indicate that the element is optional, the + to indicate "one or more" and the comma to indicate that the elements must be included in the document in the order shown.

Next we show a requirement for one or more author elements to nest within the authors element:

```
<!ELEMENT authors (author+)>
```

The title element contains only text and is declared like this:

```
<!ELEMENT title (#PCDATA)>
```

This declares this element as comprising normal characters, which the XML specification defines as **parsed character data** or **PCDATA**. The reserved character # indicates that #PCDATA is a reserved word. You cannot use the # character in your own names. Why is this called parsed character data? Simply because the text within the element will have been processed by the parser and any entity replacements, such as we saw when we used the entity &contents; earlier, will have been made.

The next few elements are similar:

```
<!ELEMENT author (#PCDATA)>
<!ELEMENT publisher (#PCDATA)>
<!ELEMENT pages (#PCDATA)>
<!ELEMENT isbn (#PCDATA)>
```

The price is also a PCDATA element, but contains an attribute. We declare this attribute as having a name "currency", containing character data (CDATA) and being a required part of the element:

```
<!ELEMENT price (#PCDATA)>
<!ATTLIST price currency CDATA #REQUIRED>
]>
```

If we put this together with the XML for the books themselves, we have our first complete, well-formed and valid XML document:

```
<?xml version = "1.0"?>
<!DOCTYPE books [
<!ELEMENT books (book)*>
<!ELEMENT book (title, authors, publisher, pages?, isbn, price+)>
<!ELEMENT authors (author+)>
<!ELEMENT title (#PCDATA)>
<!ELEMENT author (#PCDATA)>
<!ELEMENT publisher (#PCDATA)>
<!ELEMENT pages (#PCDATA)>
<!ELEMENT isbn (#PCDATA)>
<!ELEMENT price (#PCDATA)>
<!ATTLIST price currency CDATA #REQUIRED>
]>
<books>
  <book>
    <title>Clouds to Code</title>
    <authors>
      <author>Jesse Liberty</author>
    </authors>
    <publisher>Wrox Press</publisher>
    <pages>393</pages>
    <isbn>1-861000-95-2</isbn>
    <price currency = "USD">40.00</price>
  </book>
  <book>
    <title>Beginning Active Server Pages</title>
    <authors>
      <author>Francis</author>
      <author>Kauffman</author>
      <author>Llibre</author>
      <author>Sussman</author>
      <author>Ullman</author>
    </authors>
    <publisher>Wrox Press</publisher>
    <pages>653</pages>
    <isbn>1-861001-34-7</isbn>
    <price currency = "USD">39.99</price>
  </book>
</books>
```

DTD Internal and External Subsets

The DTD can either be internal to the XML document, as we have just seen for the book catalog, or it can be in an external file referenced from the document. These are referred to in the XML recommendation as the **internal** and **external subsets**. The external subset is more appropriate when documents are sharing a DTD, as is the case for the tour operator example. It is possible to use both internal and external subsets, in which case the internal definitions take precedence where there is a conflict. This can occasionally be useful where an existing DTD almost matches a need, although it is as well to be careful when combining the two forms.

We can use the example above with an external DTD instead. Take all the declarations between the square brackets of the DOCTYPE declaration,

```
<!ELEMENT books (book)*>
<!ELEMENT book (title, authors, publisher, pages?, isbn, price+)>
<!ELEMENT authors (author+)>
<!ELEMENT title (#PCDATA)>
<!ELEMENT author (#PCDATA)>
<!ELEMENT publisher (#PCDATA)>
<!ELEMENT pages (#PCDATA)>
<!ELEMENT isbn (#PCDATA)>
<!ELEMENT price (#PCDATA)>
<!ATTLIST price currency CDATA #REQUIRED>
```

and save them in a separate file called `validbooks.dtd` in the same folder as the book catalog XML file. Then modify the DOCTYPE declaration of the catalog file to read:

```
<?xml version = "1.0"?>
<!DOCTYPE books SYSTEM "validbooks.dtd">
<books>
  ...
</books>
```

A validating parser will treat this document in just the same way as the earlier example with the DTD inline.

Now let's look at the declaration types in more detail, starting with the element type declaration.

Element Type Declaration

In our example of the book catalog, we covered this declaration in some detail. The element declaration indicates whether the element contains further elements, text (PCDATA) or both (known as a mixed element). It uses operators to give an idea of whether elements are compulsory or optional, how many times they occur and the order in which they occur. We saw four of these operators (`, ?+*`) earlier. This is the full set:

Symbol	Meaning
,	strict order
?	optional
+	one or more
*	zero or more
|	select one
()	group

The pipestem (|) is used to indicate that one of a number of elements must be present. The book catalog does not provide a good example of this, but later in the case study, we will see that we restrict message types that are passed between Centaur and the tour operator system to one of five types with the element type declaration:

```
<!ELEMENT centaur (quoterequest | quoteresponse | bookrequest | bookresponse |
error)>
```

Attribute List Declaration

In our book catalog, we used a simple attribute list declaration to indicate that the price element must contain a currency attribute:

```
<!ATTLIST price currency CDATA #REQUIRED>
```

We could restrict the content of the attribute using a statement such as:

```
<!ATTLIST price currency (USD|GBP) #REQUIRED>
```

In this case, the currency could only take one of the two values representing US dollars or British pounds.

The keyword `#REQUIRED` indicates that the attribute must be present in every occurrence of the `price` start tag within the document. There are three alternatives to this.

We could declare a default attribute value:

```
<!ATTLIST price currency (USD|GBP) "USD">
```

In this case, if the `price` element is used without an attribute, the value will be assumed to be `USD`. We have still restricted the possible values to `USD` and `GBP`, but this could be replaced by `CDATA` in the attribute list declaration if we wanted to allow any value.

We could use the keyword `#IMPLIED` to indicate that the attribute has no provided default value and its presence is not required in the start tag:

```
<!ATTLIST price currency CDATA #IMPLIED>
```

Finally, the value may be fixed so that it cannot be over-ridden when the element is used:

```
<!ATTLIST price currency CDATA #FIXED "USD">
```

Attribute values declared with the `#FIXED` keyword are special cases of default attributes. If the `price` element is used without an attribute, the value will be assumed to be `USD` as before. However, the value cannot be over-ridden, so if the attribute is used explicitly within an element, its value must match that in the attribute list declaration.

There are many other attribute types that we shall cover briefly here because of their importance for designing your own applications. Apart from `ID` and `IDREF`, which we'll look at next, none of these are used in the Centaur case study and we will not meet any of them again in this book.

ID and IDREF Attributes

You will be familiar with giving an HTML anchor element a name so that it can be the target of a link within a document:

```
Have a look at my <A href="#book">book</A>.
      .
      .
<A name="book">XML Design and Implementation</A>
```

The `ID` and `IDREF` attributes allow us to do similar things within an XML document. Any element can have an attribute declared as an ID to allow it to be the target of a link. The declaration:

```
<!ELEMENT book (title, authors, publisher, pages?, isbn, price+)>
<!ATTLIST book destination ID #REQUIRED>
```

would insist that every book has an attribute declaration with the name `destination` and a value that can be used to locate it as the target of a link. Each occurrence of the `destination` attribute within the document must have a unique value.

The starting point of the link would then need an attribute of type `IDREF` identifying the destination. For example, we could have `bookref` elements that may optionally contain an `IDREF`:

```
<!ELEMENT bookref (#PCDATA)>
<!ATTLIST bookref target IDREF #IMPLIED>
```

It is also possible to reference several `ID`s by using the `IDREFS` attribute declaration:

```
<!ELEMENT bookref (#PCDATA)>
<!ATTLIST bookref targets IDREFS #IMPLIED>
```

If we then wanted to reference several books, perhaps so that the application using the document could rapidly collect a certain subset of the entries in the catalog, we could use this in our XML document:

```
<bookref targets="book1 book2 book3">book list 47</bookref>
```

Of course, each of the books would need to be tagged. For example, the first book would be:

```
<book destination="book1">
  <title>Clouds to Code</title>
  <authors>
    <author>Jesse Liberty</author>
  </authors>
  <publisher>Wrox Press</publisher>
  <pages>393</pages>
  <isbn>1-861000-95-2</isbn>
  <price currency = "USD">40.00</price>
</book>
```

ENTITY and ENTITIES Attributes

So far, all our elements have contained other elements or parsed character data (unless they have been empty elements). What if we want an element to contain something different, such as a binary image or an Excel spreadsheet? In many cases, we would just include a reference to an external file, but if we need it to be embedded in the XML document, we must declare it using the `ENTITY` attribute. By using this attribute, we ensure that the parser does not attempt to process this element content, so it is a way of including data that would be illegal as part of a `#PCDATA` element. This is essential with binary or encoded binary data as there is otherwise no easy way of knowing that the source does not include the reserved < or `&` characters.

If I wanted to include my company logo in an XML document, I could use in my DTD:

```
<!ELEMENT logo EMPTY>
<!ATTLIST logo image ENTITY #REQUIRED>
```

In my document, I would then use an empty element:

```
<logo image="boynings.gif" />
```

So far, I have said that the image `boynings.gif` is an entity, but have said nothing more about it. We provide more information using the `ENTITY` declaration, which we shall meet in a moment.

Just as with `IDREF` and `IDREFS`, I could also use `ENTITIES` to refer to several entities in one attribute value.

NOTATION Attribute

The `NOTATION` declaration is used to indicate the format of an element. For example, the image we used above is not in XML format, but in the Graphics Interchange Format. We can use the `NOTATION` attribute to identify the allowed formats and the `NOTATION` markup declaration to identify helper applications to handle these data types.

We will do this when we look at the NOTATION markup declaration after we've looked at the ENTITY declaration in more detail a few sections further on.

NMTOKEN and NMTOKENS Attributes

The NMTOKEN attribute is used when all we want is to get a value for an attribute, perhaps to make a decision based on the value, rather than to refer to it as text. For example, we may have a technical manual, where different groups of users need to see different levels of detail. We could mark each paragraph with an indication of which users should see it.

In this case, using NMTOKEN would restrict us to naming a single group of people as possible viewers, so we could use NMTOKENS instead. In common with the ENTITY and ENTITIES and with IDREF and IDREFS, we can use NMTOKENS when we have multiple NMTOKEN values.

So we could declare:

```
<!ELEMENT para (#PCDATA)>
<!ATTLIST para view NMTOKENS #IMPLIED>
```

Then in the body of our document, place:

```
<para view="manager technician">This paragraph is to be viewed by managers and
technicians.</para>
<para view="technician">While this contains more detailed information that only
the technicians need.</para>
```

We saw earlier how we can set allowed values for attributes, so we could amend the attribute list to read:

```
<!ATTLIST para  all_access NMTOKENS "manager technician seniorManager">
```

Note that, because the individual tokens are separated by spaces, spaces are not allowed in the attribute value, so senior managers are referenced here as seniorManager.

More DTD Markup Declaration

The DTD can contain four different forms of **markup declaration**. We have already met the **element type declaration** and the **attribute-list declaration.** The other two are the **entity declaration** and the **notation declaration**.

The entity declaration provides the information for an entity reference. Earlier, I used the example of this book:

```
<book>
  <title>XML Design and Implementation</title>
  <author>Paul Spencer</author>
  <creationDate>&createdate;</creationDate>
  <content>
    &contents;
    &chapter1;
    &chapter2;
    &chapter3;
```

```
        .
        .
        .
     &index;
   </content>
</book>
```

In this, there is no indication of where to find the replacement text for the chapters and other parts of the book mentioned in the entity references. The entity declaration in the DTD resolves this by allowing us to provide the URI of the relevant documents to include.

The notation declaration helps us deal with parts of documents, such as an embedded image, that do not follow the normal XML rules. You can think of this as analogous to embedding a RealAudio™ stream in an HTML page, where the browser will need a helper application to handle the data.

Entity Declaration

When we met the `ENTITY` attribute earlier, we saw that something else was required to describe the entity we were referring to. This declaration achieves this.

This was the code we had before to reference my logo:

```
<!ELEMENT logo EMPTY>
<!ATTLIST logo image ENTITY #REQUIRED>
     .
     .
<logo image="boynings.gif" />
```

Now we just have to add the entity declaration:

```
<!ELEMENT logo EMPTY>
<!ATTLIST logo image ENTITY #REQUIRED>
<!ENTITY   boynings.gif SYSTEM "http://www.boynings.demon.co.uk/logo.gif"
           NDATA gif
>
     .
     .
<logo image="boynings.gif" />
```

I have formatted the new line slightly differently from previously since it would not fit on a single line. This style of formatting is commonly used, especially where multiple attributes are being included in an attribute list.

As you can see, we have now declared our logo as an entity. We have said where it is located by using the `SYSTEM` keyword with a Uniform Resource Identifier. We have also declared the data as `NDATA` rather than the alternative `CDATA` we have used before. This is because we no longer have character data, but data that we do not want to be parsed.

We have also said the data type is `gif`, but we have not said how to handle that. This is the function of our last declaration type, the `NOTATION` declaration, that we'll look at in the next section.

The ENTITY declaration is also used to declare text strings that will be substituted for entity references. We might want this because it makes the format of our documents clearer (as we did with the &contents; example) or because we want to repeat the same text in several places (for example, a copyright notice).

In the former case, we would be getting the information externally, and so might use the declaration:

```
<!ENTITY contents SYSTEM "file:///C:/chapters/contents/contents.xml">
```

while in the latter we might use:

```
<!ENTITY copyright "Copyright 1999 Paul Spencer">
```

Note that the built-in entity references such as < to represent <, do not require entity declarations, while any we add, such as £, do.

Notation Declaration

Earlier, we had a very brief look at the NOTATION attribute and mentioned that it was closely related to the NOTATION markup declaration. Here, we will complete the example of identifying my company logo using these.

Previously, we had this XML fragment:

```
<!ELEMENT logo EMPTY>
<!ATTLIST logo image ENTITY #REQUIRED>
<!ENTITY   boynings.gif SYSTEM "http://www.boynings.co.uk/logo.gif"
           NDATA gif
>
     .
     .
<logo image="boynings.gif" />
```

This has told us that the logo element must have an image attribute. We have also seen that this image is found at a particular URI, and that the data in the GIF format is not to be parsed.

Suppose I want to use Internet Explorer as my viewer for images. We can use the notation declaration to declare this as a handler for both gif and jpeg images. I used the default location when I installed Internet Explorer, so my declaration would look like this:

```
<!ELEMENT logo EMPTY>
<!NOTATION gif
     SYSTEM "file:///C:/Program Files/Internet Explorer/iexplore.exe">
<!NOTATION jpeg
     SYSTEM "file:///C:/Program Files/Internet Explorer/iexplore.exe">
<!ATTLIST logo
     image        ENTITY                    #REQUIRED
     format       NOTATION     (gif|jpg)    #REQUIRED
>
<!ENTITY   boynings.gif SYSTEM "http://www.boynings.co.uk/logo.gif"
           NDATA gif
>
     .
     .
<logo image="boynings.gif" format="gif" />
```

So now the logo element has both a file and a format. The file is identified by its URI using the ENTITY declaration, and the application to handle it by the `NOTATION` markup declaration.

A Note on White Space

The issue of what happens with white space (spaces, tabs, carriage returns and line feeds) vexes those coming from SGML to XML as the processing options are fewer.

Basically, white space between the end tag of one element and the start tag of the next is seen as existing only to lay the XML document out neatly, while white space between a start tag and an end tag is seen as relevant to the document and so is passed on by the parser to the application. It is then up to the application how it handles this white space. Often, it will compress multiple spaces into a single space character. This is the way HTML behaves by default, but in that case we can use the `PRE` element to ensure that white space is preserved.

With XML, it is possible to indicate to the application how we want the white space to be handled by using the `xml:space` reserved attribute. This is useful where the element contains a mix of other elements and PCDATA. The attribute can take one of two values: `preserve` or `default`.

Say we want to include some code, complete with indents, in an XML document. We could write the document like this:

```
<?xml version = "1.0"?>
<!DOCTYPE program [
<!ELEMENT program (line)*>
<!ELEMENT line (#PCDATA)>
]>
<program>
  <line>for (i = 0 ; i &lt; root.childNodes.length ; i++)</line>
  <line>  if (root.childNodes.item(i).getAttribute("href") == xlnk)</line>
  <line>  {</line>
  <line>    flag = true;</line>
  <line>    position = i;</line>
  <line>  }</line>
</program>
```

Note that, where my code uses a < character for "less than", I have used an entity reference to keep my document well-formed.

Most applications will strip what they consider to be redundant white space. We can indicate to the application explicitly that we want it to use its default white space handling, or that we want white space to be preserved. In this example, we want it to be preserved for the `line` elements, so we could write:

```
<?xml version = "1.0"?>
<!DOCTYPE program [
<!ELEMENT program (line)*>
<!ELEMENT line (#PCDATA)>
<!ATTLIST line xml:space (default|preserve) "preserve">
]>
<program>
  <line>for (i = 0 ; i &lt; root.childNodes.length ; i++)</line>
  <line>  if (root.childNodes.item(i).getAttribute("href") == xlnk)</line>
  <line>  {</line>
```

```
    <line>    flag = true;</line>
    <line>    position = i;</line>
    <line>  }</line>
  </program>
```

The parser will then indicate to the application that white space is to be preserved, and it is up to the application to handle this information.

Unlike most attributes, the `xml:space` attribute is inherited by children of the element for which it is declared, unless it is specifically over-ridden by another `xml:space` attribute. So I could have equally well made this an attribute of the `program` element.

The Standalone Attribute

Earlier, we saw the XML declaration:

```
<?xml version="1.0" encoding="UTF-8"?>
```

There is another attribute - the **standalone** attribute - that we may want to add to this.

As we have examined the structure of the DTD, we have come across instances where the parser is using the information for more than checking validity. For example, it could be using it to set a default attribute or to substitute text for an entity reference.

If these occur within the internal subset of the DTD, there is no problem. There is also no problem if we are using a validating parser as it will fetch any external DTD to validate the document and make the substitutions required. However, what about a non-validating parser? An external DTD could contain information that changes the parsed text of the document, even though the parser has no need to validate the document. Should it fetch the document to check or not?

This problem is partly solved by the `standalone` attribute. If we set our XML declaration to:

```
<?xml version="1.0" encoding="UTF-8" standalone="yes"?>
```

we are telling a non-validating parser that there is no need to fetch an external DTD to check for substitutions as there is nothing in the DTD that would affect the output of the parser.

I say this "partly" solves the problem. There remains the fact that a non-validating parser is not obliged to fetch an external DTD even if the value of `standalone` is `"no"`. This parameter is therefore an indication to the user of a document that it should only be processed through either a validating parser or a non-validating parser that is known to handle substitutions from an external DTD. Luckily for us, the parser built into IE5 is a validating parser if a DTD is present, but will act as a non-validating parser in the absence of a DTD.

Putting it all Together

An XML document can be split into three sections, each of which can contain different elements as shown here.

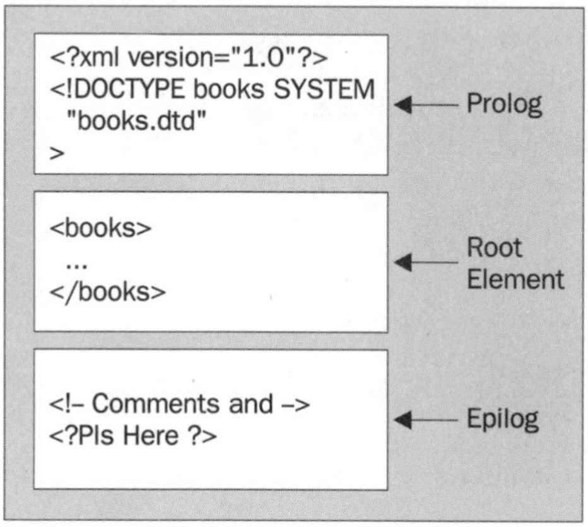

The **prolog** is before the start tag of the root element, and mainly contains the XML declaration, other processing instructions and the DTD.

The **root element** mainly contains tags, PCDATA, CDATA, processing instructions and entity references.

Finally, following the end tag of the root element, it is still possible to include processing instructions.

Any of these three sections can include white space and comments.

Now that we have a good grasp of the basics of XML syntax let's take a look at an important satellite specification which adds extra functionality to XML.

Namespaces

Having looked in some detail at the syntax of XML we now also need to take a look at **namespaces** in XML. Namespaces are indispensable if we want to be able to integrate XML data from different sources while still keeping track of which parts came from which source.

Consider a variation on the book catalog we met earlier when looking at the XML recommendation itself. This was the description of a book:

```
<book>
  <title>Beginning Active Server Pages</title>
  <authors>
    <author>Francis</author>
    <author>Kauffman</author>
    <author>Llibre</author>
    <author>Sussman</author>
    <author>Ullman</author>
```

```
    </authors>
    <publisher>Wrox Press</publisher>
    <pages>653</pages>
    <isbn>1-861001-34-7</isbn>
    <price currency = "USD">39.99</price>
  </book>
```

Now suppose we wanted to give some of these authors their proper academic title:

```
<author>Francis<title>Dr.</title></author>
```

A catalog such as this could be used by an online bookstore, which would also need a description of the customer, something like:

```
  <customer>
    <title>Mr</title>
    <forename>Paul</forename>
    <lastname>Spencer</lastname>
    <address>…</address>
    <creditcard cardtype="Visa">…</creditcard>
    <phone>…</phone>
    <email>…</email>
  </customer>
```

Now we can create an order comprising a customer and a list of books from the catalog. Although this example is a little contrived, as we could have structured our data better, you can immediately see a problem with this – the book and the customer have a title, and they mean totally different things.

```
<order>
    <title>Beginning Active Server Pages</title>
    <isbn>1-861001-34-7</isbn>
    <price currency = "USD">39.99</price>
    <title>Mr</title>
    <forename>Paul</forename>
    <lastname>Spencer</lastname>
    <address>…</address>
    <creditcard cardtype="Visa">…</creditcard>
    <phone>…</phone>
    <email>…</email>
</order>
```

This is particularly a problem if the elements with the same name but different meanings are siblings and the file is validated against a DTD. Suppose our two title elements had very different content models and that the elements in the order were not required to appear in a specific sequence within the document. In this case the parser would not be able to decide which type of title element it was dealing with and an error message would result.

What we need is some way of identifying these different meanings within the document. Namespaces achieve this, by providing a way to identify which elements should be interpreted in different ways.

Declaring and Using the Namespaces

There are clearly two, possibly three namespaces we need to use here. We need a namespace for the book definition. Perhaps the book publishers and sellers will get together and define one, but they have not yet, so let's invent our own. A namespace could be identified by URI (refer to `http://wombat.doc.ic.ac.uk/foldoc/foldoc.cgi?query=URI&action=Search`) or any other suitably long text string. Here we will invent a suitable URI without worrying for the moment what it is actually identifying. The key attribute of a URI is that it is unique, and we can achieve uniqueness simply by creating a URI on my web site, such as `http://www.boynings.co.uk/namespaces/books/`. In principle, we could then use something like `http://www.boynings.co.uk/namespaces/books/title` to identify that we are referring to the title of a book, rather than the title of a person. There are two problems with this. The first is that a URI can contain characters that would not be allowed in an XML element or attribute name. The second, and far more important from my point of view, is that if every element name had to be qualified by the string of characters in the URI, that requires a lot of typing. In fact, it would also make XML documents huge and virtually unreadable to humans. Instead, the W3C namespaces recommendation defines a shortcut that allows us to associate a short prefix with the URI:

```
<bk:books
  xmlns:bk="http://www.boynings.co.uk/namespaces/books/"
```

We have used the keyword `xmlns:` to declare our namespace as an attribute of the root element of the document. Where elements or attributes belong in this namespace, we can now use the prefix `bk:` as an **alias** for the complete namespace URI on element and attribute names.

We now have a namespace reference for the books, and can declare a similar reference for customers. We may also want a separate financial namespace relating to the credit card.

We could create an order using our three namespace definitions:

```
<?xml version="1.0"?>
<order xmlns:cust="http://www.boynings.co.uk/namespaces/customer/"
       xmlns:bk="http://www.boynings.co.uk/namespaces/book/"
       xmlns:fin="http://www.boynings.co.uk/namespaces/finance/"
>
  <cust:customer>
    <cust:title>Mr</cust:title>
    <cust:forename>Paul</cust:forname>
    <cust:lastname>Spencer</cust:lastname>
    <cust:address>…</cust:address>
    <cust:creditcard fin:cardtype="Visa">…</cust:creditcard>
    <cust:phone>…</cust:phone>
    <cust:email>…</cust:email>
  </cust:customer>
  <bk:books>
    <bk:book>
      <bk:title>Beginning Active Server Pages</bk:title>
      <bk:authors>
        <bk:author>Francis</bk:author>
        <bk:author>Kauffman</bk:author>
        <bk:author>Llibre</bk:author>
        <bk:author>Sussman</bk:author>
        <bk:author>Ullman</bk:author>
```

```
      </bk:authors>
      <bk:publisher>Wrox Press</bk:publisher>
      <bk:pages>653</bk:pages>
      <bk:isbn>1-861001-34-7</bk:isbn>
      <bk:price fin:currency = "USD">39.99</bk:price>
    </bk:book>
  </bk:books>
</order>
```

Even though we have used the three aliases, rather than the full URIs, this is a still rather longwinded. The Namespace recommendation provides two facilities to help with this – **scoping** and **default** namespaces.

Namespace Scope

If we use a namespace prefix on an element name, that prefix is assumed to apply to all descendants (including attributes) of that element unless specifically over-ridden through use of another namespace prefix. What does this mean in practice? Simply that we use the prefix once at one level of the document, then don't need to do so for descendants of that element until we meet an element from another namespace. We could therefore simplify our book order like this:

```
<?xml version="1.0"?>
<order xmlns:cust="http://www.boynings.co.uk/namespaces/customer/"
       xmlns:bk="http://www.boynings.co.uk/namespaces/book/"
       xmlns:fin="http://www.boynings.co.uk/namespaces/finance/"
>
  <cust:customer>
    <title>Mr</title>
    <forename>Paul</forname>
    <lastname>Spencer</lastname>
    <address>…</address>
    <creditcard fin:cardtype="Visa">…</creditcard>
    <phone>…</phone>
    <email>…</email>
  </cust:customer>
  <bk:books>
    <book>
      <title>Beginning Active Server Pages</title>
      <authors>
        <author>Francis</author>
        <author>Kauffman</author>
        <author>Llibre</author>
        <author>Sussman</author>
        <author>Ullman</author>
      </authors>
      <publisher>Wrox Press</publisher>
      <pages>653</pages>
      <isbn>1-861001-34-7</isbn>
      <price fin:currency = "USD">39.99</price>
    </book>
  </bk:books>
</order>
```

We now have a document that is as readable as we would have without namespaces, but have removed the ambiguity. The two `title` elements no longer have explicit namespace prefixes, but inherit the correct namespaces through their scoping. The two financial attributes, `cardtype` for the customer's credit card and `currency` for the book price, are still explicitly mentioned.

Default Namespaces

As well as declaring a namespace and using a prefix as an alias to reference it, we can declare a **default namespace**. We do this by declaring the namespace with no alias prefix. Once this is done, all elements within the scope of the definition will belong to this namespace unless they explicitly reference another.

```
<order xmlns="http://www.boynings.co.uk/namespaces/order"
       xmlns:cust="http://www.boynings.co.uk/namespaces/customer/"
       xmlns:bk="http://www.boynings.co.uk/namespaces/book/"
       xmlns:fin="http://www.boynings.co.uk/namespaces/finance/"
>
```

Here we have declared a default namespace for the `order`. So, according to the scope rules, all those tags without prefixes will be in the default namespace, in this case the namespace for the order.

The Empty Namespace

Most of the examples we have met in other chapters neither need nor use namespaces. What happens if we have a document that uses a default namespace, but we want some elements not to belong to any namespace, perhaps because they have no relevance outside the current document? In this case, we can use an empty namespace:

```
<?xml version="1.0"?>
<doc xmlns="http://www.w3.org/TR/REC-html40">
  <P>This document contains some HTML, including this <EM>table</EM></P>
  <TABLE><TR>
    <TD>This is the first cell</TD>
    <TD>And this is the second</TD>
  </TR></TABLE>
  <elem xmlns="">
    <comment>But this comment is not in any namespace</comment>
  </elem>
</doc>
```

In this example, the element `elem` does not belong in the HTML, or any other, namespace.

What Does the URI Mean?

What have our namespaces done for us? So far, they have simply ensured that all element and attribute names are unique. So what therefore is required of the URI? Simply that it is there and that it is unique, and the methods of allocating and using URIs ensure that. This confuses many people, who think that the URI should point to something useful, and many namespace identifiers are, indeed, DTDs. However, there is no requirement that it points to anything that can be understood by either a person or a computer application. In fact the W3C recommendation states when referring to the namespace declaration:

> **The attribute's *value*, a URI reference, is the *namespace name* identifying the namespace. The namespace name, to serve its intended purpose, should have the characteristics of uniqueness and persistence. It is not a goal that it be directly usable for retrieval of a schema (if any exists). An example of a syntax that is designed with these goals in mind is that for Uniform Resource Names *[RFC2141]*. However, it should be noted that ordinary URLs can be managed in such a way as to achieve these same goals.**

What Can Namespaces Do for Us?

As we have seen, currently all a namespace does is ensure that our elements and attributes are unique. However, this in itself is remarkably powerful as it potentially makes the World Wide Web our database. The most obvious way to do this is to use XML documents made available on the web to create a customized home page for myself. With messages in standard formats, there would be no difficulty in getting the local weather forecast, information on my stock portfolio and anything else that interests me. I could then use XSL stylesheets to render this as I like. And if I am going on holiday, firstly I can get special deals to places I might want to go straight onto my homepage, and nearer the time, I can just add another weather forecast. And the great thing is, I can make all this look exactly how I want it, as all I am getting from each site is the raw data marked up as XML.

And that is just the start. I recently developed a small application for marking up technical papers. The author of the paper marks each word they want defined with a specific tag, then submits the URI and the URI of a dictionary to the application. The application then puts the definitions into the paper as XML elements. Using an XSL stylesheet, the technical words appear as hyperlinks and clicking on them brings up a new window with the definition. Since I am marking up someone else's document, I do not want to risk using tag names that they are already using. By having my own namespace for the application, I can easily avoid this.

I say that "currently all a namespace can do ...". Clearly the possibilities grow once people decide that something should be at the end of the namespace URI. Although not included in the current recommendation, there is a working group addressing this and it is almost certain to happen in the future. What the possibilities are depends on the scope allowed by this new work. There could be purely a DTD or other form of schema, in which case we have access to information about the data in the element, such as the allowed values of attributes. However, there could potentially be far more. Java applets could allow us to check the semantics of a message to a degree that would be far beyond a DTD or schema. Or we could look up further information in the namespace based on data in the document. It all depends on the degree of flexibility that the World Wide Web Consortium allows when it goes to the next stage of namespace usage.

Namespaces in Centaur

So how are namespaces used in Centaur? The simple answer is that they are only used as required by XSL, as we shall see in later chapters. Why not do more? Simply because all the information in Centaur is defined by the system. One could imagine a commercial version of Centaur using a standard message set for communications with the tour operators. If this were to happen, then there would be benefits in using namespaces.

What Do I Need to Use XML?

We have seen quite a bit of XML so far, and seen that we need to do more than just send it to a browser. We have also seen that we can use XML as a messaging format between applications in a transactional environment, but we don't know what to do when we get the message.

So what do we need to make XML useful? Clearly, two things are:

- a way to display the contents of an XML document
- a way to access the contents of the document for transactional applications

The next chapter explains the Document Object Model, which gives us access to the contents of an XML document using scripting. After that, we will look at different ways of displaying XML documents, including using CSS and XSL stylesheets.

Summary

In this chapter, we have introduced some examples of uses to which XML can be put, and we have looked in some detail at the XML recommendation, including the Document Type Definition.

You now have an understanding of:

- XML itself, including the DTD
- why XML was developed
- how XML is useful in both informational and transactional contexts
- what XML namespaces are and why they are useful

You have also become familiar with some of the terminology we will be using in the rest of the book. In the next chapter we take a look at the key to manipulating XML - the object model.

3

The Document Object Model

As we saw in the last chapter, XML itself is remarkably simple - mainly a set of elements containing text and attributes. Unlike HTML, we don't even have to learn what the tags mean as they are left to us to define.

The **Document Object Model**, or DOM, is the key to manipulating the content of an XML document, since it makes the content of the document available to programs or scripts. We can access this either directly, or indirectly by using tools, such as XSL processors, where someone else has used the DOM to provide us with an interface that is easier to use for a specific purpose.

Consider our book catalogue example. Using the DOM, we can navigate through this document, selecting individual books and extracting information about them, or modifying the information they contain. As the W3C DOM recommendation puts it:

With the Document Object Model, programmers can build documents, navigate their structure, and add, modify, or delete elements and content.

Within Centaur, we will use these features of the DOM to access XML that is derived by extracting information from the database. We will use the DOM to generate HTML for display based on our XML, to create the brochure and to convert one XML document format into something that we can process more easily with a stylesheet.

In this chapter, we will:

- look at some examples of the DOM in use
- describe the structure and function of the DOM
- look at the Level 1 DOM recommendation of the W3C
- look at Microsoft's extensions to the DOM in IE5
- look at an alternative approach to parsing using the DOM
- look at the XML-related parts of the working draft for the Level 2 DOM
- develop a useful debugging tool

An Overview of the DOM

You will be familiar with the concept of an object model from Dynamic HTML, particularly as it is implemented in Internet Explorer. With this model, every HTML element is accessible through script, so I can - for example - change the style of an element. Here is a simple, but complete, HTML document that allows me to do this (`styles.htm`):

```
<HTML>
<BODY>
<DIV id="target">Pressing the buttons will allow you to change the color of this
text</DIV>
<BUTTON onclick="changeStyle('red')" type="button" id=button1
name=button1>red</BUTTON>
<BUTTON onclick="changeStyle('blue')" type="button" id=button2
name=button2>blue</BUTTON>
<BUTTON onclick="changeStyle('green')" type="button" id=button3
name=button3>green</BUTTON>
<BUTTON onclick="changeStyle('black')" type="button" id=button4
name=button4>black</BUTTON>


<SCRIPT>
function changeStyle(value)
{
     document.all.item("target").style.color = value;
}
</SCRIPT>
</BODY>
</HTML>
```

This results in a page looking like this:

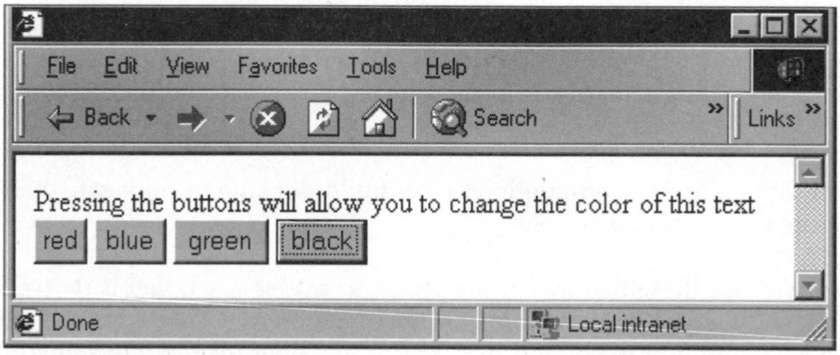

In this case, we have found an element called `target` in the `document` object. We have then set the color property of the style property to some value according to the button pressed.

The key point is that the object model comprises a set of **objects**, each of which exposes an **interface**. There may also be **collections** of objects, which have their own interfaces. In a good object model (and the W3C DOM is a good object model) these interfaces will be independent of programming language. I can therefore access my documents in a similar way from scripting languages such as ECMAScript and VBScript, or true programming languages such as Java and C++. In this chapter, we will use Microsoft's implementation of ECMAScript, called JScript.

This example is a simple use of a document object model, using, in this case, the Internet Explorer DOM. This immediately indicates one problem - I have specified the browser I am using. This page would not display correctly in Netscape Navigator, which is the reason why so many web pages have two versions with some browser-type detection code to switch between them.

It is to avoid this problem in the future that the World Wide Web Consortium has developed (and is continuing to develop) its own DOM. This DOM covers both XML and HTML, and the good news is that both the major browser manufacturers have committed to support it. Even better, both support the XML aspects of the model in their version 5 browsers.

Examples of the XML DOM in Use

Here, we will look at some of the aspects of the DOM as it applies to XML through a couple of examples. The first uses the book catalogue we developed in the last chapter to introduce some aspects of the DOM. The code for this is contained in the file `domExamples1.htm`. The second uses part of Centaur to show the DOM being used in a real application.

The Book Catalogue

Remember the book catalogue from the last chapter? We will use this to demonstrate how ECMAScript and the DOM can be used to navigate through, and extract information from, a document. Here it is again:

```
<?xml version = "1.0"?>
<!DOCTYPE books [
<!ELEMENT books (book)*>
<!ELEMENT book (title, authors, publisher, pages?, isbn, price+)>
<!ELEMENT authors (author+)>
<!ELEMENT title (#PCDATA)>
<!ELEMENT author (#PCDATA)>
<!ELEMENT publisher (#PCDATA)>
<!ELEMENT pages (#PCDATA)>
<!ELEMENT isbn (#PCDATA)>
<!ELEMENT price (#PCDATA)>
<!ATTLIST price currency CDATA #REQUIRED>
]>
<books>
  <book>
    <title>Clouds to Code</title>
    <authors>
      <author>Jesse Liberty</author>
    </authors>
    <publisher>Wrox Press</publisher>
    <pages>393</pages>
    <isbn>1-861000-95-2</isbn>
    <price currency = "USD">40.00</price>
  </book>
  <book>
    <title>Beginning Active Server Pages</title>
    <authors>
      <author>Francis</author>
      <author>Kauffman</author>
      <author>Llibre</author>
      <author>Sussman</author>
      <author>Ullman</author>
```

```
      </authors>
      <publisher>Wrox Press</publisher>
      <pages>653</pages>
      <isbn>1-861001-34-7</isbn>
      <price currency = "USD">39.99</price>
    </book>
  </books>
```

The W3C DOM provides a standard Application Programming Interface (API) for manipulating XML documents once they are loaded into memory. It does not (yet) provide an API for actually creating a DOM object, loading data into it or parsing the XML. We will therefore use proprietary Microsoft extensions for doing this. Of course, this makes this part of the code incompatible with Netscape's browser, but this is only for a small part of the code that you would use in an XML application.

Creating a DOM Object in Internet Explorer 5

To work with the script examples that follow you will need to set up a simple HTML file with a script section.

```
<HTML>
<SCRIPT>
...script code goes here ...
</SCRIPT>
</HTML>
```

Save this to disk but keep the file open for editing. That done we can begin to experiment.

The first thing we do is to use a Microsoft DOM extension to create an ActiveX object to hold our document. Here we hold a reference to this object in a variable called `source`. Insert this line into the script section of the HTML file:

```
source = new ActiveXObject("Microsoft.XMLDOM");
```

We then load the catalogue into this object, again with a Microsoft extension. We set the `async` property of the object to `false` to indicate to the browser that it should not continue processing until the document is fully loaded. We will be looking more at this property, and others related to parsing, later.

```
source.async = false;
source.load("catalog.xml");
```

When we load the document like this, it will be parsed by the `MSXML` parser built into Internet Explorer 5. If the parser finds an error, we want to see this, and Microsoft provides an interface to let us see errors detected by the parser. This code will show them to us:

```
if (source.parseError != 0)
  alert(source.parseError.reason);
```

Let's introduce a couple of errors to show this. If we change a closing tag name like this:

```
<title>Clouds to Code</name>
```

our document is no longer well-formed. Internet Explorer 5 will report this error:

If we change the start tag of this element to match the new end tag, the document will again be well-formed, but it will no longer be valid, since the DTD does not allow the element `book` to contain an element `name`. Since it is a validating parser, Internet Explorer 5 will also report this error:

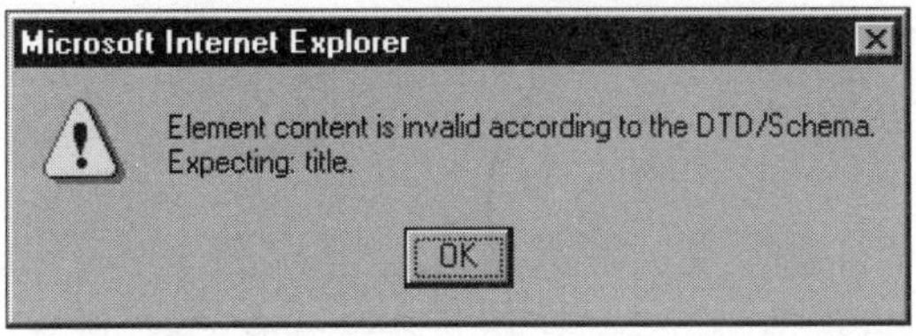

A non-validating parser would not spot this error. If, for example, we had started with an element name of `name`, decided to change it to `title` throughout the document, but missed this one instance, this could cause problems in our application.

The Root Element

We now have the document loaded, so we can start to use the W3C DOM to navigate through it.

First of all, we find the root element:

```
root = source.documentElement;
```

If we apply these two lines to the root element of the books example:

```
alert(root.nodeName);
alert(root.nodeType);
```

we will get the results:

Let's put these three lines of code into the context of the DOM. (Now we are using the W3C DOM; all references to the DOM refer to this unless I explicitly say otherwise.) The variable `source` holds a reference to a `Document` object. As such its interface exposes methods and properties that tell us about the document and allow us to create and find elements and other XML entities such as attributes and comments. Here, we find the `documentElement` of the object, which in the book catalogue is the element `books`, and assign it to a variable `root`.

`books` is an `Element` node. This exposes two interfaces, one specific to the `Element` node type, the other a more general `Node` interface that applies to all node types. The `Node` interface exposes the two properties we use here (and many more). The first, `nodeName`, is self-explanatory. The second, `nodeType`, is a numerical value indicating the type of node. The value `1` indicates that this is an element node. The complete set of values is:

Node	Value
Element node	1
Attribute node	2
Text node	3
CDATA Section node	4
Entity Reference node	5
Entity node	6
Processing Instruction node	7
Comment node	8
Document node	9
Document Type node	10
Document Fragment node	11
Notation node	12

Finding the Authors

Let's go deeper into the document and display the number of authors of the second book in our catalogue and the name of the second author of that book:

Firstly, we have to navigate to the second book. The `Node` object exposes a `childNodes` property, that returns a collection of nodes known as a **NodeList**. We can then index into this list using the `item` property to get the second book. Being ECMAScript, the index is zero-based, so we use an index value of `1`.

```
var book2 = root.childNodes.item(1);
```

The variable `book2` is a `Node` of type `Element`. The `Element` object has a method `getElementsByTagName()` that does exactly that. We will use this now to get a `NodeList` of the `author` elements:

```
var authors = book2.getElementsByTagName("author");
```

An important aspect of `getElementsByTagName()` is that it looks through all descendants (that is, children, grandchildren and so on) of the current element, not just immediate children. We have therefore not had to navigate through the `authors` element to reach the individual `author` names.

Now we can use the properties of the `NodeList` to display the number of children (i.e. `authors`) we have found:

```
alert(authors.length);
```

We can also look at the data within the second `author` element. Let's try this in two stages. Firstly, we will get the element itself:

```
author2 = authors.item(1);
```

This element contains a **Text** node. A `Text` node can only have one child, and that is the text itself. However, the DOM does not let us access this directly - in case a node has more children, we must first get a `NodeList`, then the `Text` node will be the first (and only) item in the list. `Text` nodes inherit the properties of an object type called **CharacterData**, and these include a `data` property that contains the text itself:

```
alert(author2.childNodes.item(0).data);
```

We can easily combine these two lines of code into a single line:

```
alert(authors.item(1).childNodes.item(0).data);
```

This may seem a little long-winded when we know that the second `author` node only contains text. The World Wide Web Consortium clearly felt that all node types should be treated in identical ways for consistency. Microsoft, meanwhile, felt that ease of use was equally important, and have given us an alternative:

```
alert(authors.item(1).text);
```

I much prefer this, as it is easier to write, and much clearer to read. However, we are introducing an implementation-specific property. Of course, it is easy to write code using the `text` property and do a global search and replace to replace it with `childNodes.item(0).data` before deploying the code. Alternatively, you can write a simple method that takes an element as a parameter and returns the enclosed text. Either of these would maintain simplicity while keeping your code conformant to the DOM, maintaining implementation compatibility. For simplicity, I will continue to use the Microsoft extension.

Accessing Attributes

We have seen how to navigate our way through the elements of the catalogue, so now let's see how we can read the `currency` attribute of the first book. Firstly, we navigate to the book and set a variable to the price element:

```
var book1 = root.childNodes.item(0);
var price = book1.getElementsByTagName("price").item(0);
```

Then we simply use the `getAttribute()` method of the `Element` object to read the attribute value:

```
alert(price.getAttribute("currency"));
```

This is the resulting alert message:

We could have done this another way. In the same way that we can get a `NodeList` of child Elements, we can get a collection called a `NamedNodeMap` of all the attributes of any `Node` object. Let's start by getting this collection:

```
var attributes = price.attributes;
```

Now we can get the currency attribute, which will be returned as a Node:

```
var currency = attributes.getNamedItem("currency");
```

Since this is a Node, we can extract the text using Microsoft's proprietary text property (remember - the one we are using to save typing):

```
alert(currency.text);
```

As well as getting an item from the NamedNodeMap by name, we can index into the collection. Here, we get the first item, and display it's value property. Both these methods display USD as we saw before.

```
alert(attributes.item(0).value);
```

However, we need to be aware that implementations need not preserve the order of attributes, and so indexing into the namedNodeMap is risky if it contains more than one node. In general, attributes should be accessed by name.

Adding an Element

I mentioned at the start of the chapter that we can use the DOM to create elements as well as read them. If we are to have a useful catalogue, it should at least have this book in it, so let's add it. First we create a new book element using the createElement() method of the Document object:

```
var newBook = source.createElement("book");
```

We also need a title element, and a Text node containing the title:

```
var newTitle = source.createElement("title");
var newText = source.createTextNode("XML Design and Implementation");
```

Then we use the appendChild() method of the Node object three times to create our hierarchy:

```
newTitle.appendChild(newText);
newBook.appendChild(newTitle);
root.appendChild(newBook);
```

What did we do here? Firstly, we appended the text as a child of the title element. We do this because text is contained in a node of its own. Then we appended the title to the book element. Finally, we appended this book to the root element of the document.

Now we have done this, our document is no longer valid. To make it valid again, we would have to add the remaining elements defined in the DTD. However, we can see the result of what we have done so far using a another Microsoft extension - the xml property of the Node object. This is a very useful debugging aid as it returns a representation of the node as a string:

```
alert(root.xml);
```

As you can see below, this does not give us the pretty formatting of the original, but the new book is in there as we expect.

```
Microsoft Internet Explorer                                    [X]

  ⚠️       <books>
              <book>
                      <title>Clouds to Code</title>
                      <authors>
                              <author>Jesse Liberty</author>
                      </authors>
                      <publisher>Wrox Press</publisher>
                      <pages>393</pages>
                      <isbn>1-861000-95-2</isbn>
                      <price currency="USD">40.00</price>
              </book>
              <book>
                      <title>Beginning Active Server Pages 2.0</title>
                      <authors>
                              <author>Francis</author>
                              <author>Kauffman</author>
                              <author>Llibre</author>
                              <author>Sussman</author>
                              <author>Ullman</author>
                      </authors>
                      <publisher>Wrox Press</publisher>
                      <pages>653</pages>
                      <isbn>1-861001-34-7</isbn>
                      <price currency="USD">39.99</price>
              </book>
              <book><title>XML Design and Implementation</title></book></books>

                          [      OK      ]
```

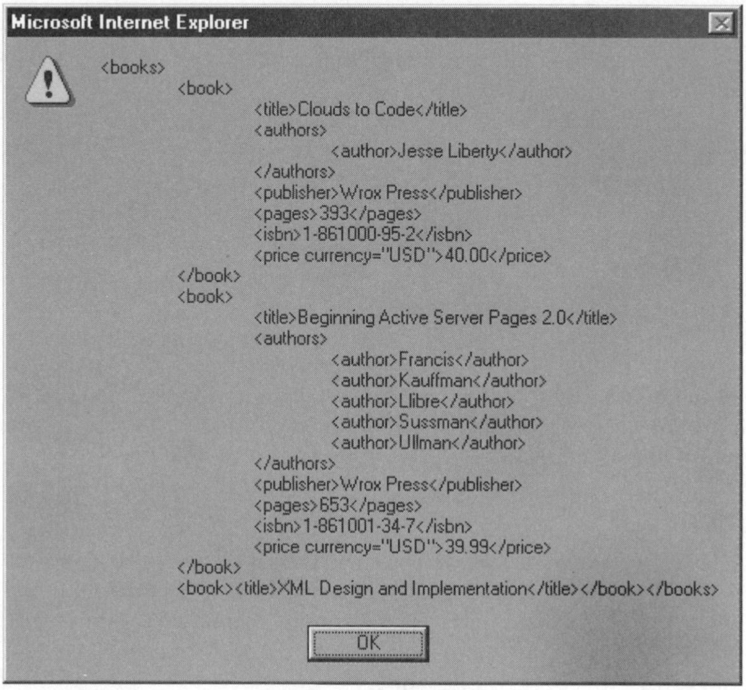

Displaying Search Results in Centaur

We have now seen how to use some of the more common parts of the DOM. Let's try putting these together into something that is used as part of Centaur.

In Centaur, when we conduct a search, we see the results in a frame on the left-hand side of the screen. At this stage, all we are seeing is the basic information about the vacations that match our search criteria:

If we were to do this in HTML, the first matching vacation would be displayed using code something like:

```
<A onclick="getTour(4)">Panorama <EM>Hotel Marhaba Palace</EM> Tunisia</A>
```

where the parameter of the `onclick` event handler is the reference `ID` of the vacation in the database.

Centaur uses Microsoft's Active Server Page (ASP) technology for running code on the server. The ASP code we use to extract information from the database would create this HTML for us. In Centaur, we are trying, wherever possible, to separate the complex database extraction from the much simpler task of displaying information on the browser, so we use XML as an intermediate data format. In this case, the XML we create from the database looks like this:

```
<results>
  <result>
    <tourid>4</tourid>
    <tourOp>Panorama</tourOp>
    <name>Hotel Marhaba Palace</name>
    <area>Tunisia</area>
  </result>
  <result>
    <tourid>3</tourid>
    <tourOp>Panorama</tourOp>
    <name>Hotel Phenicia</name>
    <area>Tunisia</area>
  </result>
  <result>
    <tourid>2</tourid>
    <tourOp>Panorama</tourOp>
    <name>Hotel Fourati</name>
    <area>Tunisia</area>
  </result>
</results>
```

As you can see, this contains the four important bits of information about each vacation - the tour operator, hotel and location for display, and the `ID` to identify the vacation when the viewer clicks on it.

Let's see how we use the DOM to create the display. The ASP code places the results in an **XML Island**. Remember that the W3C DOM does not have any means to load and parse XML. The XML Island is one Microsoft extension to do this, and is simply a proprietary tag in the HTML code that allows us to embed some XML as a string in an HTML document. We will look at the XML Island further when we discuss the Microsoft extensions to the DOM. This is what it looks like in this case:

```
<XML Id="Island">
<?xml version="1.0"?>
<%=mstrXML%>
</XML>
```

The element `XML` defines the island, which is given an `Id` of `Island`. This contains the XML declaration and a placeholder for the ASP code to write its results - the XML code we saw just now. This would work equally well without the XML declaration - it is just there for completeness.

In Centaur, the situation is complicated by the fact that the code to create the results is in one page (`getSearchResults.asp`) and the code to display them is in another (`index-1.htm`). Since this helps in the separation of data and display, we will look at how the situation is managed.

Centaur is based on three frames, called `left`, `right` and `hidden`. Since `getSearchResults.asp` does not have any display function, it exists in the hidden frame. `index-1.htm` is permanently visible in the left frame. In the code below `parent` refers refers to the window object containing the frames.

The XML island above is part of `getSearchResults.asp`, which has the following `onLoad()` function:

```
function onLoad()
{
  if(Island.readyState != "complete")
    window.setTimeout('onLoad();',200);
  else
  {
    if (Island.parseError != 0)
      alert("getSearchResults.asp: " + Island.parseError.reason);
    parent.left.domResults = Island;
    parent.left.getResults();
  }
}
```

This will be called when the page loads on the client, which will be after the ASP code has done its work and put the search results into the island. This starts by using a Microsoft DOM extension that we shall meet in a moment to check that the document is fully loaded and parsed before we continue processing. If the parser has not completed it, the function will exit and be called again after 200 ms. The four lines of code in the else clause are therefore only called once parsing is complete.

The next two lines check that the parser did not report an error. If it did, the error is reported. I have included the name of the page to make debugging easier. Many people would code this differently, so processing does not continue after the parser detects an error:

```
    if (Island.parseError != 0)
      alert("getSearchResults.asp: " + Island.parseError.reason);
    else
    {
      parent.left.domResults = Island;
      parent.left.getResults();
    }
```

However, I work on the basis that I will correct errors before deploying the code, and the style I have used is easier to read, especially in a long function. The worst that happens is that, after displaying the alert, I will get a script error reported.

Once parsing is complete, and assuming there were no errors, an object in the left frame is set to point to the island and a function called. It is this function that creates the display, as we shall see now.

The aim of the function `getResults()`, which is in the file `index-1.htm`, is to create the HTML we need to put the search results on the screen in the format we saw in the screen-shot and HTML extract earlier.

The left frame always displays index-l.htm, but it uses dynamic HTML to switch between the search results and the brochure. After declaring our variables, the first task is therefore to ensure that the results screen is being displayed:

```
function getResults()
{
  var s='';
  var i,currentNode;
  var rootResults,tempId,tempTourOp,tempName,tempArea;

  // show results screen
  displayResults();
```

We then get the root element of the results:

```
rootResults = domResults.documentElement;
```

Remember, the format of the document is:

```
<results>
  <result>
    <tourid>4</tourid>
    <tourOp>Panorama</tourOp>
    <name>Hotel Marhaba Palace</name>
    <area>Tunisia</area>
  </result>
  <result>
    <tourid>3</tourid>
    <tourOp>Panorama</tourOp>
    <name>Hotel Phenicia</name>
    <area>Tunisia</area>
  </result>
  <result>
    <tourid>2</tourid>
    <tourOp>Panorama</tourOp>
    <name>Hotel Fourati</name>
    <area>Tunisia</area>
  </result>
</results>
```

The root element is therefore the element called `results`. We will want to build up a string of text representing the HTML to display the results. We will therefore need a loop to run the formatting code once for each matching vacation. We have already met the `childNodes` property of the `Node` object. This returns a `NodeList`, and a property of a `NodeList` is its `length`. This length represents the number of `result` elements, and so allows us to control the loop:

```
  for (i = 0 ; i < rootResults.childNodes.length ; i++)
  {
```

We then get the `result` element according to our current index:

```
    currentNode = rootResults.childNodes.item(i);
```

and the text of the four elements we want:

```
    tempId = currentNode.getElementsByTagName('tourid').item(0).text;
    tempTourOp = currentNode.getElementsByTagName('tourOp').item(0).text;
    tempName = currentNode.getElementsByTagName('name').item(0).text;
    tempArea = currentNode.getElementsByTagName('area').item(0).text;
```

Again, I have used the Microsoft proprietary text property, knowing I could write my own method or do a global search and replace if I wanted to.

Once we have these, we insert them as required into a string:

```
  s += '<A style="cursor:hand" onclick="getTour(' + "'" + tempId + "'" + ')">';
  s += tempTourOp + ' <EM>' + tempName + '</EM> ' + tempArea + '</A><BR/>';
```

(I have reduced the indentation here to get the code to fit on the lines.) The need to incorporate either apostrophes or quotation marks makes this look rather more complex than it is. If we replace the variables with the literal values of the first matching vacation, the lines would look like this:

```
   s += '<A style="cursor:hand" onclick="getTour(4)">';
   s += 'Panorama <EM>Hotel Marhaba PalacepName</EM> Tunisia</A><BR/>';
```

Finally, we close the loop and use dynamic HTML to write the results to a DIV element on the displayed page:

```
  }
  tgtResults.innerHTML = s;
}
```

The complete code looks like this:

```
function getResults()
{
  var s='';
  var i,currentNode;
  var rootResults,tempId,tempTourOp,tempName,tempArea;

  // show results screen
  displayResults();

  // get the root element of the results object
  rootResults = domResults.documentElement;

  // build the results string
  for (i = 0 ; i < rootResults.childNodes.length ; i++)
  {
```

```
      currentNode = rootResults.childNodes.item(i);
      tempId = currentNode.getElementsByTagName('tourid').item(0).text;
      tempTourOp = currentNode.getElementsByTagName('tourOp').item(0).text;
      tempName = currentNode.getElementsByTagName('name').item(0).text;
      tempArea = currentNode.getElementsByTagName('area').item(0).text;

      s += '<A style="cursor: hand" onclick="getTour(' + "'" + tempId + "'" + ')">';
      s += tempTourOp + ' <EM>' + tempName + '</EM> ' + tempArea + '</A><BR/>';
    }
    tgtResults.innerHTML = s;
  }
```

About the DOM

From these examples, we can see that the DOM provides a powerful interface for manipulating our XML documents, which also has the advantage of being an agreed standard. We have navigated through documents, finding the nodes we wanted to work with, we have read tag names, attributes and data and have added nodes. Something we did not do was manipulate the DTD, and that is because the DOM does not currently support more than finding very basic information from the DTD. We also saw that Microsoft has added some extensions to the DOM. Some of these, such as the `load()` method, are essential to its use, and Netscape will provide equivalents. To maintain implementation independence, we will still therefore have to detect the browser type and write separate code for creating and parsing our DOM objects. Also, of course, we must remember that pages that deliver XML to the client will still only work in browsers from version 5 upwards.

I should point out that browsers are not the only source of XML parsers. There are several others available to build into applications. Microsoft has also stated an intention to make its MSXML parser available independently of Internet Explorer 5. A version of this parser written in Java is available from DataChannel at
`http://www.datachannel.com/xml_resources/developers/parser.shtml`.

In this section, we will look more at the structure of the DOM recommendation before taking a more formal look at the objects it makes available to us and the interfaces we can use to work with them.

Structure of the DOM

The W3C DOM is split into two **levels**. **Level 1** covers all the interfaces we have used above and is a World Wide Web Consortium recommendation. **Level 2** covers additional areas, such as event handling, and is still a working draft at the time of writing. Centaur only uses the Level 1 DOM, but we will also look briefly at Level 2 here.

The DOM covers both XML and HTML. We have already seen that HTML is an implementation of SGML, and that XML is a subset. As an implementation, HTML has a defined set of tags, and so has its own requirements in the DOM. The Level 1 DOM is therefore divided into a set of **Core** interfaces that cover both XML and HTML and a set of **HTML** interfaces that cover the specific requirements of HTML.

Since XML contains elements, such as CDATA sections, that HTML does not, it also has specific requirements. The Core interfaces are therefore further divided into **Fundamental** interfaces for those parts of the object model common to XML and HTML and **Extended** interfaces for the XML specifics.

The structure of the DOM recommendations can be represented as:

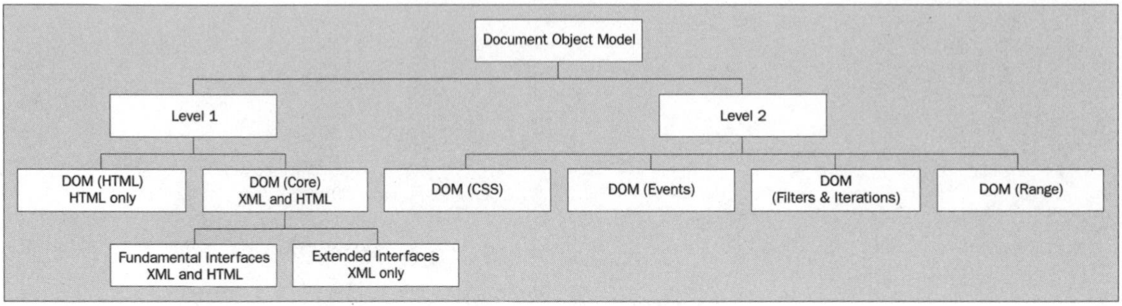

We can see here the four parts of the Level 2 DOM as well the core interfaces and HTML extensions of the Level 1 DOM.

An XML document is represented in the DOM as a **tree structure**, with the tags forming the branches and the text the leaves. Our book example:

```
<books>
  <book>
    <title>Clouds to Code</title>
    <authors>
      <author>Jesse Liberty</author>
    </authors>
    <publisher>Wrox Press</publisher>
    <pages>393</pages>
    <isbn>1-861000-95-2</isbn>
    <price currency = "USD">40.00</price>
  </book>
  <book>
    <title>Beginning Active Server Pages</title>
    <authors>
      <author>Francis</author>
      <author>Kauffman</author>
      <author>Llibre</author>
      <author>Sussman</author>
      <author>Ullman</author>
    </authors>
    <publisher>Wrox Press</publisher>
    <pages>653</pages>
    <isbn>1-861001-34-7</isbn>
    <price currency = "USD">39.99</price>
  </book>
</books>
```

can be represented as a set of nodes:

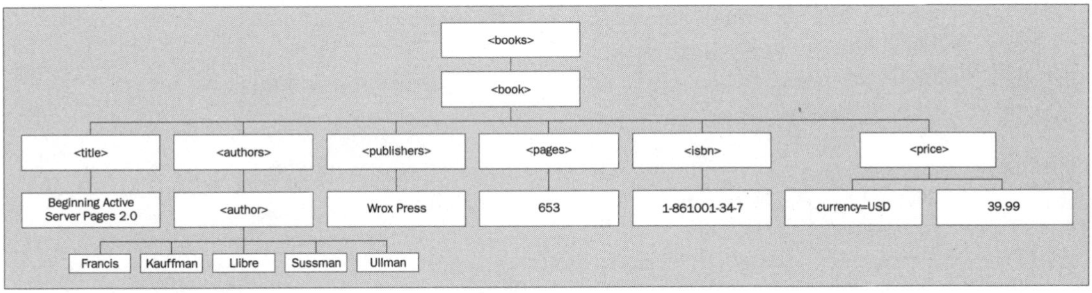

We have already used several of the DOM interfaces to manipulate these objects. Now we will look at the Core interfaces more formally.

The Level 1 DOM Interfaces

The DOM represents the entire document object as a set of interfaces that allow us to manipulate the XML data. Each has its own set of methods and properties, some of which may be inherited by other objects. For example, in the book catalogue, we used the `tagName` property of the `Node` interface on an `Element` object since the `Element` interface inherits all the methods and properties of the `Node` interface. Each of the twelve node types we saw in the table earlier inherits these methods and properties, so this is a particularly powerful interface. Similarly, we saw that `Text` nodes inherit the methods and properties of the `CharacterData` object.

Overview of the Core Interfaces

Of the interfaces defined in the DOM, Centaur uses six. These are:

- The `Document` interface, which enables querying of document properties such as the `DOCTYPE`, and provides facilities for creating nodes. This interface can also be used to return a collection of elements.
- The `Node` interface, which we have just seen provides facilities that are common to all node types. These include properties to provide information about the node, such as its `nodeType` that we used before, and methods to add, remove and copy nodes.
- The `Element` interface, which mainly provides facilities for attribute handling, since this is the only node type that has attributes.
- The `Attr` interface, which allows us to see whether an attribute is explicitly specified and find its name and value.
- The `NodeList` interface, which allows us to find the number of nodes in the collection and index into them.
- The `NamedNodeMap` interface, which lets us do the same for attributes, but also fetch, set and remove attributes by name.

Centaur uses the Microsoft `text` property extension, and so does not use two other useful interfaces:

- The `CharacterData` interface, which has properties to determine the content and length of the character data and a set of string handling methods.
- The `Text` interface, which inherits the `CharacterData` properties and methods and has a single method of its own to split text.

We will look at all these interfaces in more detail in moment. However, before that, we'll briefly mention the other DOM interfaces that we will not meet in Centaur.

- The `DOMException` interface, which tells us about errors such as an index out of range or an illegal character.
- The `DomImplementation` interface, which allows us to find a little about the implementation of the DOM in our program. Currently we can just check support for HTML and XML and the version supported.
- The `DocumentFragment` interface, which allows us to build up parts of documents. It inherits the properties and methods of the `Node` object, and does not add any more of its own.
- The `Comment` interface for creating and manipulating comments. It inherits the properties and methods of the `CharacterData` interface.

Overview of the Extended Interfaces

Although we are most interested in the DOM as it applies to XML, the interfaces above also apply to HTML. The interfaces listed below are specific to XML, since HTML has no equivalents of the objects involved.

These interfaces are:

- The `CDATASection` interface for creating and manipulating CDATA sections. It inherits the properties and methods of the `Text` interface.
- The `DocumentType` interface. As well as inheriting the methods and properties of the `Node` interface, it can tell us the `DOCTYPE` of the document and provide information about the entities and notations in it.
- The `Notation` interface, which allows us to read information about `Notation` nodes in the DTD.
- The `Entity` interface, which allows us to read information about entities we use in the XML document.
- The `EntityReference` interface, which allows entity references to be inserted into the document and accessed using the properties and methods of the `Node` interface.
- The `ProcessingInstruction` interface, which allows processing of processing instructions.

The Document Interface

The `Document` object sits right at the top of the tree. It is the only node type that cannot be created within the DOM, so implementations need to define their own methods of creating new documents. We have already seen how to do this in Internet Explorer 5.

`Document` objects can use all the properties and methods exposed by the `Node` interface, which we will look at next. It also has several properties and methods specific to dealing with `Document` objects.

Document Interface Properties

These properties allow us to find information about the document itself. Its main uses are to:

- tell us about the document itself
- tell us about the DOM implementation we are using
- find the root element of the document so we can start navigating its structure
- create nodes

doctype

This read-only property returns the document type defined in the DTD as a `DOCTYPE` object. The `DOCTYPE` interface belongs in the extended interfaces, and exposes the `name`, `entities` and `notations` of the document. Being a node, we can also use all the properties and methods of the `Node` object. Because the `doctype` refers to the DTD, the interface only applies to documents containing a DTD.

If we go back to our book catalogue example (`domExamples1.htm`), we have our document (`catalog.xml`) loaded into an object called `source`. Since the file contains a DTD, we an look at the name of the `doctype`:

```
alert(source.doctype.name);
```

This gives a result:

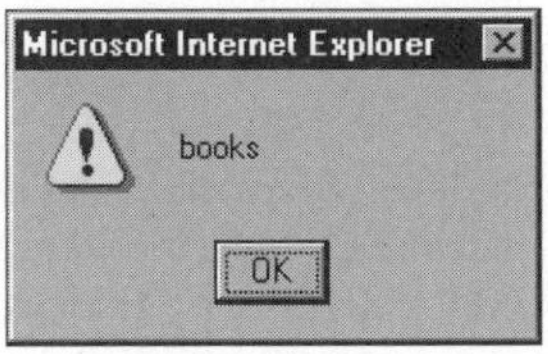

implementation

This read-only property can be used to find out which versions of XML and HTML are supported by the implementation of the DOM. It returns an object of type `DOMImplementation` which has a single method `hasFeature()`. This can be used as follows:

```
alert(source.implementation.hasFeature("XML","1.0"));
```

This will indicate whether the implementation of the DOM in Internet Explorer 5 supports version 1.0 of XML. As we would expect, the result of running this code is:

There is currently one alternative for the first parameter, and that is `HTML`. We can ask in the same way whether Internet Explorer 5 supports HTML version 4:

```
alert(source.implementation.hasFeature("HTML","4.0"));
```

This results in a response of `false`, since the HTML DOM implementation in Internet Explorer 5 is not complete.

documentElement

The final property is also read-only and returns the document element of the document. This is an essential start to any processing using the DOM, and we used it in both our examples at the start of this chapter. For the book catalogue, we used:

```
root = source.documentElement;
```

And for the example from Centaur, we used:

```
rootResults = domResults.documentElement;
```

Document Interface Methods

Most of the methods in this interface relate to creating document nodes. They are therefore similar in operation.

Creating Nodes

We have already used `createElement()` and `createTextNode()` to add a book to the catalogue. This was the code we used to create the book:

```
var newBook = source.createElement("book");
```

The `tagName` parameter (`book`) is of a data type called **DOMString**. This is defined as a sequence of unsigned short integers representing characters encoded using UTF-16 character encoding. For our purposes, it is safe to think of it simply as a string type that can handle double byte characters such as Kanji.

The full list of node types that can be created in this way is:

Method	Return Type	Parameter Types
`createElement(tagName)`	Element	The `tagName` parameter is of type DOMString
`createDocumentFragment()`	DocumentFragment	
`createTextNode(data)`	Text	The `data` parameter is of type DOMString
`createComment(data)`	Comment	The `data` parameter is of type DOMString

Method	Return Type	Parameter Types
`createCDATASection(data)`	CDATASection	The `data` parameter is of type DOMString
`createProcessing_ Instruction(target, data)`	ProcessingInstruction	The `target` and `data` parameters are of type DOMString
`createAttribute(name)`	Attr	The `name` parameter is of type DOMString
`createEntityReference_ (name)`	EntityReference	The `name` parameter is of type DOMString

getElementsByTagName(tagname)

This is the last of the Document object's methods. We met the same method in the book catalogue example, where we applied it as part of the `Element` interface.

```
var price = book1.getElementsByTagName("price").item(0);
```

The Node Interface

This is an especially important interface as all node types implement its properties and methods, most adding a few extra of their own. Its main uses are:

- to find information about nodes
- to copy, add, remove and replace nodes

Node Interface Properties

Using the properties of the node object, we can find a lot of useful information about a node.

nodeName

This is a read-only string giving the name of the node as we saw when looking at the book catalogue.

nodeValue

This is a read/write string representing the value of a node. Don't be confused into thinking that you can use this to access the text between the tags of an `Element` node. This text is in a `Text` node of its own; the value of an `Element` node is `null`. Since this is a read/write string, we can also set the value of a node. In the book catalogue example, we set the title of a new book to "XML Design and Implementation". This was set in a `Text` node called `newText`. We can use the `nodeValue` property to change this title:

```
newText.nodeValue = "XML Design and Implementation, First Edition";
alert(newText.data);
```

This results in an alert message:

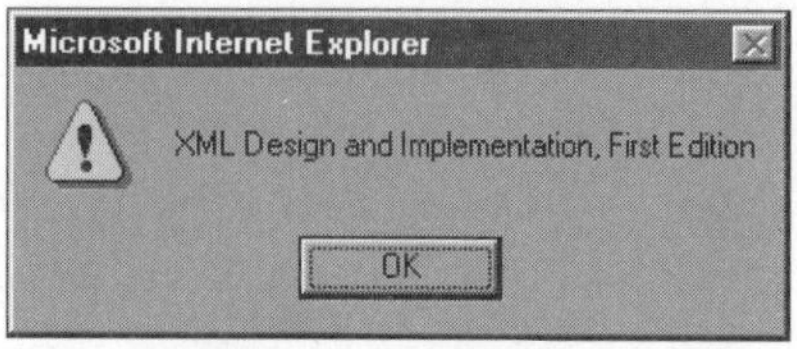
Microsoft Internet Explorer
XML Design and Implementation, First Edition
OK

When we change this node value, we do not need to re-attach it to the `title` node, the `book` node and the root element. Looking at the complete document object demonstrates that the change ripples through as we would want:

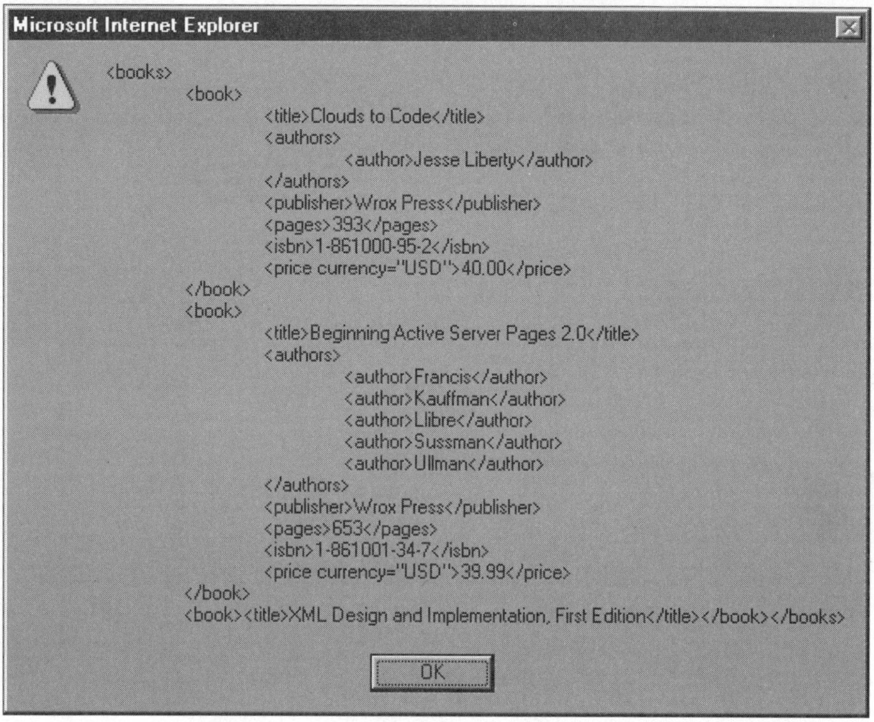
Microsoft Internet Explorer
<books>
<book>
<title>Clouds to Code</title>
<authors>
<author>Jesse Liberty</author>
</authors>
<publisher>Wrox Press</publisher>
<pages>393</pages>
<isbn>1-861000-95-2</isbn>
<price currency="USD">40.00</price>
</book>
<book>
<title>Beginning Active Server Pages 2.0</title>
<authors>
<author>Francis</author>
<author>Kauffman</author>
<author>Llibre</author>
<author>Sussman</author>
<author>Ullman</author>
</authors>
<publisher>Wrox Press</publisher>
<pages>653</pages>
<isbn>1-861001-34-7</isbn>
<price currency="USD">39.99</price>
</book>
<book><title>XML Design and Implementation, First Edition</title></book></books>
OK

nodeType

This is a read-only unsigned short representing the type of node (`Element`, `Comment` or whatever), using the values that we saw in the table earlier in the section on "The Root Element".

parentNode

This read-only property returns the parent node of a node. The parent node of either of the `book` nodes is the `books` node, so the code:

```
alert(book1.parentNode.nodeName);
```

results in:

childNodes

This read-only property returns a `nodeList` of all the children of the current node. We have already used this in the book catalogue example, where we indexed into the `nodeList` to find a specific node.

```
var book2 = root.childNodes.item(1);
```

firstChild, lastChild

These two read-only properties return the first and last children of the current node.

```
var book1     = root.firstChild();
var lastbook  = root.lastChild();
```

previousSibling, nextSibling

These two read-only properties find the next and previous siblings (that is, nodes at the same level of the hierarchy in relation to their parent). If `book1` contains the first `book` node, we can find the title of the next book:

```
alert(book1.nextSibling.getElementsByTagName("title").item(0).text);
```

This gives us a message:

attributes

This is a read-only property that returns a `namedNodeMap` of the attributes of the current `Element` node. Previously, we accessed the `currency` attribute of the `price` node in two ways. The first was by name, using the `getAttribute()` method of the `Element` object:

```
alert(price.getAttribute("currency"));
```

We also accessed it, getting the same result by retrieving all the attributes (there is only this one) into a `NamedNodeMap` and indexing into it. This uses the `attributes` property of the `Node` object:

```
alert(price.attributes.item(0).value);
```

This is an example of how we can often use either a method or property of a specific node type (in this case, the `getAttribute()` method from the `Element` interface), or use a method or property from the generic `Node` interface.

ownerDocument

The final read-only property returns a `Document` object, which is the owning document of the node.

Node Interface Methods

The methods of the `Node` interface are mainly concerned with adding, removing and copying child nodes. In Centaur, they are used for functions such as taking a vacation description from a search and adding it to the catalogue, which is held as an XML document.

We will demonstrate these by manipulating the nodes of two simple documents. These are the files:

Our source document, `nodeSource.xml`

```
<?xml version = "1.0"?>
<nodeSource>
  <source1>source element 1</source1>
  <source2>source element 2</source2>
  <source3>source element 3</source3>
  <source4>source element 4</source4>
</nodeSource>
```

and our destination document, `nodeDest.xml`

```
<?xml version = "1.0"?>
<nodeDest>
  <dest1>destination element 1</dest1>
  <dest2>destination element 2</dest2>
  <dest3>destination element 3</dest3>
  <dest4>destination element 4</dest4>
</nodeDest>
```

The code for this section is in the file `domExamples2.htm`. If you want to work through the code examples that follow yourself you can start with an HTML file like this in the same folder as the two XML files:

```
<HTML>
<SCRIPT>

   nodeSource = new ActiveXObject("Microsoft.XMLDOM");
   nodeDest = new ActiveXObject("Microsoft.XMLDOM");

   nodeSource.async = false;
   nodeSource.load("nodeSource.xml");

   if (nodeSource.parseError != 0)
      alert(nodeSource.parseError.reason);
```

```
      nodeDest.async = false;
      nodeDest.load("nodeDest.xml");

      if (nodeDest.parseError != 0)
         alert(nodeDest.parseError.reason);

      rootSource = nodeSource.documentElement;
      rootDest = nodeDest.documentElement;

   </SCRIPT>
   </HTML>
```

removeChild(oldChild)

The first method removes a child and returns it. We will remove the last node of the `source` object and return it:

```
      source4 = rootSource.removeChild(rootSource.lastChild);
      alert(source4.xml);
```

Microsoft Internet Explorer
<source4>source element 4</source4>
OK

Naturally, this will leave the source object with only three elements.

insertBefore(newChild, refChild)

We can now insert this object into the destination object. We will put it before the second element:

```
      dest2 = rootDest.childNodes.item(1);
      rootDest.insertBefore(source4,dest2);
      alert(rootDest.xml);                    //show the result
```

The destination object now looks like this:

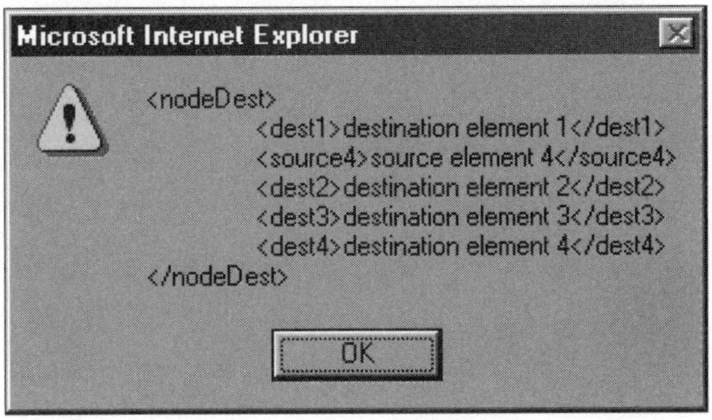
Microsoft Internet Explorer
<nodeDest>
<dest1>destination element 1</dest1>
<source4>source element 4</source4>
<dest2>destination element 2</dest2>
<dest3>destination element 3</dest3>
<dest4>destination element 4</dest4>
</nodeDest>
OK

and the source like this:

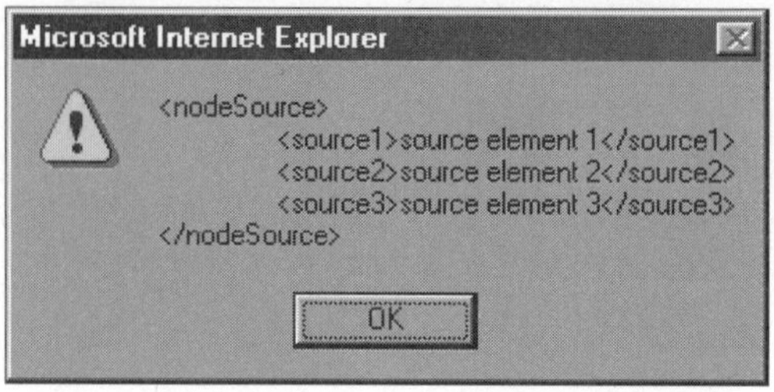
Microsoft Internet Explorer
<nodeSource>
<source1>source element 1</source1>
<source2>source element 2</source2>
<source3>source element 3</source3>
</nodeSource>
OK

This method returns the node being inserted.

replaceChild(newChild, oldChild)

We have just moved a node from one document to another in two stages - the first being to remove the node from the source document, and the second to insert it into the destination. We could do this in a single stage with `replaceChild()`. We will replace the first item with the destination with the first item of the source:

```
rootDest.replaceChild(rootSource.childNodes.item(0),rootDest.childNodes.item(0));
```

The destination and source files now look like this:

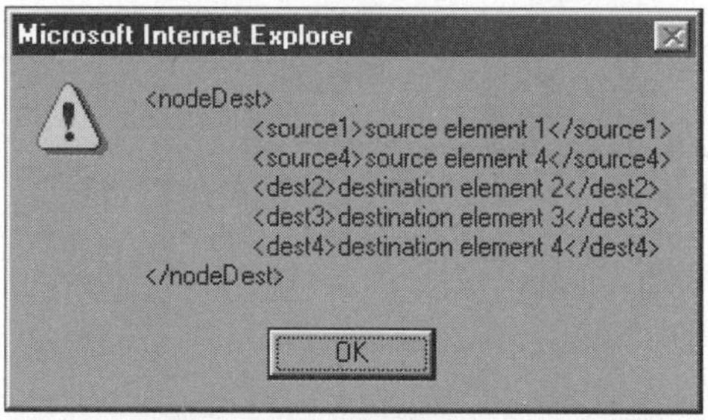
Microsoft Internet Explorer
<nodeDest>
<source1>source element 1</source1>
<source4>source element 4</source4>
<dest2>destination element 2</dest2>
<dest3>destination element 3</dest3>
<dest4>destination element 4</dest4>
</nodeDest>
OK

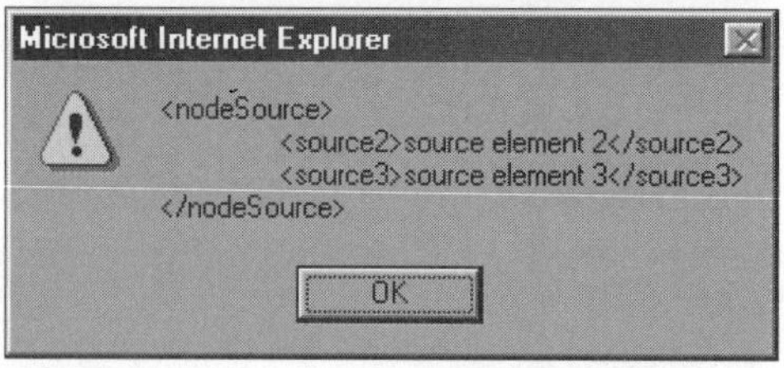
Microsoft Internet Explorer
<nodeSource>
<source2>source element 2</source2>
<source3>source element 3</source3>
</nodeSource>
OK

Note that the node has been removed from the source document. This is because a node can only have one parent, and the parent is now the root node of the destination document.

If we wanted to leave the node in the source document, we could make a copy of the node as we shall now.

cloneNode(deep) and appendChild(newChild)

The `cloneNode()` method makes a copy of the node, optionally including all sub-nodes. We will use it to make a copy of the first remaining node in the source and append it to the destination:

```
source2 = rootSource.childNodes.item(0).cloneNode(true);
rootDest.appendChild(source2);
```

These are the resulting destination and source documents:

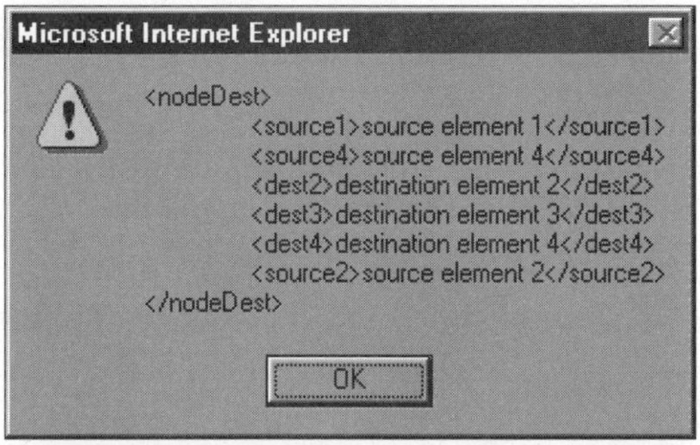
Microsoft Internet Explorer
<nodeDest>
<source1>source element 1</source1>
<source4>source element 4</source4>
<dest2>destination element 2</dest2>
<dest3>destination element 3</dest3>
<dest4>destination element 4</dest4>
<source2>source element 2</source2>
</nodeDest>
OK

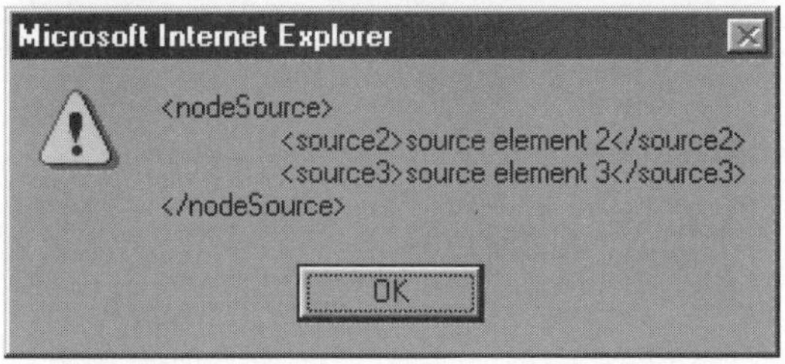
Microsoft Internet Explorer
<nodeSource>
<source2>source element 2</source2>
<source3>source element 3</source3>
</nodeSource>
OK

By setting the `deep` parameter to `true`, we clone all the sub-nodes, including the `Text` node. Had the parameter been `false`, we would only have cloned the node and any attributes. If we do this now, the `xml` property shows this as an empty element at the end of the document:

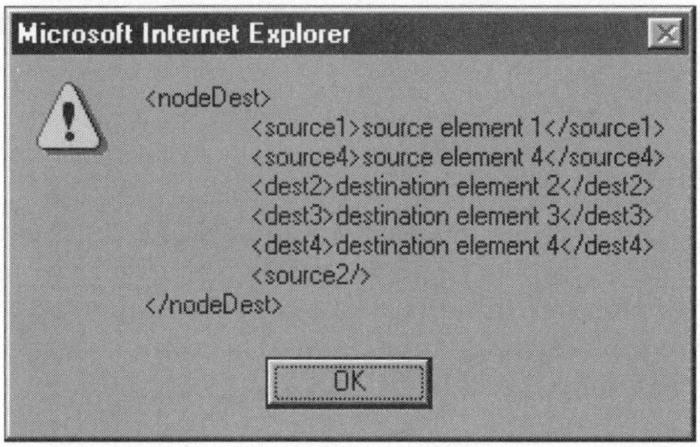
Microsoft Internet Explorer
<nodeDest>
<source1>source element 1</source1>
<source4>source element 4</source4>
<dest2>destination element 2</dest2>
<dest3>destination element 3</dest3>
<dest4>destination element 4</dest4>
<source2/>
</nodeDest>
OK

hasChildNodes()

Finally, we can test if our node has any children. If we look at the source document, we will see that it still has two, so this method returns `true`. If we deleted these children, it would return `false`.

```
alert(rootSource.hasChildNodes());
```

The NodeList Interface

We have already met the `nodeList` interface several times. A `nodeList` is an ordered collection of `Node` objects. It has a single read-only property, its `length` (of type `int`), and a single method `item(index)` to let us access the nodes in the collection.

When navigating through a tree, you will soon get familiar with the alternation between `Node` objects and `NodeList` collections as you use the `childNodes` property of the `Node` and the `item()` method of the `NodeList`. For example, consider a document:

```
<abc>
  <item>
    <item>
      <item>hello</item>
    </item>
  </item>
</abc>
```

I could navigate to the `Text` node from the root element (`abc`) like this:

```
a = root.childNodes;          // NodeList
b = a.item(0);                // Node - the first "item"
c = b.childNodes;             // NodeList
d = c.item(0);                // Node - the second "item"
e = d.childNodes;             // NodeList
f = e.item(0);                // Node - the third "item"
g = f.childNodes;             // NodeList
h = g.item(0)                 // Node - the Text node
```

Of course, in practice we would do this in fewer lines, but the alternation between `Node` and `NodeList` is still there.

The Element Interface

Most of the nodes, apart from `Text` nodes, contained within an XML document tree will usually be `Element` nodes, containing a combination of text, attributes and further elements. Since elements are nodes in an XML document, this interface inherits all the properties and methods we just met in that interface. However, elements are the only node type that has attributes, so this interface is predominantly concerned with handling these.

The main uses of the interface are:

- to find the tag name of the element
- to get, set and remove attributes
- to retrieve child elements

Element Interface Properties

This interface has a single read-only property: `tagName`. This retrieves the tag name of the element as a string, with the same result as if we had used the `nodeName` property inherited from the `Node` interface.

```
child1 = nodeSource.childNodes.item(1);
alert(child1.tagName);
```

Element Interface Methods

We have already used the `getAttribute()` method from this interface to display the `currency` attribute of a book price. This returned the attribute value as a DOMString.

```
alert(price.getAttribute("currency"));
```

Attribute Management

Attributes can be managed in two forms. Either we can set, get and remove them in DOMString form, as we did before, or we can perform the same operations on them in object form. In this case, we are manipulating them using the `Attr` interface we will meet in the moment. The full set of methods for managing attributes through the `Element` interface is:

Method	Return Type	Parameter Types
`getAttribute(name)`	DOMString	The `name` parameter is of type DOMString
`setAttribute(name, value)`	void	The `name` and `value` parameters are of type DOMString
`removeAttribute(name)`	void	The `name` parameter is of type DOMString
`getAttributeNode(name)`	Attr	The `name` parameter is of type DOMString
`setAttributeNode(newAttr)`	Attr	The `newAttr` parameter is of type Attr
`removeAttributeNode(oldAttr)`	Attr	The `oldAttr` parameter is of type Attr

getElementsByTagName(name)

There are two main ways to find elements. The first is by indexing into a `nodeList` of all the child nodes of an element, which implies that we know the position of the required element in the list. We used this to find the second book in the catalogue, since we knew that all the child nodes of the root element of the catalogue were `book` elements. The other is to get a `nodeList` of the elements by name, and we have used this as well, for example to get the `author` elements of the second book.

There is a very important difference between these two ways of finding elements. The first, using `childNodes`, fetches the immediate children of the node. The second, using `getElementsByTagName()`, fetches all descendant elements that match the `name` parameter, whether they are children, grandchildren or at any other level of the element hierarchy.

If I have a document:

```
<doc>
  <div>Here is a div that contains another div element
    <div>This is the embedded div</div>
  </div>
  <div>And this has nothing embedded</div>
</doc>
```

Then, from the root element, `root.getElementsByTagName()` will find all three `div` elements, while `root.childNodes` will return only the two immediate children of the root element. It would actually be quite hard to extract just these two if the root elements also had children with different names. To make this easier, Microsoft has a proprietary extension `selectNodes()` that we will meet later. This resolves the problem at the expense of losing implementation-independence.

normalize()

This method combines adjacent `Text` nodes (that is, text strings with no markup separating them). This situation can occur if multiple `Text` nodes are being added to an element. If we saved the document concerned and reloaded it, these nodes would be concatenated into a single `Text` node. We can achieve the same end using the `normalize()` method.

The Attr Interface

In describing the `Element` interface, we saw that we could work with attributes by treating them as `Attr` objects. The `Attr` interface inherits all the properties and methods of the `Node` interface, and adds three additional properties to describe the attributes.

Attr Interface Properties

The three additional properties are

- the `name` of the attribute, which is a read-only string
- the `specified` property, which is a read-only boolean (`true` or `false`)
- the `value` of the attribute which is a read/write string

The `specified` property is `true` if the attribute is explicitly given a value, either in the original document or because it has been set by the application. It is `false` if the value is the result of being set as a default in the DTD.

The NamedNodeMap Interface

While the `NodeList` interface exposes an ordered collection of nodes, the `NamedNodeMap` interface exposes an unordered collection. There are several cases in which the order of the nodes is not important, the attributes of an element being the one you are likely to meet most often. Indeed, many editing tools (including Microsoft's FrontPage 98 and Visual InterDev 6) will change the order of attributes in HTML under certain circumstances. There are other nodes, such as the `entities` and `notations` of the `Document` object that we met earlier, where the order is not important and so the objects can be collected into a `namedNodeMap`.

Nodes in the `namedNodeMap` are therefore referenced by name, not index, although an `index` property is included to allow enumeration of its contents.

The `NamedNodeMap` interface does not inherit any properties or methods, but exposes it own. Its main uses are:

- to find the number of attributes in the map
- to allow enumeration of the attributes
- to get attribute values
- to set or remove attributes

We shall look at this interface, then illustrate it with some examples.

NamedNodeMap Interface Properties

There is only one property, the read-only integer `length`. This is used to set the parameters for looping through the contents of the collection.

NamedNodeMap Interface Methods

This interface provides four methods.

getNamedItem(name)

This method gets an item from the list by name. It takes a DOMString as an argument and returns a node.

setNamedItem(arg)

This method adds a node to the collection, giving it the name that is the value of the `nodeName` of the parameter. A `namedNodeMap` can only contain a single node with a given name (just as an element can only have a single attribute with a single name). If there is already an item with this name, it is replaced and returned.

removeNamedItem(name)

This method removes an item from the list. It takes the node name as a DOMString as an argument. It returns the node, or `null` if the node does not exist.

item(index)

This method returns the item in the `nameNodeMap` from the position pointed to by the `index` parameter, which is an unsigned long. As we just saw, the `namedNodeMap` is an unordered collection, so the contents need not be held in the order they are in the document.

Example of the namedNodeMap

In this example, we will use a message from Centaur to demonstrate the use of the `namedNodeMap` property and methods. Centaur uses attributes extensively in its messaging interface, as this allows more checking using the DTD than is possible using elements. This checking is important in messaging applications, where we typically only have control over one end of the interface.

The code for this example is in the file `domExamples3.htm`. The message is in the file `message.xml`. Both these files are available via the Wrox web site, `http://www.wrox.com/`.

This is an example of such as message:

```
<centaur>
  <quoterequest>
    <qttour supplier="PNM" ref="TUMP" depdate="19990801" duration="14" />
    <qttravelers adults="2" children="1" infants="1" />
  </quoterequest>
</centaur>
```

Firstly, we will loop through the contents of the `qttour` element, extracting the attribute nodes and getting their names and values:

```
s = "";
tour = root.getElementsByTagName("qttour").item(0);
atts = tour.attributes;
for (i = 0 ; i < atts.length ; i++)
{
  s += atts.item(i).nodeName + " = ";
  s += atts.item(i).nodeValue + "\n";
}
alert(s);
```

We create the `namedNodeMap` in the line:

```
atts = tour.attributes;
```

We then use its `length` attribute to see how many times to run the loop code. This code uses two properties from the Node interface to get the information we want, which we then put in an alert message. This is the message we get:

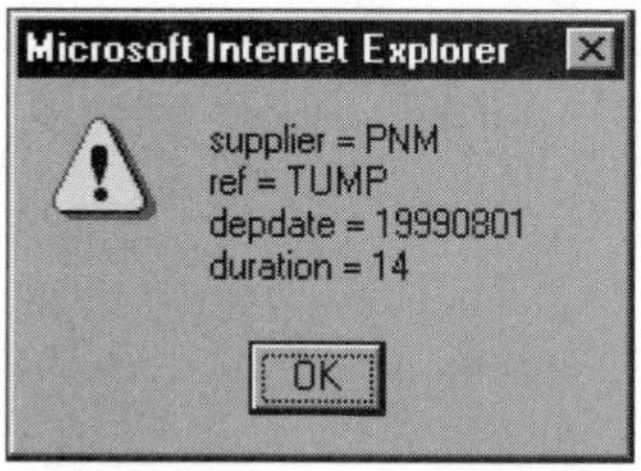

In the examples that follow, we will use this same loop code several times to see the results of our processing of the `atts` `namedNodeMap`.

We can get the `supplier` attribute by name, then display its `nodeName`:

```
alert(atts.getNamedItem("supplier").nodeName);
```

This gives the result:

If we ran the loop code now, it would show us that, although we have retrieved this node, we have not deleted it from the collection.

We can, however, use the methods of the namedNodeMap to remove the node. We can then run the loop code again:

```
atts.removeNamedItem("supplier");
s = "";
for (i = 0 ; i < atts.length ; i++)
{
  s += atts.item(i).nodeName + " = ";
  s += atts.item(i).nodeValue + "\n";
}
alert(s);
```

This leaves the collection with just three nodes:

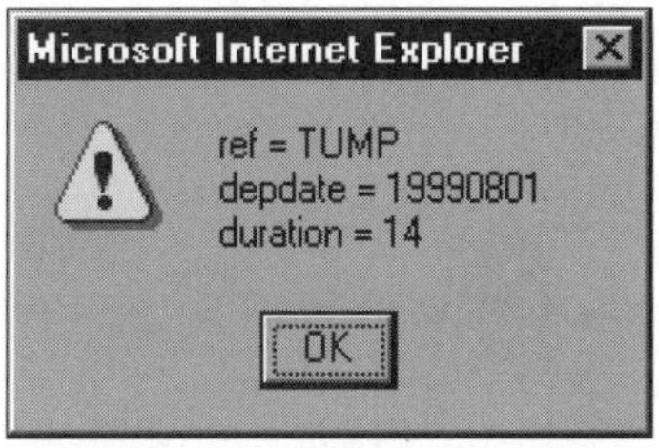

The only method we have not yet used is setNamedItem(). In the following example, we will use a method from the Document interface to create an Attr node, then a property from the Attr interface to give it a value. Finally, we will add this to the collection:

```
newAttr = source.createAttribute("supplier");
newAttr.value = "ARG";
atts.setNamedItem(newAttr);
```

Running the loop code again, results in this new collection:

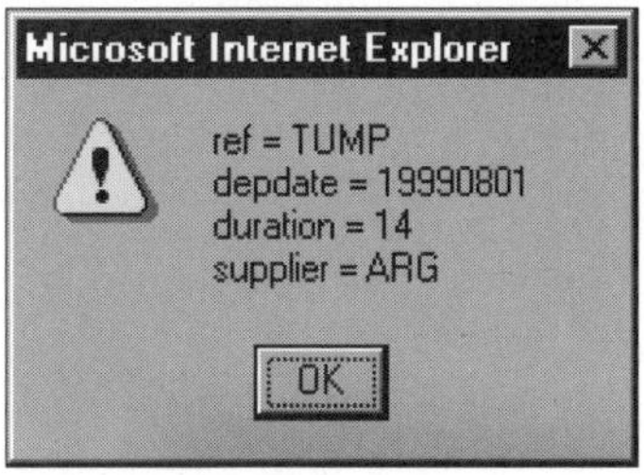

The CharacterData Interface

There is no object of the type `characterData`, but this interface is inherited by objects that contain character strings, such as `Text` nodes and `Comment` nodes. Since these are node types, the `characterData` interface inherits all the methods and properties of the `Node` interface.

The properties and methods provide standard string handling facilities.

characterData Interface Properties

There are just two properties in this interface - the `data` itself, which is returned as a string, and the `length` of the data, which is returned as an integer.

characterData Interface Methods

With the methods of this interface, we can manipulate the data itself. Earlier, we changed the string "XML Design and Implementation" to "XML Design and Implementation, First Edition" by setting a new `nodeValue` for the `Text` node. Alternatively, we could have used the `appendData()` method from this interface to just add the additional text.

substringData(offset,count)

This method extracts a substring from the data. The `offset` parameter is an unsigned long and indicates where to start the extraction. The `count` parameter indicates how many characters to extract. The substring is returned as a DOMString.

appendData(arg)

This method appends the DOMString provided in the `arg` to the end of the current data.

insertData(offset, arg) and deleteData(offset, count)

The `insertData()` method takes an `offset` parameter as an unsigned long, and inserts the DOMString provided in the `arg`. `deleteData()` deletes a number of characters given by the unsigned long `count`, starting from the `offset`.

replaceData(offset, count, arg)

This method replaces characters in the string. The `offset` parameter is an unsigned long, and indicates where to start the replacement. The `count` parameter is also an unsigned long, and indicates the number of characters to replace. The `arg` is a DOMString containing the replacement text, and can have more characters than `count`.

If we have an element `line` containing a `Text` node with the string "Now is the winter of our discontent", we can replace "winter" by "summer" with the code:

```
line.childNodes.item(0).replaceData(11,6,"summer");
```

Note that we have had to navigate from our `Element` node to its `Text` node, using `.childNodes.item(0)` since it is the `Text` node that inherits the methods of the `characterData` interface.

Microsoft's Level 1 DOM Extensions

We have seen that Microsoft's extensions to the W3C DOM fall into two categories - those, such as the `load` method of the `Document` object that are essential to use of the DOM, and those, such as the `text` property of the `Node` object that make the DOM easier to use. It is up to you whether you use any methods and properties from the latter group. They can make coding considerably simpler and more understandable, but this is at the expense of implementation compatibility. As we saw with the `text` property, you can always write your own functions and methods to duplicate those Microsoft extensions you want to use.

We have used the `xml` property of the `Node` extensively in the example code in this chapter to display the results of our processing. I use it in this way as a debugging aid during development to see the content of a node, but I have not found any need to use it in the final code of Centaur or any other developments. Later in this chapter, we will use the DOM to write a function with a similar purpose.

Since Centaur uses XSL as well as the DOM, it will only operate under Internet Explorer 5. It does not use the non-essential Microsoft extensions to any great extent, but it does use the `text` property, mainly to make code clearer to read.

All the properties and methods we'll move on to look at now are in addition to the W3C model objects and interfaces for XML. Microsoft implements the W3C DOM Level 1 Core in full.

XML Islands

As well as the extensions to the interfaces, Microsoft implements a method of embedding XML in an HTML document that it calls the **XML island**. We saw this earlier when we used Centaur as an example of XML processing using the DOM. As we saw there, the island is simply a way of embedding XML in an HTML document. This is especially useful when code on the server is being used to generate the XML, which will then be processed on the client. This is the model used in many places in Centaur, where XML is used as an intermediate format for passing data between server code and client code. The Centaur example earlier in this chapter was a case in point. Here ASP code on the server extracted data about vacations matching the search criteria and placed the results in an XML island. The client code then picked up the results, parsed the XML and processed it into displayable HTML using the DOM and script.

The Document Interface

In addition to the W3C properties and methods, Internet Explorer 5 implements a number of properties and methods mainly relating to document loading and parsing. This interface also inherits the extensions to the `Node` interface.

The main uses of the extensions are:

- to load and parse XML documents
- to find additional information about the document

Document Interface Properties

The extra properties of the IE5 `Document` interface mainly relate to parsing documents. They can be categorised as essential properties, since there are no alternative ways of achieving the same ends in the W3C recommendation.

url

This is a read-only property that returns the URL of the last document loaded.

async

This is a read/write property that enables or disables asynchronous loading of the document. You might have noticed that our examples have started with code such as:

```
source = new ActiveXObject("Microsoft.XMLDOM");
source.async = false;
source.load("catalog.xml");
```

By default, or if the `async` property is set to `true`, the `MSXML` parser will return immediately, allowing processing to continue. If that processing involves use of the document, we might try to access it before it is fully loaded and parsed.

There are two ways to avoid this. The first is to set the `async` property to `false`. The parser will then not return until it has completed its task. The second way is to test whether the parser has completed, as we shall see in a moment. We can test not only completion, but whether there is any data at all available to work with. This can be useful if we are loading a large file and want to start processing the first few records before parsing of the rest of the document is complete.

readyState, onreadystatechange and ondataavailable

These are the three properties that allow us to test for data being available. There are two occasions when we might want to do this. The first is as described above - when we want to start processing the data before the complete document has been parsed. The second is if we are accessing data in an XML island. In this case, the XML is parsed when the HTML document containing the island is loaded, and there is no opportunity to set the `async` property value. We therefore check the `readyState` before continuing processing.

The `readyState` can take one of five values:

State	Description
`UNINITIALIZED`	The XML object has been created, but no content has been loaded.
`LOADING`	The XML object is being initialised, but no data is yet being read or parsed.
`LOADED`	Data is being loaded into the object and parsed.
`INTERACTIVE`	Some data has been read and parsed, so the object model is available. However, the complete document has not been read.
`COMPLETED`	The document has been loaded and parsed.

In Centaur, we always work with complete documents, so we are most interested in a `readyState` of "`COMPLETED`". However, as mentioned previously, other values are useful when processing can start on the first few elements of a long document. We will look at use of the `readyState` in more detail when we examine the code in Centaur.

parseError

This complete interface is specific to Internet Explorer 5, and we will use it every time we parse an XML document. The properties tell us about the last error detected by the parser. How do we find out about other errors? Simple! Fix the error we know about and parse again.

If there is an error in the XML document, the error returned by the parser is an object of the type `parseError`, which exposes its own interface with a set of seven properties.

Property	Type	Description
`errorcode`	read only	An integer representing the error.
`url`	read only	The URL of the XML document containing the error.
`reason`	read only	A text representation of the reason for the error.
`srcText`	read only	The full text of the line containing the error.
`line`	read only	The number of the line containing the error.
`linepos`	read only	The character position where the error occurred.
`filepos`	read only	The absolute file position where the error occurred.

Typically, when we parse a document, we will include the code:

```
if (source.parseError != 0)
    alert(source.parseError.reason);
```

If there is an error this code will display a message box with a description of the error.

validateOnParse

This read/write property takes a value of `true` or `false` to indicate to the parser whether it should validate the document against the DTD.

```
source.validateOnParse = false;
```

Document Interface Methods

Like the properties of this interface, the IE5 method extensions to this interface perform functions for which the W3C DOM recommendation does not provide an alternative means.

load(url)

This method loads an XML document from the location specified by the URL. We have used it on several occasions in this chapter.

loadXML(xmlString)

This method loads an XML document from the string in its parameter. It is particularly useful for loading small documents. For example, we can create an XML object `xmlObj`, then put a complete XML document into it using the `loadXML()` method:

```
xmlObj = new ActiveXObject("Microsoft.XMLDOM");
str = "<?xml version='1.0'?><books><book>";
str += "<title>XML Design and Implemenation</title><author>Paul Spencer</author>";
str += "</book></books>";
xmlObj.loadXML(str);
```

Of course, all this could be done in fewer lines. As with many examples in this book, it is set out like this to make it easier to read on the printed page.

createNode(type,name,namespaceURI)

This method creates a new node as a specified namespace. We met namespaces in Chapter 2.

nodeFromID(idString)

We saw in the last chapter that nodes can have unique `ID` attributes. This method returns a node with a specified `ID`. This can be achieved in the W3C DOM by working with the `ID` as an attribute.

abort()

If a document is being loaded with the `async` property set to `true`, this method can be used to abort the loading of the document.

The Node Interface

The Microsoft extensions to the Node interface cover three main areas. These are:

- properties that relate to namespaces
- methods to make navigation through the document easier
- a method to assist with processing a document using XSL

There are also some properties to give additional information about the node.

Node Interface Properties

These are the additional properties Microsoft has implemented in Internet Explorer 5.

nodeTypeString

The W3C specifies a property `nodeType` that returns a numerical representation of the type of node. The read-only property `nodeTypeString` returns the node type as a string, such as element.

definition

Returns the node from the DTD that contains the definition of this node. Internet Explorer 5 also implements an alternative to the DTD for describing the contents of an XML document, called an XML schema. If a schema is used instead of a DTD, this property will return a definition from the schema in the same way. There are several proposals for schemas being discussed by the W3C, and we will look at some of these in Appendix D.

specified

This read-only property indicates that the node was specified directly in the XML source, rather than being implied from the DTD or schema.

namespace, prefix and baseName

`namespace` is a read-only property that returns the URI of the namespace for the node. `prefix` and `baseName` return the parts of the name before and after the colon respectively.

nodeTypedValue and dataType

These two properties relate only to documents that use the IE5 Schema rather than a DTD to define the XML document's structure. The schema allows the data type of a node to be defined, and these two read/write properties, represent the value and data type respectively.

xml and text

We have used these two properties extensively in this chapter. The former is read-only and represents the markup and data of a node as a text string. The latter is a read/write property and represents the text contained within a node. Note that this property applies not just to immediate children of the current node, but to all descendants. So with the document we just created using the `loadXML()` method of the Document object:

```
<?xml version='1.0'?>
<books>
  <book>
    <title>XML Design and Implementation</title>
    <author>Paul Spencer</author>";
  </book>
</books>
```

the code:

```
alert(root.text)
```

gives this result:

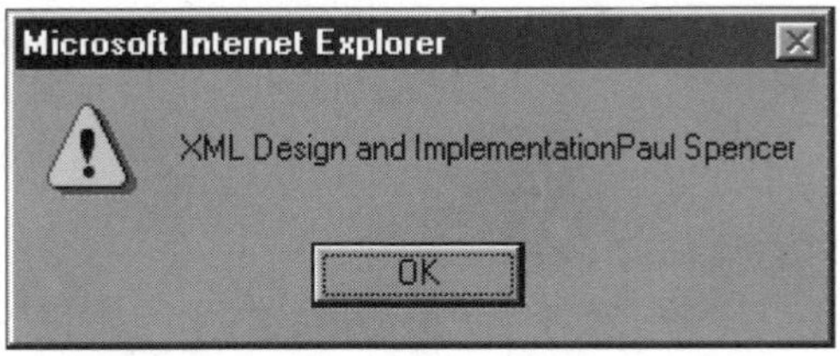

parsed

This read-only property indicates, if true, that this node and all of its descendants have been parsed. This does not imply that the parsing was successful. The value of `parseError` needs to be checked to ensure this.

Node Interface Methods

The additional methods `selectNodes()` and `selectSingleNode()` exposed by the `Node` object can be of great utility for finding specific nodes. The `transformNode()` method is essential for processing an XML document with XSL under program control. (The alternative is to specify the stylesheet in the document as we would with a CSS stylesheet and an HTML document.)

selectNodes(query) and selectSingleNode(query)

We have seen that the W3C DOM is very rigidly structured. For example, to select a single node deep in the document tree, we either use `getElementsByTagName()`, which gets all matching elements regardless of their depth below the current node, or we have to navigate through every intermediate node, selecting them each by name. This is true even if we know that the node we want is the only one of its type in the document, so there is no risk of ambiguity.

Microsoft's additional selection methods circumvent this by allowing the use of a query language. This query language is the same as the pattern matching syntax in XSL that we will see in action in more detail in Chapter 5.

> *In addition, at the time of writing Microsoft were submitting proposals to the W3C to extend this syntax. For more information visit the Microsoft XML site at* `http://www.microsoft.com/xml` *and access the XSL Reference pages.*

The first of these methods, `selectNodes()`, returns all nodes that match the query. In the simplest case, a line such as:

```
nodes = currentNode.selectNodes("item");
```

will create a `nodeList` containing only the `item` elements that are immediate children of `currentNode`. This compares to:

```
nodes = currentNode.getElementsByTagName("item");
```

which will search through all descendants for matches.

`selectSingleNode()` is used when we know there is only a single node that will match our query, and saves us having to create a `nodeList` with a single node in it. If more than one node matches the query, the method selects the first.

transformNode(stylesheet)

This method returns the result of processing the node with an XSL stylesheet. This is used in two places in Centaur. We will discuss it in detail when we look at XSL stylesheets.

The NodeList Interface

When we have iterated through `NodeLists`, we have used the length property to set a loop variable. Visual Basic and VBScript programmers in particular will be used to using the syntax:

```
For Each object in collection
…
Next
```

Microsoft has added three methods to the `NodeList` interface to support this. These are `nextNode()`, `reset()`.

`nextNode()` simply moves the iterator to the next node in the collection, and `reset()` returns the iterator to the start of the collection.

The NamedNodeMap Interface

Internet Explorer 5 adds five methods to this interface, two relating to namespaces and three relating to iterating through the nodes in the list.

getQualifiedItem(baseName,URI)

This method allows the specification of a URI to access a namespace-qualified attribute.

removeQualifiedItem(baseName,URI)

This method allows the specification of a URI to remove a namespace-qualified attribute. It returns the attribute removed.

nextNode(), reset()

As we just saw for the `nodeList`, these two methods allow us to iterate over a collection in a `namedNodeMap`.

The Simple API for XML (SAX)

We have seen that Microsoft's `MSXML` parser creates a complete internal tree structure in memory from the source document. Since Centaur is dealing with complete documents, this is what we want to do. However, what if we were dealing with a very large XML file, and just wanted to extract a small amount of information? Perhaps we have a component catalogue described as XML, and just want to work with information concerning a single component.

In this case, there is another approach to parsing XML. Instead of building a complete tree, we can work at another level, traversing the document and informing the calling application of parsing events such as meeting the start of a new element. A group of people have developed such an interface, and many XML parsers, including those from IBM and Sun, implement it, either instead of, or in addition to, the tree-based interface. Although MSXML does not support SAX, there are add-ons available from third parties to provide this support.

Three key figures in SAX development were Tim Bray, co-author of the XML recommendation, Peter Murray-Rust, developer of the Chemical Markup Language and the Jumbo XML browser and Dave Megginson, developer of the Ælfred XML parser. Many others were involved in creating SAX, since it was developed through a public mailing list. Dave Megginson has links to sources of SAX parsers and tools on his web site at `http://www.megginson.com/SAX`.

To see how a SAX parser operates, let's take a very simple document:

```
<?xml version="1.0">
<doc>
<name>Paul Spencer</name>
</doc>
```

The events the parser would report are:

```
start document
start element: doc
start element: name
characters: Paul Spencer
end element: name
end element: doc
end document
```

An application could, for example, monitor these events as they occur when parsing a long document, then read into memory only those parts of the tree in which it is interested. For more information on SAX, Dave Megginson's web site, referenced above, is a good starting point.

The Level 2 DOM

As already mentioned, the Level 2 DOM is still a working draft within the W3C, and is not currently implemented in Internet Explorer 5 or any other commercial browser, and is therefore not used within Centaur. Here, we will just get a flavour of the additional facilities it will offer to XML users.

Filters and Iterators

We saw when looking at the Microsoft extensions to the DOM that they contain methods for iterating through the collections `NodeList` and `NamedNodeMap`. The W3C is also working in this area with the Level 2 DOM. The Level 2 DOM iterators will allow similar ways of iterating through collections without having to find the length of the collection and use an index. They will not be restricted to these two collection types, but will also be able to process objects such as a complete document.

The advantage of using this type of iterator over other methods such as a `for` loop with an index is that the code does not have to know anything about the structure of the collection it is navigating. This both simplifies code and makes it more likely to be re-usable.

The Level 2 DOM also includes the ability to apply filters to collections. For example, in Centaur, we will have two types of adult traveler, one with an attribute `type` with value `contact`, and one without. Using a filter makes it easy to select either one type or the other. With the DOM Level 2, we would use filters by iterating through a collection, using a filter expression to filter out those elements that do not match the expression criteria.

Range

The `range` interface in the Level 2 DOM allows us to select part of an XML document to work with by specifying start and end points. The Level 1 DOM makes it easy to select a node and its descendants, but the `range` interface extends this to selecting areas of the document that can start in the child of one node and end in the child of another. In fact, the flexibility of selecting start and end points for the range is such that we can place them in the middle of a text node if we so wish.

Why might we want to do this? Imagine you are writing a word processor that uses XML as its native format. If your user now wants to cut a section that starts in the middle of one paragraph and ends in the middle of another, you can use the `range` interface to specify the start and end of the selection.

Let's Try It

We have now learned about XML and understand the DOM though a combination of examples and descriptions of the interfaces provided by both the W3C DOM and the Microsoft through its extensions. Let's complete this chapter by putting some of this to use by creating a function that takes some XML and displays its structure.

We will use the book catalogue file we have seen before:

```
<?xml version = "1.0"?>
<!DOCTYPE books [
<!ELEMENT books (book)*>
<!ELEMENT book (title, authors, publisher, pages?, isbn, price+)>
<!ELEMENT authors (author+)>
<!ELEMENT title (#PCDATA)>
<!ELEMENT author (#PCDATA)>
<!ELEMENT publisher (#PCDATA)>
<!ELEMENT pages (#PCDATA)>
<!ELEMENT isbn (#PCDATA)>
<!ELEMENT price (#PCDATA)>
<!ATTLIST price currency CDATA #REQUIRED>
]>
<books>
  <book>
    <title>Clouds to Code</title>
    <authors>
      <author>Jesse Liberty</author>
    </authors>
    <publisher>Wrox Press</publisher>
    <pages>393</pages>
    <isbn>1-861000-95-2</isbn>
    <price currency = "USD">40.00</price>
  </book>
  <book>
    <title>Beginning Active Server Pages 2.0</title>
    <authors>
      <author>Francis</author>
      <author>Kauffman</author>
      <author>Llibre</author>
      <author>Sussman</author>
      <author>Ullman</author>
    </authors>
    <publisher>Wrox Press</publisher>
    <pages>653</pages>
```

```
      <isbn>1-861001-34-7</isbn>
      <price currency = "USD">39.99</price>
    </book>
  </books>
```

We will write a program to display the tree structure of this file like this:

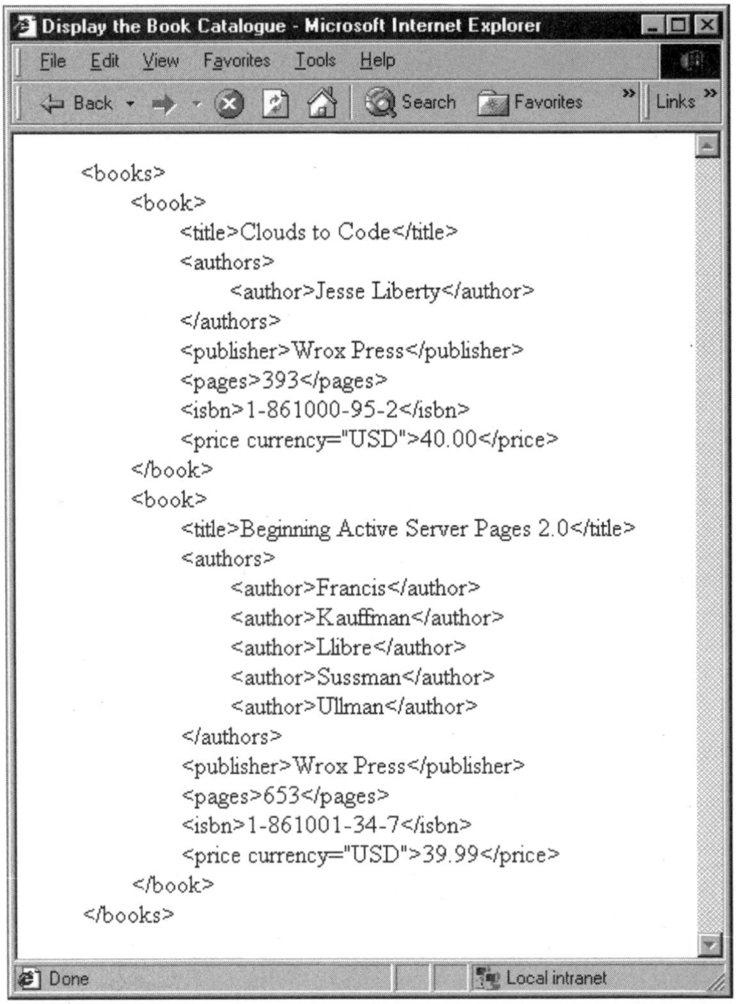
Display the Book Catalogue - Microsoft Internet Explorer
File Edit View Favorites Tools Help
Back
Search
Favorites
Links
<books>
<book>
<title>Clouds to Code</title>
<authors>
<author>Jesse Liberty</author>
</authors>
<publisher>Wrox Press</publisher>
<pages>393</pages>
<isbn>1-861000-95-2</isbn>
<price currency="USD">40.00</price>
</book>
<book>
<title>Beginning Active Server Pages 2.0</title>
<authors>
<author>Francis</author>
<author>Kauffman</author>
<author>Llibre</author>
<author>Sussman</author>
<author>Ullman</author>
</authors>
<publisher>Wrox Press</publisher>
<pages>653</pages>
<isbn>1-861001-34-7</isbn>
<price currency="USD">39.99</price>
</book>
</books>
Done
Local intranet

And this is the code we will use to display it (`catalog.htm`):

```
<HTML>
<HEAD>
  <TITLE>Display the Book Catalogue</TITLE>
</HEAD>

<BODY onLoad="onLoad()">

  <DIV id = "tgtResult"></DIV>
```

```
<SCRIPT Language="JScript">

var strDisplayTree = "";

function onLoad()
{
  var root,source,strResult;

  source = new ActiveXObject("Microsoft.XMLDOM");
  source.async = false;
  source.load("catalog.xml");

  if (source.parseError != 0)
    alert(source.parseError.reason);

  root = source.documentElement;
  displayTree(root);
  tgtResult.innerHTML = strDisplayTree;
}

function displayTree(base)
{
  var i,win,indent;

  indent = "2em";

  if (base.nodeType == 3)       // node is a TEXT node
    strDisplayTree += "<SPAN>" + base.data + "</SPAN>";

  else if  (base.nodeType == 1)  // node is an ELEMENT node
  {
    strDisplayTree += "<DIV Style='margin-left:" + indent + "'>&lt;" +
                      base.tagName + getAttributes(base)+ ">";
    for (i = 0 ; i < base.childNodes.length ; i++)
        displayTree(base.childNodes.item(i));
    strDisplayTree += "&lt;/" + base.tagName + ">" + "</DIV>";
  }
  else
    alert("This function only handles Text and Element nodes. Your document
     contains a node of type: " + base.nodeType + ", " + base.nodeStringType);
}

function getAttributes(elem)
{
  var i;
  var strResult = "";

  xmapAtts = elem.attributes;
  for (i = 0 ; i < xmapAtts.length ; i++)
    strResult += ' ' + xmapAtts.item(i).name + '="' + xmapAtts.item(i).value +
      '"';
  return(strResult);
}
</SCRIPT>
</BODY>
</HTML>
```

Let's go through this a bit at a time. As you can see, most of the work is done in the script. In fact, the only significant HTML is:

```
<DIV id = "tgtResult"></DIV>
```

which just puts a placeholder for the script to write the HTML it creates for itself. This is a common approach when using the DOM to process XML for display.

The onLoad() Function

The function `onLoad()` is where we load the XML file.

First we create an object model object with:

```
source = new ActiveXObject("Microsoft.XMLDOM");
```

We then load the document, making sure that the parser will not process it until loading is complete:

```
source.async = false;
source.load("catalog.xml");
```

If the document parses correctly, we find the root element called `books` and continue by calling the function that builds up the HTML to display:

```
root = source.documentElement;
displayTree(root,0);
```

Finally, we display it:

```
tgtResult.innerHTML = strDisplayTree;
```

Of course, we might have an error in the document. If so, we want to see it. The two lines:

```
if (source.parseError != 0)
  alert(source.parseError.reason);
```

achieve this.

The displayTree() Function

The function `displayTree()` creates a string of HTML by extracting the text from `Text` nodes and building tags from element names. It also indents the elements according to their level in the source tree and calls another function `getAttributes()` to create the attribute strings. As you can see, it only handles these two element types.

The function first sets a variable to the amount we want to indent each level of the tree:

```
indent = "2em";
```

Then we handle `Text` nodes, by placing the text in an HTML `SPAN` element:

```
if (base.nodeType == 3)      // node is a TEXT node
  strDisplayTree += "<SPAN>" + base.data + "</SPAN>";
```

If we have an `Element` node, we need to build up an HTML `DIV` element so the block goes on a new line. This element is given a style to indent it. We will see in a moment how this works. We then put in the opening angle bracket of the start tag using an entity reference. If we used < instead of `<`, the HTML parser would, of course, treat it as the start of a new tag when we come to write the string into the document. We then complete the start tag with the element name, any attributes and an end tag. We could escape the end tag with an entity reference, but there is no need:

```
else if  (base.nodeType == 1)  // node is an ELEMENT node
{
  strDisplayTree += "<DIV Style='margin-left:" + indent + "'>&lt;" +
                    base.tagName + getAttributes(base)+ ">";
```

With the start tag in place, we then go through the contents, calling `displayTree()` recursively for each node:

```
for (i = 0 ; i < base.childNodes.length ; i++)
      displayTree(base.childNodes.item(i));
```

Each time we do this with another `Element` node, we place the new `DIV` within the `DIV` of its parent. Each `indent` therefore starts at the indented position of its parent, giving us the progressive indentation we want.

Finally, we supply an end tag:

```
  strDisplayTree += "&lt;/" + base.tagName + ">" + "</DIV>";
```

If any other node type is found, we display an error message.

```
else
  alert("This function only handles Text and Element nodes. Your document
  contains a node of type: " + base.nodeType + ", " + base.nodeStringType);
```

Please feel free to implement the display of these instead of allowing them to cause an error. You will then have a useful tool for debugging XML code. I have a slightly modified form of this function in a separate file `utils.js`, which I attach to files during testing by adding the following line just before the `<SCRIPT>` tag that starts my main script:

```
<SCRIPT src="utils.js"></SCRIPT>
```

The modification I have made is to open a new window to display the tree. This is particularly useful when working in frames. This is done by renaming the function above to `buildTree()` and adding a new `displayTree()` function:

```
function displayTree(base)
{
  buildTree(base);

  win = window.open("about:<HTML></HTML>","","resizable=yes");
  win.document.body.insertAdjacentHTML('BeforeEnd', strDisplayTree);
}
```

Of course, I also have to change the recursion in the new `buildTree()` function to call `buildTree()` rather than `displayTree()`.

The getAttributes() Function

This is the final function required to display the book catalogue. It starts by creating a `namedNodeMap` of the attributes:

```
xmapAtts = elem.attributes;
```

Then for each one, it creates a text string in the style `attribute="value"`. The complete string is then returned to the calling function:

```
for (i = 0 ; i < xmapAtts.length ; i++)
  strResult += ' ' + xmapAtts.item(i).name + '="' +
               xmapAtts.item(i).value + '"';
return(strResult);
```

That's it – you have an XML file and an HTML file containing JScript to access and display it through the DOM.

In the next three chapters we will use other examples to display XML documents in several different ways, introducing more technologies as we go.

Summary

The Document Object Model is the key to working with XML documents. It allows us to look at their structure, and to read and modify their content. All manipulation of XML uses the DOM in some way, be it directly or through other software such as an XSL processor.

Through the examples and the descriptions, you now have a good understanding of:

- how the W3C Level 1 DOM model allows us to work with XML documents
- how the Microsoft extensions provide necessary enhancements for document loading and parsing
- how the Microsoft extensions add additional features to simplify the sometimes verbose syntax of the W3C DOM at the expense of implementation independence
- an alternative, event-based, approach to parsing XML documents
- how the Level 2 DOM will add iterators and filters and allow the manipulation of ranges within XML documents in an implementation-independent way

Not only have we learnt enough to start developing XML applications, we have created our first one by displaying the structure of the book catalogue.

4

Displaying XML

In the two previous chapters we looked at the skeleton of XML and saw how to use the DOM to manipulate the content of XML documents. Now we're going to start putting some flesh onto those bones.

In this and the next chapter we'll look at how to satisfy another important requirement of our Centaur application – displaying XML in a browser. Generally, people refer to this display process as **rendering**, which is the term I'll use from now on.

With HTML, the browser understands the markup and will display it without the use of any styling mechanism (although HTML has *some* rudimentary styling options, such as the `<B>` tag). Stylesheets are therefore a welcome addition to HTML that give more flexibility to document designers, but they are not *required* (indeed, the web worked well without stylesheets for years).

XML, however, is different. The markup is not standardized and the browser does not know how to render it. This is because, with XML, authors can create their own tag set, giving the browser little chance of knowing how to display the resulting document. Stylesheets and other display mechanisms are therefore an *essential* part of rendering XML.

In this chapter, I will demonstrate three ways to display XML, leaving a further two until later. Each method has its own applications, and it is useful to know them all so that you can choose the most appropriate in any situation. The good news is that the various mechanisms can be flexibly combined to get the best from each.

IE5 provides a *sixth* method to display your XML document. All you need to do with this method is send the document to the browser with a `.xml` extension – IE5 has a default stylesheet that will show the document structure rather as our `displayTree()` function did in the last chapter. In fact, it is rather cleverer than `displayTree()` in that it allows sections of the tree to be collapsed.

By the end of this chapter, you will:

- be able to render XML using Cascading Stylesheets
- be able to render XML using the DOM and some scripting
- be able to navigate through an XML file using databinding
- understand when each is applicable

Don't forget that you can download the code used in this chapter by pointing your browser at `www.wrox.com` *and navigating to the* Source Code *page for this book.*

Let's begin by looking at the first of our display methods – **Cascading Stylesheets** (CSS).

Rendering with CSS

In case you are wondering, yes, this is the good old Cascading Stylesheets we know and love. Old? Well it is in Internet terms, and especially when compared to the other technologies we are discussing here.

Cascading stylesheets exist in two forms – CSS1, which was accepted as a recommendation by the W3C in December 1996, and CSS2, which added more functionality and was accepted in May 1998.

The recommendations can be found at `http://www.w3.org/TR/REC-CSS1` *and* `http://www.w3.org/TR/REC-CSS2.`

As you might expect, CSS1 covers all the basic facilities you might want in a stylesheet, while CSS2 adds some very useful additional facilities, such as the ability to specify table layouts.

Cascading Stylesheets can exist in a variety of locations: in their own file; in the `<HEAD>` part of an HTML or XML file; or within a start tag for an HTML element. The **cascading** in the title refers to how the stylesheet rules cascade through embedded elements according to a set of priorities that depend on where the stylesheet is placed (among other considerations).

In this section, I will provide a brief introduction to Cascading Stylesheets through examples, but for a fuller explanation, see either the recommendations (which are very clearly written), or a book dedicated to the subject such as Frank Boumphrey's *Style Sheets for HTML and XML* (Wrox Press, ISBN 1-861001-657). However, if you refer to Frank's book, remember that the sections on XSL refer to an early submission to the W3C, not the current version of the recommendation or its implementation in IE5.

Let's start with a basic HTML file and see how it interacts with a stylesheet. Here, we'll use a file called `macbeth.htm`. This contains an extract from the Bard of Avon's famous Scottish tragedy, and the stylesheet information on how to display it. Here's the file in full before we discuss it:

```
<HTML>

<HEAD>
  <!--
  Text placed in the public domain by Moby Lexical Tools, 1992.
  SGML markup by Jon Bosak, 1992-1994.
```

```
  XML version by Jon Bosak, 1996-1997.
  HTML extract by Paul Spencer 1998
  This work may be freely copied and distributed worldwide.
  -->

  <STYLE type="text/css">
  Body
  {
    font-family: Times, serif;
    font-size: 10pt;
  }

  .emph
  {
    display: inline;
    color: Green;
    font-style: italic;
  }

  .acttitle
  {
    font-family: Arial, sans-serif;
    font-size: 14pt;
    font-weight: bold;
    color: red;
    text-align: center;
    margin-bottom: 10px;
  }

  .scenetitle
  {
    font-family: Arial, sans-serif;
    font-size: 12pt;
    font-weight: bold;
    color: red;
    text-align: left;
    margin-bottom: 10px;
  }

  .stagedir
  {
    font-size: 12pt;
    font-weight: bold;
    font-style: italic;
  }

  .speaker
  {
    font-family: Arial,sans-serif;
    font-style: italic;
    font-weight: bold;
    margin-top: 10px;
    color: blue;
  }

  .line{}
  </STYLE>
</HEAD>
```

```
<BODY>
  <DIV Style="
        font-family: Arial, sans-serif;
        font-size: 20pt;
        font-weight: bold;
        color: red;
        text-align: center;">

    <DIV Style= "margin-bottom: 10px;">
      The Tragedy of Macbeth
    </DIV>

    <DIV Style="
          font-size: 14pt;
          margin-bottom: 10px;">
      SCENE  Scotland: England.
    </DIV>

    <DIV Style="display: none">
      MACBETH
    </DIV>

  </DIV>

  <DIV class="acttitle">ACT I</DIV>

  <DIV Class="scenetitle">SCENE I.  A desert place.</DIV>
  <DIV Class="stagedir">Thunder and lightning. Enter three Witches</DIV>

  <DIV Class="SPEAKER">First Witch</DIV>
  <DIV Class="line">When shall we three meet again</DIV>
  <DIV Class="line">In thunder, lightning, or in rain?</DIV>

  <DIV Class="SPEAKER">Second Witch</DIV>
  <DIV Class="line">When the hurlyburly's done,</DIV>
  <DIV Class="line">When the battle's lost and won.</DIV>

  <DIV Class="SPEAKER">Third Witch</DIV>
  <DIV Class="line">That will be ere the set of sun.</DIV>

  <DIV Class="SPEAKER">First Witch</DIV>
  <DIV Class="line">Where the place?</DIV>

  <DIV Class="SPEAKER">Second Witch</DIV>
  <DIV Class="line">Upon the heath.</DIV>

  <DIV Class="SPEAKER">Third Witch</DIV>
  <DIV Class="line">There to meet with <SPAN Class="emph">Macbeth</SPAN>.</DIV>

</BODY>
</HTML>
```

To illustrate the alternative ways of defining styles, I have put some styles in the `<HEAD>` part, and declared others within individual tags. How did I decide when to use which type? In this case, it was simple. I have declared the styles within the tags for the elements that only occur once (such as the play title), while declaring other (repeated) elements as **classes**, each with its own style. The class is simply an instruction to the processor to tell it which style to use.

One aim of CSS is to allow content providers to provide content, and more artistic types to supply the styles. To do this, it is generally better to put the styles in a separate file. Using the 'separate file' technique would also allow any play marked up in the same manner to be displayed using a single stylesheet. If we were to do this, we would reference the separate file by changing the `HEAD` element of the HTML file to:

```
<HEAD>
  <!--
   ...
  -->
<LINK rel="stylesheet" type="text/css" href="macbeth.css">
</HEAD>
```

and the style declarations would be exactly as they are in the HTML file, but picked up from the `macbeth.css` file we've just specified.

OK, back to the straight HTML file. When displayed, the output should look similar to this:

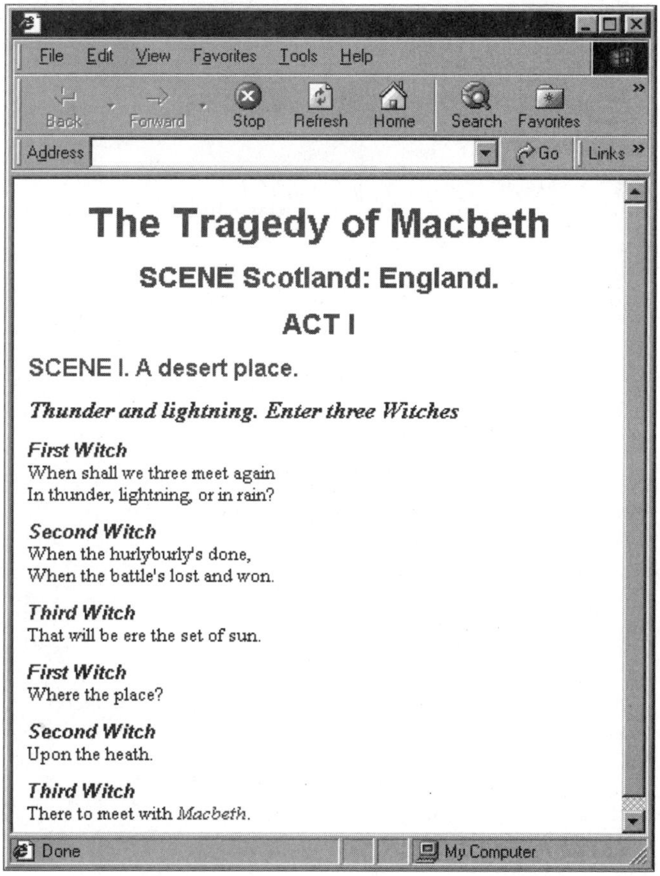

Let's look at the file in detail. Firstly, the <STYLE> element:

This starts by declaring the base font for the document as 10pt Times, or, if the Times font is not available, as any typeface with serifs:

```
<STYLE type="text/css">
  Body
  {
    font-family: Times, serif;
    font-size: 10pt;
  }
```

Any content between tags in the class `acttitle` (the dot before the name indicates that this is a class of element) will be rendered in 14 point Arial (or any sans-serif font if Arial is not available), in bold and centered on the page. There will be a 10-pixel margin below it and the text will be red:

```
  .acttitle
  {
    font-family: Arial, sans-serif;
    font-size: 14pt;
    font-weight: bold;
    color: red;
    text-align: center;
    margin-bottom: 10px;
  }
```

Any tags in the class `scenetitle` are rendered in a similar way. Now we come to the class `stagedir`:

```
  .stagedir
  {
    font-size: 12pt;
    font-weight: bold;
    font-style: italic;
  }
```

Here, we inherit the base font of the <BODY> element – which cascades through the file as the 'default' unless we override it with something more specific – but change the size, weight and style.

The character speaking the lines has their own blue italic `Arial` style, with some space above:

```
  .speaker
  {
    font-family: Arial,sans-serif;
    font-style: italic;
    font-weight: bold;
    margin-top: 10px;
    color: blue;
  }
```

Each *line* of speech uses the base style, because we don't specify any style attributes inside the curly brackets:

```
  .line{}
```

Since the `line` class is not adding any further styles, we could leave it out of the style definitions and even delete the style completely. It is only there so that we can change it independently of the base style if we want to in the future.

That covers the main parts of the document, which will provide suitable formatting for almost all the text in the rest of the play. There is some additional text, and hence some additional markup, just before the play's text starts:

```
<DIV Style="
      font-family: Arial, sans-serif;
      font-size: 20pt;
      font-weight: bold;
      color: red;
      text-align: center;">

  <DIV Style= "margin-bottom: 10px;">
    The Tragedy of Macbeth
  </DIV>

  <DIV Style="
        font-size: 14pt;
        margin-bottom: 10px;">
    SCENE  Scotland: England.
  </DIV>

  <DIV Style="display: none">
    MACBETH
  </DIV>
</DIV>
```

This has used **inline styles** to define appearance. The DIV in which all these elements appear defines a style, then the title and scene inherit this, making changes as necessary. Note that the play has a sub-title **Macbeth**, which I decided not to display. And for those who think the scene setting indicates that Scotland is part of England, it refers to the fact that the play is set mostly in Scotland, but part of the play (Act 4 Scene 3 for the pedantic) is set in England.

And that's it. There is obviously a lot more to learn about Cascading Stylesheets, what they can do, and how inheritance works, but this example has shown us the basic elements.

The aim of CSS is to separate content from style, and it is clear that it goes some way to achieving this. Later on, though, we will see some of its limitations – especially in the XML world – and look at how XSL overcomes these. However, CSS should *not* be written off, as you'll see in a moment, when we use CSS to render XML.

CSS and XML

Let's look at the extract from the Scottish play described in XML, rather than the straight HTML we saw before. Here's the file, `macbethcss.xml` :

```
<?xml version="1.0"?>
<play>
  <title>The Tragedy of Macbeth</title>

  <fm>
    <P>Text placed in the public domain by Moby Lexical Tools, 1992.</P>
    <P>SGML markup by Jon Bosak, 1992-1994.</P>
    <P>XML version by Jon Bosak, 1996-1997.</P>
    <P>This work may be freely copied and distributed worldwide.</P>
  </fm>

  <scndescr>SCENE  Scotland: England.</scndescr>

  <playsubt>MACBETH</playsubt>

  <act>
    <title>ACT I</title>
    <scene>
      <title>SCENE I.  A desert place.</title>

      <stagedir>Thunder and lightning. Enter three Witches</stagedir>

      <speech>
        <speaker>First Witch</speaker>
        <line>When shall we three meet again</line>
        <line>In thunder, lightning, or in rain?</line>
      </speech>

      <speech>
        <speaker>Second Witch</speaker>
        <line>When the hurlyburly's done,</line>
        <line>When the battle's lost and won.</line>
      </speech>

      <speech>
        <speaker>Third Witch</speaker>
        <line>That will be ere the set of sun.</line>
      </speech>

      <speech>
        <speaker>First Witch</speaker>
        <line>Where the place?</line>
      </speech>

      <speech>
        <speaker>Second Witch</speaker>
        <line>Upon the heath.</line>
      </speech>
```

```
        <speech>
          <speaker>Third Witch</speaker>
          <line>There to meet with <emph>Macbeth</emph>.</line>
        </speech>

      </scene>
    </act>
  </play>
```

Jon Bosak, who is a key player in the world of XML and SGML, has marked up all the known plays of Shakespeare in both SGML and XML, and made them freely available on the Internet. The listing above is an extract from his work. To me, this file is easier to read than the HTML equivalent with its use of classes, because the tag names we've used are more intuitive and descriptive.

Let's see what we have to do to render this file using a CSS stylesheet. Firstly, we need to tell the XML document what stylesheet to use by adding the following (highlighted) line to the top of the file:

```
<?xml version="1.0"?>
<?xml-stylesheet type="text/css" href="macbethxml.css"?>
<play>
<title>The Tragedy of Macbeth</title>
```

This inserted line indicates that we will render this file with a separate stylesheet, `macbethxml.css`. Here's the separate stylesheet file in full:

```
play
{
  font-family: Times, serif;
  font-size: 10pt;
}

emph
{
  display: inline;
  color: Green;
  font-style: italic;
}

fm
{
  display: none;
}

title
{
  display:block;
  font-family: Arial, sans-serif;
  font-size: 20pt;
  font-weight: bold;
  color: red;
  text-align: center;
  margin-bottom: 10px;
}
```

```
scndescr
{
  display:block;
  font-family: Arial, sans-serif;
  font-size: 14pt;
  font-weight: bold;
  color: red;
  text-align: center;
  margin-bottom: 10px;
}

playsubt
{
  display:none;
}

act title
{
  font-size: 14pt;
}

scene title
{
  font-size: 12pt;
  text-align: left;
}


stagedir
{
  display:block;
  font-size: 12pt;
  font-weight: bold;
  font-style: italic;
}

speaker
{
  display:block;
  font-family: Arial,sans-serif;
  font-style: italic;
  font-weight: bold;
  margin-top: 10px;
  color: blue;
}

line
{
  display:block;
}
```

This is very similar to before, but this time we have declared some elements as having a display style of `block`. In HTML, some elements, such as `DIV`, are defined as being in a block of their own, with a new line before and after. Others, such as `SPAN`, are defined as being inline, so that the text flow continues from the previous element and into the next. XML does not, as we know, define how its elements should be displayed, so we explicitly use a display style of `block` to force the element into a block of its own.

The effect of this stylesheet is so similar that the screen display is indistinguishable from the previous rendering:

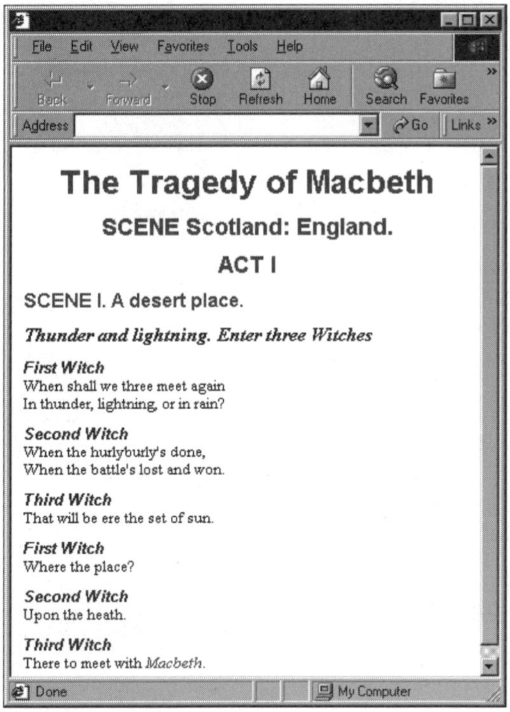

So how does the stylesheet differ from what we did before? Firstly, we no longer put our text in `DIV` elements with classes to define the style. We can define our own element types and directly assign styles to them using the meaningful names of the elements. Since we are working with element names, not classes, we no longer prefix the names with a period (`.`). Secondly, we have three different styles applied to elements called `title`, depending on whether they are the title of the *play*, the *act* or the *scene*. This is done by taking the base `title` as:

```
title
{
  display:block;
  font-family: Arial, sans-serif;
  font-size: 20pt;
  font-weight: bold;
  color: red;
  text-align: center;
  margin-bottom: 10px;
}
```

Then we use **contextual selectors** as defined in the CSS specifications. This means that the `scene title` style:

```
scene title
{
  font-size: 12pt;
  text-align: left;
}
```

inherits the rest of the style properties from the `title` style. This is because, in this context, the `title` element is a direct descendant of the `scene` element, and the style properties for the `scene` element override the font size and text alignment specified in the `title` element:

```
<scene>
      <title>SCENE I.  A desert place.</title>
```

Advantages and Disadvantages of Styling with CSS

There are some clear benefits of styling XML with CSS. Principally, CSS is already standardized, and CSS1, at least, is well-supported by browsers. It is a relatively simple standard and allows a wide range of formatting, including paragraph numbering. Since styling XML with CSS is almost identical to styling HTML, it is very easy to pick up and learn.

On the other hand, it is limited to adding style to existing (static) content. It cannot change the order of the content or modify it in other ways. It cannot perform calculations, or make decisions based on the content, or store variables for later use.

Later, we will meet a vacation described in an XML file. Here is an extract:

```
<?xml version="1.0"?>
<tours>
  <tour>
    <touroperator>
      <code>PNM</code>
      <name>Panorama</name>
      <logourl>Logos/panorama.gif</logourl>
      <email>vacation@boynings.co.uk</email>
    </touroperator>
```

When we display this in the Centaur application, we want to ignore the tour operator name and code, but use the `logourl` to get a logo, and put the `email` address near the bottom of the document within an `<A></A>` tag pair. CSS will have problems with most of this.

It is clear from these examples that XML documents fall into two main categories – those, like the Scottish play, that are a static string of text marked up for display, and those, like the vacation description, that comprise data elements that we want to dynamically manipulate and display. CSS handles the first type well, but is a non-starter when it comes to the second, which requires us to either manipulate the document object model or use XSL to display successfully. Which brings us to our next rendering technique, which uses the DOM that we met in the last chapter.

Rendering Using the Document Object Model

It is possible to display XML by using the DOM and a scripting language to write information to an HTML element that will be displayed using DHTML. In fact, we did that in the last chapter. Let's try again with an example that is about as simple as it gets (`title.htm`):

```
<HTML>
<BODY onLoad = "onLoad()">

<DIV Id="domTarget" Style="color:blue; font-size: 24pt"></DIV>
```

```
<XML Id = "dom">
<?xml version = "1.0"?>
<document>
  <text>XML Design and Implementation</text>
</document>
</XML>

<SCRIPT Language="JScript">
function onLoad()
{
    if (dom.parseError != 0)
    alert(dom.parseError.reason);

  var root = dom.documentElement;
  domTarget.innerText = root.childNodes.item(0).text;
}
</SCRIPT>
</BODY>
</HTML>
```

This document may be short, but it contains the three sections common to all documents that display XML using the DOM and script: the `<DIV>` element, the `<XML>` element, and the `<SCRIPT>` element.

It also introduces the concept of the **XML island** – an XML document embedded *inside* an HTML document. The island is contained within the `XML` element and can be accessed by the `Id` (dom) of this element.

The XML document content itself is simply:

```
<?xml version = "1.0"?>
<document>
  <text>XML Design and Implementation</text>
</document>
```

The HTML file has two other sections – the target location for the generated text:

```
<DIV Id="domTarget" Style="color:blue; font-size: 24pt"></DIV>
```

and the script:

```
<SCRIPT Language="JScript">
function onLoad()
{
    if (dom.parseError != 0)
    alert(dom.parseError.reason);

  var root = dom.documentElement;
  domTarget.innerText = root.childNodes.item(0).text;
}
</SCRIPT>
```

Viewing the file in IE5 gives us what we would expect – the XML `<text>` element is rendered in the defined style:

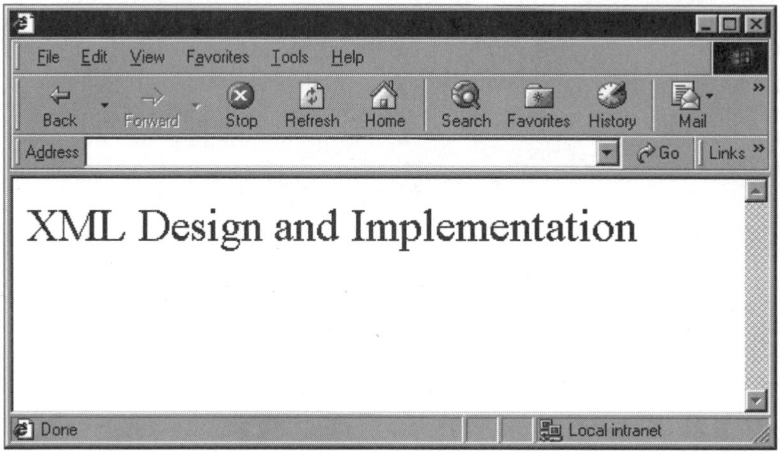

This is all fairly self-explanatory. As before, we check for parser errors in the script. If there are any, this will cause an alert followed by a script error, as `dom.documentElement` will not be recognized. This error could be avoided with an `else` statement, but I feel this adds complexity to the layout for no benefit since we would correct the error anyway.

Assuming there are no errors, we just write the text to the target `<DIV>`, using its `innerText` property, from which it will be displayed using the inline CSS style.

Working with the DOM like this is useful for simple bits of display, or where there is a lot of manipulation to do as in the `displayTree()` example. In particular, using the DOM, we get access to the PCDATA (i.e. the text between tag pairs).

Now, let's take a look at the final rendering technique in this chapter – **databinding**.

Rendering Using Databinding

The term **databinding** will be familiar to anyone who has used Microsoft products to display database information using HTML, and this gives a clue to its use with XML. This technology is part of Microsoft's proprietary ActiveX Data Object (ADO) technology, so the usual warning about trading off the benefits of the technology against the lack of browser-independence applies.

Databinding and XML

Databinding is simply a method for binding data to controls within HTML pages. When the page is rendered, the data is pulled from the **data source object** referenced in the HTML. This data source object could be – for example – a database recordset, or a comma delimited file. Of most interest to us, however, is that it can be an XML document, either as a separate file or embedded in the HTML as an island.

When we discuss databinding, we are in the pseudo-database world, even if our "database" is actually an XML document. Clearly then, databinding requires a document to have a regular structure. Since we are treating our document as a database, we need to think in terms of records and fields. A simple document will therefore have a root element, with records as children of this. Each record will have its fields as children. The skeleton structure will therefore be something like this:

```
<database>
  <record>
    <field1>data</field1>
    <field2>data</field2>
    <field3>data</field3>
  </record>
  <record>
    <field1>data</field1>
    <field2>data</field2>
    <field3>data</field3>
  </record>
</database>
```

We could embed this in an XML document (`datacells.htm`) and use databinding to display it as a table:

```
<HTML>
<BODY>

<XML ID="dso">
<database>
  <record>
    <field1>data</field1>
    <field2>data</field2>
    <field3>data</field3>
  </record>
  <record>
    <field1>data</field1>
    <field2>data</field2>
    <field3>data</field3>
  </record>
</database>
</XML>

<TABLE DATASRC="#dso" BORDER=1>
  <TR>
    <TD><SPAN DATAFLD="field1"></SPAN></TD>
    <TD><SPAN DATAFLD="field2"></SPAN></TD>
    <TD><SPAN DATAFLD="field3"></SPAN></TD>
  </TR>
</TABLE>

</BODY>
</HTML>
```

Here, the XML island contains our database of information (the datasource). The HTML references this via the datasource name:

```
<TABLE DATASRC="#dso" BORDER=1>
```

and displays the data content:

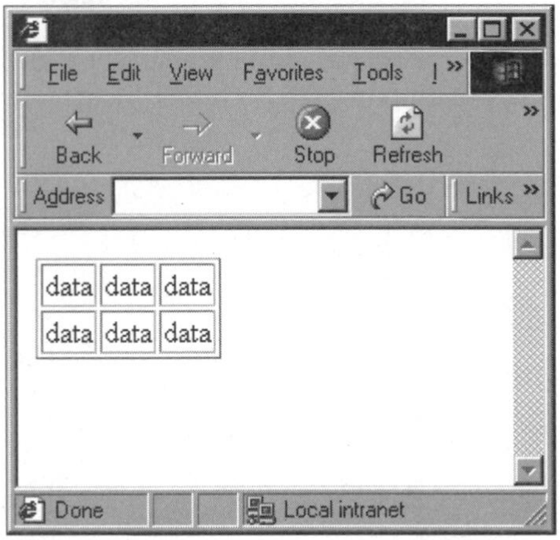

Effective, but dull. Let's change our data and try again:

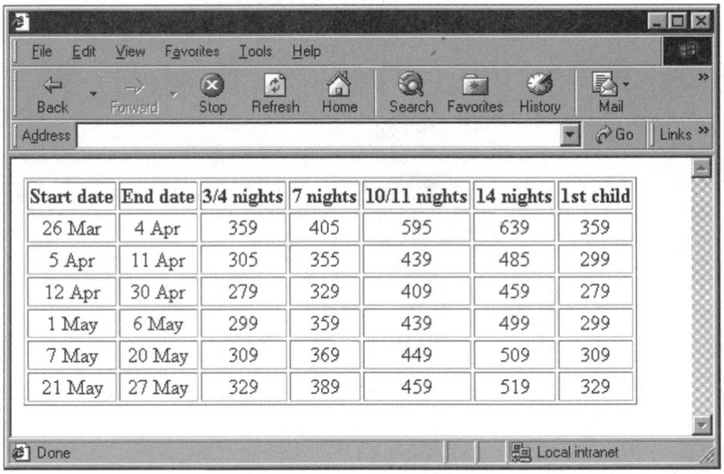

Start date	End date	3/4 nights	7 nights	10/11 nights	14 nights	1st child
26 Mar	4 Apr	359	405	595	639	359
5 Apr	11 Apr	305	355	439	485	299
12 Apr	30 Apr	279	329	409	459	279
1 May	6 May	299	359	439	499	299
7 May	20 May	309	369	449	509	309
21 May	27 May	329	389	459	519	329

This screenshot shows a vacation price table similar to those we will meet later in our study of the Centaur application. The XML file we are displaying is shown below:

```
<?xml version="1.0"?>
<pricetable>
  <row>
    <startdate>26 Mar</startdate>
    <enddate>4 Apr</enddate>
    <price1>359</price1>
    <price2>405</price2>
    <price3>595</price3>
    <price4>639</price4>
    <price5>359</price5>
  </row>
  <row>
```

```
    <startdate>5 Apr</startdate>
    <enddate>11 Apr</enddate>
    <price1>305</price1>
    <price2>355</price2>
    <price3>439</price3>
    <price4>485</price4>
    <price5>299</price5>
  </row>
  <row>
    <startdate>12 Apr</startdate>
    <enddate>30 Apr</enddate>
    <price1>279</price1>
    <price2>329</price2>
    <price3>409</price3>
    <price4>459</price4>
    <price5>279</price5>
  </row>
  <row>
    <startdate>1 May</startdate>
    <enddate>6 May</enddate>
    <price1>299</price1>
    <price2>359</price2>
    <price3>439</price3>
    <price4>499</price4>
    <price5>299</price5>
  </row>
  <row>
    <startdate>7 May</startdate>
    <enddate>20 May</enddate>
    <price1>309</price1>
    <price2>369</price2>
    <price3>449</price3>
    <price4>509</price4>
    <price5>309</price5>
  </row>
  <row>
    <startdate>21 May</startdate>
    <enddate>27 May</enddate>
    <price1>329</price1>
    <price2>389</price2>
    <price3>459</price3>
    <price4>519</price4>
    <price5>329</price5>
  </row>
</pricetable>
```

Since the data is now larger, I have extracted it to a new file called `dso2.xml`. The HTML to display this (`dso2.htm`) now looks like:

```
<HTML>
<BODY>

<XML ID="dso" src="dso2.xml"></XML>

<TABLE DataSrc="#dso" Border="1">
  <THEAD>
    <TH>Start date</TH>
    <TH>End date</TH>
    <TH>3/4 nights</TH>
```

```
      <TH>7 nights</TH>
      <TH>10/11 nights</TH>
      <TH>14 nights</TH>
      <TH>1st child</TH>
    </THEAD>
    <TR>
      <TD Style="text-align:center"><SPAN DataFld="startdate"></SPAN></TD>
      <TD Style="text-align:center"><SPAN DataFld="enddate"></SPAN></TD>
      <TD Style="text-align:center"><SPAN DataFld="price1"></SPAN></TD>
      <TD Style="text-align:center"><SPAN DataFld="price2"></SPAN></TD>
      <TD Style="text-align:center"><SPAN DataFld="price3"></SPAN></TD>
      <TD Style="text-align:center"><SPAN DataFld="price4"></SPAN></TD>
      <TD Style="text-align:center"><SPAN DataFld="price5"></SPAN></TD>
    </TR>
  </TABLE>

  </BODY>
  </HTML>
```

The structure is much the same, except that we have put in some column headings. It would not be complex to use the DOM to extract these from the XML document and insert them into the resulting display using dynamic HTML.

In the current example, we can also see a different form of XML island. Previously, we used the XML island to embed XML code in our file. Here, we are linking to an *external* XML file:

```
<XML ID="dso" src="dso2.xml"></XML>
```

Later, we will display a similar table using XSL. Databinding, however, lets us do something really powerful – we can navigate through a set of records:

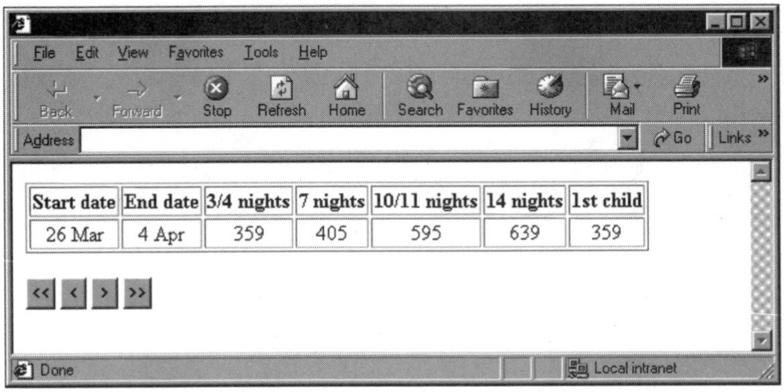

All we have to do is move the binding from the `TABLE` element (which caused the data source to iterate through all the records) to the `TD` element, and then add some navigation code:

```
<HTML>
<BODY>

<XML Id="dso" Src="dso2.xml"></XML>
```

```
<TABLE Border="1">
  <THEAD>
    <TH>Start date</TH>
    <TH>End date</TH>
    <TH>3/4 nights</TH>
    <TH>7 nights</TH>
    <TH>10/11 nights</TH>
    <TH>14 nights</TH>
    <TH>1st child</TH>
  </THEAD>
  <TR>
    <TD Style="text-align:center">
      <SPAN DataSrc="#dso" DataFld="startdate"></SPAN>
    </TD>
    <TD Style="text-align:center">
      <SPAN DataSrc="#dso" DataFld="enddate"></SPAN>
    </TD>
    <TD Style="text-align:center">
      <SPAN DataSrc="#dso" DataFld="price1"></SPAN>
    </TD>
    <TD Style="text-align:center">
      <SPAN DataSrc="#dso" DataFld="price2"></SPAN>
    </TD>
    <TD Style="text-align:center">
      <SPAN DataSrc="#dso" DataFld="price3"></SPAN>
    </TD>
    <TD Style="text-align:center">
      <SPAN DataSrc="#dso" DataFld="price4"></SPAN>
    </TD>
    <TD Style="text-align:center">
      <SPAN DataSrc="#dso" DataFld="price5"></SPAN>
    </TD>
  </TR>
</TABLE>

<BR>
<INPUT Type=BUTTON Value="<<" onclick="dso.recordset.MoveFirst()">
<INPUT Type=BUTTON Value=" < " onclick="previous()">
<INPUT Type=BUTTON Value=" > " onclick="next()">
<INPUT Type=BUTTON Value=">>" onclick="dso.recordset.MoveLast()">

<SCRIPT Language = "JScript">
function previous()
{
  dso.recordset.MovePrevious();
  if (dso.recordset.BOF)
    dso.recordset.MoveFirst();
}

function next()
{
  dso.recordset.MoveNext();
  if (dso.recordset.EOF)
    dso.recordset.MoveLast();
}
</SCRIPT>
</BODY>
</HTML>
```

I have reformatted the code for the table purely to avoid lines wrapping on the page.

This code uses an ADO Recordset object to let us navigate through the data (these recordsets also give us access to the ADO API beyond these basic recordset navigation methods). To find out more about ADO, try looking at Wrox Press's *ADO 2.0 Programmer's Reference* (ISBN 1-861001-835).

We now have a simple interface that allows us to navigate through the data in our file just as if it were a database with a front-end.

We are using four `recordset` methods: `MoveFirst()`, `MoveNext()`, `MovePrevious()`, and `MoveLast()`. We tie these methods to the buttons that appear on the form:

```
<INPUT Type=BUTTON Value="<<" onclick="dso.recordset.MoveFirst()">
<INPUT Type=BUTTON Value=" < " onclick="previous()">
<INPUT Type=BUTTON Value=" > " onclick="next()">
<INPUT Type=BUTTON Value=">>" onclick="dso.recordset.MoveLast()">
```

We also need checks for the beginning and end of the data:

```
function previous()
{
  dso.recordset.MovePrevious();
  if (dso.recordset.BOF)
    dso.recordset.MoveFirst();
}

function next()
{
  dso.recordset.MoveNext();
  if (dso.recordset.EOF)
    dso.recordset.MoveLast();
}
```

With these in place, we simply click on the buttons and go.

That was a quick introduction to databinding. It is possible to use the technique on more complex data structures by adding more `DataFld` attributes, but the main point to remember is that, however simple or complex your data source, it must have a regular structure. Provided that the structure is regular, we can use elements and scripts to navigate around in it.

> *There is more information available on databinding, and on ADO in general on the Microsoft Developer network web site at* `http://msdn.microsoft.com`.

Summary

This chapter has been about the basics of displaying XML in different ways, each with different benefits and disadvantages, and hence with different uses. We have seen that:

- CSS is good for displaying unstructured XML such as textual documents, where the order of display is the same as the order of elements in the XML document.
- The DOM allows us to manipulate not only the order of elements, but the PCDATA as well.
- Databinding allows easy display of highly structured XML documents in tables or by stepping through the data.

In the next chapter we'll look at the Extensible Stylesheet Language (XSL) in depth, and see how this technology can be combined with other rendering options to get the best from each in different circumstances. All of this will contribute to understanding how our Centaur application displays XML in the user's browser.

5

XSL in Theory and Practice

In the last chapter, we looked at three ways of processing XML for display: styling with Cascading Stylesheets; manipulating the Document Object Model and displaying the results with Dynamic HTML; and using Databinding to display regularly structured information. All these mechanisms predate XML, although they complement it well.

In this chapter, we'll look at the Extensible Stylesheet Language – XSL – that is being developed specifically for rendering XML. XSL is still a working draft, and is certain to change before the final recommendation is released.

Meanwhile, Microsoft has based the XSL implementation in IE5 on the status of the XSL draft at the time they had to freeze the code. So there are two major health warnings – the standard will change and the initial IE5 implementation does not quite match the current draft.

We'll start by looking at the working draft itself. As we go through the draft, we'll see how the IE5 implementation differs, and use some examples in IE5. Next, we'll summarize the differences between the draft and IE5, with examples you can try in the browser. Then we'll apply our knowledge to some more IE5 examples and see how XSL allows us to use XML documents in environments running other browsers.

By the end of this chapter, you will:

- understand the concepts behind XSL
- understand the XSL working draft and how the IE5 implementation supports this
- understand how to render linear documents (like the Scottish play) and non-linear documents (like a vacation description) with XSL
- know how to process XSL on the server
- have learnt how to combine the different rendering mechanisms to get the best solution to a particular problem
- have built one of the screens that we will use in the case study

This chapter is based on the W3C working draft dated 16 December 1998. You can find this at `http://www.w3.org/TR/WD-xsl`.

What is XSL?

XSL is a technology for transforming and styling XML. XSL comprises two main elements – a **transformation** language and a **formatting** language.

The transformation language takes a well-formed XML document (it can also be a valid document through having a DTD and matching its requirements) and transforms it into an alternative XML format. In a moment, we will look at why we might want to do this.

The formatting language is analogous to CSS, in that it describes how the information provided by the transformation should be formatted for display. In fact, this language is derived in many aspects from CSS, one difference being that it uses XML syntax rather than the CSS syntax.

Displaying an XML document with XSL is therefore a two-stage process, as shown in the diagram below:

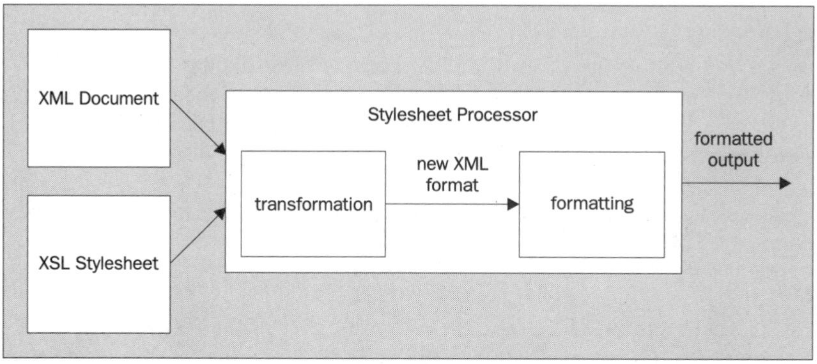

The first stage, the transformation, is the major difference from CSS as it allows us to reorganize the content of the document. As well as leaving out some content, much as we left out the subtitle of the Scottish play when we used CSS in the last chapter, we can add content and move content around. It is this that gives XSL much of its power.

Both the transformation and the formatting aspects of XSL are somewhat controversial, as is the inclusion of them both in the same working draft. By the time the recommendation is released, it may well split into two by separating the transformation and formatting elements into different recommendations. The transformation language is controversial mainly because transformations can be achieved through the DOM. However, as we shall see, XSL is simpler, to the extent that Microsoft has included pattern-matching elements based on those of XSL into its DOM extensions. Netscape prefers the DOM approach, and XSL is not included in Communicator 5.

The formatting language is controversial mainly because we already have one in CSS. However, CSS is targeted entirely at the Web, while XSL is intended for a variety of output media. Using the XSL formatting objects also creates a neater stylesheet since the transformational and formatting aspects are expressed in the same syntax (XML). IE5 implements only the transformational aspects of the working draft. It can do this by creating well-formed HTML directly from the transformation stage. We will look at this in more detail later.

First though, let's get a closer view of the working draft itself.

An Introduction to the XSL Working Draft

Let's start from the beginning. An XSL transformation takes well-formed XML as a **source tree**. It processes this to produce a **result tree** that can then be styled with a set of **formatting objects**. The source tree, result tree and stylesheet are three totally separate entities. Of course, we are familiar with this tree metaphor from the `displayTree()` function we developed earlier in Chapter 3. We can add these to the diagram we had before:

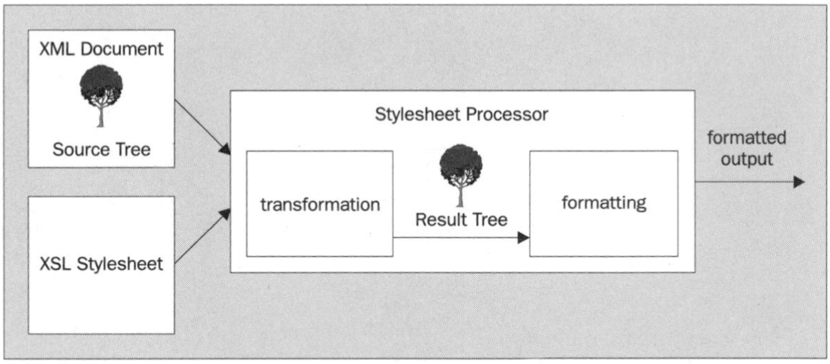

The stylesheet describes the rules for transformation and formatting based on the XML elements in the source tree. This means that a single stylesheet can apply to multiple XML source documents, as long as they are sufficiently similar. What does "sufficiently similar" mean? That depends on the stylesheet. It could be as simple as including the same element types, or it could also refer to the structure of the document. As an example, it would be simple to construct a single XSL stylesheet that could handle any book that uses a set of XML element types defined by a publisher.

Here is a paragraph from the working draft that is critical to the implementation in IE5:

> **XSL does not require result trees to use the formatting vocabulary and thus can be used for general XML transformations. For example, XSL can be used to transform XML to "well-formed" HTML, that is, XML that uses the element types and attributes defined by HTML.**

This not only allows us to produce well-formed HTML (including CSS formatting), it also allows us to produce any other XML document we want, as we shall see in a moment. In Centaur, we will use the IE5 version of XSL to produce well-formed HTML. The process is similar to the diagram above, but ignores the formatting process by including CSS stylesheet information in the resulting HTML:

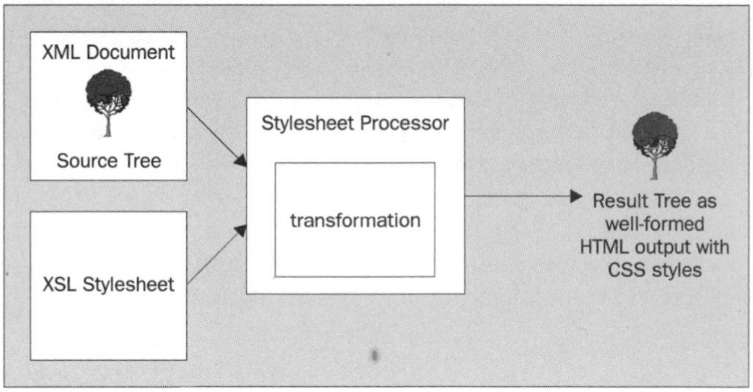

XSL transformations rely on the concepts of **pattern matching** and **templates**. As an XML document is processed with a stylesheet, the processor will look in the stylesheet for patterns, it will then try to match these patterns in the XML document. When it finds a match, it will process the matching nodes (there may be more than one) using rules held in templates in the stylesheet. These templates have rules for both the transformations *and* the formatting to be applied.

The XSL processor is directly instructed to apply a template to a match using an `xsl:apply-templates` instruction. As we shall see in a moment, a template can include further pattern-matching and instructions to apply further templates. It is this that gives XSL its power.

The overall process is shown in the diagram:

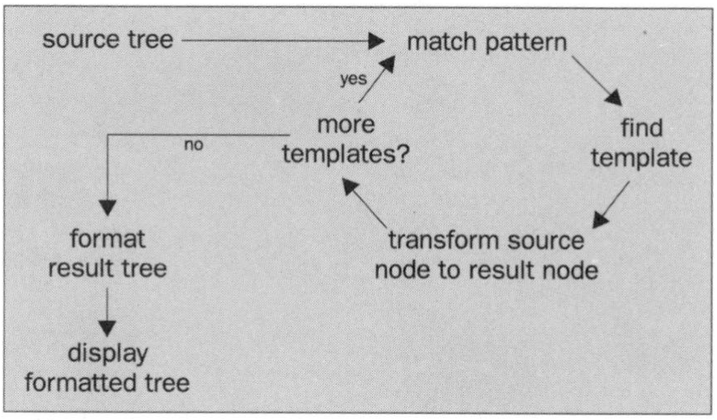

This shows how the first stage is to match a pattern from the stylesheet with a node or nodes in the source tree (that is, the XML document we are styling). When a match is found, the stylesheet processor finds the appropriate template rule and transforms the nodes from the source tree into nodes in the result tree. If the template rule indicates that further templates should be applied, the process starts again by finding new matching nodes. If there are no more templates to process, then the formatting and display can start. In a moment, we will work through some examples that illustrate how this process happens.

An Introduction to XSL Transformation

We have already seen that, in theory, XSL can be used to transform one XML format into another. Why do we want to do that? Here are a couple of reasons:

As we have just seen, one reason is to produce a well-formed HTML document. Remember that HTML and XML are related, one being a *subset* and one an *implementation* of SGML. We mentioned in Chapter 2 that the normal HTML markup you see around is not well formed – for example, because of the lack of closing tags on some elements. However, it is possible to write well-formed HTML, simply by adding closing tags (as in `<P>This is a paragraph</P>`) or using the empty tag format (for example `<BR />`). So we can use XSL to convert an XML document into well-formed HTML for display. However, if we do this, we must take into account that a document can only have one external stylesheet, and the XSL sheet will take priority.

We can also use XSL to convert one XML format into another. We may be collecting information from various sources that do not all use the same format for the data. For example, we showed some alternative representations of a book catalogue earlier.

In this chapter, we'll use an XML description of a vacation. Part of this describes the tour operator as:

```
<touroperator>
  <code>PNM</code>
  <name>Panorama</name>
  <logourl>Logos/panorama.gif</logourl>
  <email>vacation@boynings.co.uk</email>
</touroperator>
```

The same information could equally well be represented in XML as:

```
<touroperator code="PNM" logourl=" Logos/panorama.gif">
  <name>Panorama</name>
  <email>mailto:vacation@boynings.co.uk</email>
</touroperator>
```

The information is the same, but the markup is different. Hence the code used to define display will be different. Normally, you would hope to avoid this, for example through adherence to a DTD, but there will be times on the Web when this translation is needed. An example would be if, instead of holding vacation information ourselves in Centaur, we wanted to search the Web for vacations from different suppliers. Perhaps these suppliers publish their brochures in XML on the Web, but have not developed a common DTD. We could use a different stylesheet to pre-process the results from each operator then use common processing from there on.

Pre-processing with XSL could also help us with the sticky problem of DTD version control. I have yet to see a good example of handling multiple versions of DTDs. The best I have found is in the Open Financial Exchange (OFX) standard (see `http://www.ofx.net/ofx/` for more information). In this, changes that leave the DTD compatible with older DTDs are indicated by incrementing the minor number of the version tag (for example, from 1.3 to 1.4). Changes that result in a new DTD that is not compatible with older versions require a change to the major number (for example, from 1.5 to 2.0). This allows DTD versions to be specified, but only so that documents using an incompatible version can be rejected. An alternative approach could be to use an XSL stylesheet to convert between an old version and a newer one before starting other processing.

OK, enough theory. Let's take a closer look at an XSL stylesheet.

A Simple Stylesheet

Here is a simple XSL stylesheet for us to analyze – it's in the format of the December working draft. In a moment, we will look at the equivalent using the IE5 syntax. Don't worry about the specifics of the syntax – we will be looking at that in more depth later. This example is modified slightly from one in the working draft (section 2.1):

```
<xsl:stylesheet
  xmlns:xsl="http://www.w3.org/TR/WD-xsl"
  xmlns:fo="http://www.w3.org/TR/WD-xsl/FO"
  result-ns="fo">
  <xsl:template match="/">
    <fo:basic-page-sequence font-family="serif">
      <xsl:apply-templates/>
    </fo:basic-page-sequence>
  </xsl:template>
```

```
  <xsl:template match="doc">
    <xsl:apply-templates/>
  </xsl:template>

  <xsl:template match="para">
    <fo:block font-size="10pt" space-before="12pt">
      <xsl:apply-templates/>
    </fo:block>
  </xsl:template>
</xsl:stylesheet>
```

Remember, you cannot use this stylesheet in IE5 as the browser does not support formatting objects (invoked in the `<fo:...></fo:...>` *elements) and has a slightly different syntax for transformation.*

This stylesheet would act on an XML document with a `doc` root element containing a series of `para` elements.

The document starts with the `xsl:stylesheet` element:

```
<xsl:stylesheet
  xmlns:xsl="http://www.w3.org/TR/WD-xsl"
  xmlns:fo="http://www.w3.org/TR/WD-xsl/FO"
  result-ns="fo">
```

XSL relies on the use of namespaces, which we looked at briefly in Chapter 2. Namespaces for XML were introduced as a means of ensuring that the element and attribute names in an XML document are unique, and that is why they are being used here. Although the namespace declarations here use URIs to identify the namespaces, they are used *solely* for this purpose – the XSL processor will not try to access the URI to retrieve anything.

The `xsl:stylesheet` element indicates that the stylesheet will use two namespaces `http://www.w3.org/TR/WD-xsl` and `http://www.w3.org/TR/WD-xsl/FO`. The former declares all the possible *transformational* elements, and the latter the *formatting* elements. In the stylesheet, these are identified by prefixing element names with `xsl:` and `fo:` respectively. The attribute `result-ns="fo"` indicates that our output tree uses the formatting object vocabulary.

If we were constructing an HTML document instead, we would use:

```
<xsl:stylesheet
  xmlns:xsl="http://www.w3.org/TR/WD-xsl"
  xmlns="http://www.w3.org/TR/REC-html40"
  result-ns="">
```

In this case, the value of `result-ns` can be an empty string as HTML is the default namespace – a concept we shall meet again later.

Let's go back to our original example. Having indicated that this is an XSL stylesheet, we can start on the templates. The first matches the root node:

```
<xsl:template match="/">
```

> **Note that the root node is not the same as the root element, but is the root of the document tree. It has a single child, which is the root element of the document. We will look at the implications of this when we look at our first example in IE5.**

Next, we define the font for this as being any serif font:

```
    <fo:basic-page-sequence font-family="serif">
```

The `basic-page-sequence` formatting object is used to describe the general layout for a Web page. This formatting will be inherited by any further elements unless over-ridden by a further `font-family` attribute. Having defined all we wish to at this level, we ensure that all immediate child nodes are processed using `xsl:apply-templates`, and then put in the closing tags for each element:

```
      <xsl:apply-templates/>
    </fo:basic-page-sequence>
  </xsl:template>
```

Let me re-iterate how `xsl:apply-templates` operates here, since it is so key to the understanding of XSL, both in the working draft and the IE5 implementation. Having found the template to apply to the root node, the XSL processor started to apply the instructions in the template. The first was a formatting instruction. The second was an instruction to apply further templates. At this point, the processor looks for templates to apply to children of the root node. It will find the single child of the root node – the document's root element. Since this also has an `xsl:apply-templates` rule, it will continue to work through these children, and other descendants specified by further `xsl:apply-templates` rules, until it is not told to apply more templates. At this point, it will work back up through the tree, close the `fo:basic-page-sequence` formatting element and exit the template. This is illustrated in the diagram at the end of this section.

As the XSL processor works on the XML source document, it will find `para` elements as children of the root element. It will then find the template:

```
  <xsl:template match="para">
    <fo:block font-size="10pt" space-before="12pt">
      <xsl:apply-templates/>
    </fo:block>
  </xsl:template>
```

and place a 12-point space before the paragraph and apply a font size of 10pt to all the text. This template also has an `xsl:apply-templates` element. This is required as the `para` elements themselves are not text – the text is in a `Text` node that is a child of the `para` element. So why not build a template for these? This is not necessary as XSL has a built-in default template to extract the value of the `Text` node (which is the text itself) and copy it directly to the result tree:

```
<xsl:template match="text()">
  <xsl:value-of select="."/>
</xsl:template>
```

XSL has one further built-in template rule:

```
<xsl:template match="*|/">
  <xsl:apply-templates/>
</xsl:template>
```

This ensures that processing starts with the root node (/) and continues at any point where a match is not found (*). We could therefore have left out the template for the doc element, since all we did was duplicate this template. The pipestem (|) is used as an "or" connector to indicate that this will match either pattern (root node or wildcard). If we put in our own rules, they will override these built-in rules. An instance of this is where you do not want all the text in your document to appear in the output. For example, you might have a single document with multiple audiences, where each audience uses its own stylesheet to display only the level of detail required. The built-in rules would ensure that all elements cause their children to be processed, and that all Text nodes are copied to the output. You could override the former with the rule:

```
<xsl:template match="*">
</xsl:template>
```

Now, no processing will occur on elements that are not explicitly matched in other rules.

This processing sequence in this example is summed up in this diagram:

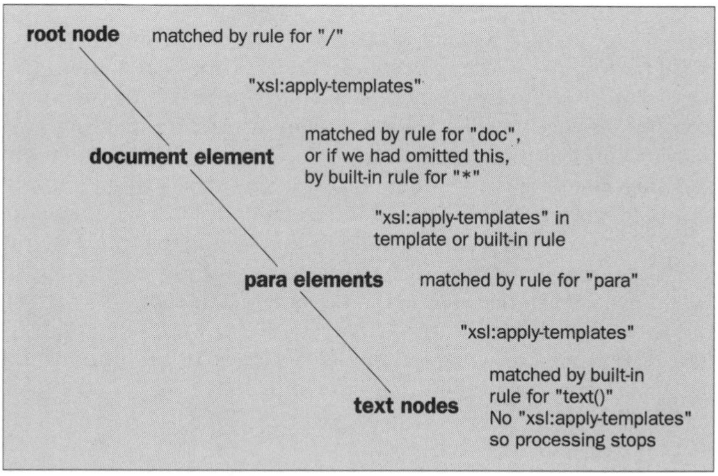

Now let's take a look at how these manifest themselves in IE5.

The XSL Stylesheet In IE5

Here is the same stylesheet, modified to operate with IE5:

```
<?xml version="1.0"?>
<xsl:stylesheet
  xmlns:xsl="http://www.w3.org/TR/WD-xsl"
  xmlns="http://www.w3.org/TR/REC-html40"
  result-ns="">
```

```
   <xsl:template match="/">
   <HTML>
     <BODY>
       <DIV style="font-family:serif">
         <xsl:apply-templates select="doc" />
       </DIV>
     </BODY>
   </HTML>
   </xsl:template>

   <xsl:template match="doc">
       <xsl:apply-templates/>
   </xsl:template>

   <xsl:template match="para">
     <DIV style="font-size:10pt; margin-top:12pt">
       <xsl:value-of />
     </DIV>
   </xsl:template>
</xsl:stylesheet>
```

If we apply this to a simple document (`first.xml`):

```
<?xml version="1.0"?>
<?xml-stylesheet type="text/xsl" href="first.xsl"?>
<doc>
  <para>This is the first paragraph</para>
  <para>And this is the second</para>
</doc>
```

we get the result:

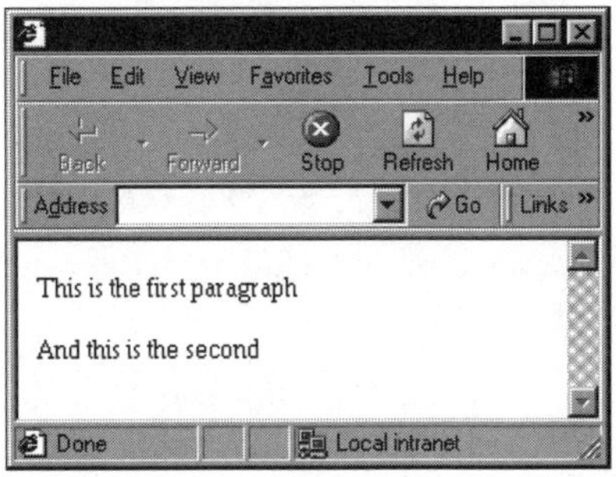

Let's have a look at the differences. Firstly, we are now using the HTML 4.0 namespace as the default namespace in the stylesheet, as we described above:

```
xmlns="http://www.w3.org/TR/REC-html40"
```

Following this, we use the template for our root node to build the framework for an HTML document:

```
<xsl:template match="/">
  <HTML>
    <BODY>
      <DIV style="font-family:serif">
        <xsl:apply-templates select="doc" />
```

```
        </DIV>
      </BODY>
    </HTML>
    </xsl:template>
```

The formatting that we previously placed in an XSL formatting object, we now have in an inline CSS style instruction in the HTML <DIV> tag. Since we have defined a template for unmatched elements, we will use a specific template for the element doc. This template just ensures that processing continues with sub-elements:

```
  <xsl:template match="doc">
        <xsl:apply-templates/>
    </xsl:template>
```

Finally, we put our para elements inside HTML DIV elements, applying the styling we previously applied using formatting objects:

```
  <xsl:template match="para">
      <DIV style="font-size:10pt; margin-top:12pt">
        <xsl:value-of />
      </DIV>
    </xsl:template>
```

Here, we use the xsl:value-of rather than the xsl:apply-templates element. This ensures that the content (that is, the text) of the element is displayed, but the XSL processor does not search for further templates.

Next, let's go into more depth on the pattern matching facilities that XSL gives us.

Pattern Matching

In this section, we will use pattern matching from the December XSL working draft. The IE5 implementation is very similar, and I will point out differences when they occur.

In our previous examples we saw statements like these:

```
  <xsl:template match="/">
  <xsl:template match="para">
```

Here, the first line matches the root node, the second matches elements called para.

Let's look at a slightly more complex example. Consider this extract from an XML document describing a vacation (we will meet the full document later in this chapter):

```
  <?xml version="1.0"?>
  <tours>
    <tour>
      <resort>
        <facilities>
          <facility>restaurants</facility>
```

```
        <facility>evening entertainment</facility>
        <facility>nightclubs</facility>
      </facilities>
    </resort>
    <vacation>
      <purposes>
        <purpose logourl="Logos/sumsun.gif">Summer Sun</purpose>
        <purpose logourl="Logos/winsun.gif">Winter Sun</purpose>
      </purposes>
      <name>Hotel Aziza</name>
      <facilities>
        <facility>Air conditioning</facility>
        <facility>Outdoor pool</facility>
        <facility>Indoor pool</facility>
        <facility>Lounge</facility>
        <facility>Bar</facility>
        <facility>Cafe</facility>
        <facility>Restaurant</facility>
        <facility>Shops</facility>
      </facilities>
    </vacation>
  </tour>
</tours>
```

We'll discuss this example in detail below. Since we will be discussing this as a hierarchy of nodes, it is useful to see it as a tree structure as well (I have not included all the `facility` elements):

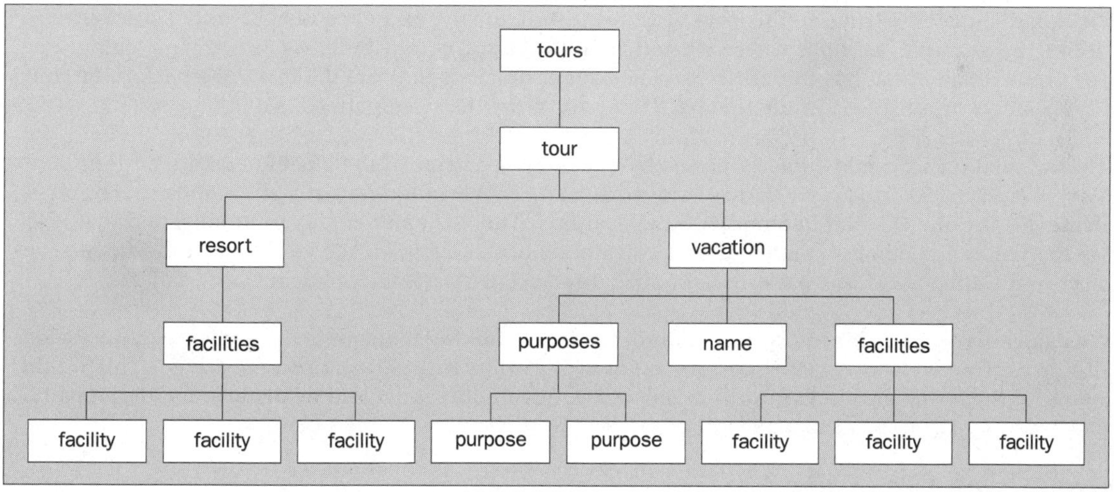

Matching Elements

We have seen that we can match the `tours` element with a pattern of `tours`. XSL uses the syntax familiar from matching files in file system hierarchies to find deeper elements. The `tour` element could therefore be matched as `/tours/tour`. In the same way, we could match the resort facilities using `/tours/tour/resort/facilities/facility`.

XSL uses the concept of a current element. We will meet this concept more when we discuss the `xsl:for-each` element, but at the moment we just need to remember that the starting point for our pattern matching might not be the root node. This is again analogous to a file system. If you are in DOS and have changed to the directory `\WINDOWS`, issuing a command `DIR SYSTEM` will give a directory listing of the directory `\WINDOWS\SYSTEM`, not `\SYSTEM`. In XSL, we can ensure that we look for descendants of the root node by placing a `/` at the start of the pattern. Of course, DOS uses the `\` rather than `/`, but the principle is the same.

It is possible to use some short cuts when doing this. By using `/` between names, we are selecting immediate children. We can instead use `//` to select *all* descendants. Thus `/.//resort//facilities` will select all resort facilities in the same way we did above, while `/.//facilities` will select all facilities, whether for the resort or the vacation. In this case, the period [`.`] represents the current node.

Matching Attributes

So far, we have looked at matching on element names. We can also match on attribute names and values. Attributes are treated just like child elements, but are prefixed with the `@` symbol. We could, for example, match the `logourl` attribute of any element using the pattern `/.//@logourl`.

Matching on Descendants

Just now, we matched all `logourl` attributes. What if instead we want to match the `purpose` elements that have a `logourl` attribute? In that case, we can add a test to the `purpose` element by specifying a pattern `/.//purpose[@logourl]`. The pattern will only be matched if the test inside the square brackets is true. In this case, it is just testing for the existence of a `logourl` attribute. Unlike the example just now, where we matched the `logourl` attribute, we are now matching the `purpose` element that has this attribute. The square brackets indicate the test to be performed, but any elements or attributes inside them are not part of the matched pattern.

If we wanted to, we could extend this test by checking the value of the attribute with a pattern `/.//purpose[@logourl="Logos/sumsun.gif"]`. We would now match a single `purpose` element – the one relating to Summer Sun vacations. There is another way to do this, and that is to use the `text()` method to match on the `Text` node of the element. We could select the same `purpose` element with the pattern `/.//purpose[text()="Summer Sun"]`.

We can easily extend this test. If we had more tours in our XML document, we might want to select all `tour` elements whose vacation element has a `purpose` with the `sumsun.gif` logo. This would match all the Summer Sun vacations in our XML document, and could be achieved with the pattern `/.//tour[vacation/purpose/@logourl="Logos/sumsun.gif]`.

Matching on Ancestors

XSL includes an `ancestor()` function to select ancestors of the current node. If our current node were the `facilities` node of the `vacation` element, we could find the parent vacation name with `ancestor(vacation)/name`. In the same way that descendants can be anywhere below the current node in the hierarchy, ancestors can be anywhere above it. They do not have to be immediate parents.

Matching on Position

We can match on the position of an element using four special tests:

- `first-of-any()` matches if the node being tested is the first element child
- `last-of-any()` matches if the node being tested is the last element child
- `first-of-type()` matches if the node being tested is the first element child of its element type
- `last-of-type()` matches if the node being tested is the last element child of its element type

Look at the bullet points above. The last bullet has space below it, but the others do not. This would be a good example of special processing for a `last-of-type()` when matching `bullet` elements within a `section`.

Let's mark up the text above as XML (`bullet.xml`):

```
<?xml version="1.0"?>
<?xml-stylesheet type="text/xsl" href="bullet.xsl"?>
<doc>
  <line>We can match on the position of an element using four special
    tests:</line>
  <bullet>first-of-any() matches if the node being tested is the first element
    child</bullet>
  <bullet>last-of-any() matches <em>if</em> the node <i>being</i> tested is the
    last element child</bullet>
  <bullet>first-of-type() matches if the node being tested is the first element
    child of its element type</bullet>
  <bullet>last-of-type() matches if the node being tested is the last element
    child of its element type</bullet>
  <line>Look at the bullet points above. The last bullet has space below it, the
    others do not. This would be a good example of special processing for a last-
    of-type() when matching bullet elements within a section.</line>
</doc>
```

Suppose a `line` element has a 12pt space below it. For the `bullet` element, we could achieve the formatting we have on this page by using one template rule for the normal `bullet` elements, but a different rule for the `last-of-type()` inserting a 12pt space after the element.

IE5 does not implement these methods, but provides alternatives by allowing indexing into a collection, such as the collection of `bullet` elements above, and finding the last member of the collection.

We can use our bullet point example to illustrate both the XSL working draft and the IE5 implementation. We want to put a 12pt space below the last bullet. We will emphasize that we have done this by rendering the last bullet point in a bold font. We will also italicize the first bullet point to illustrate indexing into the collection. The code to do this is (`bullet.xsl`):

```
<?xml version="1.0"?>
<xsl:stylesheet
  xmlns:xsl="http://www.w3.org/TR/WD-xsl"
  xmlns="http://www.w3.org/TR/REC-html40"
  result-ns="">
```

```
<xsl:template match="/">
<HTML>
  <BODY>
      <xsl:apply-templates select="doc" />
  </BODY>
</HTML>
</xsl:template>

<xsl:template match="doc">
    <xsl:apply-templates/>
</xsl:template>

<xsl:template match="line">
  <DIV style="margin-bottom:12pt">
    <xsl:value-of />
  </DIV>
</xsl:template>

<xsl:template match="bullet">
  <DIV>
    * <xsl:value-of />
  </DIV>
</xsl:template>

<xsl:template match="bullet[0]">
  <DIV style="font-style:italic">
    * <xsl:value-of />
  </DIV>
</xsl:template>

<xsl:template match="bullet[end()]">
  <DIV style="margin-bottom:12pt; font-weight:bold">
    * <xsl:value-of />
  </DIV>
</xsl:template>

</xsl:stylesheet>
```

You can see in this that we have explicitly matched the `doc` and `line` elements, putting a 12pt space below the latter:

```
<xsl:template match="doc">
      <xsl:apply-templates/>
</xsl:template>

<xsl:template match="line">
    <DIV style="margin-bottom:12pt">
      <xsl:value-of />
    </DIV>
</xsl:template>
```

We match the first `bullet` element by using an index value of zero. This is rendered in italics:

```
<xsl:template match="bullet[0]">
 <DIV style="font-style:italic">
 * <xsl:value-of />
</DIV>
</xsl:template>
```

Other bullet elements simply have the prefix * . The last template matches bullet elements where end() returns true:

```
<xsl:template match="bullet[end()]">
  <DIV style="margin-bottom:12pt; font-weight:bold">
    * <xsl:value-of />
  </DIV>
</xsl:template>
```

These are rendered in bold with a space below them. They are also prefixed by an asterisk and a space. Don't worry about how the XSL processor knows whether to use the specific templates or the more general one for the first and last bullet elements – we will see this in a moment. The result of this processing is:

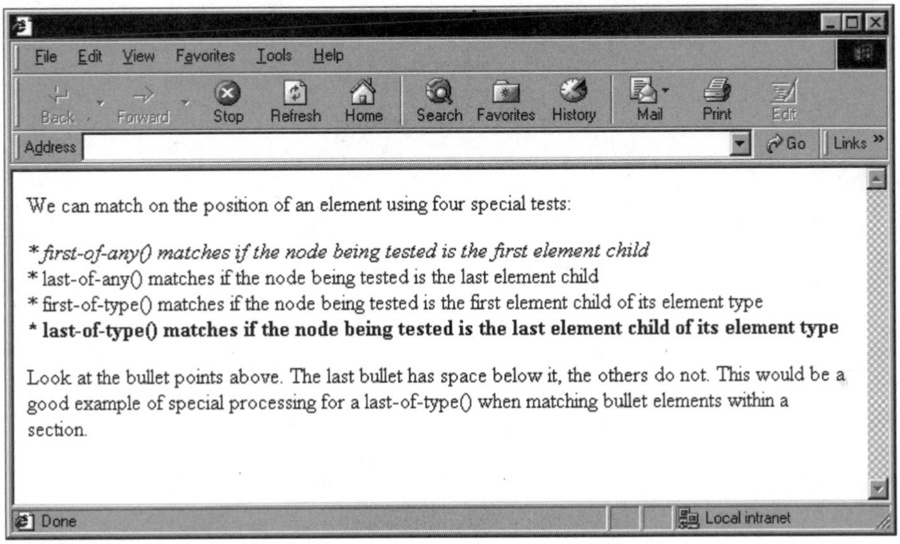

Boolean Tests

We can also test using boolean operators such as and, or and not(). Examples of these are:

bullet[first-of-type() or last-of-type()] matches the first and last bullet elements

bullet[first-of-type() and last-of-type()] matches a bullet element only if it is the *only* bullet child of its parent.

In our original vacation example, purpose[not(@logourl)] would match purpose elements without a logourl attribute if there were any.

IE5 uses a different syntax from the working draft. In fact, it uses two syntaxes, since there are alternatives to some operators. The equivalent operators for IE5 are:

<table>
<tr><th>Operator</th><th>Shortcut</th><th>Description</th></tr>
<tr><td>and</td><td>&&</td><td>Logical-and</td></tr>
<tr><td>or</td><td>||</td><td>Logical-or</td></tr>
<tr><td>not, not()</td><td></td><td>Negation</td></tr>
</table>

Matching on ID

In Chapter 2, we introduced the ID and IDREF attributes that allow us to link elements within an XML document. The XSL working draft includes an id() function for matching elements that contain specific IDs. For this to work, IDs and IDREFs must be suitably declared in the DTD. This allows XSL to follow links within a document. IE5 does not support the id() function.

Consider the following:

```
<?xml version="1.0"?>
<tours>
  <vacation>
    <name id="h1">Hotel Aziza</name>
    <rating value="4" />
    <seeAlso ref="h2">Hotel Fourati</seeAlso>
  </vacation>
  <vacation id="h2">
    <name>Hotel Fourati</name>
    <rating value="3" />
  </vacation>
</tours>
```

Then if our current node were the vacation at the Hotel Aziza, the pattern id(seeAlso/@ref) would match the Hotel Fourati.

The working draft hints that the function name may change in the future from id() *to* idref().

Special Characters

We have already met special characters such as / for the root node, . for the current element and // to select from descendants rather than children. There are a few other special characters we can use:

.. matches the parent of the current node. Again, this is familiar from file system usage.

* can be used as a wild card. We have used it to select all elements not explicitly matched. We can also it more generally, for example, @* selects all attributes of the current node.

| is used to select alternatives. Remembering that XML names are case sensitive, while HTML names are not, the string B | b | emph | EMPH | Emph will match all the likely ways that people might specify bold text in HTML. We will see later that this can be useful when an XML document can contain HTML over which we have no control.

Matching non-Element Nodes

So far, we have matched elements and their attributes. XML contains other node types, and XSL can be used with comment and processing instruction nodes in much the same way, using the built-in functions `comment()` and `pi()`.

Conflicting Matches

It is possible that more than one template will be found that applies to the same source node. In fact, this will almost always be true since all nodes will match the built-in rule:

```
<xsl:template match="*|/">
  <xsl:apply-templates/>
</xsl:template>
```

The following rules show how the working draft indicates which template should be selected. IE5 uses a different mechanism, which we will look at afterwards.

Stylesheets may import other stylesheets. Template rules have an **importance** based on whether they are included in the stylesheet or are imported from another stylesheet. To quote the working draft:

> **Rules and definitions in the importing stylesheet are defined to be more important than rules and definitions in any imported stylesheets. Also rules and definitions in one imported stylesheet are defined to be more important than rules and definitions in previous imported stylesheets.**

So, when there are multiple matches,

> **...all matching template rules that are less important than the most important matching template rule or rules are eliminated from consideration.**

The built-in template rules are treated as though they were imported before any other imported stylesheets and so will not take priority over rules we write ourselves.

In practice, this means that templates are selected in the following order:

Most important	Templates in the main stylesheet
	Templates in the stylesheet whose import was defined nearest the bottom of the main stylesheet
	Templates in other imported stylesheets, working up the main stylesheet
Least important	The built-in templates

It is also possible to set a **priority** for a template rule. The priority is a positive or negative integer, the default being zero. To quote the working draft again:

> **The priority of a rule is specified by the priority attribute on the rule. The value of this must be a real number (positive or negative).**
>
> **It is an error if this leaves more than one matching template rule. An XSL processor may signal the error; if it does not signal the error, it must recover by choosing from amongst the matching template rules that are left the one that occurs last in the stylesheet.**

Conflicting Matches in IE5

IE5 supports neither importance (it does not support importing stylesheets) nor priority. Instead, it works through templates from the bottom of the stylesheet upwards, looking for the first match. That is why, in our bullet point example, we had the specific templates for the first and last `bullet` elements below the more general one for the other `bullet` elements. If you try moving the general `bullet` template below the others, you will see that all `bullet` elements use this template.

> **As you can see, the pattern matching in XSL is extremely flexible and powerful. Remember also that you can use this form of pattern matching within the DOM, although you should be aware that is currently a Microsoft proprietary extension to the DOM.**

Having looked in detail at the important pattern matching ideas, let's move on to how we deal with the nodes that we've selected.

Transformation

Once patterns have been matched, we need to do something with the nodes that are returned, and that is where the **transformation** and **formatting** parts of XSL come into play.

Transformation of the XML source is one of the great powers of XSL. While some documents (such as the Scottish play we rendered with CSS in the last chapter) are linear in nature, others are not. With the former, elements appear on the screen in the order they appear in the source document. In the latter, they do not.

The extract from a vacation description we have just seen is a good example. We could pull the data from the database as we want it displayed, including extracting some elements more than once. In fact, this is what we would do if we were to render the document using HTML. However, if we then wanted to change the format of the display, we would have to change chunks of complex database handling code. And believe me, while developing Centaur, I changed the appearance of the vacation details screen several times.

Instead, we can pull the data from the database in a convenient XML format and render it as we wish. Of course, "convenient" could be convenient for the database extraction, or convenient for the XML rendering. The final format chosen will always be a compromise.

Remember that, at the time of writing, XSL was still in draft, although the changes and level of editorial comment indicate that the transformational aspects are close to completion. IE5 implements most of the transformation part of this draft, and also some legacy parts from the previous draft. Chief among these is the ability to include script within a stylesheet. This is no longer included in the present working draft (16 December 1998), although it is always possible that it will be replaced in the final version.

Transformation Instructions

Here is a summary of the transformation instructions and their associated actions:

xsl:apply-templates

We have already seen this element, which directs the XSL processor to find the appropriate template to apply based on the results of the pattern in the `match` attribute.

xsl:import

As we've already seen, it's possible for one stylesheet to import another. For example, we might have a set of tags that we display the same way in several applications. We could include templates for these in a stylesheet we import when required. Because of the rules for selecting templates that we saw earlier, we can always override individual templates if we need to.

All `xsl:import` elements must occur at the start of the stylesheet. They use an `href` attribute to locate the stylesheet to import:

```
<xsl:stylesheet xmlns:xsl="http://www.w3.org/TR/WD-xsl">
  <xsl:import href="html.xsl"/>
  ...
```

Remember, IE5 does not support importing stylesheets.

xsl:for-each

This evaluates an XSL pattern in the `select` attribute, and applies the same template to each node found.

For example, here is an extract from the document we met earlier:

```
<?xml version="1.0"?>
<tours>
  <tour>
    <resort>
      <facilities>
        <facility>restaurants</facility>
        <facility>evening entertainment</facility>
        <facility>nightclubs</facility>
      </facilities>
    </resort>
  </tour>
</tours>
```

If we were processing the template for the `tours/tour` node, we could process each of the facility elements with:

```
<xsl:for-each select="resort/facilities/facility">
  <LI><xsl:value-of/></LI>
</xsl:for-each>
```

With HTML as our result namespace, this would cause each of the `facility` elements to be shown in a list.

`xsl:for-each` is the element that allows us to process non-linear documents. In our examples so far, we have put nodes in our result tree in the same order that we find them in the source tree. Using `xsl:for-each`, we can extract individual nodes of the source tree as and when we like. Later in this chapter, we will look in detail at a linear example (the Scottish Play) and a non-linear example (the description of a vacation).

xsl:value-of

This evaluates an XSL pattern in the `select` attribute and inserts the resulting value into the template node as text. It is generally used to extract the text node from within an element.

Using XSL to Apply Numbering

The XSL working draft provides two mechanisms for providing numbering in the result tree:

- `xsl:number` can be used to supply numbers based on the position of elements in the source tree.
- `xsl:counter` and its related elements allow the stylesheet to hold counters that can be controlled within the stylesheet.

IE5 uses different mechanisms, which we look at in a moment.

Using xsl:number

This defines a number based on the position of the current node in the source tree. This is a very flexible mechanism for numbering sections of a document. It is possible to include or exclude parent numbering and to change the style of the numbers, using, for example, Roman numerals or letters rather than Arabic numerals.

The following example would number the resort facilities:

```
<xsl:template match="/.//resort/facilities/facility">
  <fo:block>
    <xsl:number/>
    <xsl:text>. </xsl:text>
    <xsl:apply-templates/>
  </fo:block>
<xsl:template>
```

This example uses the `xsl:text` element. This puts the enclosed text as a `Text` node in the result tree. When we are creating HTML as our result tree, we do not need this as the text will be placed in the document at the point it appears in the source tree.

The working draft provides a more complex example for numbering chapters and appendices in a book:

```
<xsl:template match="title">
  <fo:block>
     <xsl:number level="multi"
                 count="chapter|section|subsection"
                 format="1.1. "/>
     <xsl:apply-templates/>
  </fo:block>
</xsl:template>
```

```
<xsl:template match="appendix//title" priority="1">
  <fo:block>
     <xsl:number level="multi"
                 count="appendix|section|subsection"
                 format="A.1. "/>
     <xsl:apply-templates/>
  </fo:block>
</xsl:template>
```

In this case, title elements will be matched elsewhere and this template used. The priority mechanism is used to ensure that a title within an appendix will use the second template. The only difference between the templates is in the numbering scheme used, where a sub-section within a chapter will be numbered in the style 1.1.1, while in an appendix it would be A.1.1.

It is the attribute `multi` that ensures that the full numbering is used rather than just the sub-section itself. The `count` attribute uses a match pattern to specify which elements should be included in the count, while the `format` attribute specifies the format of the numbering scheme.

Using xsl:counter

While `xsl:number` bases its output on the position of an element in the *source* tree, `xsl:counter` and its related elements `xsl:counters`, `xsl:counter-increment` and `xsl:counter-reset` base their output on the position of an element in the *result* tree.

This example from the working draft will number all `note` elements in the output in the order they appear:

```
<xsl:template match="note">
  <xsl:text> (Note </xsl:text>
  <xsl:counter-increment name="note"/>
  <xsl:counter name="note"/>
  <xsl:text>).</xsl:text>
</xsl:template>
```

The element `xsl:counter-increment` increments the counter each time the template creates a result node based on a `note` element in the source tree. `xsl:counter` then copies this number to the result tree. With the addition of the `xsl:text` elements, the overall effect for the first note will be to output the text "`(Note 1).`".

There may be times when elements with the same name are nested within each other, as we would with `DIV` elements in HTML. In this case, XSL supplies an element `xsl:counters` that can be used to maintain multiple lists reflecting this nesting.

The other element in this group is `counter-reset`. This takes `name` and `value` attributes, so the counter can be set to any value. If no `value` attribute is included, it defaults to zero. The counter selected is the one with the correct name within the containing element in the result tree. If there is no containing element, the document root is used. If there is no matching counter, one is created, so this is a useful way of creating a new counter.

The `xsl:counter` and `xsl:counters` elements can use a `format` attribute to define their output style in the same way as `xsl:number`.

Numbering with IE5

IE5 supports numbering based on the order of elements in the source tree through a variety of elements. The main ones are covered here, although there are others for providing additional information and formatting.

- `xsl:absoluteChildNumber()` returns the number of the node relative to all siblings.
- `xsl:ancestorChildNumber()` returns the number of the nearest ancestor of a node with the requested node name.
- `xsl:childNumber()` returns the number of the node relative to siblings of the same node name.
- `xsl:depth()` returns the depth within the document tree at which the specified node appears.
- `formatNumber()` formats the supplied number using the specified format.

More information on XSL numbering in IE5 can be found on the Microsoft Web site at `http://www.microsoft.com/workshop/xml/xsl/reference/xslmethods.asp`.

Conditional Processing

XSL provides two means for conditional processing of the source tree:

- `xsl:if`
- `xsl:choose`

IE5 supports both. Let's look at what they do.

xsl:if

This element allows simple `if-then` processing within a template. Note that there is no support for `if-then-else` processing – this must be done using `xsl:choose`. `xsl:if` has a single parameter, `test`, that takes a select pattern as its value.

If we only wanted to see a list of resort facilities in our vacation example, we could place a comma after each element (except the last) using:

```
<xsl:template match="resort/facilities/facility">
  <xsl:apply-templates/>
  <xsl:if test=".[not(last-of-type())]">, </xsl:if>
</xsl:template>
```

xsl:choose

As we just saw, `xsl:if` is very limited through the absence of an `else` statement. `xsl:choose` and its related elements `xsl:when` and `xsl:otherwise` allow implementation of the familiar `switch`-type statement as an alternative. The working draft provides a self-explanatory example of using this construct to output items in an ordered list using arabic numerals, letters, or roman numerals depending on the depth to which the ordered lists are nested:

```
<xsl:template match="orderedlist/listitem">
  <fo:list-item indent-start='2pi'>
    <fo:list-item-label>
      <xsl:choose>
        <xsl:when test='ancestor(orderedlist/orderedlist)'>
```

```
          <xsl:number format="i"/>
        </xsl:when>
        <xsl:when test='ancestor(orderedlist)'>
          <xsl:number format="a"/>
        </xsl:when>
        <xsl:otherwise>
          <xsl:number format="1"/>
        </xsl:otherwise>
      </xsl:choose>
      <xsl:text>. </xsl:text>
    </fo:list-item-label>
    <fo:list-item-body>
      <xsl:apply-templates/>
    </fo:list-item-body>
  </fo:list-item>
</xsl:template>
```

There's yet another weapon in the XSL armory – **macros**.

Macros

XSL allows the developer to re-use parts of templates though the use of **macros**. There is currently discussion within the working group as the whether the name "macro" will be retained or changed. IE5 has no support for macros.

An example from the working draft is the production of a warning paragraph that can be used as part of several templates:

```
<xsl:macro name="warning-para">
  <fo:block-level-box>
    <fo:block>
      <xsl:text>Warning! </xsl:text>
      <xsl:contents/>
    </fo:block>
  </fo:block-level-box>
</xsl:macro>

<xsl:template match="warning">
  <xsl:invoke macro="warning-para">
    <xsl:apply-templates/>
  </xsl-invoke>
</xsl:template>
```

The macro is declared using an `xsl:macro` element with a `name` attribute. The macro itself just looks like any other template rule, other than the use of the `xsl:contents` element.

The macro is invoked using the `xsl:invoke` element. This element will first produce an output based on its contents (in this case, the result of the `xsl:apply-templates` element). It passes this to the macro, where it is inserted to replace the `xsl:contents` element. The results of processing this with the macro are then passed back to the calling template, where they form a fragment of the result tree.

In this case, if the content of the warning element were text, this text would be passed to the macro, which would add the text "Warning! " to the beginning, then format the result according to the `<fo:>` elements in the macro.

The result is the same as if the template had been:

```
<xsl:template match="warning">
  <fo:block-level-box>
    <fo:block>
      <xsl:text>Warning! </xsl:text>
      <xsl:apply-templates/>
    </fo:block>
  </fo:block-level-box>
</xsl:template>
```

xsl:text

We have already met `xsl:text` on several occasions in the examples we have used above. It simply places the text within the element into the result fragment. White space is preserved within the text, so the "Warning!" we produced with the macro is followed by a space, *before* the text that is added by the `xsl:apply-templates` element. The same function can be achieved in IE5 using `xsl:eval`, although (as mentioned earlier), if we are creating HTML – as we do when using XSL in Centaur – the text can be placed straight into the template.

Adding other Node Types

Other node types can be added to the result tree through the use of the `xsl:pi`, `xsl:comment`, `xsl:element` and `xsl:attribute`. These add processing instructions, comments, elements and attributes respectively. For example, consider this fragment of the vacation information we saw earlier:

```
<?xml version="1.0"?>
<tours>
  <tour>
    <vacation>
      <purposes>
        <purpose logourl="Logos/sumsun.gif">Summer Sun</purpose>
        <purpose logourl="Logos/winsun.gif">Winter Sun</purpose>
      </purposes>
    </vacation>
  </tour>
</tours>
```

Here, we would want to produce an HTML image element from the `logourl` attributes of the `purpose` elements. With HTML as our default output namespace, we can use the following:

```
<xsl:template match="purposes">
  <IMG>
    <xsl:attribute name="src">
      <xsl:value-of select="@logourl"/>
    </xsl:attribute>
  </IMG>
</xsl:template>
```

For the first of the `purpose` elements, this will create this HTML:

```
<IMG src=" Logos/sumsun.gif" />
```

In the working draft, but not in IE5, we can define multiple attributes using **attribute sets**. In this example, we could define all images to be of the same size using:

```
<xsl:attribute-set name="images">
  <xsl:attribute name="width">112</xsl:attribute>
  <xsl:attribute name="height">66</xsl:attribute>
</xsl:attribute-set>
```

The template would then change to be:

```
<xsl:template match="purposes">
  <IMG>
    <xsl:attribute name="src">
      <xsl:value-of select="@logourl"/>
    </xsl:attribute>
    <xsl:use attribute-set="images"/>
</IMG>
</xsl:template>
```

Note that attribute sets are very similar to macros (although multiple sets can be merged, which is not possible with macros). It is therefore possible that they will be removed from the final recommendation.

xsl:copy

Our final element type is `xsl:copy`, which merely copies its contents from the source tree to the result tree. This is extremely useful, for example, to copy well-formed XML to the output. We use this in Centaur to allow the tour operator to pre-format some information using a restricted set of HTML elements.

That concludes our look at the transformation elements. The differences between the working draft and the IE5 implementation are summarized briefly later in this chapter, and in more detail in Appendix F.

Next, we'll take a quick look at XSL's formatting principles.

Formatting Overview

In the examples above, we have used several of the formatting objects included in the XSL working draft. This part of the working draft is described as a "work in progress", and the current draft is clearly full of gaps. While it is *likely* that changes will be made to the transformation part of the specification, it is *certain* that changes will be made to the formatting part, both to fill the gaps and to align the terms further with CSS terminology. This will overcome many of the complaints that XSL is defining a new formatting vocabulary when we already have one in CSS. IE5 does not implement this part of the draft at all, so it is not used in Centaur. For this reason, I will just give you an overview here.

The formatting objects in XSL provide functionality very similar to that of CSS2. Currently, there are aspects, such as tables, where the coverage is less good than CSS, and others areas where it is better. To give an idea of the scale of the formatting draft, this section of the XSL draft occupies around two thirds of the specification, or over a hundred pages when I printed it out.

The XSL formatting model is defined in terms of **rectangular areas**, which reserve space in the formatted result and contain content, and **spaces**, which reserve space, but cannot hold content. It is possible that non-rectangular areas will be added to the model in the future. The variety of formatting objects and properties is very broad, allowing anything that might reasonably be required in a Web page, and most things that could be wanted in print.

For full details the formatting objects, look at the Formatting section in the working draft, at http://www.w3.org/TR/WD-xsl

XSL Support in IE5

IE5 and the XSL working draft have been developed in parallel. In IE5, Microsoft attempted to track the specification as it was developing from the draft issued on 18 August 1998 to that of 16 December 1998. Inevitably, they had to freeze the software at some point, and the result is that there are parts of the specification that were removed in the second version that are still implemented in IE5, and others that were added that are not included. However, Microsoft has committed to implement the final recommendation when it is issued.

Apart from the elements that are supported, IE5 beta 2 differs from the current XSL draft by not having built-in rules.

A summary of the elements and operators supported in IE5, along with some of the methods, is provided in Appendix F – *XSL Support in IE5*. The full documentation is available at `http://www.microsoft.com/workshop/xml/xsl/reference/start.asp`.

So far in this chapter, we have looked at the XSL working draft for stylesheets to use with XML. From now on, we will concentrate exclusively on IE5, working through two examples, one using a linear document (the Scottish play again), and the other a structured extract from a database (the description of a vacation).

Putting XSL to Work

From here on we'll look at how we can use XSL in practice in IE5. Firstly, we will render the extract from the Scottish play using XSL. This play is an example of a **linear** document, where the order of elements in the result tree matches that in the input tree. Next, we will render a complete vacation description from the case study. This is an example of a **non-linear** XML document. In this case, the XSL stylesheet defines the order of elements in the result tree, picking content from the source document as it requires it. Finally, we will see how we can process XSL on the server, allowing us to realize some of the advantages of the technology while maintaining compatibility with legacy browsers.

XSL and Linear Documents

Here is the complete stylesheet (`macbeth.xsl`) that will render the Scottish play we've seen in previous chapters – this rendering will present the play to us in a similar-looking form. (You may want to refresh your memory of the play's XML document structure by referring back to Chapter 4). We'll talk our way through the XSL stylesheet shortly, but for the moment here is the full listing so that you can familiarize yourself with its contours:

```
<?xml version="1.0"?>
<xsl:stylesheet
  xmlns:xsl="http://www.w3.org/TR/WD-xsl"
  xmlns="http://www.w3.org/TR/REC-html40"
  result-ns="">

<xsl:template match="text()">
     <xsl:value-of/>
</xsl:template>

<xsl:template match="/">
<HTML>
<BODY>
  <DIV>
    <xsl:apply-templates select="play" />
  </DIV>
</BODY>
</HTML>
</xsl:template>

<xsl:template match="*" priority="-1">
  <xsl:apply-templates />
</xsl:template>

<xsl:template match="emph">
  <SPAN Style=  "font-style: italic;
          color: green;">
    <xsl:apply-templates />
  </SPAN>
</xsl:template>

<xsl:template match="fm">
  <DIV Style="display:none">
    <xsl:apply-templates />
  </DIV>
</xsl:template>

<xsl:template match="play/title">
  <DIV Style=  "font-family: Arial, sans-serif;
        font-size: 20pt;
        font-weight: bold;
        color: red;
        text-align: center;
        margin-bottom: 10px">
    <xsl:value-of />
  </DIV>
</xsl:template>

<xsl:template match="scndescr">
  <DIV Style=  "font-family: Arial, sans-serif;
        font-size: 14pt;
        font-weight: bold;
        color: red;
        text-align: center;
        margin-bottom: 10px">
    <xsl:value-of />
  </DIV>
</xsl:template>
```

```
<xsl:template match="playsubt">
  <DIV Style="display:none">
    <xsl:apply-templates />
  </DIV>
</xsl:template>

<xsl:template match="act/title">
  <DIV Style=  "font-family: Arial, sans-serif;
         font-size: 14pt;
         font-weight: bold;
         color: red;
         text-align: center;
         margin-bottom: 10px">
    <xsl:value-of />
  </DIV>
</xsl:template>

<xsl:template match="scene/title">
  <DIV Style=  "font-family: Arial, sans-serif;
         font-size: 12pt;
         font-weight: bold;
         color: red;
         text-align: left;
         margin-bottom: 10px">
    <xsl:value-of />
  </DIV>
</xsl:template>

<xsl:template match="stagedir">
  <DIV Style=  "font-size: 12pt;
         font-weight: bold;
         font-style: italic">
    <xsl:value-of />
  </DIV>
</xsl:template>

<xsl:template match="speaker">
  <DIV Style=  "font-family: Arial,sans-serif;
         font-size: 10pt;
         font-style: italic;
         font-weight: bold;
         margin-top: 10px;
         color: blue">
    <xsl:value-of />
  </DIV>
</xsl:template>

<xsl:template match="line">
  <DIV Style=  "font-family: Times, serif;
         font-size: 10pt">
    <xsl:apply-templates />
  </DIV>
</xsl:template>

</xsl:stylesheet>
```

Before we start on the stylesheet, we also need to change one line in the XML file (`macbethxsl.xml`) to reference the XSL rather than the CSS stylesheet:

```
<?xml version="1.0"?>
<?xml-stylesheet type="text/xsl" href="macbeth.xsl"?>
<play>
```

As you can see, what we have done is embed the CSS stylesheet information in the XSL sheet. This may appear pointless – why not just use CSS? The simple answer is that we are introducing techniques that will be useful later to render non-linear XML in ways that are not possible with CSS alone.

The first line of the stylesheet uses an XML declaration to indicate that this is an XML document, which it is since XSL stylesheets use the XML syntax.

```
<?xml version="1.0"?>
```

This is followed by a root element that indicates: that this is an XSL stylesheet; that it creates an HTML output file; and that it uses the specified namespaces:

```
<xsl:stylesheet
  xmlns:xsl="http://www.w3.org/TR/WD-xsl"
  xmlns="http://www.w3.org/TR/REC-html40"
  result-ns="">
```

We then put in our standard line to make IE5 process the text nodes:

```
<xsl:template match="text()">
     <xsl:value-of/>
</xsl:template>
```

This is a different approach from the one we took earlier in the chapter in our stylesheet `first.xsl`. If you remember, in that case, we explicitly used `xsl:value-of` in the template for the `para` element so that the text from the element would be copied to the result tree and displayed. That works because the `para` element contains only text. In our version of the Scottish play, we have allowed the line elements to contain both text *and* further elements (the `emph` element in the last line). We therefore need to use `xsl:apply-templates` to cause this element to be processed. Since we cannot use `xsl:value-of` in the `line` element, we use a separate template to match all `Text` nodes and ensure they are displayed.

We then provide a template rule for the root node:

```
<xsl:template match="/">
<HTML>
<BODY>
  <DIV>
    <xsl:apply-templates select="play" />
  </DIV>
</BODY>
</HTML>
</xsl:template>
```

Remember that IE5 does not support built-in template rules. If it did, the rule above would take precedence over the default rule. Since the XSL processor will simply replace XSL elements with the result of processing the matched elements, the line:

```
    <xsl:apply-templates select="play" />
```

tells the processor to replace it with the results of processing the element `play`, styling these results with the templates that follow. The result is put inside the `DIV` element, which is inside the `BODY` of the HTML. Since `play` is the root element, the entire document will be processed.

The XSL processor will then search the templates for one that matches. We can see that the `play` does not have a template of its own – that is, there is no template starting `<xsl:template match="play">`. The XSL processor therefore defaults to using the template that is included for all those elements not *explicitly* matched:

```
<xsl:template match="*" priority="-1">
  <xsl:apply-templates />
</xsl:template>
```

In a browser that complied with the December XSL working draft, this would have a low importance as a built-in template. Since we are using IE5, which does not support the built-in templates, we ensure that other templates are checked for a match *before* invoking this default, by placing it *above* all the other templates. This is because IE5 checks templates from the bottom of the file upwards. According to the draft, doing this would cause an error, since this template will match all patterns that are also matched more explicitly. We have therefore given this template a low priority to avoid this situation.

The play `title` matches the rule:

```
<xsl:template match="play/title">
  <DIV Style=  "font-family: Arial, sans-serif;
      font-size: 20pt;
      font-weight: bold;
      color: red;
      text-align: center;
      margin-bottom: 10px">
    <xsl:value-of />
  </DIV>
</xsl:template>
```

and so is displayed in this style. The Act and Scene titles match their own rules and so gain their own styles. For the `scene`, this is:

```
<xsl:template match="scene/title">
  <DIV Style=  "font-family: Arial, sans-serif;
      font-size: 12pt;
      font-weight: bold;
      color: red;
      text-align: left;
      margin-bottom: 10px">
    <xsl:value-of />
  </DIV>
</xsl:template>
```

What if we had included a template with `match="title"`? If it had been placed below the more specific `title` templates, such as `scene/title`, it would have caused a match on all `title` elements. If we had put it above, all the `title` elements would already have been processed, so the new template would never have been invoked.

Inside the `DIV` element, we have used an `xsl:value-of` element. This will cause any text inside the element to be copied to the output tree, but no further processing of child elements will take place. Any further markup will be ignored, with just the enclosed text being processed. If we want further processing, we use `xsl:apply-templates`. This has been done with the `line` element to allow the `emph` elements to be processed.

What if, instead of defining a style for the `emph` elements, we just want some HTML markup (that does the same job) to be copied to the output tree? We can achieve this with `xsl:copy`.

The file `macbethxslbold.xml` replaces the last line element with:

```
        <line>There to meet with <B>Macbeth</B>.</line>
```

A new stylesheet, `macbethbold.xsl` replaces the template for `emph` with one for `B`:

```
<xsl:template match="B">
  <xsl:copy>
    <xsl:apply-templates />
  </xsl:copy>
</xsl:template>
```

That's all there is to it – the text will be copied to the output tree with its tags as we want, and processing will continue with any child elements.

XSL and Non-Linear Documents

Just now, we used templates to define rules for the XSL processor. The other way that XSL can be used is to access the individual elements of the document *directly*, rather than working through the elements in linear sequence. To do this, we need to know the structure of the document. Of course, the linear and non-linear techniques can be combined, and both can be combined with CSS and direct manipulation through the object model. We will use a description of a vacation to demonstrate all these techniques.

The Code to Display

This vacation description (tour.xml) is the most complex XML document we have seen so far, so is worth examining in detail. Here's the full listing that we'll be working with:

```
<?xml version="1.0"?>
<?xml-stylesheet type="text/xsl" href="tour.xsl"?>
<tours>
  <tour>
    <touroperator>
      <code>PNM</code>
      <name>Panorama</name>
```

```
    <logourl>Logos/panorama.gif</logourl>
    <email>vacation@boynings.co.uk</email>
  </touroperator>
  <resort>
    <worldarea>North Africa</worldarea>
    <area>Tunisia</area>
    <name>Hammamet</name>
    <summary>Guarded by its 15th century fortress, the town of Hammamet spreads
     out along the curve of the Cap Bon Bay with its miles of golden beaches.
    </summary>
    <description><P>Hammamet is one of the largest and most established of
     Tunisian resorts, and has been sympathetically developed over the years,
     resulting in a long line of widely spaced low level hotels stretching north
     and south from the centre of town. Many of our hotels are situated on the
     resort's wide sandy main beach and are set in acres of their own colourful
     gardens.</P><P>Hammamet has first class sport facilities including tennis.
     horse riding and watersports. There are two excellent golf courses The
     Yasmine — an 18 hole, 72 par course and the 45 hole Citrus.</P><P>In the
     old town...restaurants.</P><P>Evening entertainment.... enjoy their evening
     entertainment.</P><P>The more energetic can dance the night away at a
     number of nightclubs including the fantastic Manhattan, probably the equal
     of any big city discotheque.</P><P>It is easy to travel around Hammamet. A
     Noddy Train operates between most hotels and the town centre during the
     high season, or you can catch one of the many reasonably priced
     taxis.</P></description>
    <facilities>
      <facility>restaurants</facility>
      <facility>evening entertainment</facility>
      <facility>nightclubs</facility>
    </facilities>
    <photourl>Photos/ham.jpg</photourl>
  </resort>
  <vacation>
    <id>1</id>
    <ref>TUAA</ref>
    <purposes>
      <purpose logourl="Logos/sumsun.gif">Summer Sun</purpose>
      <purpose logourl="Logos/winsun.gif">Winter Sun</purpose>
    </purposes>
    <name>Hotel Aziza</name>
    <rating src="Logos/Q.gif">4</rating>
    <summary><P>Consistently voted one of our best four star hotels by our
     clients, the attractive <I>Hotel Aziza</I> offers comfortable
     accommodation, a good range of facilities and a relaxing atmosphere.
     Featured by Panorama for over 6 years.</P><P>Situated right on the beach,
     in a lovely setting, this hotel is built in a typical Moorish style. Across
     the road there is a small, commercial centre with some shops. Hammamet town
     centre is three kilometres away.</P></summary>
    <notes>Breakfast is buffet style. Lunch is waiter service and evening meal
    is a combination of buffet and waiter service.</notes>
    <facilities>
      <facility>Air conditioning</facility>
      <facility>Outdoor pool</facility>
      <facility>Indoor pool</facility>
      <facility>Lounge</facility>
```

```
      <facility>Bar</facility>
      <facility>Cafe</facility>
      <facility>Restaurant</facility>
      <facility>Shops</facility>
    </facilities>
    <photourl>Photos/aziza.jpg</photourl>
    <pricetable>
      <block>
        <accommodation>Bed and Breakfast</accommodation>
        <headings>
          <col>3/4</col>
          <col>7</col>
          <col>10/11</col>
          <col>14</col>
          <col>1st child</col>
        </headings>
        <row>
          <startdate>26 Mar</startdate>
          <enddate>4 Apr</enddate>
          <prices>
            <price>359</price>
            <price>405</price>
            <price>595</price>
            <price>639</price>
            <price>359</price>
          </prices>
        </row>
        <row>
          <startdate>5 Apr</startdate>
          <enddate>11 Apr</enddate>
          <prices>
            <price>305</price>
            <price>355</price>
            <price>439</price>
            <price>485</price>
            <price>299</price>
          </prices>
        </row>
        <row>
          <startdate>12 Apr</startdate>
          <enddate>30 Apr</enddate>
          <prices>
            <price>279</price>
            <price>329</price>
            <price>409</price>
            <price>459</price>
            <price>279</price>
          </prices>
        </row>
        <row>
          <startdate>1 May</startdate>
          <enddate>6 May</enddate>
          <prices>
            <price>299</price>
            <price>359</price>
            <price>439</price>
            <price>499</price>
            <price>299</price>
          </prices>
        </row>
```

```
            <row>
              <startdate>7 May</startdate>
              <enddate>20 May</enddate>
              <prices>
                <price>309</price>
                <price>369</price>
                <price>449</price>
                <price>509</price>
                <price>309</price>
              </prices>
            </row>
            <row>
              <startdate>21 May</startdate>
              <enddate>27 May</enddate>
              <prices>
                <price>329</price>
                <price>389</price>
                <price>459</price>
                <price>519</price>
                <price>329</price>
              </prices>
            </row>
          </block>
          <pricecomment>Prices are based on two persons sharing a twin bedded room
           with private bath/shower separate wc, TV, mini bar and balcony or
           terrace, on a bed and breakfast basis. Three bedded rooms available
          (third bed only suitable for a child under 12 years). </pricecomment>
        </pricetable>
      </vacation>
    </tour>
  </tours>
```

This document comprises a mixture of textual descriptions and a structured pricing table, which makes it very suitable for demonstrating the power and flexibility of XSL.

We have already met parts of this document; the following figure shows the tree structure of the complete document:

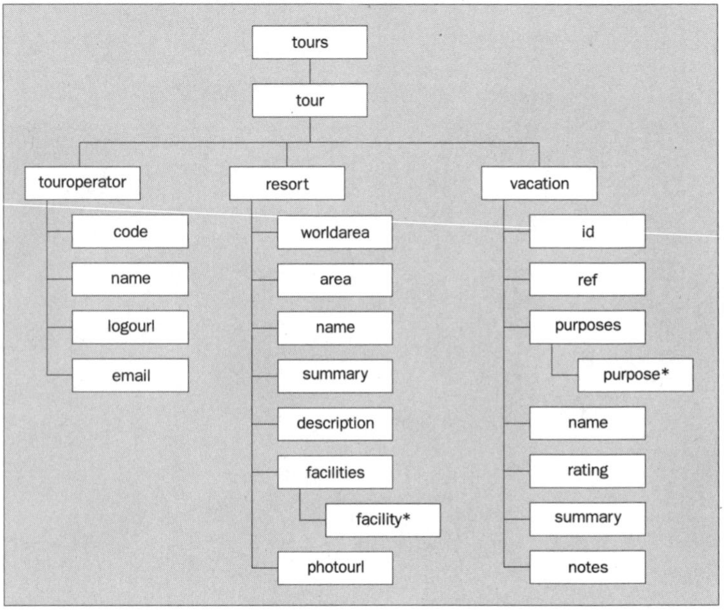

Note that the two elements marked with asterisks can occur more than once, and that some elements can contain a restricted range of HTML markup (to break up the text into paragraphs and include bold and italic text, for example).

The tree diagram shows how the document is split into three main sections, describing the tour operator, the resort and the specific vacation respectively. These sit within the element `tours/tour`. The root element `tours` could be seen as unnecessary, but I have retained it because it costs little and allows us, if required, to include multiple tours within the same XML document without changing the stylesheet.

The tour operator description:

```
<touroperator>
  <code>PNM</code>
  <name>Panorama</name>
  <logourl>Logos/panorama.gif</logourl>
  <email>vacation@boynings.co.uk</email>
</touroperator>
```

is simple, just comprising a code, the tour operator's name, a reference to its logo and an email address. (I have used a dummy email address on my own site so that I can keep my inbox clear). The resort description is similar in style (I have cut some of the text to make the structure clearer), but the description contains some HTML `P` elements and the `facility` can be repeated an arbitrary number of times:

```
<resort>
  <worldarea>North Africa</worldarea>
  <area>Tunisia</area>
  <name>Hammamet</name>
  <summary>Guarded by … golden beaches.</summary>
  <description><P>Hammamet is...priced taxis.</P></description>
  <facilities>
    <facility>restaurants</facility>
    <facility>evening entertainment</facility>
    <facility>nightclubs</facility>
  </facilities>
  <photourl>Photos/ham.jpg</photourl>
</resort>
```

The description of the hotel is more complex, and has a few areas that will be of interest when we render the file:

```
<vacation>
  <id>1</id>
  <ref>TUAA</ref>
  <purposes>
    <purpose logourl="Logos/sumsun.gif">Summer Sun</purpose>
    <purpose logourl="Logos/winsun.gif">Winter Sun</purpose>
  </purposes>
  <name>Hotel Aziza</name>
  <rating src="Logos/Q.gif">4</rating>
  <summary><P>Consistently...kilometres away.</P></summary>
  <notes>Breakfast...waiter service.</notes>
  <facilities>
```

```
        <facility>Air conditioning</facility>
        <facility>Outdoor pool</facility>
        <facility>Indoor pool</facility>
        <facility>Lounge</facility>
        <facility>Bar</facility>
        <facility>Cafe</facility>
        <facility>Restaurant</facility>
        <facility>Shops</facility>
      </facilities>
      <photourl>Photos/aziza.jpg</photourl>
      <pricetable>
        <block>
          <accommodation>Bed and Breakfast</accommodation>
          <headings>
            <col>3/4</col>
            <col>7</col>
            <col>10/11</col>
            <col>14</col>
            <col>1st child</col>
          </headings>
          <row>
            <startdate>26 Mar</startdate>
            <enddate>4 Apr</enddate>
            <prices>
              <price>359</price>
              <price>405</price>
              <price>595</price>
              <price>639</price>
              <price>359</price>
            </prices>
          </row>
             .
             .
             .
          <row>
            <startdate>21 May</startdate>
            <enddate>27 May</enddate>
            <prices>
              <price>329</price>
              <price>389</price>
              <price>459</price>
              <price>519</price>
              <price>329</price>
            </prices>
          </row>
        </block>
        <pricecomment>Prices are...12 years). </pricecomment>
      </pricetable>
    </vacation>
```

Firstly, the `purpose` elements in this file have attributes. These `logourl` attributes describe where to find a logo to display. The `rating` element is similar, although in this case, the rating itself will indicate how many times to display the rating logo (this gives us a guide to the quality of the hotel). In the tour operator's paper brochure, this is shown as:

The Qs indicate that this hotel has a rating of 4. Like the `resort` element, the `vacation` element has multiple facilities. The `vacation` element also has a highly structured extract from a price table. Since this is a demonstration system, I will admit to taking a short cut here. While the element names in other areas reflect the *nature* of the data, here they reflect the *layout.* This works in this application because we are only using the price table for display as a *guide* to prices. When a quotation is required, we access the tour operator system directly to ensure we get the latest prices. Had we wanted to obtain prices from the information in the XML file, we would have to structure it so that the prices are better described. For example, we could have done it like this:

```
<pricetable>
  <priceschedule>
    <accommodation>Bed and Breakfast</accommodation>
    <priceblock>
      <startdate>26 Mar</startdate>
      <enddate>4 Apr</enddate>
      <prices>
        <price nights="3/4">359</price>
        <price nights="7">405</price>
        <price nights="10/11">595</price>
        <price 639</price>
        <price 359</price>
      </prices>
    </priceblock>
      .
      .
      .
    <priceblock>
      <startdate>21 May</startdate>
      <enddate>27 May</enddate>
      <prices>
        <price nights="3/4">329</price>
        <price nights="7">389</price>
        <price nights="10/11">459</price>
        <price nights="14">519</price>
        <price nights="1st child">329</price>
      </prices>
    </priceblock>
  </priceschedule>
  <pricecomment>Prices are...12 years). </pricecomment>
</pricetable>
```

For display, we could take the column headings from the attributes in the `price` elements of the first `priceblock` element, knowing that we have a regular structure.

OK, let's get back to our working example. Eventually, we would like this XML document to be displayed like this:

Let's examine how we get from the document structure to the rendered page. My first step is to create a rough cut that lets me see how the page will look.

A Page Mock-up

For structured documents like this vacation information, I find that the easiest way to develop the stylesheet is to mock up the page using something like FrontPage 98, then modify the code produced and make any other changes. Here is the HTML that FrontPage created to generate my mock-up screen (`tour.htm`):

```
<html>

<head>
<title>Hotel Aziza</title>
</head>

<body>

<p align="center"><img src="Logos/panorama.gif" width="430" height="91"
alt="panorama.gif (2539 bytes)"></p>

<table border="0" width="100%">
  <tr>
    <td width="50%" valign="top">put images for vacation purposes here<p>Vacation
    destination: Hammamet, North Africa</p>
    <p>Description here (1st para is emphasised)</td>
```

```
    <td width="50%"><img src="Photos/ham.jpg" width="300" height="208"
    alt="ham.jpg (8995 bytes)"></td>
  </tr>
</table>

<p align="left">The following facilities are available in Hammamet:</p>

<ul>
  <li><p align="left">facility</p>
  </li>
  <li><p align="left">and another</p>
  </li>
</ul>

<table border="0" width="100%">
  <tr>
    <td width="50%"><img src="Photos/aziza.jpg" width="300" height="221"
    alt="aziza.jpg (11489 bytes)"></td>
    <td width="50%" valign="top" rowspan="2">Tour Name<p>Summary (1st para is
    emphasised)</p>
    <p>Facilities</p>
    <p>Notes</td>
  </tr>
  <tr>
    <td width="50%"><table class="priceTable" border="1" width="100%"
    bgcolor="yellow">
      <tr>
        <td width="25%">Vacation</td>
        <td width="75%" colspan="3"> </td>
      </tr>
      <tr>
        <td width="25%">Vacation Reference</td>
        <td width="75%" colspan="3"> </td>
      </tr>
      <tr>
        <td width="25%">Accommodation</td>
        <td width="75%" colspan="3"> </td>
      </tr>
      <tr>
        <td width="25%">Nights</td>
        <td width="25%" align="middle">7</td>
        <td width="25%" align="middle">14</td>
        <td width="25%" align="middle">Ex Week</td>
      </tr>
      <tr>
        <td width="25%">1 May - 12 May</td>
        <td width="25%" align="middle">515</td>
        <td width="25%" align="middle">595</td>
        <td width="25%" align="middle">91</td>
      </tr>
    </table>
    </td>
  </tr>
</table>

<table border="0" width="100%">
  <tr>
    <td width="50%" align="middle"><p align="center">Add to brochure</td>
    <td width="50%" align="middle">Quote me!</td>
```

```
  </tr>
</table>

<p align="left">Send an <a href="mailto:vacations@boynings.demon.co.uk">E-mail</a>
to the tour operator</p>
</body>
</html>
```

And here's the mock-up screen that this HTML produces:

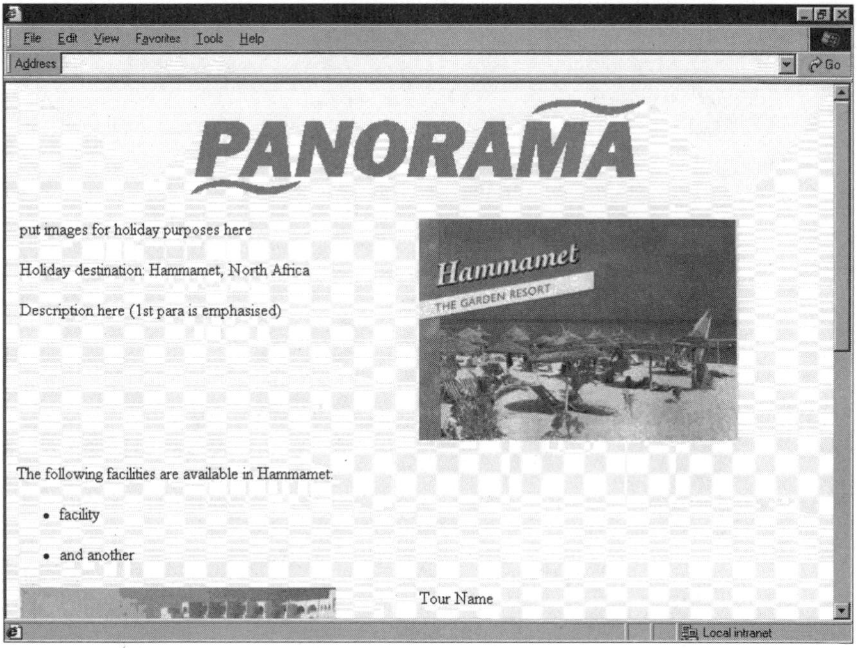

This prototyping exercise leads us to ask a few questions before we go any further:

Q. Do we want image sizes in the XML document?
A. Putting in the image sizes improves the appearance while the images are downloading, but at the expense of forcing the tour operators to provide the information. Better to leave them out, other than for images where we know the sizes (such as the "vacation purposes" logos).

Q. Should the images have `alt` attributes to display if the user has images turned off?
A. We expect people looking for vacations to want to see the images, so there is no need for `alt` attributes, which would again force the tour operators to add information.

Q. Is it right to enforce table widths?
A. There are several formatting questions – like this one – that are best answered once several real pages have been rendered. In this case, I decided not to put in fixed widths, but let the photos take what they needed, and use the remainder of the screen width for the text.

Q. Is it best to emphasize the first paragraph of text information?
A. I decided to leave this to the tour operator by allowing a limited degree of HTML markup within these descriptions.

Q. Why is the vacation rating not shown?
A. Simple! I didn't think of it at the time. Which begs the real question...

Q. How do we show the vacation rating?
A. Ideally, we would repeat an image as we saw with the "Q" logos earlier (we'll cover this in detail shortly).

Let's take this process on a stage.

The tour.xsl Stylesheet

With this rough idea of how the screen should look, we can then generate a first pass of the stylesheet (`tour.xsl`). The complete listing follows below: there's lots of it, but we step through the important bits shortly. For the moment, we will display the vacation rating as a number of asterisks that matches the rating value. Later, we will see how to change this into the Q logo image we want.

```
<?xml version="1.0"?>
<xsl:stylesheet
  xmlns:xsl="http://www.w3.org/TR/WD-xsl"
  xmlns="http://www.w3.org/TR/REC-html40"
  result-ns="">

<xsl:template match="text()">
  <xsl:value-of/>
</xsl:template>

<xsl:template match="/">
<HTML>
<BODY>

<xsl:for-each select="tours/tour">

  <!-- ================================== -->
  <!-- start with the tour operator logo -->
  <!-- ================================== -->

 <DIV align="center">
    <IMG>
      <xsl:attribute name="src">
        <xsl:value-of select="touroperator/logourl"/>
      </xsl:attribute>
    </IMG>
  </DIV>

  <!-- ================================================================ -->
  <!-- this  displays the "purposes" logos and the purposes themselves. -->
  <!-- ================================================================ -->

 <DIV align="center">
    <TABLE border="0">
      <TR>
```

```
        <xsl:for-each select="vacation/purposes/purpose">
          <TD>
            <IMG width="112" height="66">
              <xsl:attribute name="src">
                <xsl:value-of select ="@logourl"/>
              </xsl:attribute>
            </IMG>
          </TD>
        </xsl:for-each>
      </TR>
      <TR align="center">
        <xsl:for-each select="vacation/purposes/purpose">
          <TD><xsl:value-of/></TD>
        </xsl:for-each>
      </TR>
    </TABLE>
  </DIV>

  <!-- ============================== -->
  <!-- This is the resort information -->
  <!-- ============================== -->

<DIV align="center">Vacation destination: <xsl:value-of select="resort/name"/>,
<xsl:value-of select="resort/area"/>, <xsl:value-of
select="resort/worldarea"/></DIV>
  <BR />
  <DIV Style="text-align:center; font-weight:bold; font-style:italic">
  <xsl:value-of select="resort/summary" /></DIV>
  <BR />

  <IMG align="right">
    <xsl:attribute name="src">
      <xsl:value-of select="resort/photourl"/>
    </xsl:attribute>
  </IMG>

  <xsl:apply-templates select="resort/description" />

  <BR/>
  <TABLE align="center"><TR>
    <TD valign="top">Available in <xsl:value-of select="resort/name"/>:</TD>
    <TD valign="top">
      <UL>
        <xsl:for-each select="resort/facilities/facility">
          <LI><xsl:value-of/></LI>
        </xsl:for-each>
      </UL>
    </TD>
  </TR></TABLE>

  <!-- =============================== -->
  <!-- This is the vacation information -->
  <!-- =============================== -->

  <TABLE border="0">
    <TR>
      <TD>
        <IMG>
          <xsl:attribute name="src">
            <xsl:value-of select="vacation/photourl"/>
```

```
      </xsl:attribute>
    </IMG>
  </TD>

  <TD width="50%" valign="top" rowspan="2">
    <DIV style="font-weight:bold"><xsl:value-of select="vacation/name"/></DIV>

    <!-- The vacation rating goes in here -->
    <xsl:apply-templates select="vacation/rating" />
    <!-- end of vacation rating -->

    <DIV><xsl:apply-templates select="vacation/summary"/></DIV>
    <UL>
      <xsl:for-each select="vacation/facilities/facility">
        <LI><xsl:value-of/></LI>
      </xsl:for-each>
    </UL>
    <DIV><xsl:apply-templates select="vacation/notes"/></DIV>
  </TD>
</TR>

<!-- =============== -->
<!-- the price table -->
<!-- =============== -->

<TR>
  <TD>
    <TABLE border="1" Style="font-size:9pt; background:yellow;">
    <!-- to use the full table width, some headings use colspan="10".
         The alternative is to calculate the number of pricing columns -->
      <TR>
        <TD>Vacation</TD>
        <TD colspan="10"><xsl:value-of select="vacation/name"/></TD>
      </TR>
      <TR>
        <TD>Vacation Ref.</TD>
        <TD colspan="10"><xsl:value-of select="vacation/ref"/></TD>
      </TR>
      <TR>
        <TD>Accommodation</TD>
        <TD colspan="10">
        <xsl:value-of select="vacation/pricetable/block/accommodation"/></TD>
      </TR>
      <TR>
        <TD>Nights</TD>
        <xsl:for-each select="vacation/pricetable/block/headings/col">
          <TD align="middle">
          <xsl:value-of/>
          </TD>
        </xsl:for-each>
      </TR>
      <xsl:for-each select="vacation/pricetable/block/row">
        <TR>
          <TD>
            <xsl:value-of select="startdate"/> - <xsl:value-of
            select="enddate"/>
          </TD>
          <xsl:for-each select="prices/price">
            <TD align="middle">
              <xsl:value-of/>
```

```
                </TD>
              </xsl:for-each>
            </TR>
          </xsl:for-each>
          <TR><TD colspan="10">
            <DIV><xsl:apply-templates
            select="vacation/pricetable/pricecomment"/></DIV>
          </TD></TR>

        </TABLE>
      </TD>
    </TR>
  </TABLE>
  <BR/>

  <!-- ================= -->
  <!-- the E-mail option -->
  <!-- ================= -->

 <DIV>Send an
    <A>
      <xsl:attribute name="href">
        <xsl:eval>"mailto:"</xsl:eval><xsl:value-of select="touroperator/email"/>
      </xsl:attribute>
    E-Mail</A>
  to the tour operator</DIV>

</xsl:for-each>
</BODY>
</HTML>
</xsl:template>

<xsl:template match = "*">
  <xsl:apply-templates />
</xsl:template>

<xsl:template match="B|b|I|i|STRONG|strong|Strong|EM|em|Em|P|p|DIV|div|Div">
  <xsl:copy>
    <xsl:apply-templates />
  </xsl:copy>
</xsl:template>


<xsl:template match="vacation/rating">
  <xsl:script><![CDATA[
    function massageRating(n)
    {
      var string = "";

      for(var i = 0 ; i < n ; i++)
        string += "*";
      return(string);
    }
  ]]></xsl:script>
  <DIV>
    <xsl:eval>massageRating(this.text)</xsl:eval>
  </DIV>
</xsl:template>


</xsl:stylesheet>
```

This stylesheet uses a mixture of the techniques we have already discussed, but in a context where many of the XML elements are accessed *directly* from the stylesheet. This is done by replacing `xsl:apply-templates` with `xsl:value-of` elements. The difference is that the former processes all child nodes, including both `Text` nodes and `Element` nodes, while the latter just fetches the value (that is, the *text*) to be extracted. For those elements where we are allowing the tour operator to include some HTML markup, we therefore stick with `xsl:apply-templates`.

The tour operator is limited to just a few HTML elements, which will allow them to specify paragraph breaks and to apply bold and italic styles to the text. Since each of these has alternatives in HTML, several variations on these HTML elements are allowed:

```
<xsl:template match="B | b | STRONG | Strong | strong | I | i | EM | Em | em | P |
p| DIV | Div | div">
  <xsl:copy>
    <xsl:apply-templates />
  </xsl:copy>
</xsl:template>
```

XSL allows one looping element: `xsl:for-each`. We have used this to iterate through multiple elements such as the price table and the facilities:

```
        <xsl:for-each select="resort/facilities/facility">
          <LI><xsl:value-of/></LI>
        </xsl:for-each>
```

The HTML anchor tag `IMG` requires an attribute, which is added using the `xsl:attribute` element as we saw earlier in the chapter.

```
            <IMG width="112" height="66">
              <xsl:attribute name="src">
                <xsl:value-of select ="@logourl" />
              </xsl:attribute>
            </IMG>
```

The treatment of the e-mail address is similar:

```
<A>
  <xsl:attribute name="href">
    <xsl:eval>"mailto:"</xsl:eval><xsl:value-of select="touroperator/email" />
  </xsl:attribute>
E-Mail</A>
to the tour operator</DIV>
```

Again we use the `xsl:attribute` element. The `xsl:eval` element is used to compute text, here adding the text "`mailto:`" to the front of the e-mail address taken from the XML document. An implementation compliant with the W3C draft would use `xsl:text` rather than `xsl:eval`, since that is the syntax in the draft.

Note that there is no white space (a space character or new line) between the text "`E-Mail`" and the following tag. Any white space would be compressed to a single space, which would appear underlined as part of the link. Instead, we have a new line after, which serves our purpose of adding a single space between "`E-Mail`" and the following word.

The XSL processor in IE5 allows script to be embedded in the stylesheet, and we have used this to display a number of asterisks dependent on the value in the `rating` element. As mentioned earlier in the chapter, this use of script was included in an earlier draft of XSL, but was removed from the December 1998 draft. It is likely to be restored at some stage. I have included this example here, although I would not recommend using this technique unless and until it is put back into the recommendation. If you have a requirement that cannot be met by XSL without scripting, there are other ways around the problem as we shall see in a moment.

The script is declared in the template rule:

```
<xsl:template match="vacation/rating">
  <xsl:script><![CDATA[
    function massageRating(n)
    {
      var string = "";

      for(var i = 0 ; i < n ; i++)
        string += "*";
      return(string);
    }
  ]]></xsl:script>
  <DIV>
    <xsl:eval>massageRating(this.text)</xsl:eval>
  </DIV>
</xsl:template>
```

We have declared the script inside a CDATA element. This is not always necessary, but it ensures that the processor will not trip up on XML reserved characters.

The script is called from the line:

```
<xsl:eval>massageRating(this.text)</xsl:eval>
```

This is called when the processor finds a match for `vacation/rating`, and so applies this template. The function takes as its parameter the text of the current element. The `this` keyword is used as an identifier for this element. In this case, the parameter will be the digit "4". This is used in the loop to cause a string of four asterisks to be built and returned. I included this as an example of script being used within a stylesheet, but it is not *quite* achieving the objective we want, since it is causing asterisks rather than the "Q" image to be displayed. Let's correct this as a demonstration of another way of using XSL with XML.

Using XSL From Within HTML

We have just used the XSL processor in IE5 by sending the browser an XML page with a reference to the stylesheet. An alternative is to call the processor using the `transformNode()` method of the DOM from within an HTML page.

Why would we want to do this, when it means more work and more documents (since we now have to create both our XML document and our stylesheet, *and* an HTML page to combine them)? There are several reasons. If we want to run client-side code, we need to use an HTML page – unless we embed the code in a stylesheet. We will meet this circumstance within Centaur. A more important reason, perhaps, is that one of the main uses of XML is to separate content from style. We might want to use the same information to produce different types of output: a vacation itinerary with one stylesheet, and an invoice with another. In that case, we can use HTML to allow the choice to be made, using client-side code. Apart from reducing the load on the server, this means that more complex applications can be run by small companies whose Web sites are hosted by Internet Service Providers (ISPs) that do not allow server-side code to be used. In a moment, we will use the technique on an example from Centaur where we want to do a little manipulation on the XML before we render it.

To achieve what we had just now when we sent the `tour.xml` page directly to the browser, we can create an HTML page (`renderTour.htm`) with an `onLoad()` event handler:

```
<HTML>
<BODY onLoad="onLoad()">

<SPAN Id="tourTarget"></SPAN>

<SCRIPT>
function onLoad()
{
  var tour = new ActiveXObject("Microsoft.XMLDOM");
  tour.async = false;
  tour.load("tour.xml");
  if (tour.parseError != 0)
    alert(tour.parseError.reason);

  var style = new ActiveXObject("Microsoft.XMLDOM");
  style.async = false;
  style.load("tour.xsl");
  if (style.parseError != 0)
    alert(style.parseError.reason);

  document.all.item("tourTarget").innerHTML = tour.transformNode(style);
}
</SCRIPT>
</BODY>
</HTML>
```

The first block of `onLoad()` code loads the XML page in the same way that we have seen before, checking for parser errors after loading. The next block is similar, loading the stylesheet, which is, after all, just another XML document. The final line is the one that does the transformation:

```
  document.all.item("tourTarget").innerHTML = tour.transformNode(style);
```

This takes the document object (`tour`), and transforms it using the stylesheet `style`. We then use dynamic HTML to write the result tree (which will be an HTML document fragment) to the location `tourTarget`, which is the `id` of a `SPAN` element in the HTML document:

```
<SPAN Id="tourTarget"></SPAN>
```

elsewhere in the document. Strictly, we should delete the `xml-stylesheet` processing instruction from the XML document, but in practice this is not necessary, so we can use the same file as before.

However, rather than just display the document as before, we want to make it display the image defined in the `src` attribute of the `rating` element a number of times depending on the value of the `rating` element. We can do this by altering the XML before it is sent to the XSL processor. Effectively, we want to duplicate our element:

```
<rating src="Logos/Q.gif">4</rating>
```

a number of times according to the value. Then, in the stylesheet, we can ignore the value and just put in the image each time we meet this element.

Here is the complete HTML source to do this and display the result:

```
<HTML>
<BODY onLoad="onLoad()">

<SPAN Id="tourTarget"></SPAN>

<SCRIPT>
function onLoad()
{
  var tour,style,root,vacation;

  tour = new ActiveXObject("Microsoft.XMLDOM");
  tour.async = false;
  tour.load("tour.xml");
  if (tour.parseError != 0)
    alert(tour.parseError.reason);

  style = new ActiveXObject("Microsoft.XMLDOM");
  style.async = false;
  style.load("renderTour.xsl");
  if (style.parseError != 0)
    alert(style.parseError.reason);

  root = tour.documentElement;
  vacation = root.childNodes.item(0).getElementsByTagName("vacation").item(0);

  massageRating(vacation);

  document.all.item("tourTarget").innerHTML = tour.transformNode(style);
}

function massageRating(vacation)
{
  var i,rating,source;

  rating = vacation.getElementsByTagName("rating").item(0);

  for(var i = 1 ; i < rating.text ; i++)
  {
    source = rating.cloneNode(true);
    vacation.appendChild(source);
  }
}
</SCRIPT>
</BODY>
</HTML>
```

We have now used the DOM to find the `vacation` element in the `onLoad()` function. This is passed to the function `massageRating()`, which uses a loop to create copies of the `rating` node and add them to the `vacation` node.

To render this, we delete the old template for `vacation/rating` and replace the call to that with:

```
<!-- The vacation rating goes in here -->
<xsl:for-each select="vacation/rating">
  <IMG>
    <xsl:attribute name="src">
      <xsl:value-of select="@src" />
    </xsl:attribute>
  </IMG>
</xsl:for-each>
<!-- end of vacation rating -->
```

This iterates through the `rating` elements, ignoring the value in the `Text` element, which we have already used to create the duplicates, and displaying an image just as we have before.

Having spent some time looking chiefly at the client-side, let's now turn to the server-side.

XSL (Server-side)

We have rendered our XML with several techniques so far. These have involved different numbers of visits to the server to get information. One fact not always appreciated is that server load is affected far more by the number of page requests than by the size of each page. Of course, the network is affected by both, so there is a balance to strike: between sending redundant information in case it is needed later, and sending the minimum possible to keep the network traffic down – which risks having to return to get more later.

In the early days of HTML, there was no choice – if you sent something to the browser, it got displayed. Dynamic HTML and then HTML 4 improved the position by allowing information to be sent, but not *displayed* until the user took some action on the browser. The display could then be activated by script from within the page. This is often used on Web sites to expand tables of contents.

XML goes a stage further in giving the Web site designer complete control over what is sent to the client. We exploit this feature to a great extent in the case study.

Processing Models for Client-Server Interaction

Let's look at the models we have had so far.

The first was an HTML page with CSS styles as inline styles, and inside a `STYLE` element. Just one visit to the server and we had the page. The disadvantage was that the styles were mixed with the content.

Instead, we could use a separate stylesheet, as we did with XML and CSS. The following graphic summarizes this model:

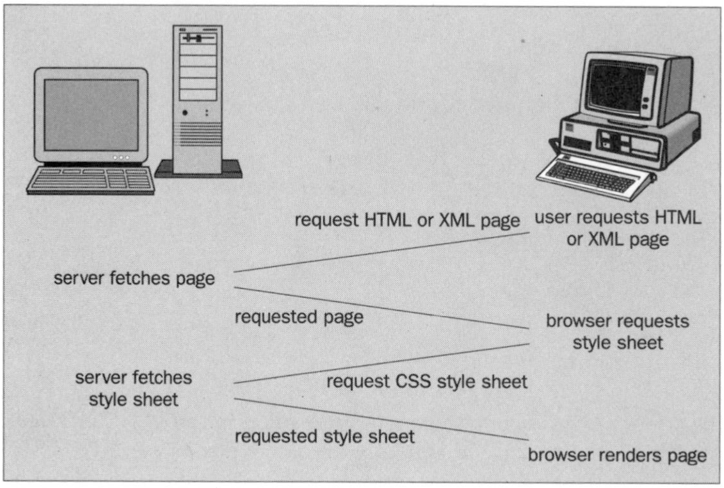

This represents *two* round trips to the server.

This model was also the one we used to get an XSL stylesheet from an XML page. Once we moved to a model that meant getting both the XML and XSL from a single page, three visits to the server were required, as shown below:

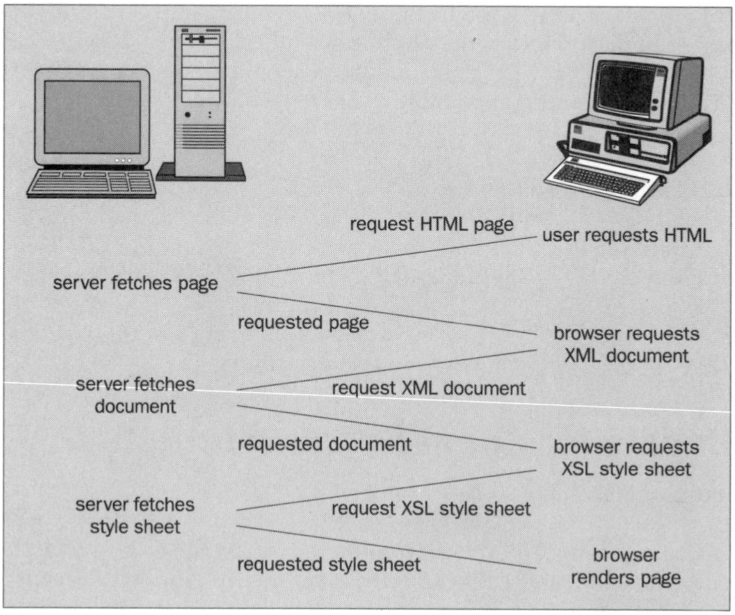

Although two or three round trips may be required, the client now has the document in its memory and can process it without further visits to the server. So, for example, a form can be built with drop-down lists that change according to the entries in other form elements without further visits to the server.

Although not used in the Centaur case study here, I found this useful when I was developing a quotation system used by a sales representative on a notebook PC. Once they have used the system once, all the information needed to change the form according to context is held in the XML document in the browser cache.

All the processing up to this point has been on the client – all the server has done is deliver the pages. However, there are two good reasons for processing on the server, which we will look at now. The examples here use Microsoft's Active Server Page (ASP) technology and so require an ASP-capable server, such as Microsoft's Internet Information Server (IIS) 4 or Personal Web Server (PWS) 4.

Why Process on the Server?

The first reason to process on the server is to run code that *must* be server-based. A prime example of that is database extraction code. Although Centaur uses database code extensively, we will demonstrate the technique for delivering the XML and stylesheet using fixed text. We will create an XML document in an ASP page and deliver this page to the client, which will then pick up the stylesheet reference from the page, fetch the stylesheet and render the page. The stylesheet will be the same as we used earlier in the chapter to display documents with a `doc` element containing `para` elements.

Here is the ASP code (`first.asp`), written in VBScript:

```
<%
      CRLF = Chr(13) & Chr(10): TAB = Chr(9)

      strXML = "<?xml version=""1.0""?>" & CRLF
      strXML = strXML & "<?xml-stylesheet type=""text/xsl"" href=""first.xsl""?>"
               & CRLF
      strXML = strXML & "<doc>" & CRLF
      strXML = strXML &  "<para>This is the first para</para>" & CRLF
      strXML = strXML &  "<para>And this is the second</para>" & CRLF
      strXML = strXML & "</doc>"

      Response.ContentType = "text/xml"
      Response.Write strXML
%>
```

The `<%` and `%>` delimiters are the means of telling the server that the code is to run there, rather than on the client. As you can see, we are building up a string of XML code, then sending it to the client using the ASP `Response.Write` method, which sends the results of our script back to the client. The line:

```
      Response.ContentType = "text/xml"
```

sets HTTP header information to inform the client that the content it is getting is in XML format.

Clearly, we can't cover ASP in detail here. However, if you want to learn more, I learnt about ASP from these Wrox books: *Beginning ASP 2.0 (ISBN 1-86100-1347)* and *Professional ASP 2.0 (ISBN 1-86100-1266).*

If we access this page from the client, and then right click with the mouse on the page and View Source, we will see that the content of the page is now XML:

```
<?xml version="1.0"?>
<?xml-stylesheet type="text/xsl" href="first.xsl"?>
<doc>
<para>This is the first paragraph</para>
<para>And this is the second</para>
</doc>
```

The display in the browser will be the same as when we viewed it earlier.

The second important reason to process on the server is that we have assumed so far – in fact insisted – that the user has a copy of IE5. This may be acceptable in an Intranet environment, but it will be some time before the majority of browsers on the wider Internet support XML. The time you decide to wait before using pages that require an XML browser depends on how important the use of XML is compared to the number of users who will not be able to use your site.

Requesting either `tour.xml` or `renderTour.htm` from an earlier version of Internet Explorer, or from any version of Netscape, will result in an error. This means that there is an immediate benefit from processing the XML on the server. You could ask, "Why not do the whole thing in HTML in the first place?" – and that's a perfectly valid question. My response would be that XML provides a good intermediate data format. This allows you to write your relatively complex database access code – once – to extract the XML, and then play around with a simpler stylesheet until you have the display result you want. This also allows two or more people to work independently on the development. In the case of Centaur, I defined the XML format I wanted and developed the stylesheet using the file above, while someone else was writing the Active Server Page code to produce this format from a database.

With a more text-based document such as an instruction manual, it can still be worth writing the document as XML and processing using stylesheets, as you can then develop different stylesheets for different audiences. In this case, we could use the facilities provided by ASP to detect the browser type. If it is IE5, we could send the XML and XSL directly to the client, otherwise we could process on the server to generate HTML.

Of course, there are disadvantages to processing on the server, and I see it as mainly an interim measure until there is better browser support for XML. Apart from the additional processing caused by having to do the rendering on the server, there is no client-based processing of the data, so we are back to the server for every little display change. Processing on the client allows changes to be made using script and dynamic HTML without requiring further server access.

We have been discussing processing the XML with a stylesheet on the server to give us browser independence. Of course, any database access will require *some* server-side processing, so we can think of two levels of processing – extracting information from the database on the server, and presenting the resulting XML with an XSL stylesheet, to the client. This requires an XSL-aware client (in our case IE5), but the technique is important, so we will cover it.

Let's Try It

Let's put some of these ideas about processing on the server into practice. First, we need to make some changes to our file `renderTour.htm` to create `renderTour.asp`:

```
<%@ LANGUAGE = JScript %>
<%

  var tour,style,root,vacation,result;

  tour = Server.CreateObject("Microsoft.XMLDOM");
  tour.async = false;
  tour.load(Server.MapPath("tour.xml"));
    if (tour.parseError != 0)
    Response.Write(tour.parseError.reason);

  style = Server.CreateObject("Microsoft.XMLDOM");
  style.async = false;
  style.load(Server.MapPath("renderTour.xsl"));
  if (style.parseError != 0)
    Response.Write(style.parseError.reason);

  root = tour.documentElement;
  vacation = root.childNodes.item(0).getElementsByTagName("vacation").item(0);

  massageRating(vacation);

  result = tour.transformNode(style);
  Response.Write(result);


function massageRating(vacation)
{
  var i,rating,source;

  rating = vacation.getElementsByTagName("rating").item(0);

  for(var i = 1 ; i < rating.text ; i++)
  {
    source = rating.cloneNode(true);
    vacation.appendChild(source);
  }
}
%>
```

The file now has a `.asp` extension to indicate to the Web server that it has to process it before sending it to the client. Even if you are not familiar with Active Server Pages, the code here is easy to follow with a minimum of explanation.

As we saw a moment ago, the `<% %>` tags indicate to the server those bits of the code that it needs to process. In this case, this means *everything*, and the result will be the HTML page sent to the browser (try View Source in your browser if you want to see this). It is important to remember when writing code to process on the server that the result is the HTML page, so client-side constructs such as `alert()` and `writeln()` will not work. Instead, we use `Response.Write()` to write text to the output HTML. We use this both for the error messages, and for the resulting HTML:

```
Response.Write(result);
```

Similarly, the construction:

```
tour = new ActiveXObject("Microsoft.XMLDOM");
tour.async = false;
tour.load("tour.xml");
```

results in two client-side operations , which need to be replaced with the server-side equivalents:

```
tour = Server.CreateObject("Microsoft.XMLDOM");
tour.async = false;
tour.load(Server.MapPath("tour.xml"));
```

The remaining code, including the function to put in the asterisks, runs unchanged.

The result of this is a page we can view on Netscape (I am using version 4) as well as Internet Explorer:

XSL, the DOM and Pattern Matching

We have seen that the DOM can be used to retrieve nodes for processing. For example, we retrieved the vacation rating by navigating the tree within the `onLoad()` then the `massageRating()` functions:

```
root = tour.documentElement;
vacation = root.childNodes.item(0).getElementsByTagName("vacation").item(0);
rating = vacation.getElementsByTagName("rating").item(0);
```

We have also seen that XSL has a pattern-matching mechanism that lets us find the same information using a familiar hierarchical notation. Working from the root node, we would find the rating value:

```
<xsl:value-of select="/tours/tour/vacation/rating" />
```

The latter is obviously a much simpler syntax and, as we saw earlier in the chapter, Microsoft supports this type of pattern-matching when working with the DOM. We could therefore change the three lines of JScript code above to read:

```
  rating =
tour.documentElement.selectNodes("/.//tours/tour/vacation/rating").item(0).text;
```

or, if we are certain that this is the only `rating` element in the document:

```
  rating = tour.documentElement.selectSingleNode("/.//rating").text;
```

Clearly, we couldn't replace the three lines above while they are in separate functions. We could instead combine the functions. The following version of the `onLoad()` function shows both the lines above, with the second commented out. Commenting out the first instead gives the same result.

```
function onLoad()
{
  var tour,style,root,vacation,rating,i,source;

  tour = new ActiveXObject("Microsoft.XMLDOM");
  tour.async = false;
  tour.load("tour.xml");
  if (tour.parseError != 0)
    alert(tour.parseError.reason);

  style = new ActiveXObject("Microsoft.XMLDOM");
  style.async = false;
  style.load("renderTour.xsl");
  if (style.parseError != 0)
    alert(style.parseError.reason);

  rating =
tour.documentElement.selectNodes("/.//tours/tour/vacation/rating").item(0).text;
//  rating = tour.documentElement.selectSingleNode("/.//rating").text;

  for(var i = 1 ; i < rating.text ; i++)
  {
    source = rating.cloneNode(true);
    vacation.appendChild(source);
  }

  document.all.item("tgtTour").innerHTML = tour.transformNode(style);
}
```

Again, it is up to you whether you use these extensions. If you do, you will be writing code that is specific to Microsoft implementations. On the other hand, there are times when it becomes much simpler to use these constructs. I was recently writing a page to produce a table of contents from an XML file. Only the top-level headings were to be included, with a plus sign (+) placed before those that had lower level entries. Clicking on the plus sign expanded the sub-tree. Applying the principle to this chapter would give an XML source:

```
<chapter>
  <heading>
    XSL in Theory and Practice
    <heading>What is XSL?</heading>
     <heading>An Introduction to the working draft</heading>
     <heading>An Introduction to XSL Transformation</heading>
     <heading>A Simple Stylesheet</heading>
     <heading>The XSL Stylesheet In IE5</heading>
.
.
.
    <heading>XSL and Non-Linear Documents
      <heading>The Code to Display</heading>
      <heading>A Page Mock-up</heading>
      <heading>The tour.xsl Stylesheet</heading>
      <heading>Using XSL From Within HTML</heading>
    </heading>
    <heading>
      XSL (server-side)
      <heading>Processing Models for Client-Server Interaction</heading>
      <heading>Why Process on the Server?</heading>
      <heading>Let's Try It</heading></heading>
    </heading>
    <heading>XSL, the DOM and Pattern Matching</heading>
    <heading>Summary</heading>
  </heading>
</chapter>
```

Using Microsoft's extensions, I can get all the second level headings using the line:

```
headings1 = root.selectNodes("/.//heading/heading");
```

Try the same using the W3C DOM. You might be surprised how much more difficult it is.

Summary

In this chapter, we have looked in detail at the XSL working draft, and at IE5's XSL implementation. We've seen how XSL can be used to render XML pages, either through a reference in the stylesheet, or by reference in HTML or Active Server pages.

Previously, we have seen that CSS is a simple rendering mechanism for documents that need no manipulation on the client, while the DOM allows complex manipulation of both the document elements and the document text. XSL stylesheets combine these features – we can use them to change the order and content of the source document as well as apply styles to it.

In this chapter, we have seen:

- how to find elements in the source document and transform these elements into new XML elements
- how to interpret these new elements as HTML
- that XSL running on the client is good for manipulating XML for display in arbitrary formats
- that XSL complements CSS by providing a transformation mechanism that allows use of CSS as a styling mechanism
- that the DOM can be used for manipulation of document content *before* rendering with XSL
- that we can generate an XML file with server-side code and render it using XSL on the client
- that XSL processing can also take place on the server, allowing HTML to be sent to clients without XSL support. (However, this approach loses some of the benefits of XML)

In the next chapter, we'll take a look at some more sophisticated XML techniques – these will prepare us for discussing the Centaur case study in more detail.

6

Further XML Techniques

So far, we have introduced XML and its related recommendations and described them in some detail where appropriate. As we have done this, we have introduced various techniques that are relevant to the case study. In the next chapter, we will start to look into the case study itself in more detail, but first, we will look at some more useful techniques we will be using later.

In this chapter, we will:

- find how to check that we are using a browser capable of displaying our XML pages
- compare two ways of using code to generate XML
- compare two ways of keeping data related to our Web site on the client
- compare two ways of storing data on the server
- use a Microsoft component to send data from an Active Server Page to an HTTP server

Browser Detection

As I am sure you are aware, different browsers support different subsets of, and extensions to, the various Internet standards. It is therefore often useful to be able to determine the browser in use. This is not strictly an XML issue, but since the XML technology is new, the level of support varies from none (version 3 browsers and Navigator 4), through "a little" (IE4) to "quite a bit" (IE5 and Navigator 5).

Browser capabilities can be detected on the client or on the server, either by detecting the browser type and version or by looking for specific capabilities. The latter is often useful (after all, while Internet Explorer and Navigator have around 90% of the market, that leaves millions of other browsers in use). I would certainly suggest that approach if looking to see whether a browser supports, for example, frames. However, XML support is not included in the capabilities, so we have to look specifically for the IE5 browser type. We will do that now, using client-side ECMAScript code, since that is the approach used in Centaur.

Detecting Browser Type

There are two properties of the `navigator` object, which represents the browser, that give the information we require. The following simple script (`browser.htm`) displays the properties of the browser it is being run in.

```
<HTML>
<BODY>
<SCRIPT>
  var property;
  var str = "";

  for(property in navigator)
    str += property + ": " + navigator[property] + "\n";
  alert(str);
</SCRIPT>
</BODY>
</HTML>
```

When I ran this in the beta version of IE5, I got the following:

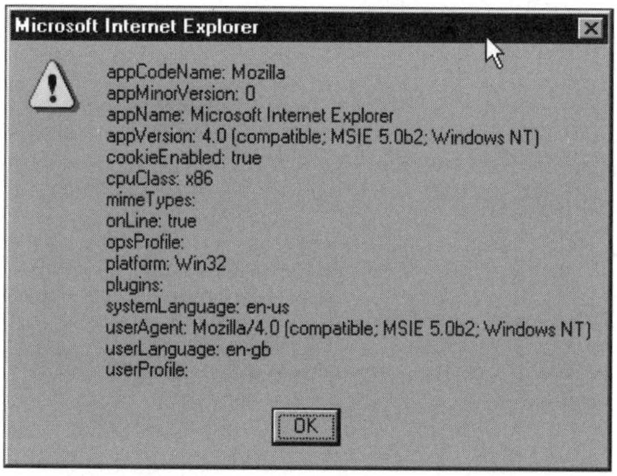

It would appear from this, that all I need to do is find the string MSIE 5 in the `appVersion` property and I will have detected my browser. Internet Explorer 4.01 has an `appVersion` 4.0 (compatible; MSIE 4.01;Windows 95), which makes me think that just looking at this property will be sufficiently robust to cope with future versions of IE5.

With that in mind, here is the start of the `onLoad()` function of Centaur's index page:

```
function onLoad()
{
  var strButtons = '<INPUT type="button" value = "New Brochure" onClick =
"enter()"><INPUT
                   type="button" value = "Restore Brochure" onClick =
"restore()">';

  if (navigator.appVersion.indexOf("MSIE 5") != -1)
  {
    // we're OK - it's IE5
    version.style.display = "none";
    buttons.innerHTML = strButtons;
```

Functions such as this need a little care in design. Firstly, in this page, I have hidden all script from browsers that do not implement JavaScript by enclosing all my script between HTML comment delimiters (`<!-- ... -->`). Some books recommend it for all script, but in our case this is the only page where I do not know that the browser supports my script.

Because some browsers do not support the script, the page I display in these other browsers must be the page I want for browsers other than IE5. So there is no use using script to hide portions of the page that I do not want displayed in these browsers. Instead, we must use the script to hide and add portions for IE5 users only.

Hence, once we have detected that the browser is IE5, we hide some text that says that the browser is not compatible with Centaur, then add the text for the buttons.

As an example, we can compare the Centaur welcome screen in IE5 and Navigator 4. Here is `index.htm` as it appears in IE5:

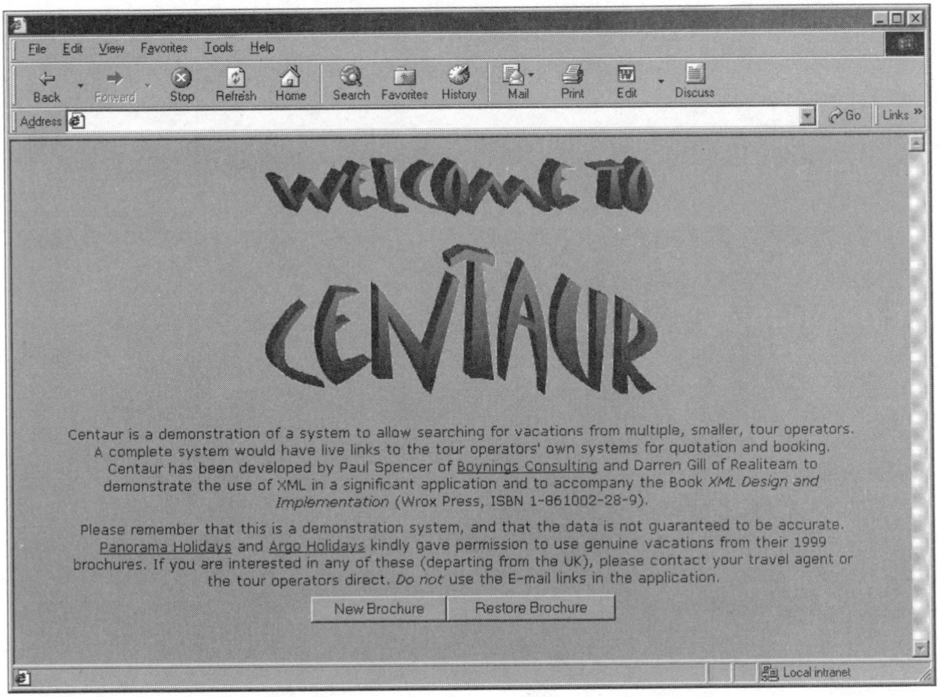

And here is the same page as displayed in Netscape Communicator 4.5:

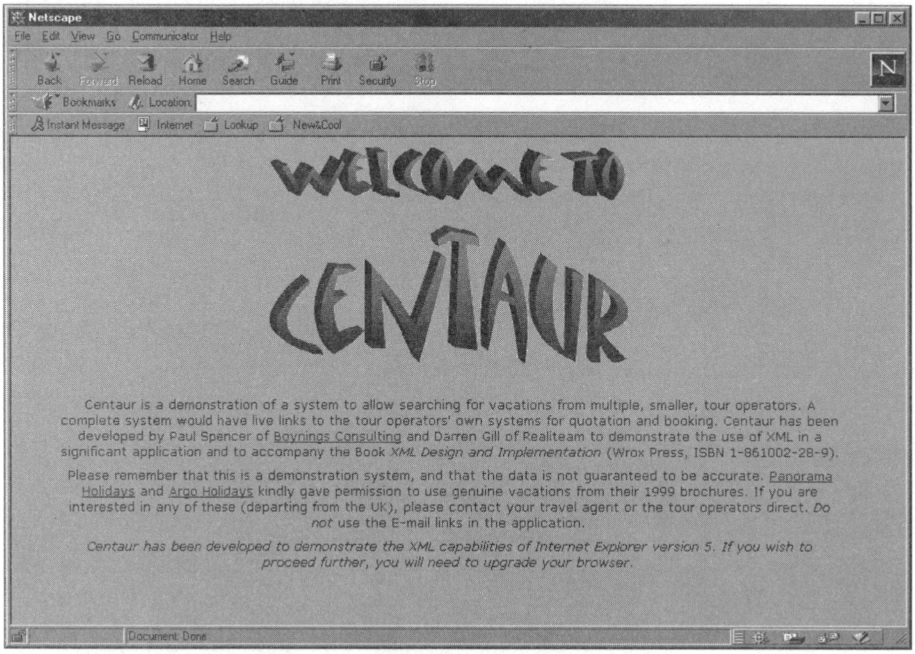

Checking That Cookies are Enabled

We use a similar technique to detect whether the user has cookies enabled. Since Centaur relies on cookies, we warn the user that the application will not operate correctly without them.

The navigator object has a property `cookieEnabled` that allows us to test for this. We simply test the property and warn the user if cookies are disabled. Here is the full `onLoad()` function, including both the browser type and cookie test:

```
function onLoad()
{
  var strButtons = '<INPUT type="button" value = "New Brochure" onClick =
"enter()"><INPUT
                     type="button" value = "Restore Brochure" onClick =
"restore()">';

  if (navigator.appVersion.indexOf("MSIE 5") != -1)
  {
    // we're OK - it's IE5
    version.style.display = "none";
    buttons.innerHTML = strButtons;

    // new check that cookies are enabled
    if (navigator.cookieEnabled == false)
      alert("This application requires cookies to be enabled. Please enable
        cookies and reload the page");
  }
}
```

Building XML from Script

Many XML applications will need to use script to build up XML. This is done in several places within Centaur, most noticeably when the details of a tour are built from the database. There are two basic ways to build the XML – as a text string or as a data object. We will look at both of these, then compare them.

Building XML as a Text String

Let's build a simple piece of XML and put it in the document as an XML island. Our code could look like this (`xmlAsString.asp`):

```
<% option explicit %>
<%
Dim strXML

  strXML = "<result>" & tagIt("tourid",1,"")
  strXML = strXML & tagIt("tourOp", "Panorama","")
  strXML = strXML & tagIt("name","Hotel Aziza","")
  strXML = strXML & tagIt("area", "Tunisia","")
  strXML = strXML & "</result>"

function tagIt(strTag, strData, strAttr)
'Purpose: Utility function to help mark up XML
  if strData <> "" then
    tagIt = "<" & strTag & " " & strAttr & ">" & strData & "</" & strTag & ">"
  else
    tagIt = "<" & strTag & " " & strAttr & " />"
  end if
end function

%><HTML>
<BODY onLoad="displayTree(Island.documentElement,0)">
<XML Id="Island">
<%=strXML%>
</XML>

<Script Language = "JScript" src="utils.js"></Script>
</BODY>
</HTML>
```

When we developed the `displayTree()` function in the chapter on the DOM (Chapter 3), we mentioned placing it in a separate file so we could include it when we needed it. We are doing just that in this example, using the line:

```
<Script Language = "JScript" src="utils.js"></Script>
```

and the result will look like this:

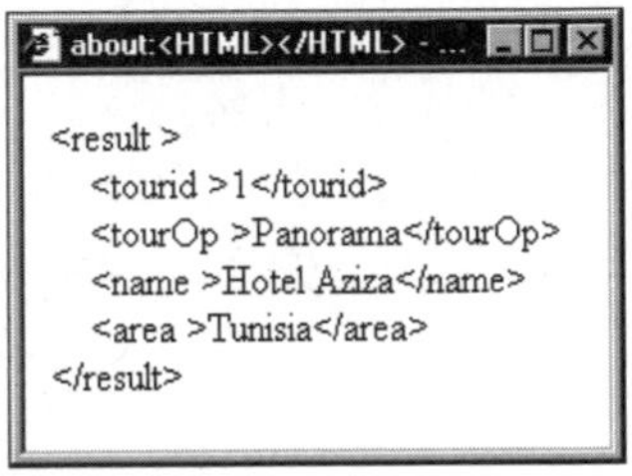
about:<HTML></HTML> - ...
<result >
<tourid >1</tourid>
<tourOp >Panorama</tourOp>
<name >Hotel Aziza</name>
<area >Tunisia</area>
</result>

Here, the key to building up the XML as a text string is our `tagIt()` function:

```
function tagIt(strTag, strData, strAttr)
'Purpose: Utility function to help mark up XML
  if strData <> "" then
    tagIt = "<" & strTag & " " & strAttr & ">" & strData & "</" & strTag & ">"
  else
    tagIt = "<" & strTag & " " & strAttr & " />"
  end if
end function
```

This is another useful function that takes as parameters a tag name, some data and an attribute string and returns these as a well-formed XML string. If the element has no content, an empty element tag is created, otherwise an element with content is created.

Building XML as a DOM Object

The second way to build XML is using the document object model. We discussed the document object model in Chapter 3, where we used it to manipulate and display XML. However, it can be used equally well to *build* XML.

Here is the code to build the same output as we just saw when building the XML as a string (`xmlAsDOM.asp`):

```
<% option explicit %>
<%
Dim xmlDoc
Dim root
Dim mstrXML

  set xmlDoc = Server.CreateObject("Microsoft.XMLDOM")
  set root = xmlDoc.createElement("result")

  AppendChild(root, "tourid", "1")
  AppendChild(root, "tourOp", "Panorama")
  AppendChild(root, "name", "Hotel Aziza")
  AppendChild(root, "area", "Tunisia")

  mstrXML = root.xml


  Sub AppendChild(parent, strTag, strData)
  Dim child

  Set child = xmlDoc.createElement(strTag)
  child.text = strData
  parent.appendChild(child)

  End sub

%>
<HTML>
<BODY onLoad="displayTree(Island.documentElement,0)">
<XML Id="Island">
<% =mstrXML %>
</XML>
```

```
<Script Language = "JScript" src="utils.js"></Script>
</BODY>
</HTML>
```

As you can see, this code creates a new XML document:

```
    set xmlDoc = Server.CreateObject("Microsoft.XMLDOM")
```

and then a root element:

```
    set root = xmlDoc.createElement("result")
```

Then, just as we used the `tagIt()` function before, we use `AppendChild()` to create the child elements and add them to the root element. However, there is one difference from the `tagIt()` function. That took a parameter of a string representing the attributes as name/value pairs. If we are creating our elements using the DOM, we cannot do this. We would need to create them explicitly using the `setAttribute()` method of the `Element` object.

Finally, in the main function, the XML object is turned back into a string using Microsoft's proprietary `.xml` property, so it can be put into the XML island for the JScript `displayTree()` function to access:

```
mstrXML = root.xml
```

XML as DOM vs. XML as String

So should you create your XML using the object model or as text? Ultimately, that is your own decision. I have not conducted benchmarks to compare the performance of the two methods. The DOM method has the advantage that it is almost impossible to create XML that is not well-formed. This is all too easy with the string method, although our `tagIt()` function makes it less likely. However, the string method, using the `tagIt()` function, makes it slightly easier to add attributes.

With IE5, it is simple to convert between DOM and text using the `.xml` property of the `Node` object or the `loadXML()` method of the `Document` object.

Keeping Your Data Available

Cookies

In the past, if you wanted to store data that is generated in a Web page, you used cookies. A cookie is a piece of text stored on the client machine. However, some people are nervous about cookies, and often disable them in their browser. So first, the truth about cookies.

What is a Cookie?

A cookie is simply a small piece of named data stored by the browser. Both Netscape Navigator and Internet Explorer can use cookies, so they are a popular means of storing information.

I say that cookies are small – any browser implementing the cookie specification can limit the size of an individual cookie to four kilobytes, and the number of cookies stored by a single site to twenty. There is also an overall maximum of 300 cookies, and, while a browser may store more, it is not compelled to.

So what is the use of cookies? The most common is to remember information that you have sent to a site, for example to indicate that you have registered for a Web site. When I first accessed the Microsoft Developer Network (MSDN) site, I had to register. Now, if I access the site from my PC, I just access the page like any other, because Microsoft has stored relevant information in a cookie on my PC. However, if I am using somebody else's PC, MSDN will not know who I am, and so ask me to register again. So from this point of view, cookies are extremely valuable.

However, in this example, when I use somebody else's PC, because cookies are stored on the client, I am giving them future access to this information and the ability to log on to MSDN using my identity. This is alright in a low security scenario such as this, but would not be acceptable on higher security sites, such as a bank.

Cookies are also used to track your navigation of a site. At the simplest level, the Webmaster can improve a site by seeing how people navigate it. At a deeper level, this information can be used for marketing purposes. One of the best known exponents of this use of cookies is `http://www.doubleclick.com`.

A third use for cookies is simply to pass information between pages on a Web site. We do that in Centaur: on the welcome page, there are two buttons – one to start a new brochure and one to open an existing one. What happens when a button is pressed? This page, `index.htm`, calls the main frames page `main.htm`. This, in turn, loads `search.asp` into the right frame and `index-1.htm` into the left frame. `index-1.htm` is the page that needs to know which button you pressed. How does it do this? `index.htm` sets a cookie, and `index-1.htm` reads it. This is taken one stage further in ASP, which uses a cookie (`ASPSESSIONID`) to carry context across HTTP requests and enables the Session object to work. The session object is another way to pass information between pages, and is used in Centaur, for example, to display information from the quotation request on the screen that is used to request a booking.

What Do People Object to?

People have three main areas of dislike about cookies.

The first is that, because the Web page can write to their hard disk, they are worried about viruses. This concern can be dismissed instantly – a cookie cannot write programs to your disk, so there is no risk of viruses.

The second perceived risk is that people can read information from the PC. Again, this is an illusion – the only information that can be read is the data in the cookie. And what is that data – it is information you have voluntarily provided or that the Web site has been able to find about you through your navigation. A cookie cannot, for example, reveal your email address unless you have chosen to provide it to the Web site (for example, as a part of registering for access to the site). Equally, if you have provided your email address to a site, it cannot be read by people on other sites.

So the only aspect left is tracking your navigation. If this concerns you, turn cookies off in your browser. However, if you do, you will make browsing many sites, including Centaur, much harder for yourself.

How are Cookies Set by Client Code?

Let's start by looking at an example. The start-up of Centaur is as good as any. This is the relevant part of `index.htm`:

```
function restore()
{
  document.cookie = 'restore=true';
  document.location.replace('main.htm');
}

function enter()
{
  document.cookie = 'restore=false';
  document.location.replace('main.htm');
}
```

This is about the simplest form of a cookie. It sets one parameter – `restore` – to a value of `true` or `false`. The cookie itself is stored as a string of parameter/value pairs, so if I set another parameter, it would also be stored, and I could read the value of either or both parameters from another page.

A cookie has four properties of its own that determine its life, its accessibility and its security. In most cases, setting the desired life of the cookie, through the **expiry** property, is the most useful. In the example above, we did not set any expiry time, so the cookie will expire at the end of the session. If we wished this to last longer, we could set an expiry date in the JScript `GMTString` format. To expire the cookie after a period of a month, we could simply write:

```
var expiry = new Date();
expiry.setMonth(expiry.getMonth() + 1);
if (expiry.getMonth() > 11)
  expiry.setMonth(0);
document.cookie = 'restore=false;expires=' + expiry.toGMTString;
```

Note that cookies should be set with reference to Greenwich Mean Time (GMT), as we have in the last line here.

The cookie has two properties that determine who can access it. Obviously, if I reveal my email address to one Web site, I don't want every other site able to read it. By default, only pages on the same site and in the same directory (or a sub-directory) of the page that set the cookie can read it. However, the page setting the cookie can open it up to a wider audience. For example, on my network, my Centaur pages are on `http://server/Wrox`, and the pages for this chapter are in a sub-directory called `ch6`. I could allow any pages on the Wrox Web on my server to access the cookie by setting the **path** property, for example:

```
document.cookie = 'restore=false;path=/Wrox';
```

or any pages on my server with:

```
document.cookie = 'restore=false;path=/';
```

The second property controlling access is **domain**. This allows me to change the domains that have access to the cookie. This is useful when a company is big enough to have several Web servers. So, for example, if my Centaur pages were on, say `wrox.boynings.co.uk`, I could allow all pages on all servers in the `boynings` domain access to my cookie using:

```
document.cookie = 'restore=false;path=/;domain=boynings.co.uk';
```

Of course, as the person setting the cookie, I am the one controlling who can read it. If I say "no", it stays "no".

The final property of cookies controls security. Clearly, it could be useful for secure sites to store some information, such as an account number, that have a higher level of security. What is the point of using a secure protocol like HTTPS if a secure page stores information back on the user's computer that can be accessed from non-secure pages? For that reason, the boolean property **secure** is provided. If set to "`true`", the cookie can only be retrieved using the secure HTTPS protocol.

Retrieving Cookies with Client Code

Because cookies are stored as a string, they are retrieved as a string. Unfortunately, JScript does not provide dedicated cookie reading methods, so the string methods must be used. To find the values of individual parameters saved in the cookie, you can use `string.indexOf()` and `string.subString()` methods. In Centaur, we just look for the complete name/value pair that we want:

```
    if(document.cookie.indexOf("restore=true") != -1)
      restoreBrochure();
```

IE5 Persistence

With IE5, Microsoft has introduced another means of storing data that can be used in later sessions. This is implemented as an IE5 **behavior** – another new concept with this release of Microsoft's browser. In this book, I am concentrating on using the XML features of IE5, and sticking to familiar concepts where possible. To fully describe behaviors and the persistence model is therefore beyond the scope of this book, but I shall briefly discuss persistence so that you know when it is appropriate to consider it and find out more.

IE5 behaviors are simply a means of encapsulating functionality in re-usable scripts. They can be thought of in the same way as CSS styles – while a style indicates how an HTML element should appear, a behavior defines, well ... how it should behave. An example would be to write some script to make an element fly on from the left of the screen. This could be encapsulated in a behavior, then applied to any element simply by including a reference to the behavior in the element tag just as you would with a style.

As I mentioned, persistence is an alternative to cookies as a way of storing data for use on other pages or in later sessions. Although it can be used wherever a cookie is used, it has two disadvantages over cookies: it is dependent on the client browser being IE5 and it is more long-winded to implement. It should therefore be used mainly where the limitations of cookies (which, after all, were designed for holding small amounts of data) are not appropriate. The most likely uses will be in storing complete Web pages and in storing variable data held in Web pages.

As more and more Web sites are allowing the user to customize pages to their needs, Web servers are being loaded with data for millions of individual users. How much easier if this were to be held on the client instead. Over time, the use of persistence is likely to lead to more and more sites allowing customized page setup. Of course, they will need to implement two mechanisms – persistence for IE5 users and server-based for the rest. However, they may feel that, as IE5 usage increases, it is worth their while to develop code specifically for this browser. On an intranet, the same issues do not arise, and an IE5-based intranet can use persistence as much as it likes.

How does this affect XML? In Centaur, we store the brochure on the client as a cookie. This could be stored using persistence instead. It is unlikely that the brochure will exceed the 4kB cookie limit, so a cookie is easier to use. However, a commercial version might want to switch to a persistence model to be safe when there are more vacations to choose from.

Now think of other applications of XML. One that I have implemented (on IE4) is a sales quotation system. This uses dynamic HTML to access price information stored in an XML file to provide a self-contained application. The advantage of XML here is that, once used, the data is sitting in the local browser cache, so later use of the system does not require connection to the server. Clearly, persistence is an alternative way to achieve this, providing more control over what is stored.

That is all I plan to discuss in relation to persistence. More information is available on the Microsoft Web site `http://www.microsoft.com/workshop/author/behaviors/overview.asp`.

Storing Data on the Server

Because XML is used to represent data, many people get confused between this and relational databases. There is no doubt that XML was designed to represent data in a human-readable and machine-readable form so it can be processed and/or displayed. However, it is possible to use XML for long-term storage of variable data in the same way that a database stores the information.

Currently, the boundary is reasonably clear – a relational database (and most databases in use are relational) holds multiple tables of data with relationships between them. XML holds hierarchical data and has no way of indicating relationships other than the parent/child relationship. Furthermore, databases have huge amounts of code to enable searching and to ensure, for example, that interrupted transactions do not corrupt the database, thereby preventing people reading any data that is halfway through being updated. XML has some searching capability (especially with Microsoft's extensions to the DOM), but none of the integrity and locking found in conventional databases. However, it is clear that people are thinking of XML more and more as a transactional data storage format and that some of the standard database facilities will be added to help with this.

So today, data can be stored in several formats, such as relational databases, flat files, spreadsheets, object databases and XML files. Let's have a look at data storage in Centaur to compare the benefits of two of these, XML files and relational databases.

The aim of Centaur is to store non-varying data on the Centaur server and leave varying data on the tour operator servers. When I say "non-varying", I really mean varying slowly, and where failing to implement a change sufficiently quickly does not have serious consequences. For example, the description of a hotel could change because they build a new swimming pool, but failing to mention this will not matter too much. More likely is that prices will change during the season as tour operators try to manage their inventory, and basing quotations on these prices can have serious consequences if they are out of date (as we saw in Chapter 1, when I mentioned an airline that was fined for selling seats at a price that was in an out-of-date price list on its Web site).

However, Centaur is built on the model of the vacation brochure; if you look at the price tables, you are getting a guide to the prices, but you are referred to the tour operator system for a final quotation. Of course, by keeping the data in a relational database, we can easily vary this model and allow the tour operator to update the database more dynamically. This has benefits in restricting the number of round trips to the tour operator system at the risk of allowing quotations from an out-of-date database.

The main advantage of storing data as XML is that, each time a vacation is displayed, the server only has to retrieve a file rather than perform complex database queries. A second advantage that goes with this is that the queries would not have to be written in the first place. If you look at `tour.asp`, you will see well over 500 lines of script devoted to building the XML from the database. If you look at the welcome screen of Centaur, you will see that Darren Gill helped with the coding. Remembering that Darren is considerably bigger than I am, and that he wrote the server-side code in this page, I have no intention of telling him that his 500 lines of script are unnecessary, even though storing each vacation as an XML file would have eliminated the need for it.

What is the disadvantage of this approach? The main one is as I indicated above – if we were to make the pricing information more dynamic and use it for calculations, it would be much better if it were held in a database. Before making the decision, we would also have to look at how the information reaches Centaur from the tour operator system. For this pilot, that was a lot of scanning and typing (much of the latter being undertaken by my daughter, Nicola). In a real system, we would define a DTD for transferring the information as XML from the tour operator and automating its input to Centaur. Now, the database is (reasonably) normalized, that is, there is little repeated information. That would not be true of XML documents where every vacation in one resort would probably include the same resort information. If we were to store some information in the database and some as XML pages, we either need to ask for the data twice, or build both the database and the XML pages from the source information. We would need something akin to Darren's work in `tour.asp` to achieve this.

So what is the conclusion? In the end, every designer has to make his or her own decisions, and hopefully learn from the experience. I would hate to undertake a project and learn nothing, so here is how I would do it next time ...

This demonstrator has not shown the load on the server, but I suspect that it would be as well to reduce it. However, I would not want to ask the tour operators for data in two formats, especially as there is a risk that the data could differ between them where they overlap. So I would stick with the database as it is currently designed, but would write code to generate the changed XML pages, perhaps once a day if the database has changed, and store these on the server for retrieval by the user. This gives the best of both worlds, and retains the flexibility to use the pricing information from the database. The disadvantages are that information could be slightly out of date, and the need for some additional disk storage for the pages. But disks are cheap, so that won't worry me.

Sending XML Between Application Tiers

As previously explained, Centaur is a three tier application that uses XML as a data format for communications between the middle tier (Centaur) and server tier (tour operator). The middle tier will use active server pages to send messages and receive responses. What constraints will this put on the tour operator server?

Clearly, there must be some communications protocols below the XML level. In our case, the basic protocols will be **TCP/IP** (Transmission Control Protocol / Internet Protocol) – the communications layers of the Internet. Above that, we will use **HTTP** (Hypertext Transfer Protocol) – the protocol of the World Wide Web. There is no need to describe HTTP here any more than there was when discussing cookies (which are a part of the HTTP specification). Microsoft has implemented the functions we need in the `XMLHttp` component (known as the `XMLHttpRequest` object on the Microsoft site) introduced with IE5.

This component is a part of the IE5 XML parser `MSXML.DLL`. At the time of writing, this was not available separately from IE5, although Microsoft has indicated that it will be in the future. It can therefore be used in client code running in IE5, or in Active Server Pages providing IE5 is installed on the server. This is how we use it in Centaur. The Centaur code is described in Chapters 8 and 9. In this section, our examples will be for exchanging messages between the client and a Web server.

`XMLHttp` allows us to send data to any HTTP server and receive the response either as text or as parsed XML. When the response is parsed, validation is disabled in the parser. As we shall see, Centaur uses a technique to ensure that the messages are validated before being used.

These are the methods and properties associated with `XMLHttp`:

Method or Property	Description
`abort`	Cancels the current HTTP request.
`getAllResponseHeaders`	Retrieves the values of all the HTTP headers.
`getResponseHeader`	Retrieves the value of an HTTP header from the response body.
`open`	Initializes a `Microsoft.XMLHttp` request, and specifies the method, URI, and authentication information for the request.
`readyState`	Represents the state of the request.
`responseBody`	Represents the response entity body as an array of unsigned bytes.
`responseStream`	Represents the response entity body as an `IStream`.
`responseText`	Represents the response entity body as a string.
`responseXML`	Represents the response entity body as parsed by the MSXML DOM parser.
`send`	Sends an HTTP request to the server and receives a response.
`setRequestHeader`	Specifies the name of an HTTP header.
`status`	Represents the HTTP status code returned by a request.
`statusText`	Represents the HTTP response line status.

XMLHttp Properties and Methods

Here, we will look at the most important of these methods. Visit the Microsoft Web site at `http://www.microsoft.com/workshop/xml/xmldom/reference/IXMLHttpRequest_interface.asp` for information on the others.

open

The `open` method initializes the request, setting the parameters required. There can be up to five parameters:

The first parameter, `method`, is the HTTP method used in the request, such as "PUT" or "POST". You will probably be familiar with the "POST" method from sending forms from a Web page.

The second parameter is the URL itself, and needs no explanation.

The third parameter indicates whether the call is to be **asynchronous**. This indicates that further processing can continue while the messages are being sent, and is similar to asynchronous use of the XML parser. When we use the parser, we have always included a line like:

```
domBrochure.async = false;
```

This forces the parser to complete its work before continuing. The alternative is to set `async` to `true`, and then use a handler for the `onreadystatechange` event to test whether the parser has completed its work before using the XML. You can think of this like the spell checking in Microsoft Word. In early versions of Word, you called the spell checker from a menu and it checked the document. This is synchronous operation. In more recent versions, you can ask the spell checker to operate continuously in the background and report errors. This is asynchronous operation.

The last two parameters relate to authentication and submit a user name and password to the remote application. If the user name is missing, but the remote application requires the user to log on, a logon window will be displayed.

The following line of code will initialize a request to use the POST method, sending synchronously to a URL of TransactionURL with no security:

```
httpObj.open("POST", "xmlReceive.asp", false);
```

setRequestHeader

This sets parameters in the HTTP header. For example, we are sending our data as XML. We therefore set the header:

```
httpObj.setRequestHeader("Content-type", "text/xml");
```

IE5 will recognize the message as XML if this line were omitted. However, I believe it is good practice to include it.

send

The `send` method sends the message and gets the response. It takes a single parameter indicating the message to send, which can be a string or a DOM object. If the `open` method was called with `async` set to `true`, the `send` method returns immediately. If `async` was set to `false`, the method returns once it has a complete response or times out. The `send` method has a return value to indicate whether the send was successful or not.

The following line will send the message "Hello to all our readers".

```
httpObj.send("<message>Hello to all our readers</message>");
```

responseText

The `responseText` property is simply the returned data represented as a string. Here, we set a variable to this string:

```
strResult = httpObj.responseText;
```

responseXML

The `responseXML` property is similar to `responseText`, but the data is returned as an XML object, having been parsed but not validated. Here, we put the response into an XML DOM object:

```
xmlResult = httpObj.responseXML;
```

XMLHttp in Action

The following shows about the simplest example possible of using `XMLHttp`. There are two files – `xmlSend.htm` sends an XML message to `xmlReceive.asp`. This file receives the message, parses it as an XML document and returns the same message with an extra bit tacked on. The original file, `xmlSend.htm`, receives this, parses it and displays the text.

`xmlSend.htm` looks like this:

```
<HTML>
<BODY>
<SCRIPT>
  var httpObj;

  httpObj = new ActiveXObject("Microsoft.XMLHTTP");
  httpObj.open("POST", "xmlReceive.asp", false);
  httpObj.setRequestHeader("Content-type", "text/xml");
  httpObj.send("<message>Hello to all our readers</message>");

  document.write(httpObj.responseText);

</SCRIPT>
</BODY>
</HTML>
```

This creates an XMLHttp object called httpObj, loads it with the text <message>Hello to all our readers</message>, then sends it to the page xmlReceive.asp using the HTTP POST method.

Having sent the message, we receive the message response with the responseText method, writing the result to the screen.

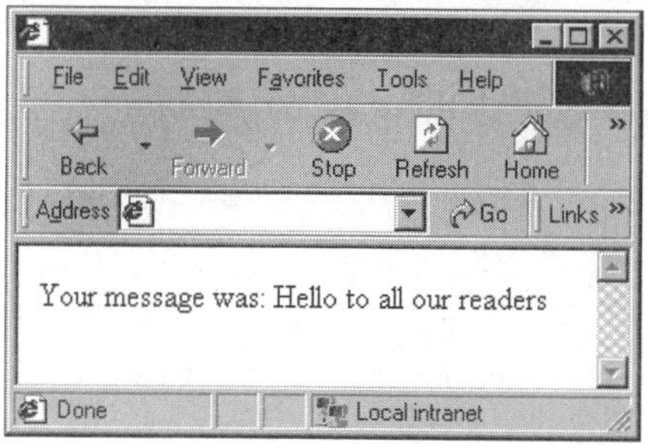

So what is xmlReceive.asp doing to receive and respond to the message? This is pretty simple:

```
<%
Dim xmlReq
Dim message

  Set xmlReq = Server.CreateObject("Microsoft.XMLDOM")
  xmlReq.load(Request)
  if xmlReq.parseError <> 0 then
    Response.Write xmlReq.parseError.reason
  end if

  message = "<reply>Your message was: " & xmlReq.text & "</reply>"
  Response.Write message
%>
```

The message is loaded into a new XML object with the code:

```
Set xmlReq = Server.CreateObject("Microsoft.XMLDOM")
  xmlReq.load(Request)
```

After checking for errors, the text is extracted and returned as an XML message within a new element and with an extra bit of text added to the front:

```
message = "<reply>Your message was: " & xmlReq.text & "</reply>"
  Response.Write message
```

That was a simple example of XMLHttp being used on the client. We will see more complex examples when we look at the messaging between Centaur and the tour operating systems.

XMLHttp in Centaur

In Centaur, we use XMLHttp in ASP code on the server to request quotations and make bookings. The code is similar in both cases. This is from quoteResults.asp:

```
Set HttpObj = Server.CreateObject("Microsoft.XMLHTTP")
HttpObj.open "POST",TransactionURL,false
HttpObj.setRequestHeader "Content-type", "text/xml"
HttpObj.send s
strResult = HttpObj.responseText
```

Before reaching this bit of code, we have set a string `s` to the XML data we want to send to the tour operator. This is sent synchronously, using the POST method to a URL we have previously pulled out from the database. There is no reason not to use a synchronous send as there is no further processing we want to do before getting the response. We then get the result as a string. Why a string? Because we want to validate it, which we can do by assigning it to an XML island, so it will be parsed on the client when the page is retrieved from the server:

```
<XML Id="xmlQuote"><% =strResult %></XML>
```

Summary

In this chapter, we have looked at additional techniques employed within Centaur, most of which are concerned with the application of XML.

The specific techniques we looked at were:

- browser detection
- building XML from script
- keeping data available through cookies and persistence
- storing data on the server as XML or in a database
- sending data from the middle to the server tier of three tier applications such as Centaur

In the next chapter we will delve into the structure of the Centaur application.

7

Under the Hood of Centaur

Introduction

Now that we have an understanding of the system, the problem it is addressing and the technologies it uses, we can look more closely at how it fits together.

In this chapter, we will see how the pages fit together to form the Web application. For the simpler pages, we will also look at the code. In later chapters, we will look in more detail at the XML-related code and the code that extracts data from the database. We will not look in detail at every line since much is simple display code or repetitions of techniques that we will have looked at. All the code is available from the Wrox web site at `http://www.wrox.com` via the **Catalog > Source Code** menu option.

By the end of this chapter, you will:

- understand the Centaur logical and physical data models
- know which pages in the application perform which tasks
- understand the structure of the displayed pages and how they interact
- know about the coding of some of the simpler pages

Don't worry about the difference between logical and physical data models here, as all will be explained soon.

The Centaur Database

Centaur holds all its information in a SQL Server database. Appendix A shows you how to build this database if you have SQL Server on your PC. Those with the skills will be able to install the system on other databases such as Microsoft Access. (We will provide an Access version of the database to download from the Wrox Web site.) However, the system has only been tested in the SQL Server environment. There are three main objects in this database – the tour operator, the resorts and the tours themselves. Since we are using a relational database, we have to model these objects as a set of **tables**.

The Logical Model

This diagram shows the relationships between data items in Centaur. This is known as the logical data model:

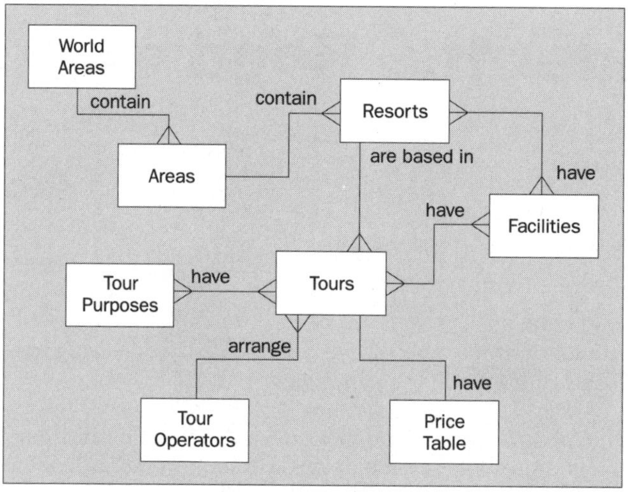

Firstly let me explain the diagramming method for those that are not familiar with data models. Each box is a logical entity in the system, and the lines show the relationships between them. These relationships are decribed with words.

So this part of the diagram shows that tours have price tables:

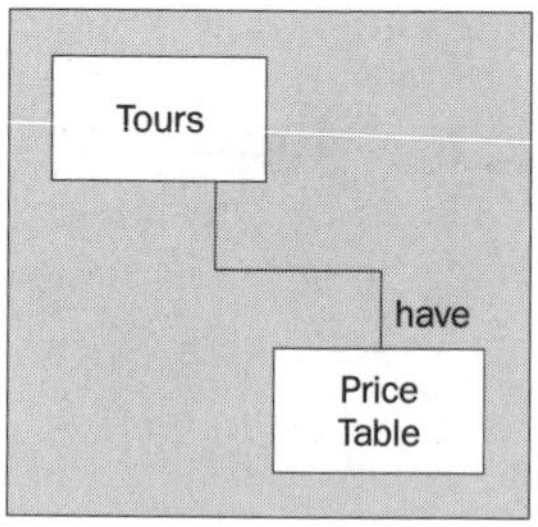

It goes a step further. You will see that some connections have a symbol that resembles crows' feet on the end. The fact that this one does not indicates that each tour has a single price table. This is known as a **one-to-one** relationship.

Let's have a look at a couple of parts of the diagram that have crows' feet:

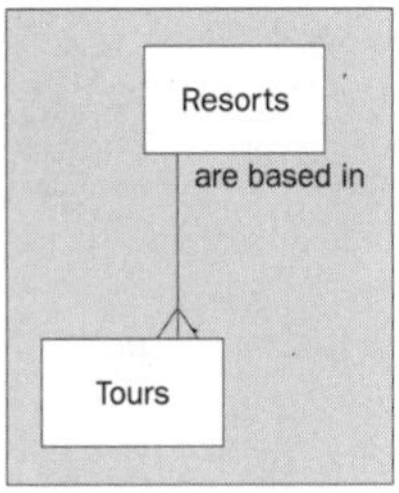

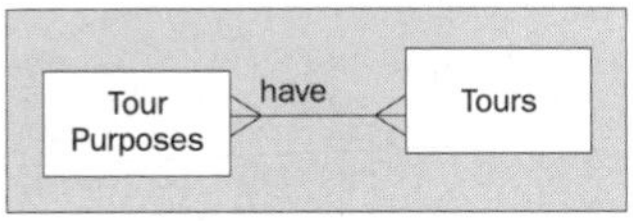

The first of these shows that many tours can be based in a single resort. Put simply, this means that a town can have several hotels, but each hotel is in a single town. This is known as a **one-to-many** relationship. The second, rather logically called a **many-to-many** relationship, shows that any tour can have several purposes (for example, a hotel with several golf courses nearby may be listed under "Summer Sun" and "Activities") and that a single purpose can apply to several tours - there is more than one "Summer Sun" vacation.

The Physical Model

Once we have a logical model, we can start thinking about how to represent this in a relational database management system such as SQL Server by thinking in terms of the **physical model**. In general, each entity in the logical model will correspond to a table in the physical model. Unfortunately, a relational database cannot build a many-to-many relationship between tables. We therefore need to add additional tables to break each many-to-many relationship down into two one-to-many relationships. Don't worry about the details of this – I will explain in a moment.

The other thing we need not worry about here is database **normalization**. Normalization is the process of organizing information in the most concise way by analyzing dependencies and reducing the repetition of information. For example, a company may take orders from customers. We could model an order in our database using the information:

Customer Name
Customer Invoice Address
Customer Delivery Address
Customer Purchasing Contact
Customer Phone Number
Customer Fax Number
Order Number
Item Number
Item Code
Item Description
Order Quantity
Price

And that would just be the start. I have left out much essential information such as delivery date. It is clearly better to describe the customer in one table, some information about the order in another (with a reference number so which know which customer is involved), each line of the order in a third and then refer to another table of products. The process of normalization is designed to present us with the most efficient structures for the data. There are times when it is best not to fully normalize a database. This is usually because the more the information is separated into tables in this way, the more work the database management system has to do and the slower it becomes.

> *For more information on the process of database table normalization visit* `http://www.bsbpa.umkc.edu/sward/mis552/CH05/index.htm` *or* `http://www.cba.nau.edu/morgan-j/class/subtop2_3/sld001.htm`

So let's have a look at the physical model of our Centaur database. This diagram was produced in Microsoft's Visual InterDev and shows all the field names in each table. Although this tool can be used to create the database, in this case it has just been used to create the diagrams used here:

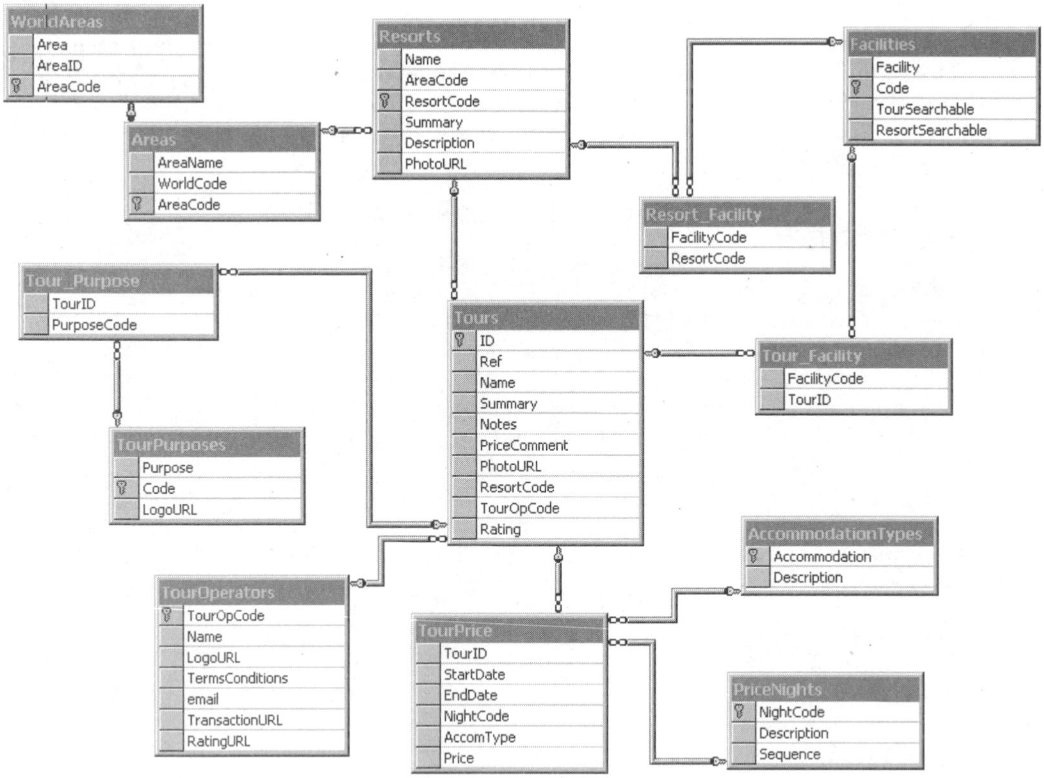

This diagram shows each of the thirteen tables in the Centaur database and the links between them. Each table comprises a set of **fields**, so, for example, the `Tours` table contains ten fields:

Field	Purpose
ID	The unique internal identifier for the tour
Ref	The tour operator's tour reference
Name	The name of the tour. This is always the hotel name
Summary	A summary description
Notes	Some notes to display about this tour
PriceComment	Text to display at the end of the price table
PhotoURL	The URL of the picture to display for this tour.
ResortCode	The code for the resort.
TourOpCode	The code for the tour operator
Rating	The rating of the tour to display in the tour details

The `Tours` table is the hub of the application. Every tour will have information relating to each of the items it contains. In fact, we can look at them in Visual InterDev by changing the display options for the `Tours` table:

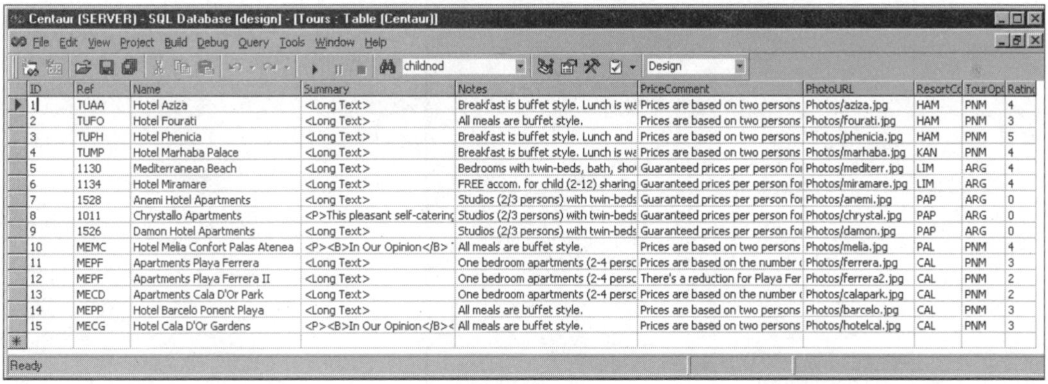

ID	Ref	Name	Summary	Notes	PriceComment	PhotoURL	ResortCo	TourOp	Rating
1	TUAA	Hotel Aziza	<Long Text>	Breakfast is buffet style. Lunch is wa	Prices are based on two persons	Photos/aziza.jpg	HAM	PNM	4
2	TUFO	Hotel Fourati	<Long Text>	All meals are buffet style.	Prices are based on two persons	Photos/fourati.jpg	HAM	PNM	3
3	TUPH	Hotel Phenicia	<Long Text>	Breakfast is buffet style. Lunch and	Prices are based on two persons	Photos/phenicia.jpg	HAM	PNM	5
4	TUMP	Hotel Marhaba Palace	<Long Text>	Breakfast is buffet style. Lunch is wa	Prices are based on two persons	Photos/marhaba.jpg	KAN	PNM	4
5	1130	Mediterranean Beach	<Long Text>	Bedrooms with twin-beds, bath, sho	Guaranteed prices per person fo	Photos/mediterr.jpg	LIM	ARG	4
6	1134	Hotel Miramare	<Long Text>	FREE accom. for child (2-12) sharing	Guaranteed prices per person fo	Photos/miramare.jpg	LIM	ARG	4
7	1528	Anemi Hotel Apartments	<Long Text>	Studios (2/3 persons) with twin-beds	Guaranteed prices per person fo	Photos/anemi.jpg	PAP	ARG	0
8	1011	Chrystallo Apartments	<P>This pleasant self-caterinç	Studios (2/3 persons) with twin-beds	Guaranteed prices per person fo	Photos/chrystal.jpg	PAP	ARG	0
9	1526	Damon Hotel Apartments	<Long Text>	Studios (2/3 persons) with twin-beds	Guaranteed prices per person fo	Photos/damon.jpg	PAP	ARG	0
10	MEMC	Hotel Melia Confort Palas Atenea	<P><B>In Our Opinion</B>	All meals are buffet style.	Prices are based on two persons	Photos/melia.jpg	PAL	PNM	4
11	MEPF	Apartments Playa Ferrera	<Long Text>	One bedroom apartments (2-4 persc	Prices are based on the number	Photos/ferrera.jpg	CAL	PNM	3
12	MEPF	Apartments Playa Ferrera II	<Long Text>	One bedroom apartments (2-4 persc	There's a reduction for Playa Fer	Photos/ferrera2.jpg	CAL	PNM	2
13	MECD	Apartments Cala D'Or Park	<Long Text>	One bedroom apartments (2-4 persc	Prices are based on the number	Photos/calapark.jpg	CAL	PNM	2
14	MEPP	Hotel Barcelo Ponent Playa	<Long Text>	All meals are buffet style.	Prices are based on two persons	Photos/barcelo.jpg	CAL	PNM	3
15	MECG	Hotel Cala D'Or Gardens	<P><B>In Our Opinion</B><	All meals are buffet style.	Prices are based on two persons	Photos/hotelcal.jpg	CAL	PNM	3

All fifteen vacations in our test data set are shown with the information stored about them. The field names are shown along the top, and the details of each tour in rows, making the whole thing appear much like a spreadsheet. The rows are known as **records**, and there is a record to describe each tour.

In the diagram showing all the tables, some of the fields have an image of a key beside them. This indicates that they are **key** fields, and that the content of this field is different for every record in the table. In the `Tours` table, the key field is the `ID`.

Each tour has a unique `ID`, so we can access the record for a tour by knowing the value of this field. In the `Resorts` table we can see that the key field is the `ResortCode`:

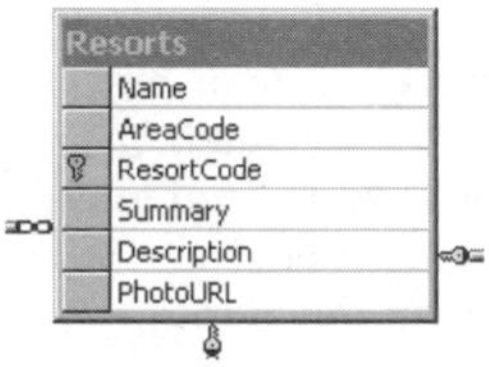

The `Tours` table also has a `ResortCode` field. We use this to access information about the resort if we know the tour `ID`. To do this, we look in the `Tours` table to find the `ResortCode` for the tour we want. We then use this value to find a record in the `Resorts` table. Since key fields must be unique, there will be only one matching record. We can then extract whatever information we want from this table.

The `ID` field in the `Tours` table, and the `ResortCode` field in the `Resorts` table are known as **primary keys**. The `ResortCode` field in the `Tours` table is known as a **foreign key**, since its purpose is to access a primary key in another table. In this case, the `ResortCode` fields have the same name in both tables, but this is not a requirement.

Note that the `PhotoURL` in the `Tours` table diagram above points to the image for this specific tour, not the image for the resort that appears near the top of the page when we look at a tour in Centaur. We can find the resort image for a specific tour by using the `ResortCode` key to find the appropriate record in the `Resorts` table, then find the `PhotoURL` from that record. This is another example of using **keys** to find information in related tables.

In Chapter 9, we will look at the code that implements these key-based relationships.

Let's have a look at what has happened to our many-to-many relationship between `tours` and `tour purposes`. The most obvious thing is that there is an additional table, called `Tour_Purpose`:

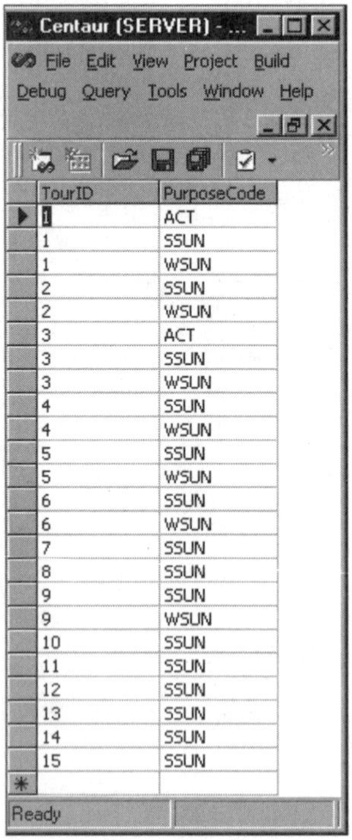

TourID	PurposeCode
1	ACT
1	SSUN
1	WSUN
2	SSUN
2	WSUN
3	ACT
3	SSUN
3	WSUN
4	SSUN
4	WSUN
5	SSUN
5	WSUN
6	SSUN
6	WSUN
7	SSUN
8	SSUN
9	SSUN
9	WSUN
10	SSUN
11	SSUN
12	SSUN
13	SSUN
14	SSUN
15	SSUN

Each tour has one or more `PurposeCodes`. If you look at the Centaur application, when you get the details on, say, Hotel Aziza (which the previous diagram showed as having an `id` of 1), you will see that it has images and text corresponding to Activities, Summer Sun and Winter Sun. So this table acts as a link between the `Tours` table and the `TourPurposes` table, breaking the many-to-many relationship down into two one-to-many relationships that can be modeled in a relational database.

The Centaur Application

We have already seen how the user might use Centaur in Chapter 1, now we will look at what is happening inside the application when they use it.

As shown below, Centaur is split into two main parts, the Interactive System that handles searching for vacations and viewing the details, and the Transactional System that handles quotation and booking. There is also a page, `server.asp`, that provides an emulation of the tour operators' own systems. This will be treated as part of the transactional system.

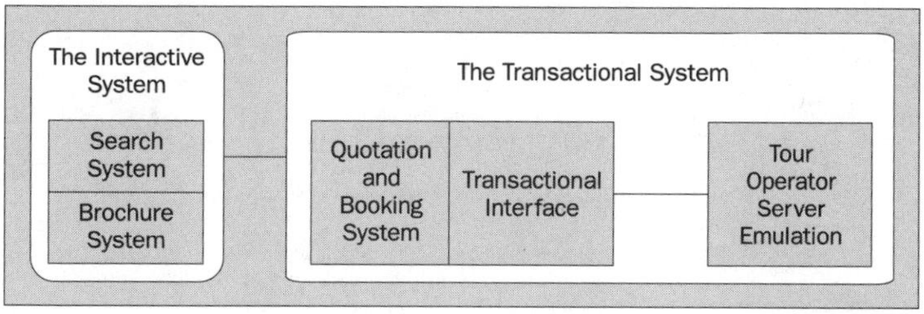

Like any Web application, Centaur comprises a set of **pages**. The pages that make up the application are:

General pages	Interactive System pages	Transactional System pages
`main.htm`	`index-1.htm`	`quoteForm.asp`
`index.htm`	`getSearchResults.asp`	`quoteResults.asp`
`bye.htm`	`prepareResults.asp`	`bookForm.asp`
`error.asp`	`search.asp`	`bookResults.asp`
	`tour.asp`	

The diagram below shows, at a high level, how the pages of the interactive system fit together. This also shows the two pages used during system startup, `index.htm`, which is the welcome page, and `main.htm`, which is the frameset page, since Centaur uses frames.

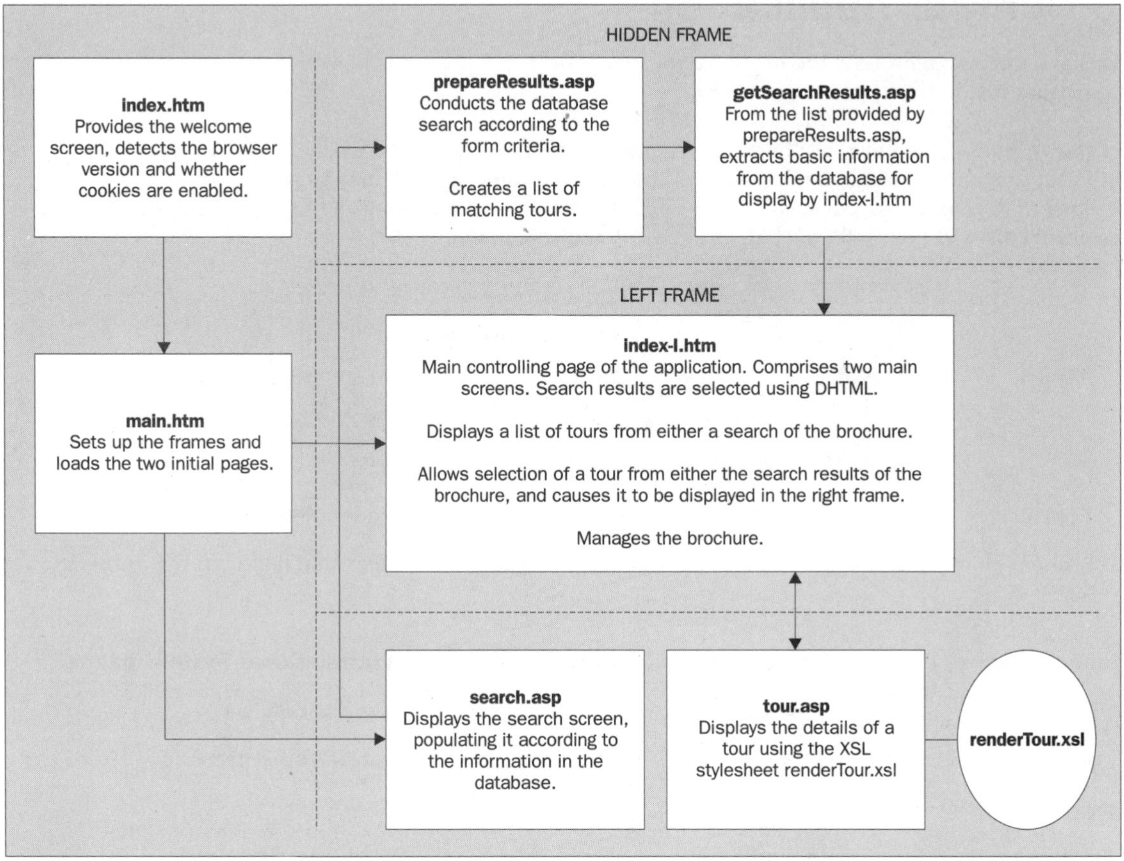

This shows how, once the system has started, it uses three frames. One of these is displayed on the left side of the screen, and contains the results of searches and the brochure, another is displayed on the right-hand side and shows the search form and the details of vacations. The third frame has a width of zero, so is not displayed. This is used by two pages, `prepareResults.asp` and `getSearchResults.asp`, that do not display results, but instead create results for other pages to use. Of course, we can alter the width of that frame, and I did this during debugging to see any error messages that were displayed.

Once the user clicks on the button to get a quotation, we enter the transactional system. This comprises four pages, and a page to simulate the tour operators' systems. This simulation is loaded into the hidden frame, the other pages into the right-hand frame:

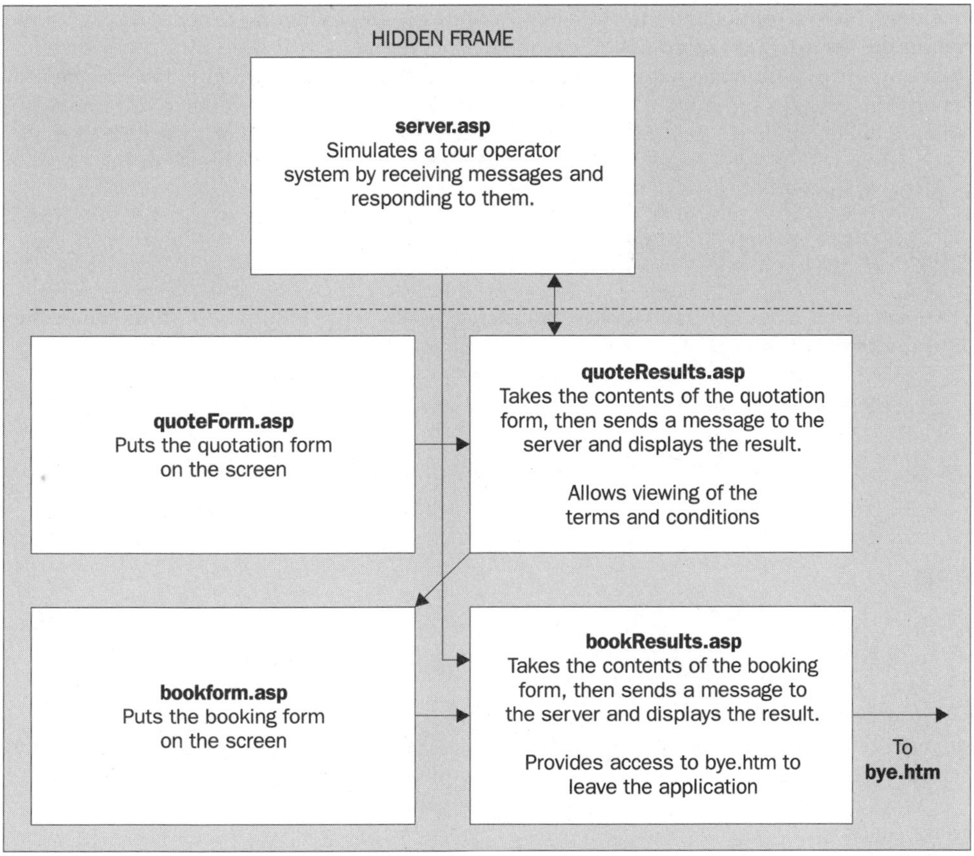

There are also a few other files. Each frame has a CSS stylesheet, `centaur-l.css` for the left frame and `centaur-r.css` for the right. There are two XSL stylesheets, `renderTour.xsl` for displaying vacation details and `booking.xsl` for displaying the results of making a booking. There is also a global file `global.asa` which we'll discuss in a moment.

There are several scripting languages commonly used to develop Web applications, one of which is JavaScript, with its standardized form ECMAScript and its Microsoft implementation JScript. In most cases, these can be treated as equivalents, although JScript has proprietary Microsoft extensions. ECMAScript is by far the most commonly used scripting language for code that is to run on the client, since it is implemented by most modern browsers, although there are small differences between implementations. Since we are writing purely for IE5, we can safely use JScript on the client.

We are using a Microsoft Internet Information Server (IIS) or Personal Web Server (PWS) to serve Active Server Pages (ASP). ASP pages can be written in either JScript or VBScript. The latter is Microsoft's own scripting language, based on Visual Basic. Traditionally, ASP server script is written in VBScript, and that is the convention followed here.

When an ASP page is requested by the browser, assuming the page contains script for the server-side, HTML and client-side script, the code in the page executes in the following order. First any code that needs to run on the server is executed. Then the resultant Web page is loaded into the browser. And following that any script within the page is executed. A very common technique is to use the server-side code of an ASP page to put information into the client-side code that is sent to the browser. For example, when a call is made to the ASP page concerned, the server may extract the ID of the vacation it is dealing with from the database, then add it to a URL that is included in the client code like this, in place of the <% =TourID %> expression:

```
<form method="post" id="quoteform" action="quoteResults.asp?tourid=<% =TourID %>">
```

If the TourID extracted from the database on the server side has the value '123', then when the page is loaded into the browser the HTML will read:

```
<form method="post" id="quoteform" action="quoteResults.asp?tourid=123">
```

Similar methods are used, for example, to put XML code into XML islands within the HTML code on a page.

Global.asa

The file global.asa is a text file that is held on the server and contains information about the application, such as code that should execute when the application is first run or when a new session is started by a new user accessing the application.

In our case, most of the file was generated by Visual InterDev when the system was first built and serves to set up parameters for the database when the application starts.

One important piece is:

```
        '''''''''''''''''''''''''''''''''''''''''''''''''''''''''''''''''''''
        'Change the following to your server name and location of the Centaur DTD
        '''''''''''''''''''''''''''''''''''''''''''''''''''''''''''''''''''''
        svrName = "SERVER"
        Application("dtd") = "http://server/Wrox/centaur.dtd"
```

My server is called "SERVER". If you are building Centaur on your own system using the files from the Wrox web site at http://www.wrox.com, you will need to change this variable. You will also need to change the value of the application variable dtd to the URL of the DTD on your system. Instructions for setting up your system are given in Appendix A, and in the installation program's help files.

In Chapter 1, we said that a limit was placed on the number of vacations that would be displayed as the result of a search. This is held as an application level variable in global.asa:

```
Application ("MAX_TOURS_IN_FIND") = 10
```

Because this variable is held at the application level, it is permanently available when the application is running. We could have put it in the one page that uses it (prepareResults.asp). The reason it is held in global.asa is to keep all configuration information in one place.

Starting up the System

When you first access Centaur, you will see the welcome page `index.htm`. Microsoft IIS servers are configured by default to use `default.htm` as a home page. Centaur therefore includes a page `default.htm` that simply redirects to `index.htm`. This is a simple page giving some information about the system and providing a couple of buttons. As with several other pages, there is no XML content. Of course, this page could be written in XML, but I see little point in doing this when HTML does the job adequately.

What would be the impact of writing simple pages like this in XML? At the simplest level, it would only be usable in IE5. Now, I am a realist. I have developed Centaur partly as an XML demonstrator, but I am aware that if I were to exploit the system commercially, it would not be much use were it only to work with a single (and very new) browser. So I would have to start processing the XML with an XSL style sheet on the server. And what would I be sending to the client? An HTML page, just like I am doing now.

So let's keep XML in its place for the moment. The technology is great on Intranets, where you have control of the browser, great for demonstrations and for doing IE5 specific versions of pages, great where data is coming from a database and can be rendered on the server with XSL, but there is still a role for HTML at the moment. Of course, when HTML is re-written as an XML language with native browser support for standard styles, all this will change.

So back to `index.htm`. The page contains three short JScript functions:

```
<SCRIPT>
//<!--
function onLoad()
{
  var strButtons = '<INPUT type="button" value = "New Brochure" onClick =
"enter()"><INPUT type="button" value = "Restore Brochure" onClick = "restore()">';

  if (navigator.appVersion.indexOf("MSIE 5") != -1)
  {
    // we're OK - it's IE5
    version.style.display = "none";
    buttons.innerHTML = strButtons;

    // new check that cookies are enabled
    if (navigator.cookieEnabled == false)
      alert("This application requires cookies to be enabled. Please enable
      cookies and reload the page");
  }
}

function restore()
{
  document.cookie = 'restore=true';
  document.location.replace('main.htm');
}

function enter()
{
  document.cookie = 'restore=false';
  document.location.replace('main.htm');
}
//-->
</SCRIPT>
```

We looked at detecting the browser type and whether cookies are enabled using the onLoad() function in the last chapter. The other functions merely set a value in a cookie according to which button has been pressed. This cookie will be accessed later by index-1.htm to determine whether or not it is to load an existing brochure.

Pressing either of these buttons takes you onto the page main.htm. This just creates three frames, one on the left for the search results and brochure, one on the right for vacation details and the forms for quotations and booking, and the hidden frame we discussed earlier.

At start-up, the screen shows the search form search.asp in the right-hand frame. The left-hand frame always shows the page index-1.htm, and uses dynamic HTML to select whether the search results or brochure are displayed. If you selected a New Brochure on the title screen, you will see an empty search results page here. If you selected Restore Brochure, it will show the brochure (providing one has previously been saved). You can switch between the displays at any time using buttons on the screen. We will look at how the brochure is saved and restored in a moment.

Moving Through the Search System

The detail of how the search system works will be discussed in the next chapter. This introduction, with the diagram earlier, will serve to help you find your way around the Centaur code. The same is true when we move onto the transactional system in a moment.

The search form contains drop-down menus and check boxes populated using information from the database. If you select some of these and click on the Search Now button, you will see the results of the search appear in the left frame (if you had brochure view selected here, it will switch to a results view). What is happening is that search.asp is sending the form contents to prepareResults.asp, which is loaded into the hidden frame. This page takes the form data and carries out the searches required to find which vacations match the specified criteria. If there are none or too many, it displays a suitable message, otherwise it calls the page getSearchResults.asp, which replaces it in the hidden frame. Of course, since these pages are being put in the hidden frame, the search form remains visible on the screen in the right-hand frame.

The page getSearchResults.asp uses ASP code to get some basic information about the vacations found. This information comprises the Tour ID (which is used throughout Centaur as the means of identifying a tour) and the information needed to display the results of the search on the results page. The data is put as XML into an XML island (called Island) in the format:

```
<results>
  <result>
    <tourid>1</tourid>
    <tourOp>Panorama</tourOp>
    <name>Hotel Aziza</name>
    <area>Tunisia</area>
  </result>
</results>
```

Of course, there could be many individual result elements.

The onLoad() script checks for parser errors and passes the result to the results page (index-1.htm) for display:

```
function onLoad()
{
  Island.onreadystatechange = onLoad;
  if(Island.readyState == 4)
  {
    if (Island.parseError != 0)
      alert("getSearchResults.asp: " + Island.parseError.reason);
    parent.left.domResults = Island;
    parent.left.getResults();
  }
}
```

This code starts by ensuring that the XML is fully loaded and parsed, using techniques we have met before. It then sets a variable `domResults` in the left frame (`parent.left`) to point to the XML island and calls a function in that page. We are therefore creating XML in one frame and using it in another. This technique is often useful in frame-based applications.

Why are we passing this as XML? We are back to separating the extraction of data from the database from the display of that data. I can change the display in the relatively simple JScript function `getResults()`, rather than having to deal with the database extraction code. We will look at `getResults()` more closely in a later chapter.

Displaying Vacation Details

This is simplicity itself for us now we know about XSL. Clicking on a vacation passes the vacation ID to a page `tour.asp` that gets the full vacation details as XML then passes them to the browser with an XSL stylesheet. There is one slight complication here relating to the brochure that we will look at in a moment.

The Brochure

The pages above are all that is needed to search for a vacation and display the details. However, in Chapter 1 we mentioned an electronic brochure, and here we will look at how that works. As well as seeing how it works now, we will look at some design decisions that were made to allow later enhancements.

The brochure is held internally as an XML object, holding all the information from the vacation details. When the Add to brochure button at the bottom of the vacation details is pressed, a copy of the node is made and passed to the `addToBrochure()` function of `index-1.htm` in the left frame. We have to make a copy rather than just pass the original as a node can only have one parent, and we do not want to remove it from the page we are displaying.

The `addToBrochure()` function adds the node to the brochure object, then causes the brochure to be displayed, and the vacation `ID` to be added to an XML island called `BrochureToSave`. If you look, you will see that, although the complete vacation details are stored in the brochure, only the `ID` is used when a vacation is selected for display. Equally, only the `ID` is stored in `BrochureToSave`. The structure of this also allows a quoted price to be included, although this has not been implemented in this version of Centaur. So why keep the complete brochure internally? The reason is simply that I thought it might be useful later to have this available, and it was simple to do.

The brochure can be easily saved as a cookie, and then restored. When it is restored, the brochure is regenerated by retrieving the details of each vacation according to its `ID`. If you create a large brochure, save it, then go back to welcome page and restore it, you will see this happening. It is easier to see on a slow system!

Off-line working with the brochure

Although only the vacation `ID`s are stored, it is possible to retrieve the brochure when off-line. Depending on your cache settings and when you last accessed the pages, you may need to select File | Work Offline in IE5 to do this. Offline working is achieved by ensuring that all the needed information will be available. The vacation details themselves will be available as we only allow a vacation to be added to the brochure when it is displayed on the screen. That just leaves the page to restore the brochure. We ensure this is in the cache by using a page we know will have been accessed previously – `tour.asp`. The page `tour.asp` contains code that handles both the display of a vacation and the display of the brochure, and does one or the other depending on a flag that has been set. It is because of the need for this that the `onLoad()` function looks in a cookie (the value of which is set on the basis of whether brochure restoration is required) for a parameter to know whether it is loading the details of a single vacation or the complete brochure. This is the complication I mentioned earlier.

The Transactional System

Once a vacation is displayed in the right-hand frame, clicking on Quote me! enters the transactional system. This is a relatively simple implementation of one side of the transactions needed to provide a quotation and book and vacation. As mentioned previously, the tour operator system would normally supply the other end of the transaction, but we simulate this with an ASP page, `server.asp`. This transactional system is kept simple to expose the XML, rather than the needs of a complex transactional interface. A full commercial system would use the additional facilities offered by components such as MTS (Microsoft Transaction Server) and MSMQ (Microsoft Message Queue Server) to ensure the integrity of the message exchanges. The Wrox book "*Professional MTS and MSMQ with VB and ASP*" by Alex Homer and David Sussman (ISBN 1-861001-46-0) explains how to use these.

The Quotation System

The first page to be accessed is `quoteForm.asp`. This is a traditional HTML form page that sends the user-entered information to `quoteResults.asp`.

This page sends the request for a quotation to the tour operator system and receives the reply. The information needed for this exchange of messages is partly obtained from the form contents, and partly from the database. Some of this information is also saved as **session variables**, so it can be used by the booking form.

Session variables are a feature of ASP that allow values to be set in one page and then used in another page during the same session. They are stored in an object called the **session** object, one of which is created for each user session. In this case, we are simulating the tour operator system for both quotation and booking. Both these functions result in a price being returned to the client. For the quotation, we generate a random number for this, so we save it as a session variable and retrieve it when a booking is made to ensure that we return the same price.

The XMLHttp component we met in the last chapter is used to send and receive the messages. There are two ways we could receive our message – using either responseText or responseXML. The latter parses the response, while the former does not. However, responseXML switches off validation in the parser, which we do not want since we are dealing with systems not under our control. So instead of using responseXML, we use responseText and write the text into an XML Island so it will be parsed and validated when the page is loaded into the client. Carrying out this parsing on the client also takes some load off the server.

The display of quoteResults.asp is split into two halves, the quotation results themselves and the tour operator's terms and conditions. As with the search results and the brochure, dynamic HTML is used to switch between the two. This approach avoids loading the terms and conditions, then having to reload the quotation results.

The Booking System

The booking system is similar in structure to the quotation system. This is reflected in the very similar names of the files: bookForm.asp and bookResults.asp.

Like quoteForm.asp, bookForm.asp just creates an HTML form. In this case, the exact format of the form (such as the number of children to include) is based on the values previously sent to quoteResults.asp and saved as session variables.

bookResults.asp communicates with the tour operator server in just the same way as quoteResults.asp. However, the resulting response message, and hence the display, is more complex, so, as we shall see when we look at the code in detail, we use XSL to style the result rather than the DOM and JScript.

Summary

In this chapter, we found our way around the Centaur application. We saw:

- how the necessary information is structured in the logical data model
- how this has to change to be represented in a relational database
- how the Centaur pages fit together

Next we will look in detail at the functions and code of the interactive parts of the system.

8

The Interactive System

This chapter walks us through the parts of the application that the user interacts with. This part of the system enables the user to:

- Search for vacations that match their requirements
- View information about the vacation(s)
- Optionally save the vacation details in an electronic brochure
- Restore a previously saved electronic brochure

Take a look at the figure below:

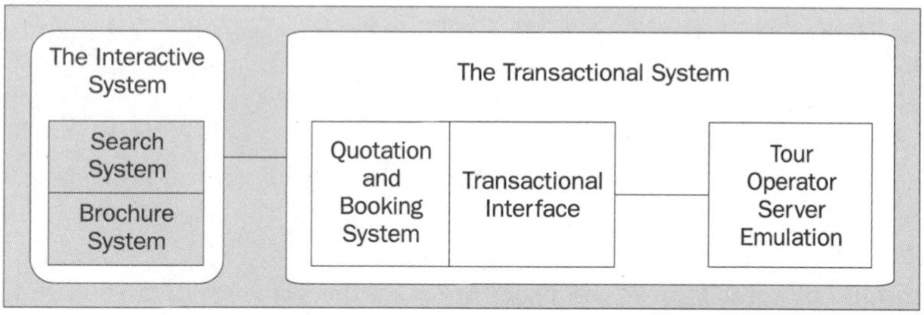

You can see that the **Interactive System** is linked to the **Transactional System**, which we'll examine in the next chapter. For the moment, just remember that the Transactional System is designed to:

- Generate price quotation information based on the user's chosen vacation
- Allow the user to book vacations with an external tour operator

In this chapter, we'll look at the Search System and the implementation of the electronic brochure in the Interactive System. Specifically, we will:

- ❑ see how the search system operates
- ❑ see how vacation details are displayed
- ❑ see how the brochure is used
- ❑ see how price information could be added to the brochure

We'll start by looking at the index-1.htm page, which appears in the left frame of the first page that appears after clicking the New Brochure button on Centaur's splash screen:

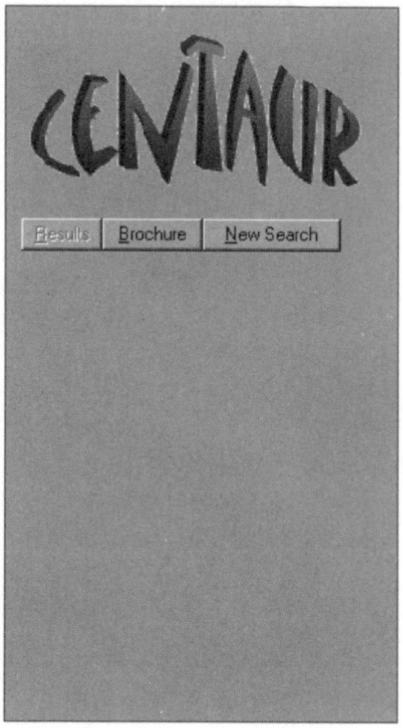

The index-l.htm Page

This page is the key to the Interactive System. It displays the search results and the brochure, and provides the buttons and links that allow the user to:

- ❑ start a new search
- ❑ display the details of a vacation from the search results or from a saved brochure
- ❑ save the brochure

Although the button to put a vacation in the brochure is on the vacation details screen, the code to perform this function is in the index-1.htm page, which is why we'll look at it here.

The functions in the index-1.htm page all run on the client, and are divided into three groups:

Group	Function
Common	`onLoad()`
	`displayBrochure()`
	`displayResults()`
Search Results	`getResults()`
	`getTour(tourId)`
Brochure	`brochureOnLoad()`
	`addToBrochure(newNode)`
	`updateBrochure()`
	`removeFromBrochure(i)`
	`addPrice(id, price)`
	`restoreBrochure()`
	`nextBrochureIndex()`

We can cover the common functions quickly. The `onLoad()` function merely calls the function `brochureOnLoad()`, which we will look at shortly. The other two functions use DHTML to switch the display between the brochure and the search results.

The next group of functions is more interesting. The function `getResults()` takes the XML supplied as the result of a search and displays it on the screen using the DOM, while `getTour()` calls a function to retrieve the details of a vacation. We will look at these when we go through the search system.

We will look at the last group of functions next, as we walk through the processes of the Interactive System. The main processes are:

- Conducting a search
- Creating and saving a brochure
- Restoring a saved brochure

Conducting a Search

When Centaur is loaded, `index-1.htm` is loaded into the left frame and `search.asp` into the right frame:

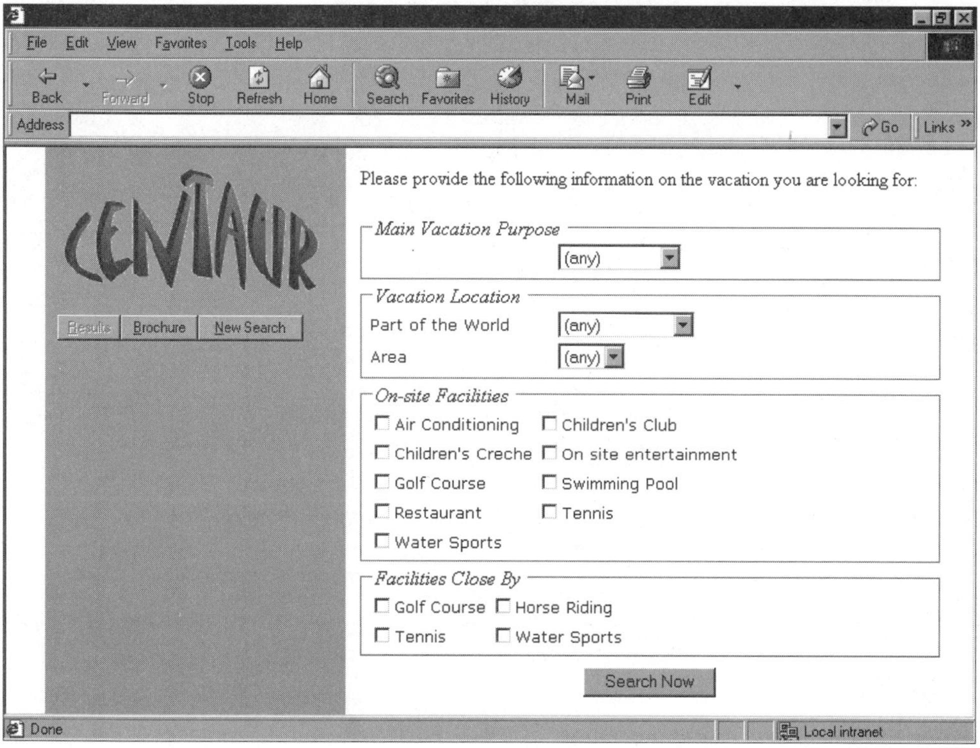

The next figure gives an overview of how this is done, and shows how the pages of the interactive system combine to perform the search and report the results:

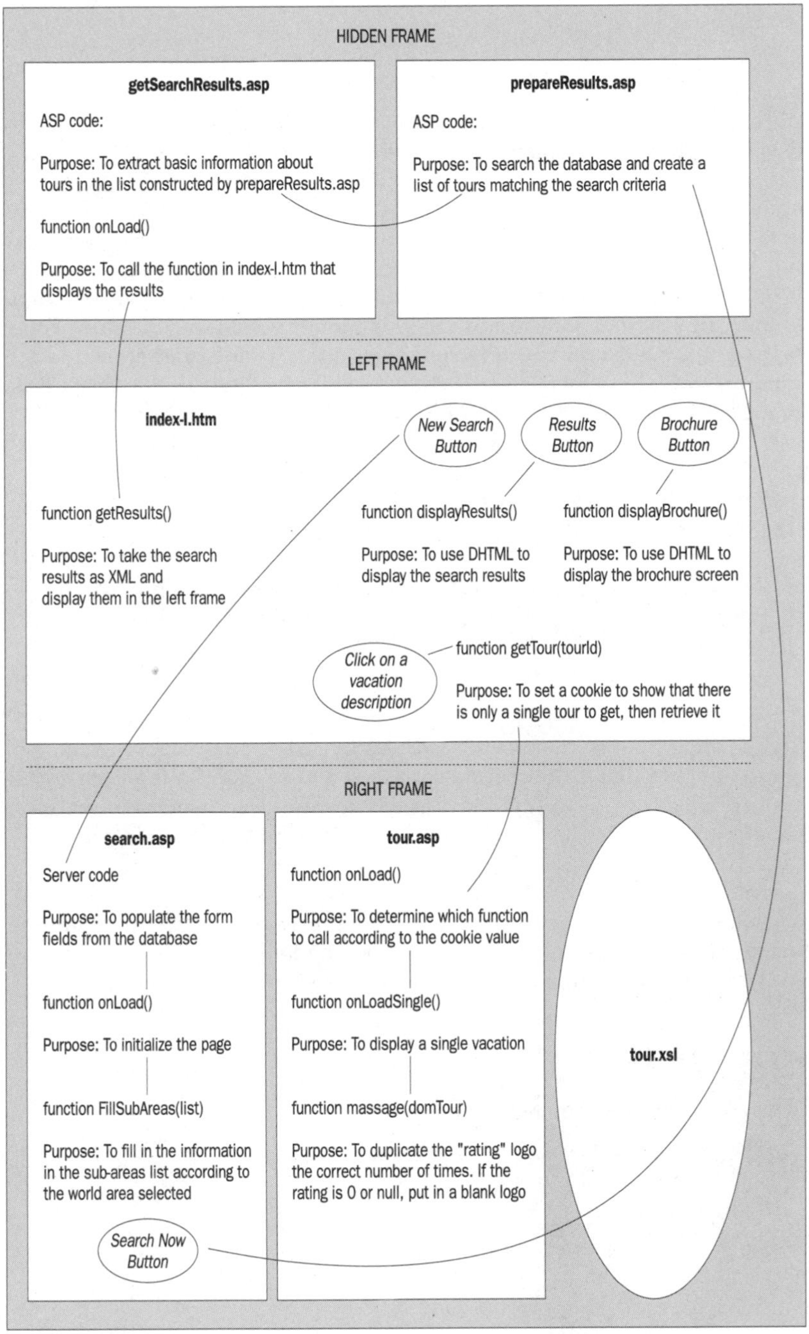
HIDDEN FRAME
getSearchResults.asp
ASP code:
Purpose: To extract basic information about tours in the list constructed by prepareResults.asp
function onLoad()
Purpose: To call the function in index-l.htm that displays the results
prepareResults.asp
ASP code:
Purpose: To search the database and create a list of tours matching the search criteria
LEFT FRAME
index-l.htm
New Search Button
Results Button
Brochure Button
function getResults()
Purpose: To take the search results as XML and display them in the left frame
function displayResults()
Purpose: To use DHTML to display the search results
function displayBrochure()
Purpose: To use DHTML to display the brochure screen
Click on a vacation description
function getTour(tourId)
Purpose: To set a cookie to show that there is only a single tour to get, then retrieve it
RIGHT FRAME
search.asp
Server code
Purpose: To populate the form fields from the database
function onLoad()
Purpose: To initialize the page
function FillSubAreas(list)
Purpose: To fill in the information in the sub-areas list according to the world area selected
Search Now Button
tour.asp
function onLoad()
Purpose: To determine which function to call according to the cookie value
function onLoadSingle()
Purpose: To display a single vacation
function massage(domTour)
Purpose: To duplicate the "rating" logo the correct number of times. If the rating is 0 or null, put in a blank logo
tour.xsl

We will now look at all of this in more detail. We'll start with the `search.asp` page.

search.asp

This page starts with a chunk of server-side code that generates the search form based on the contents of the database. This ensures that only valid options can be selected on the form.

Generating the form and drop-down lists in this way has advantages and disadvantages. The *advantage* is that maintenance is easy: if a tour operator introduces a new destination, and we load the data into the database, it will automatically appear the next time that the search form is loaded. The *disadvantage* is that it is difficult to make the search form content different from the database contents. For example, brochures tend to indicate whether a swimming pool is indoor or outdoor. I have two daughters who are keen swimmers, and if we go on vacation somewhere that is not guaranteed to be warm, we simply *must* have an indoor pool. So why not list both of these as facilities in the form? But if I do that, what happens if I'm a user that doesn't care whether the pool is indoors or out? I don't have a facility that just says "pool", so I start to need specific code to handle that. My decision in this case was just to list a pool and allow the tour operator to show in the vacation details whether it is indoors or out. The alternative approach is to hard-code all the form fields. But if I do that, I must change my HTML every time the database changes.

The search starts when the user of Centaur presses the Search Now button at the bottom of the search form. This causes the form contents to be sent to the page `prepareResults.asp`.

prepareResults.asp

This page is loaded into the hidden frame (that is, the one we defined in `main.htm` as having zero width), since it has no display content. This allows the search form to remain visible in the right frame. The purpose of `prepareResults.asp` is to find the `ids` of vacations that match the search criteria. Once it has found the matching tours, it creates a list of their `ids`, which it stores in the session variable `TourList`.

`prepareResults.asp` also has an `onLoad()` function that takes an appropriate action based on the number of tours found. If there are no tours found, or the number is so large that we do not want to send the list back to the client without a warning, a suitable message is written to the left frame; for example:

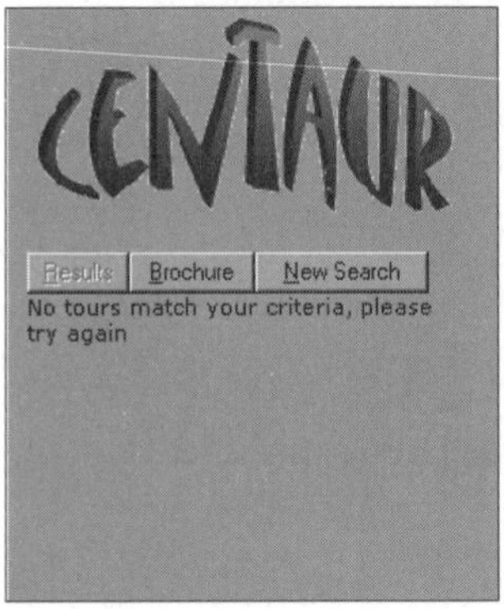

Otherwise, this page is replaced in the hidden frame by the `getSearchResults.asp` page.

Although the `prepareResults.asp` page uses no XML, you will find the full code listing for this page included in Appendix B. This page uses techniques we have covered already to access the database, but it also has some useful techniques for conducting searches using multiple criteria in several stages. However, since it uses no XML, it is time to move on ...

getSearchResults.asp

This page's aim is to get specified information from the database based on a list of tour `ids` and convert the information to XML. In many ways, the server-side code on this page is similar to the `quoteResults.asp` and `bookResults.asp` pages, which we'll look at in detail in the next chapter.

The server-side code puts its results into an XML island for client code to handle. In this case, the XML will contain the information we want to display in the search results. This will consist of information about the tours that match the user-defined search criteria:

```
<results>
  <result>
    <tourid>1</tourid>
    <tourOp>Panorama</tourOp>
    <name>Hotel Aziza</name>
    <area>Tunisia</area>
  </result>
    .
    more results
    .
</results>
```

When the page loads in the client, the `onLoad()` function sets the `resultsDOM` in the `index-1.htm` page to point to this data, parses the XML, and calls the `getResults()` function in the left frame to display the list.

The code to do this is:

```
<XML Id="Island">
<?xml version="1.0"?>
<%=mstrXML%>
</XML>

<Script Language = "JScript">

function onLoad()
// Purpose: to call the function in index-1.htm that displays the results
{
  if(Island.readyState != "complete")
    window.setTimeout('onLoad();',200);
  else
  {
    if (Island.parseError != 0)
      alert("getSearchResults.asp: " + Island.parseError.reason);
    parent.left.domResults = Island;
    parent.left.getResults();
  }
}
```

As you can see, since the XML is in an island, we are using the `readyState` property of the XML document to ensure that the XML has fully loaded before we process it.

index-l.htm

As I said before, `index-1.htm` is the main controlling page for the interactive system, so our processing returns there once we have a list of matching vacations.

First we display the results with the `getResults()` function.

getResults()

Based on vacations that match our search criteria, this function displays a summary of the results in the left-hand frame:

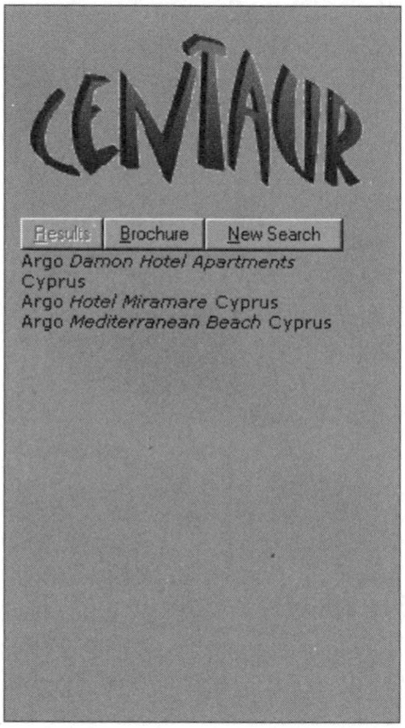

Here's the code for this part of the process:

```
function getResults()

{
  var s='';
  var i,currentNode;
  var resultsRoot,tempId,tempTourOp,tempName,tempArea;

  // show results screen and load root of the results DOM
  displayResults();
  resultsRoot = resultsDOM.documentElement;

  // build the results string
  for (i = 0 ; i < resultsRoot.childNodes.length ; i++)
  {
    currentNode = resultsRoot.childNodes.item(i);
    tempId = "'" + currentNode.getElementsByTagName('tourid').item(0).text + "'";
    tempTourOp = currentNode.getElementsByTagName('tourOp').item(0).text;
    tempName = currentNode.getElementsByTagName('name').item(0).text;
    tempArea = currentNode.getElementsByTagName('area').item(0).text;
```

```
        s += '<A style="cursor: hand" onclick="getTour(' + tempId + ')">';
        s += tempTourOp + ' <EM>' + tempName + '</EM> ' + tempArea + '</A><BR/>';
    }
//  alert(s);
    tgtResults.innerHTML = s;
}
```

This uses the document object model to produce the HTML to display. Once we know the number of vacations found,

```
for (i = 0 ; i < resultsRoot.childNodes.length ; i++)
```

we loop through them building up the string `s`, which encodes the HTML we want to display. We start by finding the current node:

```
        currentNode = resultsRoot.childNodes.item(i);
```

Next, we grab the text we want to extract for display:

```
        tempId = "'" + currentNode.getElementsByTagName('tourid').item(0).text + "'";
        tempTourOp = currentNode.getElementsByTagName('tourOp').item(0).text;
        tempName = currentNode.getElementsByTagName('name').item(0).text;
        tempArea = currentNode.getElementsByTagName('area').item(0).text;
```

Once we have this, we can add it to the string with a suitable display style and an `onclick` event handler:

```
        s += '<A style="cursor: hand" onclick="getTour(' + tempId + ')">';
        s += tempTourOp + ' <EM>' + tempName + '</EM> ' + tempArea + '</A><BR/>';
```

We could easily add more to the style, perhaps an `onMouseOver` event handler to change the color of the text of the vacation under the mouse cursor.

The next line, `alert(s);`, is for debugging and is commented out. After that, we simply use DHTML to write the string to a placeholder on the page.

Next, we need to let the user click on the vacation whose details they want to examine. This task is the responsibility of the `getTour()` function.

getTour()

When a vacation is selected for display from the search results, the `onclick` event invokes this event handler. It only contains two lines of code:

```
    document.cookie = "type=single";
    parent.right.location.href='tour.asp?tourid=' + tourId;
```

The first line sets a cookie for the `tour.asp` page to read. The second causes that page to replace the search form in the right frame. Let's see what the `tour.asp` page does for us.

tour.asp

One function of this page is to display the details of a vacation when it is selected from either the search results, or from the brochure. To do this, it creates an XML document from the information in the database and renders it using XSL.

This page also has another function. It extracts the vacation information from the database and recreates the brochure, based on the limited reference information stored when the brochure was saved after an earlier search. This additional function is the raison d'etre for the cookie we use in this application. When the cookie has a `type` of `single`, we are retrieving and displaying a single vacation. We will see how this works in detail later.

We have already met the format of the XML file we will be producing when we looked at rendering XML with XSL way back in chapter 5.

`tour.asp` is one of the largest pages in the system as there is so much XML to generate. However, we have already seen the techniques used to extract information from the database into an XML file, so we will not discuss them further here.

We have also already seen how the resulting XML is displayed using XSL. Although the stylesheet has changed slightly (to give the appearance I wanted), the techniques are exactly the same as we've already described. These techniques include the `massageRating()` function, which duplicates the `ratingURL` element the correct number of times so that the stylesheet displays the right number of stars or other rating symbol, according to the value of the `rating` element.

This completes the search system. At this stage, we have a screen with the search results on the left and the details of a specific vacation on the right:

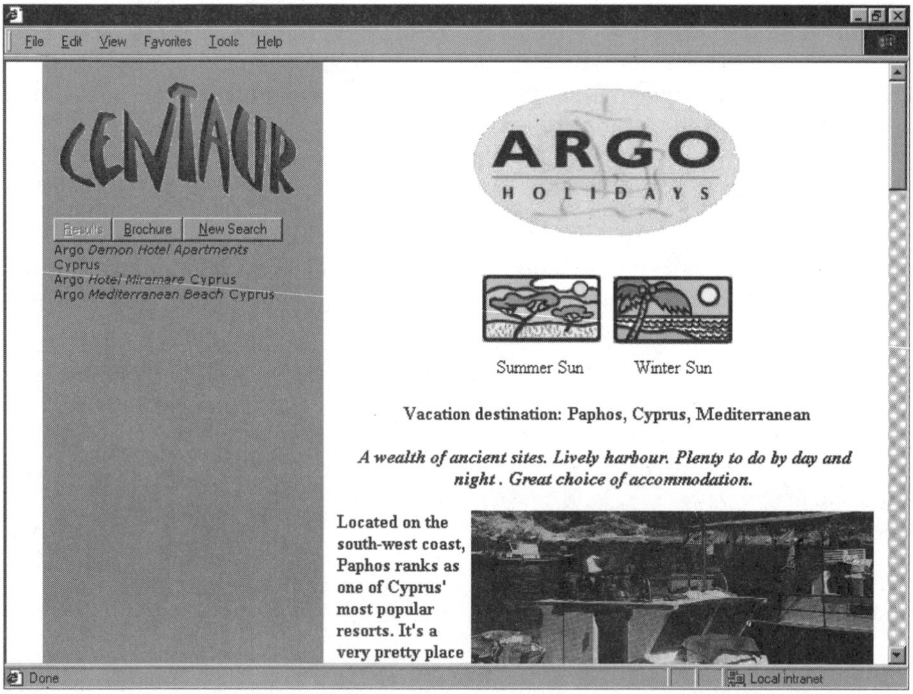

We can now go straight into the transactional system by pressing Quote Me!, but first we'll look at how we build our own customized electronic brochure, which we start doing by pressing the button Add to Brochure at the bottom of the vacation details screen.

The Brochure System

At its simplest level, the brochure reference that we store (which lets us restore our vacation details later) could simply be a list of the `id`s of the vacations. However, there are reasons for making it more complex than this.

Design of the Brochure

What are the main purposes of the brochure?

- First, to allow us to conduct multiple searches and make a collection of the vacations found – storing the `id`s would be ideal for this.
- Second, we want to be able to browse the brochure off-line. The off-line facilities of IE5 are good, and storing just the `id`s will give us the ability to browse off-line. This is because Centaur stores all the relevant information in the browser cache at this point.
- Third, once we have obtained a price quotation, perhaps it would be useful to save this in the brochure as well. We could either save just the price or also the number of travelers and the date of departure.
- At the beginning of the book, I suggested that supermarkets could set up "vacation cafes" where people can browse through vacations over a cup of coffee. While the supermarket operators would undoubtedly prefer it if people made a booking on the spot, most families go on vacation together but don't shop together, so getting an immediate decision may be impossible. In these circumstances, they could provide the facility to create a copy of the brochure (CD, diskette, or paper) that the user could take home and browse at leisure with the rest of their family. What would we needed to facilitate this? Clearly, we'd need the full XML description of the vacation and the associated images, plus some of the Centaur pages to view them. In this case, the brochure would need to store all this information (or retrieve it at the time the CD-ROM is created).

Taking these possibilities into account, we compromise in Centaur. During a session we keep a brochure as an XML object containing the full XML description of each vacation. However, when we display a vacation from the brochure, we just use the vacation `id` so that we can use the same function as we do to display a vacation from the search results. The brochure is saved to disk as a list of `id`s (in XML) with the potential to add prices if a quotation has been made, but the price is not used again in the display. When the option to restore the brochure is made on the 'Welcome' page, each vacation is retrieved from the database to repopulate the full brochure object.

Using the Brochure

When Centaur is started, a new brochure is created as an XML DOM object within `index-1.htm`:

```
function brochureOnLoad()
{
  var brochureDOM;
```

```
    // this loads a blank XML model so the parser understands the structure
    brochureDOM = new ActiveXObject("Microsoft.XMLDOM");
    brochureDOM.async = false;
    brochureDOM.load("tourStructure.xml");

    if (brochureDOM.parseError != 0)
      alert("index-1.htm brochureOnLoad(): " + brochureDOM.parseError.reason);

    brochureRoot = brochureDOM.documentElement;

    // restore the brochure if selected

    if(document.cookie.indexOf("restore=true") != -1)
      restoreBrochure();
  }
```

This not only creates the object, but also loads some XML into it. We have to do this because we need a basic brochure structure predefined for later, when we add items to a specific brochure.

The next thing we do is add a vacation to the brochure. This happens when we click the Add to Brochure button at the bottom of the vacation details screen:

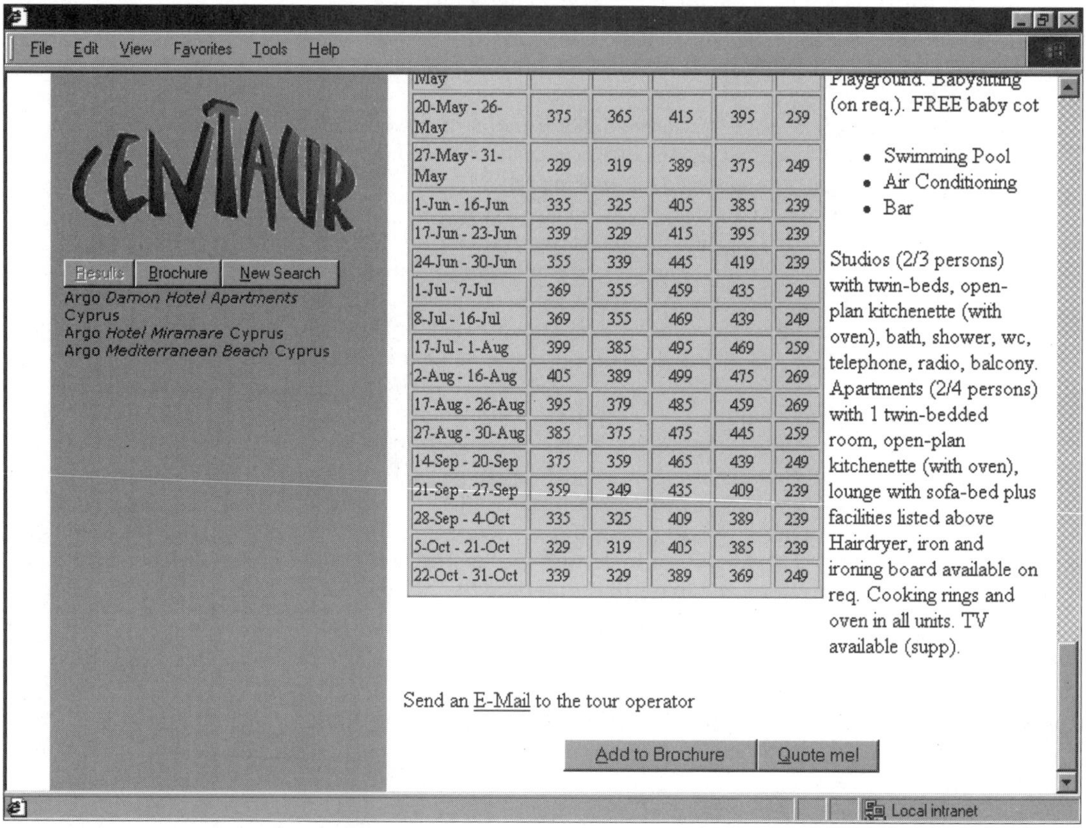

Within `tour.asp`, we make a copy of the vacation description that we have already extracted from the database, and pass this to `index-1.htm` to deal with, since the brochure is stored via `index-1.htm`. As we have seen before, we have to make a copy, because a node can only have one parent, and we *don't* want to delete the node from the vacation display. Since there is no other indication that we have added the vacation to the brochure, we also write a message to the browser status bar:

```
function addToBrochure()
{
  var newNode = root.cloneNode(true);
  parent.left.addToBrochure(newNode);
  window.status = 'This vacation has been added to your brochure. Click the
"Brochure" button to view the brochure';
}
```

For those who find the status bar too subtle, it would be easy to change this to an alert message.

Within `index-1.htm`, we find the `tour` element of the XML object (since we already have the `tours` root node in the brochure) and add it to the brochure. We then call another function to update the display of the brochure:

```
function addToBrochure(newNode)
{
  brochureRoot.appendChild(newNode.childNodes.item(0));
  updateBrochure();
}
```

Updating the brochure display is very similar to updating the search results display as we did earlier. The difference is that we also create a version of the brochure with just the tour `id` (and potentially a quoted price if that has been added to the brochure) – this means that we can save it later. The alternative to this would be to create this abbreviated form of the brochure *only* when we save it. We do it here simply because it is easier to code, although this means that this version of the brochure is created every time a new item is added.

This is the complete `updateBrochure()` function:

```
function updateBrochure()
{
  var i,currentNode;
  var tempId,quotedId,tempTourOp,tempName,tempArea,tempPrice;
  var s="<TABLE>";
  strBrochure = "<brochure>";

  for (var i = 1 ; i < rootBrochure.childNodes.length ; i++)
  // base is 1 to ignore the reference item
  {
    // get the variables we will be using
    currentNode = rootBrochure.childNodes.item(i);

    tempNode = currentNode.getElementsByTagName('touroperator').item(0);
    tempTourOp = tempNode.getElementsByTagName('name').item(0).text;
```

```
    tempNode = currentNode.getElementsByTagName('vacation').item(0);
    tempId = tempNode.getElementsByTagName('id').item(0).text;
    quotedId = "'" + tempId + "'";
    tempName = tempNode.getElementsByTagName('name').item(0).text;

    tempPrice =
    tempNode.getElementsByTagName('price').item(0).getAttribute('price');
    tempNode = currentNode.getElementsByTagName('resort').item(0);
    tempArea = currentNode.getElementsByTagName('area').item(0).text;

    // put them into a table
    s += '<TR><TD><A style="cursor:hand" onclick="getTour(' + quotedId + ')">';
    s += tempTourOp + ' <EM>' + tempName + '</EM> ' + tempArea + '</A></TD>';

    // add the trashcan for deleting items
    s += '<TD><IMG style="cursor: hand" src="Logos/bin.gif" width="32" height="32"
       onClick = "removeFromBrochure(' + i + ') "></TD></TR>';

    // put some variables into an abbreviated copy of the brochure to be saved to
    // a cookie
    strBrochure += "<h r='" + tempId + "'>" + tempPrice + "</h>";
  }
  s += "</TABLE>"
  tgtBrochure.innerHTML = s;

  strBrochure += "</brochure>";
}
```

Once a vacation is in the brochure, it can be viewed by clicking on it in the brochure display. Because we have saved it in the same format that we extracted it in from the database, we use the same function as we did earlier, when we viewed a vacation from the search results screen.

Removing an item from the brochure is just as easy. When we display the brochure, we add an image of a trash can. This image has an `onClick` event:

```
s += '<TD><IMG style="cursor: hand" src="Logos/bin.gif" width="32" height="32"
   onClick = "removeFromBrochure(' + i + ') "></TD></TR>';
```

Since this includes the position of the element in the brochure, removing the item is just a two line effort:

```
function removeFromBrochure(i)
{
  brochureRoot.removeChild(brochureRoot.childNodes.item(i));
  updateBrochure();
}
```

Saving the Brochure

We saw earlier that when we display the brochure, we also create a version suitable for saving. Here is the code within `updateBrochure()` that does this:

```
function updateBrochure()
{
  strBrochure = "<brochure>";
```

```
    for (var i = 1 ; i < brochureRoot.childNodes.length ; i++)
    {
      // code in here gets the information for the brochure

      strBrochure += "<h r='" + tempId + "'>" + tempPrice + "</h>";
    }
    strBrochure += "</brochure>";
  }
```

Much of the code in `updateBrochre()` has been omitted from this code snippet. The omitted code, among other tasks, sets the variables `tempID` and `tempPrice` to values extracted from the tour description in the XML that forms the brochure. Let's just look quickly at the line above that adds an entry to the brochure that will be saved:

```
  strBrochure += "<h r='" + tempId + "'>" + tempPrice + "</h>";
```

Firstly, the tag name and attribute name are unusually short. This is because we will be saving the brochure as a cookie, and cookies have a maximum length of 4k bytes. Each tour is held within an `h` element, with an attribute `r` that gives the tour `id`. The price is also included. We will discuss the pricing in the brochure later.

When the user presses the button to save the brochure, a simple function is called to save the XML string as a cookie, with a one-month expiry.

Of course, we could have saved the brochure as a text string rather than as XML. Let's compare examples of the strings saved for each vacation in the two cases:

xml: `<h r="1">2214</h>`

string: `1.2214:`

The former is 17 characters, the latter is 7. With XML, we could therefore store around 240 vacations (fewer once we have left space for the root element and longer `id`s). Using a text string, we could store 585. I regard a couple of hundred vacations as more than enough for our purposes and so have stuck to XML (after all, this is a case study in XML).

Having given the user the facility to save the brochure, we have to think next about how to let them restore it subsequently.

Restoring the Brochure

Once the brochure has been saved, we need to restore it if we want to view it again at our leisure. We have already seen that selecting the option from the 'Welcome' page sets a cookie, which lets `index-1.htm` know that the brochure is to be restored.

To make this happen, we are going to load `tour.asp` once for each brochure entry. Remember that we use the same page that we did for displaying the tour, so we know it will be in cache if we choose to restore the brochure while working off-line. The alternative to this is to use a separate page and load it into the hidden frame even if it is not used: this means that it will be in cache when it is needed.

First, we get the information from the cookie using JScript's string functions:

```
function restoreBrochure()
{
  cookies = document.cookie;
  pos = cookies.indexOf("Brochure=");
  if (pos != -1)
  {
    start = pos + 9;
    end = cookies.indexOf(";",start)
    if (end == -1)
      end = cookies.length;
    value = unescape(cookies.substring(start,end));
```

Note that if no brochure has been saved, the variable `pos` will be equal to `-1`: there is an `else` clause later in the code to cater for this and displays an error message.

Now that we have the cookie as a string, we can create a new XML object, load it with the brochure information, and find the root element:

```
    savedBrochureDOM = new ActiveXObject("Microsoft.XMLDOM");
    savedBrochureDOM.async = false;
    savedBrochureDOM.loadXML(value);

    if (savedBrochureDOM.parseError != 0)
      alert("index-1.htm restoreBrochure(): " +
      savedBrochureDOM.parseError.reason);

    savedBrochureRoot = savedBrochureDOM.documentElement;
```

Then we set a couple of variables we will need:

```
    brochureIndex = 0;
    numberInBrochure = savedBrochureRoot.childNodes.length;
```

Next, we get the first tour `id`, and hand control over to `tour.asp`:

```
if(brochureIndex < numberInBrochure)
    {
      tempId =
      savedBrochureRoot.childNodes.item(brochureIndex).attributes.item(0).text;

      // get the page
      document.cookie = "type=multi";
      parent.right.location.href='tour.asp?tourid=' + tempId;
    }
```

When `tour.asp` loads, it will get the details of the vacation, then call the function `nextBrochureIndex()` in `index-1.htm`. This simply gets the next index and reloads `tour.asp`. This continues until the brochure is completely loaded, at which point `nextBrochureIndex()` loads the search form. This ping-pong approach ensures that `tour.asp` has not only loaded, but has completed its processing before it is loaded again for the next page. Since restoring the brochure could take a little while, `tour.asp` keeps the user informed with a count of the pages loaded.

The Brochure and the Vacation Price

We have mentioned that since we are getting price quotations for vacations, it might be useful to store these in the brochure. Although this is not implemented in the demonstration system, hooks have been put in to simplify implementing this feature in the future.

To implement this feature, our first task would be to save the price in the brochure when a quotation is made. This would be done by the `newState()` function of `quoteResults.asp`. If the vacation was not already in the brochure, this function could either not put the price in, or it could trigger the process that adds the vacation to the brochure. There is an empty `price` element in the vacation description for this purpose, so the price would be added to this.

We could then alter `renderTour.xsl` so that the price is displayed (the functions to save and restore the brochure are already implemented). This would just store the price itself, since most people will get all their quotations for the same number of adults, children and infants. It would be possible to save more information, but you must always be aware of the limitations of cookie size.

Summary

In this chapter, we have looked at the search system and the handling of the brochure. Although you have not learnt any new techniques, you have seen how they are put to use within this part of the Centaur. We saw that the user can:

- Specify criteria for a vacation search
- View the results of this search and save them in a brochure
- Restore saved brochures for viewing

We also looked in detail at how the pages of the Interactive System implement these functions.

In the next chapter, we'll examine the processing that occurs *outside* of the Interactive System once the user has specified the criteria for their search, hit the Search Now button, and browsed through the search results. We'll see how the Interactive System communicates with the Transactional System to generate price quotations, and how the user can book their vacation with external tour operators.

9

The Transactional System

We now have a good idea of how to use XML, we know how the user interacts with Centaur, and we've seen many of the techniques used in the system. In this final chapter, we'll start to look at the XML-related aspects of the code in detail. All the code is available for download: just follow the Source Code links for this book at `www.wrox.com`.

Specifically, we'll look at the interface between Centaur and the tour operators' own systems. In the demonstration system – for simplicity – the remote systems are emulated with an Active Server Page located on the same server as the rest of the system.

Take a look at this figure:

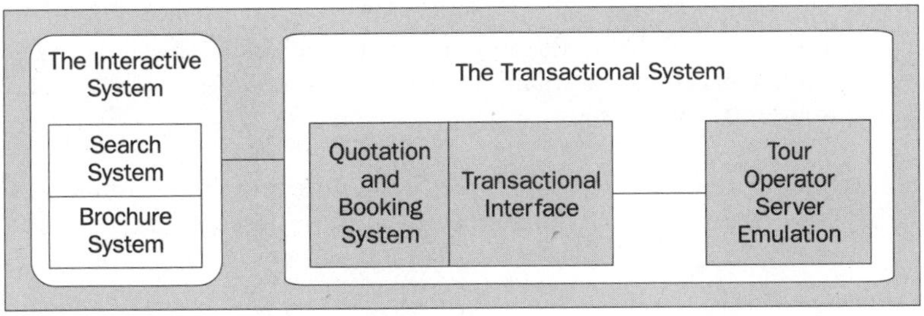

In this diagram of Centaur, we can see that the transactional system is closely associated with the Quotation and Booking System. It acts as the intermediary between this system and the code that emulates the tour operator system (which feeds Centaur with vacation data). Here, we'll look at all three aspects – Quotation and Booking, The Transactional Interface, and the Emulation.

Since we are emulating an interface where, because we don't own it, we have no control over the remote end, we will need better error checking than we have used elsewhere in the application, and we'll be using a DTD as one mechanism to achieve this.

We won't be using the transactional and message queuing facilities available in Microsoft's MTS and MSMQ products. We discussed this and gave references for more information earlier.

Here's a summary of what we'll cover in this chapter:

- the message types we will need
- the data needed in these messages
- the DTD to validate the messages
- the code within the quotation and booking pages in Centaur
- the code that provides the tour operator system emulation

We'll approach this material by considering it from the point of view of building our DTD. This will allow us to put the different parts of the application into the overall XML context. We'll begin by looking at the parts of the DTD that cater for the Quotation and Booking system.

Defining the DTD

We are only implementing five messages in our demonstration system:

- quotation request
- quotation response
- booking request
- booking response
- error response

The Messages

We will be generating a DTD called `centaur.dtd` to validate these messages. We can start by looking at the specific information that needs to be included in each message. For example, to get a quotation, we need to tell the tour operator the following: the vacation we are taking; when we are going, how long for, and how many adults, children and infants will be in the party. We will also identify the supplier as it is possible that a company trading under several names will use a single system (and hence a single URI) for all of them.

Extrapolating the same principles to the other messages, we can decide the information that needs to be included for each. The information for the four most important messages is:

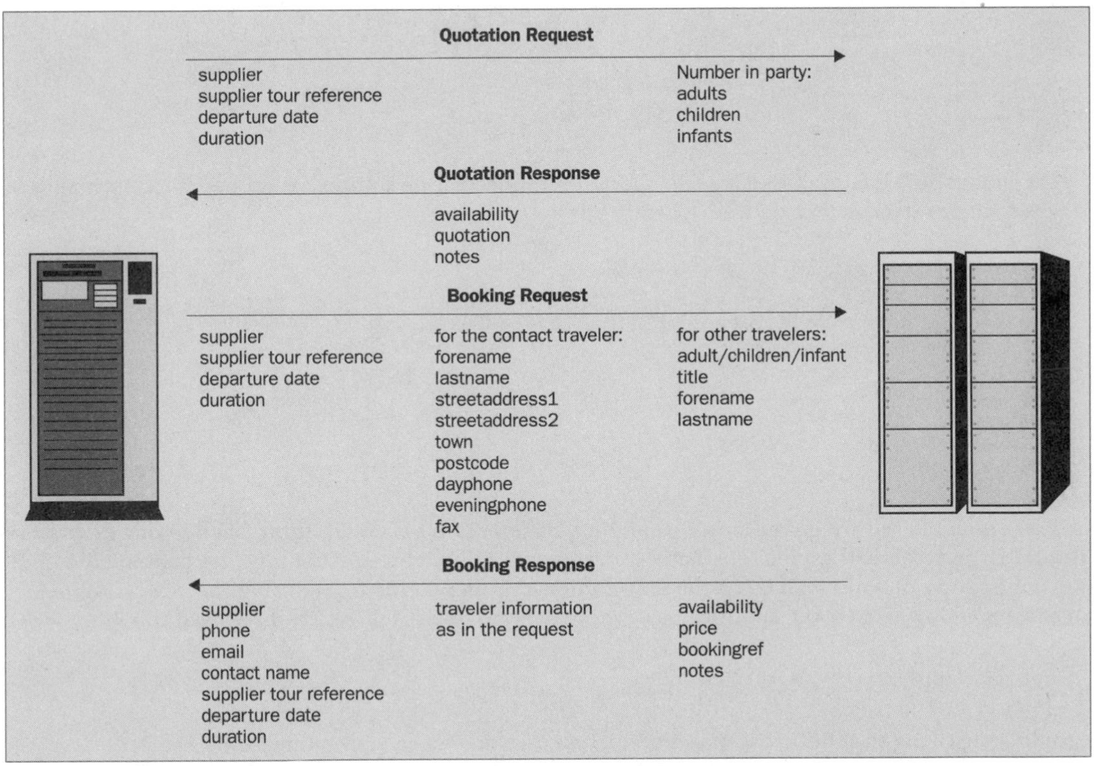

These messages, and the data that they carry, are the couriers for the Quotation and Booking system. Later, we will also add an error response for the situation where the tour operator system detects an error.

DTD Usage Issues

The use of XML for messages is relatively new, so it is inevitable that settled conventions have not yet been established. One of these conventions would cover how the DTD should be used and, specifically, whether there should be one DTD for the *complete message* set, or one per message *type*. The single DTD approach has the benefit of only having a single document to maintain, while the second approach means additional messages can be added by adding DTDs, rather than by having to modify a single DTD. This can ease version control.

In Centaur, we will use a single DTD for all our messages. It would be easy to divide this into one per message type if we decided to do that at a later date.

Now let's look at how we'll define each message in this DTD.

The Quotation Request Message

We will start all our messages with the root element `centaur`, so we define this as the `DOCTYPE` in the DTD. Each message will follow this element with its own message type. So an outline of the quotation request would be:

```
<centaur>
  <quoterequest>
    our data goes in here
  </quoterequest>
</centaur>
```

So what should our data look like for the quotation request? One option would be to use start and end tags with our data as text between them:

```
<supplier>supplier</supplier>
<ref>supplier's reference</ref>
<depdate>departure date</depdate>
<duration>duration</duration>
<travelers>
  <adults>integer</adults>
  <children>integer</children>
  <infants>integer</infants>
</travelers>
```

This looks OK, but we are going to use something different. Why? Well, think back to our discussion of the DTD, and you will remember that we can specify quite a lot of what must be contained within a tag, but nothing of what *must* be in the text node within the element. So, using the XML fragment above, we couldn't restrict the supplier names that are provided. However, if we used the line:

```
<qttour supplier="" />
```

we could restrict the suppliers that could be included in messages with a line in the DTD:

```
<!ATTLIST qttour supplier (Panorama | Argo)>
```

In practice, this might be thought rather restrictive, and would mean that we would need to rebuild the DTD every time we add a supplier. However, there will be other places in the messages where we want to check the contents of the message with a DTD.

So we will be coding our quotation request as:

```
<qttour supplier="" ref="" depdate="" duration="" />
<qttravelers adults="" children="" infants="" />
```

All the information required for a quotation (which we showed in the figure above) is included in this. Each element name is prefixed with `qt` to identify this as a **quotation transmitted** message. The **received** message elements will be prefixed with `qr` and the booking messages similarly with `bt` and `br`. There is one exception to this – in the booking message we will see that the `travelers` element is the same whether being transmitted or received, so we use the prefix `bb` to identify it as being for **both**. If we were to use a DTD per message, these prefixes would be unnecessary.

At this point, we have made two decisions that could have had different outcomes. The first was to use one DTD for the whole of the Centaur messaging, rather than one per message. Because of this, we have had to ensure that elements have different names in different messages if their content is different. That is the reason for the prefixes. This also means that adding a new message means revising this DTD rather than just adding another. Had we had one DTD per message, we would have had more DTDs to maintain, but each would have complete control over its message names.

The second decision we made was to put our data in attributes rather than as `Text` nodes within elements. This gives us shorter messages (which we have never said is an issue in Centaur) and better error checking.

We now have our complete quotation request message structure:

```
<centaur>
  <quoterequest>
    <qttour supplier="" ref="" depdate="" duration="" />
    <qttravelers adults="" children="" infants="" />
  </quoterequest>
</centaur>
```

Now, let's briefly consider the other message types.

The Quotation Response, Booking Request and Booking Response Messages

These messages are similar in style to the quotation request. To ensure that a booking is only made once for a given quotation, a simple transactional control is added. This control is embedded in the Quotation response message, which includes a sequence number set by the tour operator system, which will not be allowed to repeat for a period that is longer than the likely duration of a user session. This sequence number is returned in the booking request, ensuring that two bookings made from the same quotation will have identical sequence numbers, allowing the tour operator system to take appropriate action. Bookings made from different quotations will have different sequence numbers.

The Error Message

We also need a fifth message type, to cater for processing errors at the tour operator end of the system. For example, what happens if the tour operator system encounters an error? Perhaps there is a front-end HTTP server to handle the interface to Centaur and it detects that the main tour operator system has failed, or it identifies two bookings have the same sequence number. Let's add another message type to cover these circumstances:

```
<centaur>
  <error></error>
</centaur>
```

In this case, the error message can just be a string placed in the `error` element as a `Text` node.

Starting the DTD

We are now in a good position to start developing the DTD with which we will check the messages. We have identified five message types:

```
<!ELEMENT centaur (quoterequest | quoteresponse | bookrequest | bookresponse |
error)>
```

The first of these is the quotation request, which contains the elements `qttour` and `qttravelers` in that order:

```
<!ELEMENT quoterequest (qttour, qttravelers)>
```

Each of these is an empty element, but contains a set of attributes. We will insist that all the attributes are present for the `qttour` element since we require them all if we're to give a valid quote. However, the minimum number of travelers will be one adult, so we will not insist on including any children or infants (although in practice in the application, we do include these and set the value to zero for those lucky enough to go on vacation with no children or infants). If Centaur were to handle scheduled flights, rather than packaged vacations, we would not insist on any adult travelers, as children might well be traveling alone.

Here is the code for the `quoterequest` element:

```
<!ELEMENT qttour EMPTY>
<!ATTLIST qttour
     supplier          CDATA #REQUIRED
     ref               CDATA #REQUIRED
     depdate           CDATA #REQUIRED
     duration          CDATA #REQUIRED
>
<!ELEMENT qttravelers EMPTY>
<!ATTLIST qttravelers
     adults            CDATA #REQUIRED
     children          CDATA #IMPLIED
     infants           CDATA #IMPLIED
>
```

And that is all we have to do for this element.

The Complete DTD

The other elements are handled in similar ways.

The quoteresponse Element

The quotation response requires its own `seq` attribute to allow sequence numbering, and one more element (`qrdetails`), which has three attributes:

```
<!ELEMENT quoteresponse (qrdetails)>
<!ATTLIST quoteresponse
     seq               CDATA          #REQUIRED
>
<!ELEMENT qrdetails EMPTY>
<!ATTLIST qrdetails
     availability      (true|false)   #REQUIRED
     quote             CDATA          #REQUIRED
     notes             CDATA          #IMPLIED
>
```

The first attribute of the `qrdetails` element is the `availability`, which we will restrict to a value of `true` or `false`. The second is the price (`quote`) that the tour operator is quoting and the third allows the tour operator to optionally add some text notes to be displayed to the user.

The bookrequest Element

Here is the definition of the booking request element:

```
<!ELEMENT bookrequest (bttour,bbtravelers)>
<!ATTLIST bookrequest
     seq                CDATA #REQUIRED
>
<!ELEMENT bttour EMPTY>
<!ATTLIST bttour
     supplier           CDATA #REQUIRED
     tourref            CDATA #REQUIRED
     depdate            CDATA #REQUIRED
     duration           CDATA #REQUIRED
>
<!-- element "bbtravelers" uses the same content model for request and response --
>
<!ELEMENT bbtravelers (adult+ , child* , infant*)>
<!ELEMENT adult EMPTY>
<!ATTLIST adult
     type               (contact|normal)        #IMPLIED
     title              CDATA #REQUIRED
     forename           CDATA #REQUIRED
     lastname           CDATA #REQUIRED
     streetaddress1     CDATA #IMPLIED
     streetaddress2     CDATA #IMPLIED
     town               CDATA #IMPLIED
     postcode           CDATA #IMPLIED
     dayphone           CDATA #IMPLIED
     eveningphone       CDATA #IMPLIED
     fax                CDATA #IMPLIED
>
<!ELEMENT child EMPTY>
<!ATTLIST child
     title              CDATA #REQUIRED
     forename           CDATA #REQUIRED
     lastname           CDATA #REQUIRED
>
<!ELEMENT infant EMPTY>
<!ATTLIST infant
     title              CDATA #REQUIRED
     forename           CDATA #REQUIRED
     lastname           CDATA #REQUIRED
>
```

Again, we have the `seq` attribute to enable sequence numbering. We have allowed two `type`s of adult – the `contact` traveler, and `normal` travelers. The contact traveler is the one the tour operator will contact for queries and with travel documents. The address and other contact details are only required for this type of traveler, and so are marked as `#IMPLIED`. We could have been more rigorous here and defined the contact traveler as a separate element, thus allowing us to make all the contact details `#REQUIRED`. We also have the type itself as `#IMPLIED`, although you might think it better to use the enumerated form:

```
     type               (contact|normal)        "normal"
```

This would indicate that if the attribute is absent, it should be taken to be `normal`. However, we will be rendering the information from the booking response using XSL. If we use the enumerated form, we would have to use a test in the stylesheet that did not work in the late beta of IE5 that I was using during development.

This test would be:

```
<xsl:apply-templates select='bbtravelers/adult[not(@type="contact")]' />
```

Instead, I found I had to use:

```
    <xsl:apply-templates select='bbtravelers/adult[not(@type)]' />
```

This merely identifies the presence of the attribute `type`, *not* its value. In the stylesheet, we therefore assume that all travelers without the `type` attribute are `normal` travelers. Using the DTD to put this attribute in by default would therefore stop this part of the stylesheet working.

There is an alternative. We could automatically assume that the first adult is the `contact` traveler. In many ways, I prefer this to the rather risky fix I have used, but I have stuck with my solution on the basis that the XSL support of IE5 should improve so I can put the correct test in later.

The bookresponse Element

The booking response uses the same `bbtravelers` element as the request, so we only have two new elements to declare here:

```
<!ELEMENT bookresponse (brtour,bbtravelers,brdetails)>
<!ELEMENT brtour EMPTY>
<!ATTLIST brtour
     supplier          CDATA #REQUIRED
     phone             CDATA #REQUIRED
     email             CDATA #IMPLIED
     contact           CDATA #IMPLIED
     tourref           CDATA #REQUIRED
     depdate           CDATA #REQUIRED
     duration          CDATA #REQUIRED
>

<!ELEMENT brdetails EMPTY>
<!ATTLIST brdetails
     availability      CDATA #REQUIRED
     price             CDATA #REQUIRED
     bookingref        CDATA #REQUIRED
     notes             CDATA #IMPLIED
>
```

We have left the email address and contact name as optional, although we might think that anyone taking bookings over the Internet should be able to receive and reply to emails. The contact name is optional in case the operator is using a call center and does not want individual staff identified with a booking.

The error Element

This, the simplest of all the elements completes our DTD:

```
<!ELEMENT error        (#PCDATA)>
```

Having defined the messages that we'll be using to transfer data between the server and the tour operator, let's move on to the parts of the system that let the user interact with the Booking and Quotation system.

The Results Pages

There are two very similar pages that handle the quotation and booking messaging. These are called `quoteResults.asp` and `bookResults.asp`. The names `xxxResults` indicate that, by the time these are rendered on the client, the messaging has already been handled by the server-side code.

The following screenshot shows the screen displayed to the user once their quotation request has been processed:

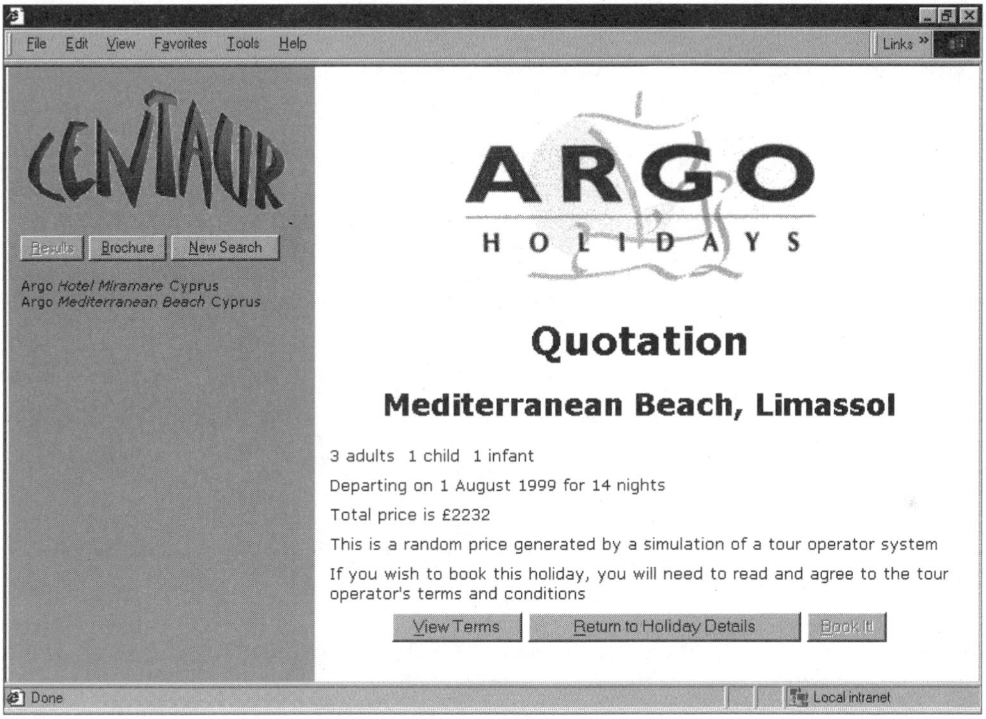

So, how do we get the user to the point where they can examine this screen? Let's look at the pages that let us return the quotation to the user. The first of these is `quoteResults.asp`.

quoteResults.asp

There are three main parts to this page:

- Some VBScript running on the *server* to extract the information required from the database
- More server-side VBScript to handle the messaging
- Some JScript running on the *client* to display the result

Since this page contains the first database extraction code we have met in the case study, we will look at it in some detail.

quoteResults.asp is retrieved from the server by placing the tour identifier in the URL. For example, if the vacation is to the Mediterranean Beach in Limassol, we would use quoteResults.asp?tourid=5. Although the tourid passed in the URL should always be an integer, it is good practice to check that it is at least numeric (rather than, say, an alphabetic character). If it is numeric it will, if necessary, be truncated to an integer. This is the code that does the checking and sets a variable id to the value of the tourid if there is no error:

```
If IsNumeric(Request.QueryString("tourid")) = True Then
    id = Request.QueryString("tourid")
  Else
    Session("Err") = "The tour id in the queryString sent to quoteResults.asp
        was not an integer. Value was """ & Request.QueryString("tourid") & """"
  Response.Redirect "error.asp"
End if
```

The id is the key information for getting information from the database. If there is an error, a message is placed in a session variable and an error page loaded. This accesses the session variable and displays its contents with a suitable message.

We will also utilize the information in the form that the user has completed. Most of this is simply retrieved as needed, but the departure date is handled separately, because it arrives in three fields and needs to be reformatted:

```
DepDate =
DateSerial(Request.Form("dep3"),Request.Form("dep2"),Request.Form("dep1"))
DepYear = Year(DepDate)
DepMonth = MonthName(Request.Form("dep2"))
DepDay = Day(Depdate)
```

Our first task is to get all the information needed for the quotation request message. The items and the sources of the information are as follows:

Data Item	Variable Name	Data Source
supplier	TourOp	TourOperators table
supplier tour reference	TourRef	Tours table
departure date	DepDate	form elements dep1, dep2, dep3
duration	n/a	form element duration
number of adults	n/a	form element adults
number of children	n/a	form element children
number of infants	n/a	form element infants

We will also be getting some extra information from the database to display on the screen, although it is *not* sent to the tour operator. Let's look at the code that does this for us.

The Database Code

We need to get information from the database, both to send to the tour operator in a quotation request, and to display on the quotation results page. The information required comes from three tables:

TourOperators	Tours	Resorts
Name	Ref	Name
LogoURL	Name	
TermsConditions	ResortCode	
TransactionURL	TourOpCode	

We will start by identifying the tour by using the tour `id` passed to the page in the `queryString`. We then get four fields relating to this tour.

- The `Ref` is the tour operator's own reference for the vacation and will be sent to the tour operator
- The `Name` will be used in the display of the results
- The `ResortCode` is used to identify a record in the `Resorts` table, from which we get the resort `Name` to display
- The `TourOpCode` similarly identifies the correct record in the `TourOperators` table, from which we get the additional information we will need, such as the URL of the tour operator system that we'll be communicating with

To get this information from the database, we use Microsoft's ADO technology. Here, we will just provide a quick sketch of how to connect to the database in an application such as this. If this makes you want to learn more about accessing databases from Active Server Pages (or about ADO in general), a good reference is Wrox Press's *ADO 2.0 Programmer's Reference* (ISBN 1-86100-1835).

The first thing we must do is open an ADO connection (`conCent`), which we will do in read only mode:

```
Set conCent = CreateObject("ADODB.Connection")
conCent.ConnectionString  = Application("conCentaur_ConnectionString")
conCent.Mode = 1 'Read Only
conCent.Open
```

We will also check for errors, and if we meet one we write a message to the client display:

```
if err then
  Response.Write "<P>Error: " & Err.description & "</P>"
  Response.End
end if
```

This error checking is fairly rudimentary, since we are only checking for errors detected by the VBScript processor. The reference book mentioned earlier covers handling ADO errors in more depth, although in practice many of these errors, if not handled in our code, will cause a VBScript error that will point us to the cause of the ADO error.

Now we can start accessing the database. Our initial identifier is the tour `id`, which identifies the record we want in the `Tours` table. This record is very important, since we use it to identify all the other information we will need. Once we have this `id`, we use it to identify the record we want:

```
Set rcsTour = conCent.Execute("SELECT Ref,name, ResortCode, TourOpCode FROM
     Tours WHERE ID = " & id)
```

From this `Tours` table, we want to get the tour operator's tour reference to put in the quotation request message. We will also want the name of the vacation (i.e. the hotel) to display to the user later:

```
TourRef = rcsTour("Ref")
TourName = rcsTour("Name")
```

We also want to get the resort name. To do this, we get the `ResortCode` from the `Tours` table, then use this to select a record from the `Resorts` table:

```
ResortCode = rcsTour("ResortCode")
    Set rcsResort = conCent.Execute("SELECT Name FROM Resorts WHERE ResortCode =
         '" & ResortCode & "'")
```

We can then get the resort name from this table:

```
Resort = rcsResort("Name")
```

We use similar techniques to get the information we want from the `TourOperators` table. This includes the URI for the tour operator's HTTP server that we will be communicating with:

```
'We want some data from the TourOperators table:
'   Name
'   LogoURL
'   TermsConditions
'   TransactionURL
TourOpCode = rcsTour("TourOpCode")

'Get Operator record
Set rcsTrOp = conCent.Execute("SELECT Name,LogoURL, TermsConditions,
    TransactionURL FROM TourOperators WHERE TourOpCode = '" & TourOpCode & "'")
TourOp = rcsTrOp("Name")
LogoURL = rcsTrOp("LogoURL")
TermsConditions = rcsTrOp("TermsConditions")
TransactionURL = rcsTrOp("TransactionURL")
```

And finally, since we have finished with our data connection, we close it and tidy it up:

```
conCent.Close
set conCent = nothing
```

This has given us all the information we need from the database. Now we can construct and send a message to the tour operator.

The Messaging Code

We have already seen the format of the quotation request message, and we'll now generate this message by combining the data we have just extracted from the database with the data in the user–submitted form. Since we are now using a DTD, we can add the XML declaration and Document Type Declaration to complete our message. Before adding the data, our message will look like this:

```
<?xml version="1.0"?>
<!DOCTYPE centaur SYSTEM "http://server/Wrox/centaur.dtd">
<centaur>
  <quoterequest>
    <qttour supplier="" ref="" depdate="" duration="" />
    <qttravelers adults="" children="" infants="" />
  </quoterequest>
</centaur>
```

Preparing the Message

As we have seen, there are two ways to create our message – as a DOM object or as a string. Since we are sending the message as a string, we will create it as a string called `s`. In doing this, we will use the `tagIt()` function we met in Chapter 6.

We start by putting the fixed text at the start. As we discussed in the earlier chapter, when we are sending a message to another Active Server Page, the easiest way is to simulate a form so we can use `Request.Form(string)` in the receiving page. To do this, we need to name the form element, which in this case we are calling `message`:

```
s = "message=<?xml version=""1.0""?><!DOCTYPE centaur SYSTEM
   ""http://server/Wrox/centaur.dtd"">"
s = s + "<centaur><quoterequest>"
```

If we were communicating instead with an HTTP server running an application to handle the XML message directly, we would leave this out and start the message with the XML declaration.
Then we build up the attributes for the `qttour` element:

```
t = "supplier=""" & TourOp & """"
t = t & " ref=""" & TourRef & """"
t = t & " depdate=""" & DepDate & """"
t = t & " duration=""" & Request.Form("duration") & """"
```

and create the element:

```
s = s & tagIt("qttour","",t)
```

The `qttravelers` element uses data from the form, so we use `Request.Form(string)` to get these, then create the element as before:

```
t = "adults=""" & Request.Form("adults") & """"
t = t & " children=""" & Request.Form("children") & """"
t = t & " infants=""" & Request.Form("infants") & """"
s = s & tagIt("qttravelers","",t)
```

We can then add the closing tags:

```
s = s & "</quoterequest></centaur>"
```

This gives us our complete string s, ready to send.

Saving the Variables

When we display the form to make the booking, it would be useful to be able to show some details that the user has already completed for the quotation. To achieve this, we will save them as **session variables** now, and get them later. We met session variables when we looked at the global.asa file in Chapter 7. They are simply variables that get stored on the server for the duration of the session, and are available for use by any Active Server Page invoked by the user of that session.

These are the variables we will save:

```
Session("supplier") = TourOp
Session("ref") = TourRef
Session("depdate") = DepDate
Session("duration") = Request.Form("duration")
Session("adults") = Request.Form("adults")
Session("children") = Request.Form("children")
Session("infants") = Request.Form("infants")
```

The first four of these are used in the booking form, the others in the emulation of the tour operator server. This emulation calculates what I refer to as a "relatively random" price. This is based on the number of travelers in the booking.

Sending the Message

We will now send the message using Microsoft's XMLHttp component:

```
Set HttpObj = Server.CreateObject("microsoft.XMLHttp")
HttpObj.open "POST",TransactionURL,false
HttpObj.setRequestHeader "Content-type", "text/xml"
HttpObj.send s
strResult = HttpObj.responseText
```

We used exactly the same principle when we looked at this interface earlier in Chapter 6.

Receiving the Response

Since the messaging is dealing with communications links and systems not under our control, we want to check for as many different errors as possible. Two obvious ones are not getting a response at all and not getting the response we want. Let's look at the latter first.

The `onLoad()` function handles not getting a response:

```
function onLoad()
{
  // Set a 20 second timeout to check for a reply
  timeout = window.setTimeout("checkResponse()",20000);
  newState();
}
```

This simply calls a function after twenty seconds to check whether there was a response:

```
function checkResponse()
{
  if(xmlQuote.documentElement == null)
    alert("There has been no response from the tour operator system");
}
```

This timeout will be cleared by code later once a valid response has been found.

We have used `responseText` to receive the reply, since we want to validate it against the DTD on the client. If we were to use `responseXML` the `MSXML` component of IE5 would switch off validation. We therefore write the response into an XML island in the page. This will get loaded and validated when the page reaches the client:

```
<XML id="xmlQuote"><% =strResult %></XML>
```

When this page is loaded, we need to ensure that it is parsed before we start using it. We have already looked at how to use the `readyState` variable to handle this. We will also look to check that there is some text in the response:

```
  else if(xmlQuote.documentElement == null)
    window.setTimeout('newState()',200);
```

If there is not, we just start the function again. Eventually, if the document is not received, the timeout set in the `onLoad()` function will trigger and display a suitable message.

After parsing (and validating against the DTD), we know we have a valid document, so we can start to process it, which is what we will look at next.

The Display Code

There are two options for displaying the response to the quotation request – via XSL or via the DOM. The message itself will be in this form:

```
<?xml version="1.0"?>
<!DOCTYPE centaur SYSTEM "http://server/Wrox/centaur.dtd">
<centaur>
  <quoteresponse seq="">
    <qrdetails availability="" quote="" notes="" />
  </quoteresponse>
</centaur>
```

We *could* use XSL to display this, but we only have three items of data here, so it is easier to use the DOM.

When the page loads in the browser, it will display this HTML, which I have reformatted slightly to look better on the printed page:

```
<DIV Class="center"><IMG src = <% =LogoURL %>></DIV>

<DIV Id="quotation">
  <H1>Quotation</H1>
  <H2><% =TourName %>, <% =Resort %></H2>
  <DIV><% =Request.Form("adults") %>
    <SPAN Id="adultTarget"></SPAN>  
    <% =Request.Form("children") %>
    <SPAN Id="childTarget"></SPAN>  
    <% =Request.Form("infants") %>
    <SPAN Id="infantTarget"></SPAN>
  </DIV>
  <DIV>Departing on
    <% =Depday %> <% =DepMonth %> <% =DepYear %>
    for <% =Request.Form("duration") %> <SPAN Id="nightTarget"></SPAN>
  </DIV>
  <DIV Id="targetPrice"></DIV>
  <DIV Id="targetNotes"></DIV>
  <DIV Id="instructions">If you wish to book this vacation, you will need to read
  and agree to the tour operator's terms and conditions</DIV>
  <DIV Class="Center">
    <button AccessKey="V" Id="terms" onClick="displayTerms()"
    type="button"><u>V</u>iew Terms</button>
    <button AccessKey="R" Id="return"
    onClick="location='tour.asp?tourid=<%=id%>'" type="button"><u>R</u>eturn to
    Vacation Details</button>
    <button AccessKey="B" Id="bookit"
    onClick="location='bookForm.asp?tourid=<%=id%>'" type="button"
    Disabled=true><u>B</u>ook It!</button>
  </DIV>
</DIV>

<DIV Id="TandC" Style="display:none">
  <DIV Class="center">
    <TEXTAREA Class="terms" rows=16 cols=90>
      <% = TermsConditions %>
    </TEXTAREA>
  </DIV>
  <DIV Class="center">
    <button AccessKey="A" Id="accept" onClick="acceptTerms()"
    type="button"><u>A</u>ccept</button>
    <button AccessKey="R" Id="reject" onClick="rejectTerms()"
    type="button"><u>R</u>eject</button>
  </DIV>
</DIV>
```

This comprises two main `DIV` elements. This is so that the user can switch between the results of the quotation and the terms and conditions without the browser having to reload the pages.

Initially, the first `DIV` is displayed. This is complicated slightly because I am a tidy person and don't like to see expressions such as 1 children in a page. We therefore have the line:

```
<% =Request.Form("children") %>
<SPAN Id="childTarget"></SPAN>  
```

The `onLoad()` function then uses DHTML to put the appropriate text into the `SPAN` element with `Id="childTarget"`:

```
if (<% =Request.Form("children") %> == 1)
  childTarget.innerText = "child";
else
  childTarget.innerText = "children";
```

The rest of the first `DIV` displays the information from the form, puts in more placeholders for the script to write to, and puts three buttons on the bottom. The first button uses DHTML to replace this screen with the terms and conditions screen, the second takes us back to the details of the vacation, and the third allows us to make a booking by taking us to the booking screen. Or at least, it *would* take us there if it were not disabled until we have looked at the terms and conditions. (As with accepting software licenses, we don't expect anyone to read them, just to click to say that they agree with them.)

The second `DIV` element is straightforward HTML that needs no comment.

We have already seen how the `onLoad()` function handles the timeout and changes some text according to the number of each type of traveler. Let's look at what else it does.

Firstly, it checks for parser–detected errors and gets the quotation response:

```
if (xmlQuote.parseError != 0)
  alert("quoteResults.asp: " + xmlQuote.parseError.reason);
domQuote=xmlQuote;
```

Then, if the quotation response contains the `error` element, we display the text:

```
root=domQuote.documentElement;
if(root.childNodes.item(0).nodeName == "error")
{
  strAlert = "There was an error in the data sent\n";
  strAlert += "The error message was: ";
  strAlert += root.childNodes.item(0).text;
  alert(strAlert);
}
```

If the error element was *not* present, we can get on with displaying the information. First we extract the values of the three atrributes:

```
else
{
  resultTour =
     root.childNodes.item(0).getElementsByTagName("qrdetails").item(0);
  resultAvailability = resultTour.getAttribute("availability");
  resultPrice = resultTour.getAttribute("quote");
  resultNotes = resultTour.getAttribute("notes");
```

Next, if the tour is available, we put the price and notes in their respective places. If it is not available, we say so and suppress the display of the booking instructions:

```
      if (resultAvailability == "true")
      {
        targetPrice.innerText = "Total price is £" + resultPrice;
        targetNotes.innerText = resultNotes;
      }
      else
      {
        targetPrice.innerText = "I'm sorry, this vacation is not available";
        instructions.style.display = "none";
      }
    }
```

That's the end of the part of the code that deals with the XML messages for the quotation. The complete code is included in Appendix B. Other code in this page is simply HTML and script to handle the display of the terms and conditions.

Having seen how we generate and display the quotation request, let's move on to see how the user books their vacation.

bookResults.asp and its Stylesheet

We will not look at this page in so much detail, as it is similar in most respects to `quoteResults.asp`. The main difference is that the amount of information returned from the server is much greater and makes it worth using XSL to render the page. The `newState()` function is therefore different (and simpler):

```
function newState()
{
  var temp,root,domBooking,style;

  // keep trying when the readyState changes
  xmlBooking.onreadystatechange = newState;

  // check that XML has loaded
  if(xmlBooking.readyState == completed)
  {
    if (xmlBooking.parseError != 0)
      alert("bookResults.asp returned message: " + xmlBooking.parseError.reason);
    domBooking = xmlBooking;

    root=domBooking.documentElement;

    if(root.childNodes.item(0).nodeName == "error")
    {
      strAlert = "There was an error in the data sent\n";
      strAlert += "The error message was: ";
      strAlert += root.childNodes.item(0).text;
      alert(strAlert);
    }
    else
    {
```

```
         style = new ActiveXObject("Microsoft.XMLDOM");
         style.async = false;
         style.load("booking.xsl");
           if (style.parseError != 0)
           alert("bookResults.asp stylesheet: " + style.parseError.reason);

         document.all.item("tgtBooking").innerHTML = domBooking.transformNode(style);
      }
   }
}
```

As you can see, this looks much like any other code used to render an XML island using an XSL stylesheet, so let's have a look at the stylesheet `booking.xsl` itself.

We want to render the returned message to give us a display like this:

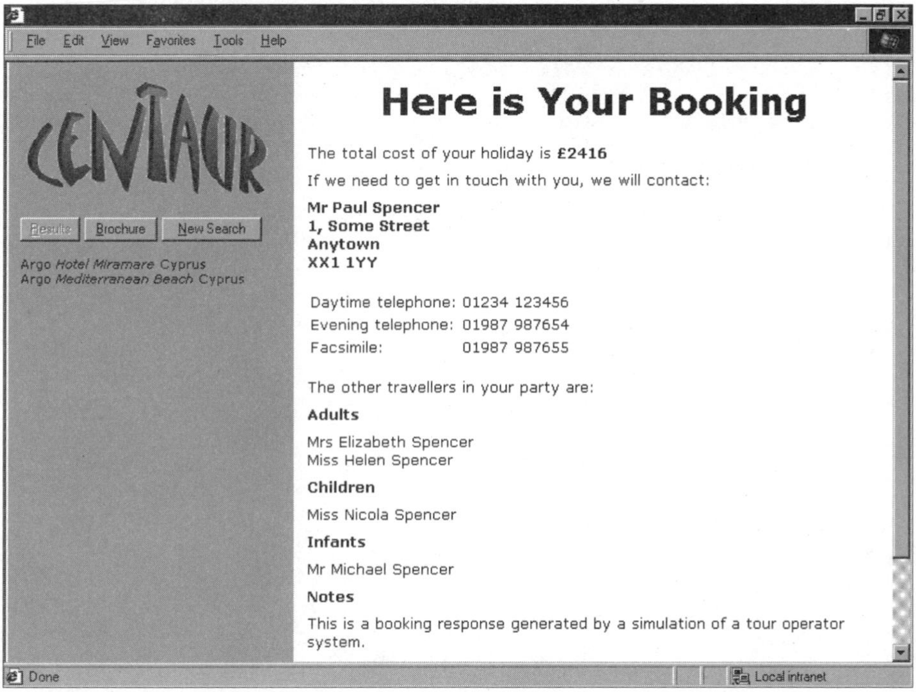

The template for the root element includes the basic elements of the HTML document we want as a result of the stylesheet:

```
<xsl:template match="/">
  <HTML>
    <BODY>
      <H1>Here is Your Booking</H1>
      <xsl:apply-templates select="/centaur/bookresponse" />
    </BODY>
  </HTML>
</xsl:template>
```

We then construct the rest of the result tree to create the display above, picking out bits of the `bookresponse` message as required. We start with the price, using a character reference for the British pound sign (£):

```
<xsl:template match="/centaur/bookresponse">
  <DIV>The total cost of your vacation is <B>&#163;<xsl:value-of
     select="brdetails/@price" /></B></DIV>
```

We then identify the contact traveler:

```
  <DIV>If we need to get in touch with you, we will contact:</DIV>
  <xsl:apply-templates select='bbtravelers/adult[@type="contact"]' />
```

and put in the relevant details using another template:

```
<xsl:template match="bbtravelers/adult[@type='contact']">
  <DIV Style="font-weight:bold">
    <xsl:value-of select="@title" />
    <xsl:value-of select="@forename" />
    <xsl:value-of select="@lastname" /><BR />
    <xsl:value-of select="@streetaddress1" /><BR />
    <xsl:if match="*[not(@streetaddress2='')]">
    <xsl:value-of select="@streetaddress2" /><BR />
                                            </xsl:if>

    <xsl:value-of select="@town" /><BR />
    <xsl:value-of select="@postcode" /><BR /><BR />
    <TABLE>
      <TR>
        <TD>Daytime telephone:</TD>
        <TD><xsl:value-of select="@dayphone" /></TD>
      </TR>
      <TR>
        <TD>Evening telephone:</TD>
        <TD><xsl:value-of select="@eveningphone" /></TD>
      </TR>
      <TR>
        <TD>Facsimile:</TD>
        <TD><xsl:value-of select="@fax" /></TD>
      </TR>
    </TABLE>
  </DIV>
</xsl:template>
```

After putting in a bit of text, we then identify the other adults:

```
  <xsl:apply-templates select='bbtravelers/adult[not(@type)]' />
```

We apply simpler pattern matches to find the children and infants:

```
  <DIV Style="margin-top:6pt; margin-bottom:6pt; font-weight:bold">Children</DIV>
    <xsl:apply-templates select='bbtravelers/child' />
    <DIV Style="margin-top:6pt; margin-bottom:6pt; font-weight:bold">Infants</DIV>
    <xsl:apply-templates select='bbtravelers/infant' />
```

We then add any notes from the tour operator:

```
<DIV Style="margin-top:6pt; margin-bottom:6pt; font-weight:bold">Notes</DIV>
<DIV><xsl:value-of select="brdetails/@notes" /></DIV>
```

and finally the contact details for the tour operator, and a button to go to the exit screen:

```
<DIV Style="margin-top:12pt">My name is <xsl:value-of select="brtour/
@contact" />. You can contact me on <xsl:value-of select="brtour/
@phone" /> or by
<A>
  <xsl:attribute name="href">
    <xsl:eval>"mailto:"</xsl:eval><xsl:value-of select="brtour/@email"/>
  </xsl:attribute>
E-Mail</A>.
Please quote reference <B><xsl:value-of select="brdetails/
    @bookingref" /></B>.</DIV>
<DIV class="Center" Style="margin-top:12pt">
  <button AccessKey="E" onClick="location=
  bye.htm'" type="button"><u>E</u>xit</button>
</DIV>
```

The Server Emulation

Since we do not have real tour operators to communicate with, Centaur includes a simple emulation of a tour operator system, as an Active Server Page. Although this code is not strictly part of the product, it is the only place where we read and manipulate XML on the server using the DOM, so we will look at parts of it here.

We start by loading the message from the `Request` object into a new XML DOM object:

```
Set domMsg = Server.CreateObject("Microsoft.XMLDOM")
domMsg.load(Request)
```

From there, we can check for parser errors as usual. Here's how:

Checking for Errors in the Transmitted Message

Since we are running this code on the server, we cannot use the client-side `alert()` we usually employ. Instead, we will write a more comprehensive error message to a text string, before sending it back as an `error` response to the page that sent us the message:

```
if domMsg.parseError <> 0 then
  ' report an error
  strError = domMsg.parseError.reason & " at character " &
    domMsg.parseError.linepos
  Response.Write "<centaur><error>" & strError & "</error></centaur>"
```

It's always best to test error handlers, and this can be done simply by putting an error in a booking request message by changing the end tag from `<bookrequest>` to `<bookreques>`. This will send the following message (I have added the formatting – all these messages are sent on a single line):

```
<?xml version="1.0"?>
<!DOCTYPE centaur SYSTEM "http://server/Wrox/centaur.dtd">
<centaur>
  <error>
    End tag 'bookreques' does not match the start tag 'bookreques'.
    at character 504
  </error>
</centaur>
```

The `onLoad()` function of `bookResults.asp` will then cause an alert:

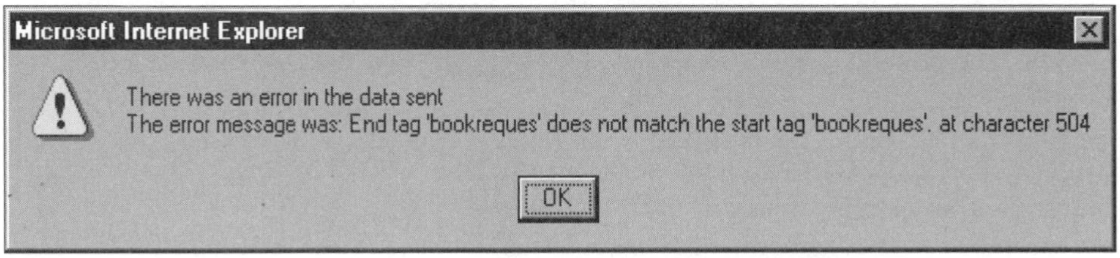

As well as errors reported by the parser, we could experience other errors. When we call the relevant functions for the two *allowed* message types, we check for *invalid* message types:

```
Set root = domMsg.DocumentElement
  ' determine the message type
  if (root.childNodes.item(0).nodeName = "quoterequest") then
    ReplyQuote()
  else
    if (root.childNodes.item(0).nodeName = "bookrequest") then
      ReplyBook()
    else
      strReply = "<centaur><error>" & root.childNodes.item(0).nodeName & " is
         not a valid message type</error></centaur>"
    end if
  end if
```

The message is placed in a string `strReply`, which gets the XML declaration and Document Type Declaration added to it when it is sent back to Centaur. The location of the DTD is stored as an Application variable in `global.asa`, simply to make it easy to change for those who decide to build their own systems:

```
Response.Write "<?xml version=""1.0""?><!DOCTYPE centaur SYSTEM """ &
   Application("dtd") & """>" & strReply
```

If I change the name of the `quoterequest` element, but keep the document well-formed by changing both start and end tags, I see a different alert:

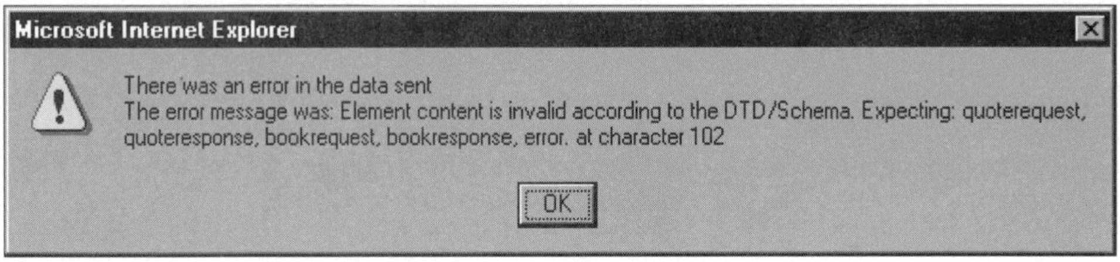

Microsoft Internet Explorer
There was an error in the data sent
The error message was: Element content is invalid according to the DTD/Schema. Expecting: quoterequest, quoteresponse, bookrequest, bookresponse, error. at character 102
OK

Having sent our booking request to the emulator, we need to generate a response.

Generating the Responses

We will start by looking at the quotation response. The booking response is similar, so we shall just look at the differences when we come to them.

The function `ReplyQuote()` simply builds up an XML message string to send back to Centaur. We start by creating text strings for the availability and notes:

```
        ' we are saying that vacations are always available
        strAvailability="true"
        ' standard set of notes
        strNotes = "This is a random price generated by a simulation of a tour
                    operator system"
```

Then we calculate a semi-random price based on the duration of the vacation and the number of adults and children travelling. As well as being used for the quotation, this price is saved so that the same price can be used for the booking:

```
    ' We shall use a formula with a base price of £200 plus between £20 and £50
    ' per day with a 40% discount for children. Infants are free.

        'Get the number of adults and children
        Set xmlTravelers =
          root.childNodes.item(0).getElementsByTagName("qttravelers").item(0)
        intAdults = xmlTravelers.getAttribute("adults")
        intChildren = xmlTravelers.getAttribute("children")
        ' And the duration
        Set xmlTravelers =
          root.childNodes.item(0).getElementsByTagName("qttour").item(0)
        intDuration = xmlTravelers.getAttribute("duration")
        ' Now do the sum
        randomize
        intPrice =  int(rnd * 30) + 20
        intQuote = intAdults * 200 + intChildren * 120
        intQuote = int(intQuote + intPrice * intDuration *
          (intAdults + intChildren * 0.6))
        ' Save the price to re-use in the booking
        session("Price") = intQuote
```

This code starts by getting the number of adults (`intAdults`), number of children(`intChildren`) and duration (`intDuration`) from the quotation request. It then invokes the random number generator to give us – you've guessed it – a random number. This will be between zero and one, so is multiplied by thirty and added to twenty. Taking the integer part of this gives us a price per night of between £30 and £50. We then generate a base price of £200 per adult and £120 per child. Finally, we do the calculation to add the variable parts of the price according to the duration. Children are charged at 60% of the adult price.

Each of the lines accessing the DOM object could, of course, use Microsoft extensions such as `SelectSingleNode`. Since this code is running on the server, there are no issues of browser compatibility, so that is not a problem here. Personally, I have got into the habit of using the W3C DOM (except where it is much harder to use than the Microsoft extensions!)

All that is left is to build up the response from the variables we have just set, and return it from the function:

```
strReply = "<centaur><quoteresponse>"
strReply = strReply & "<qrdetails availability=""" & strAvailability & """"
strReply = strReply & " quote=""" & intQuote & """"
strReply = strReply & " notes=""" & strNotes & """ />"
strReply = strReply & "</quoteresponse></centaur>"
ReplyQuote = strReply
```

The booking reply function is very similar except that it copies the complete `travelers` element from the input message to the output message. We make a copy to do this:

```
set tempNode=root.childNodes.item(0).getElementsByTagName("bbtravelers").item(0)
strReply = strReply & tempNode.cloneNode(true).xml
```

If you remember, an element can only have one parent, and attaching the element to the output message would delete it from the input message. Making the copy is not strictly necessary, since we have no further use for the input message, but it avoids confusion if we came back to modify the code later and try to use the `travelers` element of the input message again.

Summary

In this chapter, we have looked in detail at the code behind the transactional side of Centaur. This has involved us in developing a DTD, a real use of Microsoft's `XMLHttp` interface, and our first look at manipulating the XML object model on the server.

The important areas we have covered are:

- how to develop a DTD for a transactional application based on the types of data required
- how to get information from a database in an Active Server Page
- how to use the HTTP `POST` method to send messages to another ASP page as `FORM` objects
- how to receive, manipulate and respond to these messages on the server

Finally

In Chapter 1 of this book, I outlined the basic functional requirements of the Centaur system. We said then that it must:

- be able to interface with, and retrieve up-to-date data from, tour operator information databases based on search criteria the user specifies
- be able to collate that data into an integrated, sorted data set
- allow the user to select a subset of the vacations information from the data set, and persist that on the off-line client machine as a personalized brochure
- allow the user to select a vacation from the brochure, get a quotation, and if they want to, book it

As we've progressed through the book, we have built up a picture of how XML's features help us to satisfy these requirements. In the last two chapters, we have seen how Centaur's Interactive and

Transactional systems allow users to browse the available data, create unique brochures, and book vacations, using the XML technology as an organizing principle.

It should be clear from all of this that XML on its own is just an engaging set of ideas – it is only when it is linked up to an application that its power becomes apparent. XML is another – albeit powerful – tool that lets us get the job done.

I very much hope you have gained enough knowledge and interest to explore further how to put XML into action in your own work – it really is a technology for the millennium.

A

Build Your Own Centaur

You can build a Centaur application on your own server by downloading and running an installation file from the Wrox website. This installation file will allow you to install the complete code for the application, and contains scripts that will create and populate the SQL Server database that the application uses. You can also install all of the example code used in every chapter of the book. (An Access version of the database will also be made available on our website).

What Do I Need to Run Centaur?

You need to be running the following software to implement Centaur as it is demonstrated in this book:

- Microsoft NT Server
- Microsoft SQL Server (to run the database)
- Microsoft IIS 4
- Microsoft IE5 on the server (and any client machines)

We give full instructions for configuring the application across these platforms in the Installation Help Files that you download.

How Do I Download and Install the Files?

This is a simple process.

1. Navigate to the Wrox website at `www.wrox.com`.
2. Choose the Source Code option from the left-hand frame and follow the links for this book:

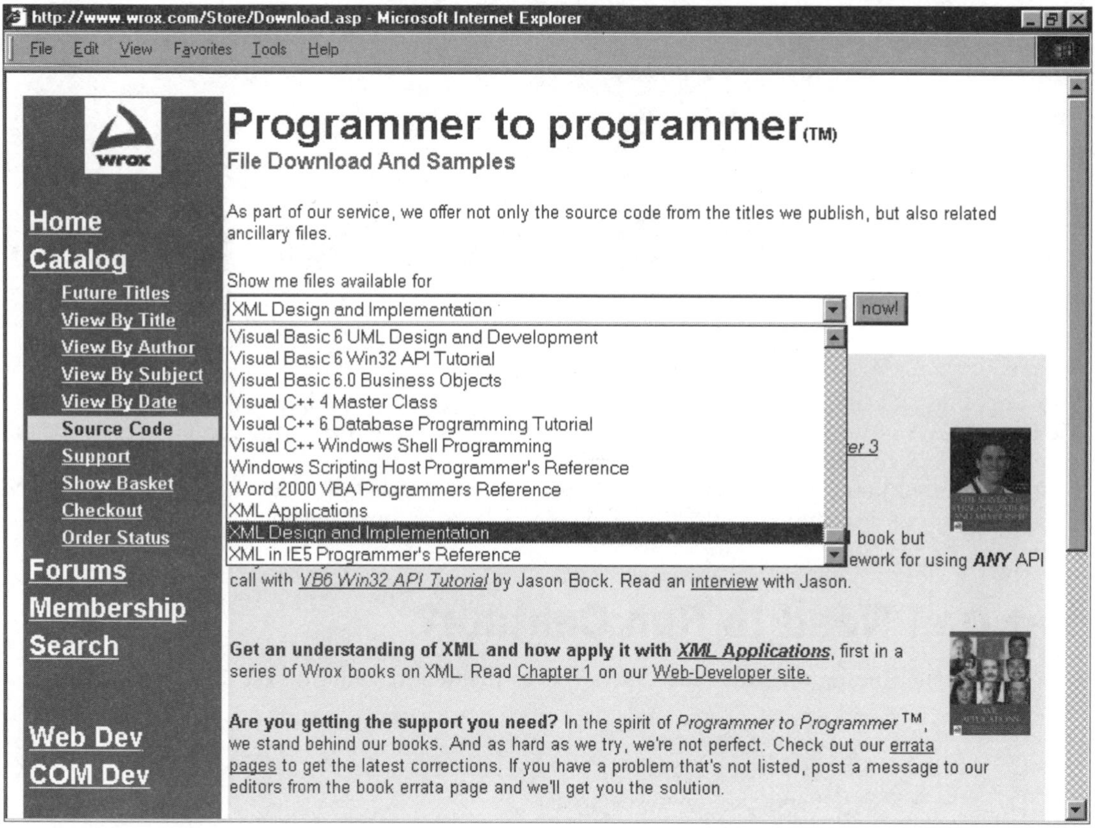

3. Select the `WROX2289.exe` download file and download it to a location of your choice.
4. Run the downloaded install file and follow the prompts to install the files that you want. There are three important points to note here:

- You have a choice of files to install. You **must** check the Centaur Sample Application check box if you want the full set of application files to install
- The destination folders for the installed Centaur files **must** be located on your **server**
- The example code from the chapters can be run on **any** machine that's running IE5 (this excludes the `.asp` files)

At this stage, you will have a Start | Programs option on your taskbar called 2289. This has options for:

- Building the SQL Server Database
- Installing Centaur as an IIS application
- Uninstalling Centaur as an IIS application
- Uninstalling the example files from your disk
- Viewing the installation help files

5. If you chose to install Centaur, you will be taken to an HTML page that takes you through the application setup process in detail. Follow the prompts in the setup program. In a nutshell, the setup process that you follow next has three main parts:

- Building the SQL Server database
- Populating the database with data
- Creating the Centaur application in IIS

The setup documentation supplied with the installation program gives you full details of these processes and any additional tweaking that is required.

Once these processes are complete, you will have:

- A fully functional Centaur application on your server
- A series of folders containing the example code for the chapters that you elected to install

You can now use and change the application and the example files to suit your own desires and experiments.

B

Selective Code Listings

prepareResults.asp

```
<%@ Language=VBScript %><%

'The form submitéd will contain information about a query
'for tours in a specific area with specific facilities required

'Page globals

Dim conCent 'Connection to Centaur DB
Dim strListFacOnTour  'List of facilities required that are at on the tour itself
Dim astrFacOnTour   'Array of  above
Dim strListFacOnResort  'List of facilities required at the tour's resort
Dim astrFacOnResort 'Array of above
Dim astrToursInArea 'An array of tours found in the area selected
Dim strToursWithFac
Dim astrToursWithFac
Dim itr 'Iterator
Dim itrFac 'Iterator
Dim frm 'The Form
Dim intMatches

Dim blnAddTour

'Get a connection object setup
     Set conCent = CreateObject("ADODB.connection")
```

```
    conCent.ConnectionString= application("conCentaur_ConnectionString")
    conCent.Mode = 1 'Read Only

    on error resume Next
    conCent.Open

    if err then
          Response.Write "<HTML><HEAD><TITLE>Centaur
Server</TITLE></HEAD><BODY><P>Failed to contact the Centaur
Server</P></BODY></HTML>"
          Response.End
    end if

    'Connect open ok

    on error goto 0

    set frm = Request.Form

    'Process the FORM to find fac_tour_ vars and fac_resort_ items sent
    for each itr in frm

          if left(itr,8) = "fac_tour" then
                strListFacOnTour = "," & Mid(itr,10) & strListFacOnTour
          elseif left(itr,10) = "fac_resort" then
                strListFacOnResort = "," & Mid(itr,12) & strListFacOnResort
          End if
    next 'itr

    'Trim any leading commas
    if len(strListFacOnResort ) then strListFacOnResort =
        mid(strListFacOnResort,2)
    if len(strListFacOnTour ) then strListFacOnTour = mid(strListFacOnTour,2)

    'Make arrays from lists
    astrFacOnTour  = Split(strListFacOnTour, "," )
    astrFacOnresort = Split(strListFacOnResort, "," )
    astrToursInArea =  Split(GetListToursInArea(frm("lstArea")),",")

    'Loop through each tour in the area and check if it has all the required
    'facilities on the tour
    for each itr in astrToursInArea

          'Assume tour is applicable
          blnAddTour = true

          for each itrFac in astrFacOnTour
                if not DoesTourHaveFacility(itr,itrFac) then
                      'Don't add this tour to the filtered list
                      blnAddTour = false
                End if
          next 'facility


          'append tour if flag true
          if blnAddTour then  strToursWithFac = "," & itr  & strToursWithFac
    next
```

```
'Drop comma prefix
if len(strToursWithFac) then
      strToursWithFac = Mid(strToursWithFac,2)

      'Iterate through this result set after converting to an array
      astrToursWithFac = Split(strToursWithFac,",")

      'Clear the string ready for the next stage of filtering
      strToursWithFac = ""

      'And then ensure that there are appropriate facilities at the resort
      for each itr in astrToursWithFac
            'Assume that the tour is ok for the final list
            blnAddTour = true
            for each itrFac in astrFacOnResort
                  if Not DoesTourResortHaveFacility(itr,itrfac) then
                        blnAddTour = false
                  End If
            next

            if blnAddTour then
                  strToursWithFac = "," & itr & strToursWithFac
            end if
      next 'itr

      'Trim a leading comma
      if len(strToursWithFac) then
            strToursWithFac = Mid(strToursWithFac,2)

            'We now have a filtered list of tours
            astrToursWithFac = split(strToursWithFac,",")

            'Store the list of acceptable tours in session
            session("TourList") = strToursWithFac

            'Decide if there are too many to display by default
            intMatches = UBound(astrToursWithFac) + 1

      else
            'There are no tours with required resort facility
            intMatches = 0
            session("TourList") = "" 'Empty the list
      end if

else
      'There are no Tours matching!
      intMatches = 0
      session("TourList") = "" 'Empty the list
end if
```

```
Function DoesTourResortHaveFacility(TourId, strFacCode)
'Determine whether the tours resort has the required resort level fac
Dim rcsResFac
Dim intRA
Dim SQL

     SQL = "Select Count(*) As NumRow FROM Resort_Facility Where FacilityCode =
     '" & strFacCode & "' AND ResortCode = (SELECT ResortCode FROM Tours
     WHERE ID = " & TourId & ")"
     set rcsResFac = conCent.Execute (SQL,intRA)
     if rcsResFac("NumRow") = 1 then
           DoesTourResortHaveFacility = True
     else
           'The resort has not got the fac
           'but the tour itself may have it
           DoesTourResortHaveFacility = DoesTourHaveFacility (TourId,strFacCode)

     end if
     rcsResFac.Close
     set rcsResFac = Nothing
End Function


Function DoesTourHaveFacility(TourID, strFacCode)
'Purpose: Determine whether the tour has the facility and
' return true if it does
Dim rcsTourfac
Dim intRA
Dim SQL
     SQL = "SELECT Count(*) AS NumRow from Tour_Facility Where TourID = " &
TourID & " AND FacilityCode = '" & strFacCode & "'"

     Set rcsTourfac = conCent.Execute (SQL,intRA)
     if rcsTourfac("NumRow") = 1 then
           DoesTourHaveFacility = True
     else
           DoesTourHaveFacility = False
     end if
     rcsTourfac.Close
     set  rcsTourfac = Nothing
End Function

Function GetListToursInArea(strAreaCode)
'Purpose: Build a list of tours in an area
Dim rcsTours
Dim strSQL
Dim intRA
Dim strList
Dim strWA       'World Area Searh field for (any) searches
Dim strPurpose 'Vacation Purpose Code
Dim strSubQuery

     'Get the vacation purpose code
     'This will be used in a Sub query to ensure the selected vacations have the
'    chosen purpose
     strPurpose = Request("Purpose")
     if strPurpose = "*" then
           'Any activty so the sub query need not be used
           strSubQuery = ""
```

```
      else
            strSubQuery = " AND Tours.ID IN (SELECT TourID FROM Tour_Purpose
            WHERE PurposeCode = '" & strPurpose & "')"
      end if


      'The area code could be * which is used to mean any!
      if strAreaCode =  "*" then
            'We need to search on World area unless that is also '*'
            strWA = request("Vacation_location")
            if strWA = "*" then
            'The search is for all areas but we include the WHERE 1=1 in case
            there is an activity requirement
                  ' i.e. the sub query may be like " AND ..."
            strSQL = "select Tours.ID as TourID from Tours  WHERE 1=1 " &
            strSubQuery
            else
            strSQL = "select Tours.ID as TourID from ((Tours Left Join
            Resorts  on Resorts.ResortCode = Tours.ResortCode) INNER JOIN Areas
            on Areas.areacode = resorts.areacode)  WHERE areas.worldcode = '" &
            strWA & "' " & strSubQuery
            end if
      else
            strSQL = "select Tours.ID as TourID from (Tours Left Join Resorts on
            Resorts.ResortCode = Tours.ResortCode)  Where AreaCode = '" &
            strAreaCode & "' " & strSubQuery


      end if
      'on error resume next
      set rcsTours = conCent.Execute (strSQL,intRA)

      if err then

            exit function
      end if

      do until rcsTours.Eof

            strList  = ","   & rcsTours("TourID")& strList
            rcsTours.MoveNext
      loop
      rcsTours.close

      'Trim any leading comma
      if len(strList) then strList = Mid(strList,2)

      'Return This list
      GetListToursInArea = strList
End Function

%><HTML>
<HEAD>
<META NAME="GENERATOR" Content="Microsoft Visual Studio 6.0">
</HEAD>
<BODY onLoad="onLoad(<%=intMatches%>)">
<Script Language = "JScript">
function onLoad(number)
{
```

```
      var str;

      parent.left.displayResults();
      if (number == 0)
            parent.left.document.all("tgtResults").innerText = "No tours match
            your criteria, please try again";
      else if (number > <%=Application ("MAX_TOURS_IN_FIND")%>)
      {
            str = "Your criteria matched " + number + " tours. Press the button
      to view them or refine your search criteria";
            str += '<P align="center"><button AccessKey="V" Id="results"
                     type="button"
                     onClick=parent.hidden.location.replace("getSearch
                     Results.asp");><u>V</u>iew Results</button>';
            parent.left.document.all("tgtResults").innerHTML = str;
      }
      else
            parent.hidden.location.replace('getSearchResults.asp');
}

</Script>

</BODY>
</HTML>
<% conCent.Close %>
```

quoteResults.asp

```
<% Option Explicit%><%
' This page uses XmlHttp to send information to the third tier in XML, get
' a response (also in XML) and display it

Dim id
Dim conCent
Dim rcsTour
Dim rcsTrOp
Dim rcsResort
Dim TourOpCode
Dim TourOp
Dim LogoURL
Dim TermsConditions
Dim TransactionURL

Dim TourRef
Dim TourOpUrl
Dim TourName
Dim ResortCode
Dim Resort
Dim WorldArea

Dim DepDate
Dim  DepYear
Dim  DepMonth
Dim  DepDay
```

```
Dim HttpObj
Dim strResult
Dim s
Dim t

      ''''''''''''''''''''''
      ' Get all the variables
      ''''''''''''''''''''''

      'Set up Data Connection
      Set conCent = CreateObject("ADODB.Connection")
      conCent.ConnectionString  = Application("conCentaur_ConnectionString")
      conCent.Mode = 1 'Read Only
      conCent.Open

      if err then
            Response.Write "<P>Error: " & Err.description & "</P>"
            Response.End
      end if

      'Get the tour record
      If IsNumeric(Request.QueryString("tourid")) = True Then
            id = Request.QueryString("tourid")
      Else
            Session("Err") = "The tour id in the queryString sent to
            quoteResults.asp was not an integer. Value was """ &
            Request.QueryString("tourid") & """"
            Response.Redirect "error.asp"
      End if
      Set rcsTour = conCent.Execute("SELECT Ref,name, ResortCode, TourOpCode FROM
      Tours WHERE ID = " & id)

      'We want some data from the Tours table:
      '     Ref
      '     Name
      TourRef = rcsTour("Ref")
      TourName = rcsTour("Name")

      'We want some data from the Resorts table:
      '     Name
      ResortCode = rcsTour("ResortCode")

      ' Get Resort record
      Set rcsResort = conCent.Execute("SELECT Name FROM Resorts WHERE
      ResortCode = '" & ResortCode & "'")
      Resort = rcsResort("Name")

      'We want some data from the TourOperators table:
      '     Name
      '     LogoURL
      '     TermsConditions
      '     TransactionURL
      TourOpCode = rcsTour("TourOpCode")

      'Get Operator record
      Set rcsTrOp = conCent.Execute("SELECT Name,LogoURL, TermsConditions,
      TransactionURL FROM TourOperators WHERE TourOpCode = '" & TourOpCode & "'")
      TourOp = rcsTrOp("Name")
      LogoURL = rcsTrOp("LogoURL")
```

```
TermsConditions = rcsTrOp("TermsConditions")
TransactionURL = rcsTrOp("TransactionURL")


'Clean up Data connection
conCent.Close
set conCent = nothing

'Now handle the date from the form, and format it for display
DepDate = DateSerial(Request.Form("dep3"),
Request.Form("dep2"),Request.Form("dep1"))
DepYear = Year(DepDate)
DepMonth = MonthName(Request.Form("dep2"))
DepDay = Day(Depdate)
''''''''''''''''''''''''''''''''''''''''''''''''''''''''''''''''''''''''''
'Now get the data into an XML message
'The format of the message is (only the white space is not put in):
'<?xml version="1.0"?>
'<!DOCTYPE centaur SYSTEM "centaur.dtd">
'<centaur>
'      <quoterequest>
'            <qttour supplier="" ref="" depdate="" duration="" />
'            <qttravelers adults="" children="" infants="" />
'      </quoterequest>
'</centaur>
'
'Note that all information is in attributes so it can be validated using
'a DTD
'
'The response will be of the form
'<centaur>
'      <quoteresponse seq="">
'            <qrdetails availability="" quote="" notes="" />
'      </quoteresponse>
'</centaur>
''''''''''''''''''''''''''''''''''''''''''''''''''''''''''''''''''''''''''

s = "<?xml version=""1.0""?><!DOCTYPE centaur SYSTEM """ &
Application("dtd") & """>"
s = s + "<centaur><quoterequest>"
t = "supplier=""" & TourOp & """"
t = t & " ref=""" & TourRef & """"
t = t & " depdate=""" & DepDate & """"
t = t & " duration=""" & Request.Form("duration") & """"
s = s & tagIt("qttour","",t)

t = "adults=""" & Request.Form("adults") & """"
t = t & " children=""" & Request.Form("children") & """"
t = t & " infants=""" & Request.Form("infants") & """"
s = s & tagIt("qttravelers","",t)

s = s & "</quoterequest></centaur>"

''''''''''''''''''''''''''''''''''''''''''''''''''''''''''''
'We also need to store all variables as session variables
'so they can be used by the booking page (bookForm.asp)
''''''''''''''''''''''''''''''''''''''''''''''''''''''''''''
Session("supplier") = TourOp
```

```
      Session("ref") = TourRef
      Session("depdate") = DepDate
      Session("duration") = Request.Form("duration")
      Session("adults") = Request.Form("adults")
      Session("children") = Request.Form("children")
      Session("infants") = Request.Form("infants")

      ''''''''''''''''''''''''''''''''''''''''
      'Now send the message to the server tier
      ''''''''''''''''''''''''''''''''''''''''
      Set HttpObj = Server.CreateObject("microsoft.xmlhttp")
      HttpObj.open "POST",TransactionURL,false
      HttpObj.setRequestHeader "Content-type", "text/xml"
      HttpObj.send s
      strResult = HttpObj.responseText 'return a string rather than XML so
      it can be validated

      function tagIt(strTag, strData, strAttr)
      'Purpose: Utility function to help mark up XML
      if strData <> "" then
            tagIt = "<" & strTag & " " & strAttr & ">" & strData & "</" & strTag &
">"
      else
            tagIt = "<" & strTag & " " & strAttr & " />"
      end if
end function
%><HTML>
<HEAD>
<LINK rel="stylesheet" type="text/css" href="centaur-r.css">
<TITLE>Quote Results</TITLE>
</HEAD>
<BODY onLoad="onLoad()">

<XML id="xmlQuote"><% =strResult %></XML>

<DIV Class="center"><IMG src = <% =LogoURL %>></DIV>

<DIV Id="quotation">
      <H1>Quotation</H1>
      <H2><% =TourName %>, <% =Resort %></H2>
      <DIV><% =Request.Form("adults") %> <SPAN
Id="adultTarget"></SPAN>  <% =Request.Form("children") %> <SPAN
Id="childTarget"></SPAN>  <% =Request.Form("infants") %> <SPAN
Id="infantTarget"></SPAN></DIV>
      <DIV>Departing on <% =Depday %> <% =DepMonth %> <% =DepYear %> for
<% =Request.Form("duration") %> <SPAN Id="nightTarget"></SPAN></DIV>
      <DIV Id="targetPrice"></DIV>
      <DIV Id="targetNotes"></DIV>
      <DIV Id="instructions">If you wish to book this vacation, you will need
      to read and agree to the tour operator's terms and conditions</DIV>
      <DIV Class="Center">
            <button AccessKey="V" Id="terms" onClick="displayTerms()"
            type="button"><u>V</u>iew Terms</button>
            <button AccessKey="R" Id="return"
            onClick="location='tour.asp?tourid=<%=id%>'"
            type="button"><u>R</u>eturn to Vacation Details</button>
            <button AccessKey="B" Id="bookit"
            onClick="location='bookForm.asp?tourid=<%=id%>'" type="button"
            Disabled=true><u>B</u>ook It!</button>
```

```
        </DIV>
</DIV>

<DIV Id="TandC" Style="display:none">
        <DIV Class="center">
                <TEXTAREA Class="terms" rows=16 cols=90>
                        <% = TermsConditions %>
                </TEXTAREA>
        </DIV>
        <DIV Class="center">
                <button AccessKey="A" Id="accept" onClick="acceptTerms()"
                type="button"><u>A</u>ccept</button>
                <button AccessKey="R" Id="reject" onClick="rejectTerms()"
                type="button"><u>R</u>eject</button>
        </DIV>
</DIV>

<SCRIPT>
var timeout
function onLoad()
{
        // Set a 20 second timeout to check for a reply
        timeout = window.setTimeout("checkResponse()",20000);
        newState();
}

function newState()
// Purpose:
// 1. to get the variables from the XML
// 2. to add the quoted price to the brochure so it can be displayed with the
vacation details.
//      (not implemented in this version)
// 3. to save the sequence number in a cookie so it can be passed in the booking
{
        var domQuote,root,sequence,resultTour,resultAvailability,resultPrice,
        resultNotes,strAlert;

        // keep trying when the readyState changes ...
        if(xmlQuote.readyState != "complete")
                window.setTimeout('newState()',200);

        // .. and if the document is empty
        else if(xmlQuote.documentElement == null)
                window.setTimeout('newState()',200);

        else
        {
                //clear the "no response" timeout
                window.clearTimeout(timeout);

                //Start by getting "adult" or "adults" etc right for the numbers
                if (<% =Request.Form("adults") %> == 1)
                        adultTarget.innerText = "adult";
                else
                        adultTarget.innerText = "adults";
                if (<% =Request.Form("children") %> == 1)
                        childTarget.innerText = "child";
                else
```

```
                childTarget.innerText = "children";
          if (<% =Request.Form("infants") %> == 1)
                infantTarget.innerText = "infant";
          else
                infantTarget.innerText = "infants";
          if (<% =Request.Form("duration") %> == 1)
                nightTarget.innerText = "night";
          else
                nightTarget.innerText = "nights";

          // Now handle the quotation response
          if (xmlQuote.parseError != 0)
                alert("quoteResults.asp: " + xmlQuote.parseError.reason);
          domQuote=xmlQuote;

          root=domQuote.documentElement;
          if(root.childNodes.item(0).nodeName == "error")
          {
                strAlert = "There was an error in the data sent\n";
                strAlert += "The error message was: ";
                strAlert += root.childNodes.item(0).text;
                alert(strAlert);
          }
          else
          {
                // save the sequence number to put in the booking request
                sequence = root.childNodes.item(0).getAttribute("seq");
                document.cookie = 'seq=' + sequence;

                resultTour = root.childNodes.item(0)
                getElementsByTagName("qrdetails").item(0);
                resultAvailability = resultTour.getAttribute("availability");
                resultPrice = resultTour.getAttribute("quote");
                resultNotes = resultTour.getAttribute("notes");
                      if (resultAvailability == "true")
                {
                      targetPrice.innerText = "Total price is £" + resultPrice;
                      targetNotes.innerText = resultNotes;
                }
                else
                {
                      targetPrice.innerText = "I'm sorry, this
                      vacation is not available";
                      instructions.style.display = "none";
                }
          }
     }
}

function checkResponse()
{
     if(xmlQuote.documentElement == null)
           alert("There has been no response from the tour operator system");
}

function displayTerms()
{
     quotation.style.display = "none";
     TandC.style.display = "";
```

```
}

function acceptTerms()
{
      quotation.style.display = "";
      TandC.style.display = "none";
      bookit.disabled=0;
}

function rejectTerms()
{
      quotation.style.display = "";
      TandC.style.display = "none";
      bookit.disabled=-1;
}

</SCRIPT>
</BODY>
</HTML>
```

C

Extensible Markup Language (XML) 1.0 Specification

This appendix is taken from the W3C Recommendation 10-February-1998 available at:

`http://www.w3.org/TR/REC-xml`

The appendix has also been edited in accordance with the list of errata of the 17-February-1999 posted at `http://www.w3.org/XML/xml-19980210-errata`

Editors:

Tim Bray (Textuality and Netscape) tbray@textuality.com
Jean Paoli (Microsoft) jeanpa@microsoft.com
C. M. Sperberg-McQueen
(University of Illinois at Chicago) cmsmcq@uic.edu

Abstract

The Extensible Markup Language (XML) is a subset of SGML that is completely described in this document. Its goal is to enable generic SGML to be served, received, and processed on the Web in the way that is now possible with HTML. XML has been designed for ease of implementation and for interoperability with both SGML and HTML.

Status of this document

This document has been reviewed by W3C Members and other interested parties and has been endorsed by the Director as a W3C Recommendation. It is a stable document and may be used as reference material or cited as a normative reference from another document. W3C's role in making the Recommendation is to draw attention to the specification and to promote its widespread deployment. This enhances the functionality and interoperability of the Web.

This document specifies a syntax created by subsetting an existing, widely used international text processing standard (Standard Generalized Markup Language, ISO 8879:1986(E) as amended and corrected) for use on the World Wide Web. It is a product of the W3C XML Activity, details of which can be found at `http://www.w3.org/XML`. A list of current W3C Recommendations and other technical documents can be found at `http://www.w3.org/TR`.

This specification uses the term URI, which is defined by [Berners-Lee et al.], a work in progress expected to update [IETF RFC1738] and [IETF RFC1808].

The list of known errors in this specification is available at `http://www.w3.org/XML/xml-19980210-errata`.

Please report errors in this document to `xml-editor@w3.org`.

Extensible Markup Language (XML) 1.0

Table of Contents

Appendices

1. Introduction

Extensible Markup Language, abbreviated XML, describes a class of data objects called XML documents and partially describes the behavior of computer programs which process them. XML is an application profile or restricted form of SGML, the Standard Generalized Markup Language [ISO 8879]. By construction, XML documents are conforming SGML documents.

XML documents are made up of storage units called entities, which contain either parsed or unparsed data. Parsed data is made up of characters, some of which form character data, and some of which form markup. Markup encodes a description of the document's storage layout and logical structure. XML provides a mechanism to impose constraints on the storage layout and logical structure.

A software module called an **XML processor** is used to read XML documents and provide access to their content and structure. It is assumed that an XML processor is doing its work on behalf of another module, called the **application**. This specification describes the required behavior of an XML processor in terms of how it must read XML data and the information it must provide to the application.

1.1 Origin and Goals

XML was developed by an XML Working Group (originally known as the SGML Editorial Review Board) formed under the auspices of the World Wide Web Consortium (W3C) in 1996. It was chaired by Jon Bosak of Sun Microsystems with the active participation of an XML Special Interest Group (previously known as the SGML Working Group) also organized by the W3C. The membership of the XML Working Group is given in an appendix. Dan Connolly served as the WG's contact with the W3C.
The design goals for XML are:

- XML shall be straightforwardly usable over the Internet.
- XML shall support a wide variety of applications.
- XML shall be compatible with SGML.
- It shall be easy to write programs which process XML documents.
- The number of optional features in XML is to be kept to the absolute minimum, ideally zero.
- XML documents should be human-legible and reasonably clear.
- The XML design should be prepared quickly.
- The design of XML shall be formal and concise.
- XML documents shall be easy to create.
- Terseness in XML markup is of minimal importance.

This specification, together with associated standards (Unicode and ISO/IEC 10646 for characters, Internet RFC 1766 for language identification tags, ISO 639 for language name codes, and ISO 3166 for country name codes), provides all the information necessary to understand XML Version 1.0 and construct computer programs to process it.

This version of the XML specification may be distributed freely, as long as all text and legal notices remain intact.

1.2 Terminology

The terminology used to describe XML documents is defined in the body of this specification. The terms defined in the following list are used in building those definitions and in describing the actions of an XML processor:

may

Conforming documents and XML processors are permitted to but need not behave as described.

must

Conforming documents and XML processors are required to behave as described; otherwise they are in error.

error

A violation of the rules of this specification; results are undefined. Conforming software may detect and report an error and may recover from it.

fatal error

An error which a conforming XML processor must detect and report to the application. After encountering a fatal error, the processor may continue processing the data to search for further errors and may report such errors to the application. In order to support correction of errors, the processor may make unprocessed data from the document (with intermingled character data and markup) available to the application. Once a fatal error is detected, however, the processor must not continue normal processing (i.e., it must not continue to pass character data and information about the document's logical structure to the application in the normal way).

at user option

Conforming software may or must (depending on the modal verb in the sentence) behave as described; if it does, it must provide users a means to enable or disable the behavior described.

validity constraint

A rule which applies to all valid XML documents. Violations of validity constraints are errors; they must, at user option, be reported by validating XML processors.

well-formedness constraint

A rule which applies to all well-formed XML documents. Violations of well-formedness constraints are fatal errors.

match

(Of strings or names:) Two strings or names being compared must be identical. Characters with multiple possible representations in ISO/IEC 10646 (e.g. characters with both precomposed and base+diacritic forms) match only if they have the same representation in both strings. At user option, processors may normalize such characters to some canonical form. No case folding is performed. (Of strings and rules in the grammar:) A string matches a grammatical production if it belongs to the language generated by that production. (Of content and content models:) An element matches its declaration when it conforms in the fashion described in the constraint "Element Valid".

for compatibility

A feature of XML included solely to ensure that XML remains compatible with SGML.

for interoperability

A non-binding recommendation included to increase the chances that XML documents can be processed by the existing installed base of SGML processors which predate the WebSGML Adaptations Annex to ISO 8879.

2. Documents

A data object is an **XML document** if it is well-formed, as defined in this specification. A well-formed XML document may in addition be valid if it meets certain further constraints.

Each XML document has both a logical and a physical structure. Physically, the document is composed of units called entities. An entity may refer to other entities to cause their inclusion in the document. A document begins in a "root" or document entity. Logically, the document is composed of declarations, elements, comments, character references, and processing instructions, all of which are indicated in the document by explicit markup. The logical and physical structures must nest properly, as described in "4.3.2 Well-Formed Parsed Entities".

2.1 Well-Formed XML Documents

A textual object is a well-formed XML document if:

- Taken as a whole, it matches the production labeled `document`.
- It meets all the well-formedness constraints given in this specification.
- Each of the parsed entities which is referenced directly or indirectly within the document is well-formed.

Document			
[1]	`document`	`::=`	`prolog element Misc*`

Matching the `document` production implies that:

- It contains one or more elements.
- There is exactly one element, called the **root**, or document element, no part of which appears in the content of any other element. For all other elements, if the **start-tag** is in the content of another element, the **end-tag** is in the content of the same element. More simply stated, the elements, delimited by start- and end-tags, nest properly within each other.

As a consequence of this, for each non-root element `C` in the document, there is one other element `P` in the document such that `C` is in the content of `P`, but is not in the content of any other element that is in the content of `P`. `P` is referred to as the **parent** of `C`, and `C` as a **child** of `P`.

2.2 Characters

A parsed entity contains **text**, a sequence of characters, which may represent markup or character data. A **character** is an atomic unit of text as specified by ISO/IEC 10646 [ISO/IEC 10646]. Legal characters are tab, carriage return, line feed, and the legal graphic characters of Unicode and ISO/IEC 10646. The use of "compatibility characters", as defined in section 6.8 of [Unicode], is discouraged.

Character Range				
[2]	Char	::=	#x9 | #xA | #xD | [#x20-#xD7FF] | [#xE000-#xFFFD] | [#x10000-#x10FFFF]	/*any Unicode character, excluding the surrogate blocks, FFFE, and FFFF. */

Production [2] is normative; in practical terms this means that newly added Unicode characters such as the Euro (`€ €`) are legal in XML documents.

The mechanism for encoding character code points into bit patterns may vary from entity to entity. All XML processors must accept the UTF-8 and UTF-16 encodings of 10646; the mechanisms for signaling which of the two is in use, or for bringing other encodings into play, are discussed later, in "4.3.3 Character Encoding in Entities".

2.3 Common Syntactic Constructs

This section defines some symbols used widely in the grammar.

`S` (white space) consists of one or more space (#x20) characters, carriage returns, line feeds, or tabs.

White Space		
[3]	S ::=	(#x20 | #x9 | #xD | #xA)+

Characters are classified for convenience as letters, digits, or other characters. Letters consist of an alphabetic or syllabic base character possibly followed by one or more combining characters, or of an ideographic character. Full definitions of the specific characters in each class are given in "B. Character Classes".

A **Name** is a token beginning with a letter or one of a few punctuation characters, and continuing with letters, digits, hyphens, underscores, colons, or full stops, together known as name characters. Names beginning with the string "`xml`", or any string which would match `(('X'|'x') ('M'|'m') ('L'|'l'))`, are reserved for standardization in this or future versions of this specification.

Note: The colon character within XML names is reserved for experimentation with name spaces. Its meaning is expected to be standardized at some future point, at which point those documents using the colon for experimental purposes may need to be updated. (There is no guarantee that any name-space mechanism adopted for XML will in fact use the colon as a name-space delimiter.)

In practice, this means that authors should not use the colon in XML names except as part of name-space experiments, but that XML processors should accept the colon as a name character.

An Nmtoken (name token) is any mixture of name characters.

<table>
<tr><th colspan="4">Names and Tokens</th></tr>
<tr><td>[4]</td><td>NameChar</td><td>::=</td><td>Letter | Digit | '.' | '-' | '_' | ':'
| CombiningChar | Extender</td></tr>
<tr><td>[5]</td><td>Name</td><td>::=</td><td>(Letter | '_' | ':') (NameChar)*</td></tr>
<tr><td>[6]</td><td>Names</td><td>::=</td><td>Name (S Name)*</td></tr>
<tr><td>[7]</td><td>Nmtoken</td><td>::=</td><td>(NameChar)+</td></tr>
<tr><td>[8]</td><td>Nmtokens</td><td>::=</td><td>Nmtoken (S Nmtoken)*</td></tr>
</table>

Literal data is any quoted string not containing the quotation mark used as a delimiter for that string. Literals are used for specifying the content of internal entities (EntityValue), the values of attributes (AttValue), and external identifiers (SystemLiteral). Note that a SystemLiteral can be parsed without scanning for markup.

<table>
<tr><th colspan="4">Literals</th></tr>
<tr><td>[9]</td><td>EntityValue</td><td>::=</td><td>'"' ([^%&"] | PEReference | Reference)* '"'
| "'" ([^%&'] | PEReference | Reference)* "'"</td></tr>
<tr><td>[10]</td><td>AttValue</td><td>::=</td><td>'"' ([^<&"] | Reference)* '"'
| "'" ([^<&'] | Reference)* "'"</td></tr>
<tr><td>[11]</td><td>SystemLiteral</td><td>::=</td><td>('"' [^"]* '"') | ("'" [^']* "'")</td></tr>
<tr><td>[12]</td><td>PubidLiteral</td><td>::=</td><td>'"' PubidChar* '"' | "'" (PubidChar - "'")* "'"</td></tr>
<tr><td>[13]</td><td>PubidChar</td><td>::=</td><td>#x20 | #xD | #xA | [a-zA-Z0-9] |
[-'()+,./:=?;!*#@$_%]</td></tr>
</table>

2.4 Character Data and Markup

Text consists of intermingled character data and markup. **Markup** takes the form of start-tags, end-tags, empty-element tags, entity references, character references, comments, CDATA section delimiters, document type declarations, and processing instructions.

All text that is not markup constitutes the **character data** of the document.

The ampersand character (&) and the left angle bracket (<) may appear in their literal form *only* when used as markup delimiters, or within a comment, a processing instruction, or a CDATA section. They are also legal within the literal entity value of an internal entity declaration; see "4.3.2 Well-Formed Parsed Entities". If they are needed elsewhere, they must be escaped using either numeric character references or the strings "&" and "<" respectively. The right angle bracket (>) may be represented using the string ">", and must, for compatibility, be escaped using ">" or a character reference when it appears in the string "]]>" in content, when that string is not marking the end of a CDATA section.

In the content of elements, character data is any string of characters which does not contain the start-delimiter of any markup. In a CDATA section, character data is any string of characters not including the CDATA-section-close delimiter, "`]]>`".

To allow attribute values to contain both single and double quotes, the apostrophe or single-quote character (') may be represented as "`'`", and the double-quote character (") as "`"`".

<table>
<tr><th colspan="4">Character Data</th></tr>
<tr><td>[14]</td><td>CharData</td><td>::=</td><td>[^<&]* - ([^<&]* ']]>' [^<&]*)</td></tr>
</table>

2.5 Comments

Comments may appear anywhere in a document outside other markup; in addition, they may appear within the document type declaration at places allowed by the grammar. They are not part of the document's character data; an XML processor may, but need not, make it possible for an application to retrieve the text of comments. For compatibility, the string "`--`" (double-hyphen) must not occur within comments.

<table>
<tr><th colspan="4">Comments</th></tr>
<tr><td>[15]</td><td>Comment</td><td>::=</td><td>'<!--' ((Char - '-') | ('-' (Char - '-')))* '-->'</td></tr>
</table>

An example of a comment:

```
<!-- declarations for <head> & <body> -->
```

2.6 Processing Instructions

Processing instructions (PIs) allow documents to contain instructions for applications.

<table>
<tr><th colspan="4">Processing Instructions</th></tr>
<tr><td>[16]</td><td>PI</td><td>::=</td><td>'<?' PITarget (S (Char* - (Char* '?>' Char*)))? '?>'</td></tr>
<tr><td>[17]</td><td>PITarget</td><td>::=</td><td>Name - (('X' | 'x') ('M' | 'm') ('L' | 'l'))</td></tr>
</table>

PIs are not part of the document's character data, but must be passed through to the application. The PI begins with a target (`PITarget`) used to identify the application to which the instruction is directed. The target names "`XML`", "`xml`", and so on are reserved for standardization in this or future versions of this specification. The XML Notation mechanism may be used for formal declaration of PI targets.

2.7 CDATA Sections

CDATA sections may occur anywhere character data may occur; they are used to escape blocks of text containing characters which would otherwise be recognized as markup. CDATA sections begin with the string "`<![CDATA[`" and end with the string "`]]>`":

CDATA Sections			
[18]	CDSect	::=	CDStart CData CDEnd
[19]	CDStart	::=	'<![CDATA['
[20]	CData	::=	(Char* - (Char* ']]>' Char*))
[21]	CDEnd	::=	']]>'

Within a CDATA section, only the CDEnd string is recognized as markup, so that left angle brackets and ampersands may occur in their literal form; they need not (and cannot) be escaped using "<" and "&". CDATA sections cannot nest.

An example of a CDATA section, in which "<greeting>" and "</greeting>" are recognized as character data, not markup:

```
<![CDATA[<greeting>Hello, world!</greeting>]]>
```

2.8 Prolog and Document Type Declaration

XML documents may, and should, begin with an **XML declaration** which specifies the version of XML being used. For example, the following is a complete XML document, well-formed but not valid:

```
<?xml version="1.0"?>
<greeting>Hello, world!</greeting>
```

and so is this:

```
<greeting>Hello, world!</greeting>
```

The version number "1.0" should be used to indicate conformance to this version of this specification; it is an error for a document to use the value "1.0" if it does not conform to this version of this specification. It is the intent of the XML working group to give later versions of this specification numbers other than "1.0", but this intent does not indicate a commitment to produce any future versions of XML, nor if any are produced, to use any particular numbering scheme. Since future versions are not ruled out, this construct is provided as a means to allow the possibility of automatic version recognition, should it become necessary. Processors may signal an error if they receive documents labeled with versions they do not support.

The function of the markup in an XML document is to describe its storage and logical structure and to associate attribute-value pairs with its logical structures. XML provides a mechanism, the document type declaration, to define constraints on the logical structure and to support the use of predefined storage units. An XML document is **valid** if it has an associated document type declaration and if the document complies with the constraints expressed in it.

The document type declaration must appear before the first element in the document.

<table>
<tr><th colspan="4">Prolog</th></tr>
<tr><td>[22]</td><td>prolog</td><td>::=</td><td>XMLDecl? Misc* (doctypedecl Misc*)?</td></tr>
<tr><td>[23]</td><td>XMLDecl</td><td>::=</td><td>'<?xml' VersionInfo EncodingDecl? SDDecl? S? '?>'</td></tr>
<tr><td>[24]</td><td>VersionInfo</td><td>::=</td><td>S 'version' Eq ("'" VersionNum "'" | '"' VersionNum '"')</td></tr>
<tr><td>[25]</td><td>Eq</td><td>::=</td><td>S? '=' S?</td></tr>
<tr><td>[26]</td><td>VersionNum</td><td>::=</td><td>([a-zA-Z0-9_.:] | '-')+</td></tr>
<tr><td>[27]</td><td>Misc</td><td>::=</td><td>Comment | PI | S</td></tr>
</table>

The XML **document type declaration** contains or points to markup declarations that provide a grammar for a class of documents. This grammar is known as a document type definition, or **DTD**. The document type declaration can point to an external subset (a special kind of external entity) containing markup declarations, or can contain the markup declarations directly in an internal subset, or can do both. The DTD for a document consists of both subsets taken together.

A **markup declaration** is an element type declaration, an attribute-list declaration, an entity declaration, or a notation declaration. These declarations may be contained in whole or in part within parameter entities, as described in the well-formedness and validity constraints below. For further information, see "4. Physical Structures".

<table>
<tr><td>[28]</td><td>doctypedecl</td><td>::=</td><td>'<!DOCTYPE' S Name (S ExternalID)? S? ('[' (markupdecl
| PEReference | S)*
']' S?)? '>'</td><td>[VC: Root Element Type]</td></tr>
<tr><td>[29]</td><td>markupdecl</td><td>::=</td><td>elementdecl
| AttlistDecl
| EntityDecl
| NotationDecl | PI
| Comment</td><td>[VC: Proper Declaration/PE Nesting]</td></tr>
<tr><td></td><td></td><td></td><td></td><td>[WFC: PEs in Internal Subset]</td></tr>
</table>

The markup declarations may be made up in whole or in part of the replacement text of parameter entities. The productions later in this specification for individual nonterminals (`elementdecl`, `AttlistDecl`, and so on) describe the declarations *after* all the parameter entities have been included.

Validity Constraint: Root Element Type

The `Name` in the document type declaration must match the element type of the root element.

Validity Constraint: Proper Declaration/PE Nesting

Parameter-entity replacement text must be properly nested with markup declarations. That is to say, if either the first character or the last character of a markup declaration (`markupdecl` above) is contained in the replacement text for a parameter-entity reference, both must be contained in the same replacement text.

Well-Formedness Constraint: PEs in Internal Subset

In the internal DTD subset, parameter-entity references can occur only where markup declarations can occur, not within markup declarations. (This does not apply to references that occur in external parameter entities or to the external subset.)

Like the internal subset, the external subset and any external parameter entities referred to in the DTD must consist of a series of complete markup declarations of the types allowed by the non-terminal symbol `markupdecl`, interspersed with white space or parameter-entity references. However, portions of the contents of the external subset or of external parameter entities may conditionally be ignored by using the conditional section construct; this is not allowed in the internal subset.

External Subset			
[30]	extSubset	::=	TextDecl? extSubsetDecl
[31]	extSubsetDecl	::=	(markupdecl | conditionalSect | PEReference | S)*

The external subset and external parameter entities also differ from the internal subset in that in them, parameter-entity references are permitted *within* markup declarations, not only *between* markup declarations.

An example of an XML document with a document type declaration:

```
<?xml version="1.0"?>
<!DOCTYPE greeting SYSTEM "hello.dtd">
<greeting>Hello, world!</greeting>
```

The system identifier "`hello.dtd`" gives the URI of a DTD for the document.

The declarations can also be given locally, as in this example:

```
<?xml version="1.0" encoding="UTF-8" ?>
<!DOCTYPE greeting [
  <!ELEMENT greeting (#PCDATA)>
]>
<greeting>Hello, world!</greeting>
```

If both the external and internal subsets are used, the internal subset is considered to occur before the external subset. This has the effect that entity and attribute-list declarations in the internal subset take precedence over those in the external subset.

2.9 Standalone Document Declaration

Markup declarations can affect the content of the document, as passed from an XML processor to an application; examples are attribute defaults and entity declarations. The standalone document declaration, which may appear as a component of the XML declaration, signals whether or not there are such declarations which appear external to the document entity.

Standalone Document Declaration			
[32]	`SDDecl`	`::= S 'standalone' Eq (("'" ('yes' | 'no') "'") | ('"' ('yes' | 'no') '"'))`	[VC: Standalone Document Declaration]

In a standalone document declaration, the value "yes" indicates that there are no markup declarations external to the document entity (either in the DTD external subset, or in an external parameter entity referenced from the internal subset) which affect the information passed from the XML processor to the application. The value "no" indicates that there are or may be such external markup declarations. Note that the standalone document declaration only denotes the presence of external *declarations*; the presence, in a document, of references to external *entities*, when those entities are internally declared, does not change its standalone status.

If there are no external markup declarations, the standalone document declaration has no meaning. If there are external markup declarations but there is no standalone document declaration, the value "no" is assumed.

Any XML document for which `standalone="no"` holds can be converted algorithmically to a standalone document, which may be desirable for some network delivery applications.

Validity Constraint: Standalone Document Declaration

The standalone document declaration must have the value "no" if any external markup declarations contain declarations of:

- attributes with default values, if elements to which these attributes apply appear in the document without specifications of values for these attributes, or
- entities (other than `amp`, `lt`, `gt`, `apos`, `quot`), if references to those entities appear in the document, or
- attributes with values subject to normalization, where the attribute appears in the document with a value which will change as a result of normalization, or
- element types with element content, if white space occurs directly within any instance of those types.

An example XML declaration with a standalone document declaration:

```
<?xml version="1.0" standalone='yes'?>
```

2.10 White Space Handling

In editing XML documents, it is often convenient to use "white space" (spaces, tabs, and blank lines, denoted by the nonterminal `S` in this specification) to set apart the markup for greater readability. Such white space is typically not intended for inclusion in the delivered version of the document. On the other hand, "significant" white space that should be preserved in the delivered version is common, for example in poetry and source code.

An XML processor must always pass all characters in a document that are not markup through to the application. A validating XML processor must also inform the application which of these characters constitute white space appearing in element content.

A special attribute named `xml:space` may be attached to an element to signal an intention that in that element, white space should be preserved by applications. In valid documents, this attribute, like any other, must be declared if it is used. When declared, it must be given as an enumerated type whose only possible values are "`default`" and "`preserve`". For example:

```
<!ATTLIST poem   xml:space (default|preserve) 'preserve'>
```

The value "`default`" signals that applications' default white-space processing modes are acceptable for this element; the value "`preserve`" indicates the intent that applications preserve all the white space. This declared intent is considered to apply to all elements within the content of the element where it is specified, unless overriden with another instance of the `xml:space` attribute.

The root element of any document is considered to have signaled no intentions as regards application space handling, unless it provides a value for this attribute or the attribute is declared with a default value.

2.11 End-of-Line Handling

XML parsed entities are often stored in computer files which, for editing convenience, are organized into lines. These lines are typically separated by some combination of the characters carriage-return (#xD) and line-feed (#xA).

To simplify the tasks of applications, wherever an external parsed entity or the literal entity value of an internal parsed entity contains either the literal two-character sequence "#xD#xA" or a standalone literal #xD, an XML processor must pass to the application the single character #xA. (This behavior can conveniently be produced by normalizing all line breaks to #xA on input, before parsing.)

2.12 Language Identification

In document processing, it is often useful to identify the natural or formal language in which the content is written. A special attribute named `xml:lang` may be inserted in documents to specify the language used in the contents and attribute values of any element in an XML document. In valid documents, this attribute, like any other, must be declared if it is used. The values of the attribute are language identifiers as defined by [IETF RFC 1766], "Tags for the Identification of Languages":

Language Identification			
[33]	LanguageID	::=	Langcode ('-' Subcode)*
[34]	Langcode	::=	ISO639Code | IanaCode | UserCode
[35]	ISO639Code	::=	([a-z] | [A-Z]) ([a-z] | [A-Z])
[36]	IanaCode	::=	('i' | 'I') '-' ([a-z] | [A-Z])+
[37]	UserCode	::=	('x' | 'X') '-' ([a-z] | [A-Z])+
[38]	Subcode	::=	([a-z] | [A-Z])+

The Langcode may be any of the following:

- a two-letter language code as defined by [ISO 639], "Codes for the representation of names of languages"
- a language identifier registered with the Internet Assigned Numbers Authority [IANA]; these begin with the prefix "i-" (or "I-")
- a language identifier assigned by the user, or agreed on between parties in private use; these must begin with the prefix "x-" or "X-" in order to ensure that they do not conflict with names later standardized or registered with IANA

There may be any number of Subcode segments; if the first subcode segment exists and the Subcode consists of two letters, then it must be a country code from [ISO 3166], "Codes for the representation of names of countries." If the first subcode consists of more than two letters, it must be a subcode for the language in question registered with IANA, unless the Langcode begins with the prefix "x-" or "X-".

It is customary to give the language code in lower case, and the country code (if any) in upper case. Note that these values, unlike other names in XML documents, are case insensitive.

For example:

```
<p xml:lang="en">The quick brown fox jumps over the lazy dog.</p>
<p xml:lang="en-GB">What colour is it?</p>
<p xml:lang="en-US">What color is it?</p>
<sp who="Faust" desc='leise' xml:lang="de">
  <l>Habe nun, ach! Philosophie,</l>
  <l>Juristerei, und Medizin</l>
  <l>und leider auch Theologie</l>
  <l>durchaus studiert mit heißem Bemüh'n.</l>
</sp>
```

The intent declared with xml:lang is considered to apply to all attributes and content of the element where it is specified, unless overridden with an instance of xml:lang on another element within that content.

A simple declaration for xml:lang might take the form:

```
xml:lang  NMTOKEN  #IMPLIED
```

but specific default values may also be given, if appropriate. In a collection of French poems for English students, with glosses and notes in English, the `xml:lang` attribute might be declared this way:

```
<!ATTLIST poem   xml:lang NMTOKEN 'fr'>
<!ATTLIST gloss  xml:lang NMTOKEN 'en'>
<!ATTLIST note   xml:lang NMTOKEN 'en'>
```

3. Logical Structures

Each XML document contains one or more **elements**, the boundaries of which are either delimited by start-tags and end-tags, or, for empty elements, by an empty-element tag. Each element has a type, identified by name, sometimes called its "generic identifier" (GI), and may have a set of attribute specifications. Each attribute specification has a name and a value.

Element				
[39]	`element`	`::=`	`EmptyElemTag`	
			`| STag content ETag`	`[WFC:` Element Type Match `]`
				`[VC:` Element Valid `]`

This specification does not constrain the semantics, use, or (beyond syntax) names of the element types and attributes, except that names beginning with a match to `(('X'|'x')('M'|'m')('L'|'l'))` are reserved for standardization in this or future versions of this specification.

Well-Formedness Constraint: Element Type Match

The `Name` in an element's end-tag must match the element type in the start-tag.

Validity Constraint: Element Valid

An element is valid if there is a declaration matching `elementdecl` where the `Name` matches the element type, and one of the following holds:

The declaration matches `EMPTY` and the element has no content.
The declaration matches `children` and the sequence of child elements belongs to the language generated by the regular expression in the content model, with optional white space (characters matching the nonterminal `S`) between each pair of child elements.
The declaration matches `Mixed` and the content consists of character data and child elements whose types match names in the content model.
The declaration matches `ANY`, and the types of any child elements have been declared.

3.1 Start-Tags, End-Tags, and Empty-Element Tags

The beginning of every non-empty XML element is marked by a **start-tag**.

Start-tag				
[40]	`STag`	`::=`	`'<' Name (S Attribute)* S? '>'`	[`WFC`: Unique Att Spec]
[41]	`Attribute`	`::=`	`Name Eq AttValue`	[`VC`: Attribute Value Type]
				[`WFC`: No External Entity References]
				[`WFC`: No < in Attribute Values]

The `Name` in the start- and end-tags gives the element's **type**. The `Name-AttValue` pairs are referred to as the **attribute specifications** of the element, with the `Name` in each pair referred to as the **attribute name** and the content of the `AttValue` (the text between the `'` or `"` delimiters) as the **attribute value**.

Well-Formedness Constraint: Unique Att Spec

No attribute name may appear more than once in the same start-tag or empty-element tag.

Validity Constraint: Attribute Value Type

The attribute must have been declared; the value must be of the type declared for it. (For attribute types, see "3.3 Attribute-List Declarations".)

Well-Formedness Constraint: No External Entity References

Attribute values cannot contain direct or indirect entity references to external entities.

Well-Formedness Constraint: No < in Attribute Values

The replacement text of any entity referred to directly or indirectly in an attribute value (other than "`<`") must not contain a <.

An example of a start-tag:

```
<termdef id="dt-dog" term="dog">
```

The end of every element that begins with a start-tag must be marked by an **end-tag** containing a name that echoes the element's type as given in the start-tag:

End-tag			
[42]	`ETag`	`::=`	`'</' Name S? '>'`

An example of an end-tag:

```
</termdef>
```

The text between the start-tag and end-tag is called the element's **content**:

Content of Elements			
[43]	content	::=	(element | CharData | Reference | CDSect | PI | Comment)*

If an element is **empty**, it must be represented either by a start-tag immediately followed by an end-tag or by an empty-element tag. An **empty-element tag** takes a special form:

Tags for Empty Elements				
[44]	EmptyElemTag	::=	'<' Name (S Attribute)* S? '/>'	[WFC: Unique Att Spec]

Empty-element tags may be used for any element which has no content, whether or not it is declared using the keyword EMPTY. For interoperability, the empty-element tag must be used, and can only be used, for elements which are declared EMPTY.

Examples of empty elements:

```
<IMG align="left"
 src="http://www.w3.org/Icons/WWW/w3c_home" />
<br></br>
<br/>
```

3.2 Element Type Declarations

The element structure of an XML document may, for validation purposes, be constrained using element type and attribute-list declarations. An element type declaration constrains the element's content.

Element type declarations often constrain which element types can appear as children of the element. At user option, an XML processor may issue a warning when a declaration mentions an element type for which no declaration is provided, but this is not an error.

An **element type declaration** takes the form:

Element Type Declaration				
[45]	elementdecl	::=	'<!ELEMENT' S Name S contentspec S? '>'	[VC: Unique Element Type Declaration]
[46]	contentspec	::=	'EMPTY' | 'ANY' | Mixed | children	

where the Name gives the element type being declared.

Validity Constraint: Unique Element Type Declaration

No element type may be declared more than once.

Examples of element type declarations:

```
<!ELEMENT br EMPTY>
<!ELEMENT p (#PCDATA|emph)* >
<!ELEMENT %name.para; %content.para; >
<!ELEMENT container ANY>
```

3.2.1 Element Content

An element type has **element content** when elements of that type must contain only child elements (no character data), optionally separated by white space (characters matching the nonterminal `S`). In this case, the constraint includes a content model, a simple grammar governing the allowed types of the child elements and the order in which they are allowed to appear. The grammar is built on content particles (`cp`s), which consist of names, choice lists of content particles, or sequence lists of content particles:

Element-content Models

[47]	children	::=	(choice | seq) ('?' | '*' | '+')?	
[48]	cp	::=	(Name | choice | seq) ('?' | '*' | '+')?	
[49]	choice	::=	'(' S? cp (S? '|' S? cp)* S? ')'	[VC: Proper Group/PE Nesting]
[50]	seq	::=	'(' S? cp (S? ',' S? cp)* S? ')'	[VC: Proper Group/PE Nesting]

where each `Name` is the type of an element which may appear as a child. Any content particle in a choice list may appear in the element content at the location where the choice list appears in the grammar; content particles occurring in a sequence list must each appear in the element content in the order given in the list. The optional character following a name or list governs whether the element or the content particles in the list may occur one or more (+), zero or more (*), or zero or one times (?). The absence of such an operator means that the element or content particle must appear exactly once. This syntax and meaning are identical to those used in the productions in this specification.

The content of an element matches a content model if and only if it is possible to trace out a path through the content model, obeying the sequence, choice, and repetition operators and matching each element in the content against an element type in the content model. For compatibility, it is an error if an element in the document can match more than one occurrence of an element type in the content model. For more information, see **Appendix E. Deterministic Content Models**.

Validity Constraint: Proper Group/PE Nesting

Parameter-entity replacement text must be properly nested with parenthesized groups. That is to say, if either of the opening or closing parentheses in a `choice`, `seq`, or `Mixed` construct is contained in the replacement text for a parameter entity, both must be contained in the same replacement text. For interoperability, if a parameter-entity reference appears in a `choice`, `seq`, or `Mixed` construct, its replacement text should not be empty, and neither the first nor last non-blank character of the replacement text should be a connector (| or ,).

Examples of element-content models:

```
<!ELEMENT spec (front, body, back?)>
<!ELEMENT div1 (head, (p | list | note)*, div2*)>
<!ELEMENT dictionary-body (%div.mix; | %dict.mix;)*>
```

3.2.2 Mixed Content

An element type has **mixed content** when elements of that type may contain character data, optionally interspersed with child elements. In this case, the types of the child elements may be constrained, but not their order or their number of occurrences:

Mixed-content Declaration				
[51]	`Mixed`	`::=`	`'(' S? '#PCDATA' (S? '|' S? Name)* S? ')*'`	
			`| '(' S? '#PCDATA' S? ')'`	[VC: Proper Group/PE Nesting]
				[VC: No Duplicate Types]

where the Names give the types of elements that may appear as children. The keyword PCDATA derives historically from the term "parsed character data".

Validity Constraint: No Duplicate Types

The same name must not appear more than once in a single mixed-content declaration.

Examples of mixed content declarations:

```
<!ELEMENT p (#PCDATA|a|ul|b|i|em)*>
<!ELEMENT p (#PCDATA | %font; | %phrase; | %special; | %form;)* >
<!ELEMENT b (#PCDATA)>
```

3.3 Attribute-List Declarations

Attributes are used to associate name-value pairs with elements. Attribute specifications may appear only within start-tags and empty-element tags; thus, the productions used to recognize them appear in "3.1 Start-Tags, End-Tags, and Empty-Element Tags". Attribute-list declarations may be used:

- To define the set of attributes pertaining to a given element type.
- To establish type constraints for these attributes.
- To provide default values for attributes.

Attribute-list declarations specify the name, data type, and default value (if any) of each attribute associated with a given element type:

Attribute-list Declaration			
[52]	`AttlistDecl`	`::=`	`'<!ATTLIST' S Name AttDef* S? '>'`
[53]	`AttDef`	`::=`	`S Name S AttType S DefaultDecl`

The Name in the AttlistDecl rule is the type of an element. At user option, an XML processor may issue a warning if attributes are declared for an element type not itself declared, but this is not an error. The Name in the AttDef rule is the name of the attribute.

When more than one AttlistDecl is provided for a given element type, the contents of all those provided are merged. When more than one definition is provided for the same attribute of a given element type, the first declaration is binding and later declarations are ignored. For interoperability, writers of DTDs may choose to provide at most one attribute-list declaration for a given element type, at most one attribute definition for a given attribute name in an attribute-list declaration, and at least one attribute definition in each attribute-list declaration. For interoperability, an XML processor may at user option issue a warning when more than one attribute-list declaration is provided for a given element type, or more than one attribute definition is provided for a given attribute, but this is not an error.

3.3.1 Attribute Types

XML attribute types are of three kinds: a string type, a set of tokenized types, and enumerated types. The string type may take any literal string as a value; the tokenized types have varying lexical and semantic constraints. The validity constraints noted in the grammar are applied after the attribute value has been normalized as described in **Section 3.3 Attribute-List Declarations**.

Attribute Types				
[54]	AttType	::=	StringType | TokenizedType | EnumeratedType	
[55]	StringType	::=	'CDATA'	
[56]	TokenizedType	::=	'ID'	[VC: ID]
			| 'IDREF'	[VC: One ID per Element Type]
			| 'IDREFS'	[VC: ID Attribute Default]
			| 'ENTITY'	[VC: IDREF]
			| 'ENTITIES'	[VC: IDREF]
			| 'NMTOKEN'	[VC: Entity Name]
			| 'NMTOKENS'	[VC: Entity Name]
				[VC: Name Token]
				[VC: Name Token]

Validity Constraint: ID

Values of type ID must match the Name production. A name must not appear more than once in an XML document as a value of this type; i.e., ID values must uniquely identify the elements which bear them.

Validity Constraint: One ID per Element Type

No element type may have more than one ID attribute specified.

Validity Constraint: ID Attribute Default

An ID attribute must have a declared default of `#IMPLIED` or `#REQUIRED`.

Validity Constraint: IDREF

Values of type `IDREF` must match the `Name` production, and values of type `IDREFS` must match `Names`; each `Name` must match the value of an ID attribute on some element in the XML document; i.e. `IDREF` values must match the value of some ID attribute.

Validity Constraint: Entity Name

Values of type `ENTITY` must match the `Name` production, values of type `ENTITIES` must match `Names`; each `Name` must match the name of an unparsed entity declared in the DTD.

Validity Constraint: Name Token

Values of type `NMTOKEN` must match the `Nmtoken` production; values of type `NMTOKENS` must match `Nmtokens`.

Enumerated attributes can take one of a list of values provided in the declaration. There are two kinds of enumerated types:

Enumerated Attribute Types				
[57]	`EnumeratedType`	`::=`	`NotationType | Enumeration`	
[58]	`NotationType`	`::=`	`'NOTATION' S '(' S? Name (S? '|' S? Name)* S? ')'`	`[VC:` Notation Attributes `]` `[VC:` One Notation per Element Type`]`
[59]	`Enumeration`	`::=`	`'(' S? Nmtoken (S? '|' S? Nmtoken)* S? ')'`	`[VC:` Enumeration `]`

A `NOTATION` attribute identifies a notation, declared in the DTD with associated system and/or public identifiers, to be used in interpreting the element to which the attribute is attached.

Validity Constraint: Notation Attributes

Values of this type must match one of the notation names included in the declaration; all notation names in the declaration must be declared.

Validity Constraint: One Notation per Element Type

No element type may have more than one NOTATION attribute specified.

Validity Constraint: Enumeration

Values of this type must match one of the `Nmtoken` tokens in the declaration.

For interoperability, the same `Nmtoken` should not occur more than once in the enumerated attribute types of a single element type.

3.3.2 Attribute Defaults

An attribute declaration provides information on whether the attribute's presence is required, and if not, how an XML processor should react if a declared attribute is absent in a document.

Attribute Defaults				
[60]	DefaultDecl	::=	'#REQUIRED' | '#IMPLIED'	
			| (('#FIXED' S)? AttValue)	[VC: Required Attribute]
				[VC: Attribute Default Legal]
				[WFC: No < in Attribute Values]
				[VC: Fixed Attribute Default]

In an attribute declaration, `#REQUIRED` means that the attribute must always be provided, `#IMPLIED` that no default value is provided. If the declaration is neither `#REQUIRED` nor `#IMPLIED`, then the `AttValue` value contains the declared **default** value; the `#FIXED` keyword states that the attribute must always have the default value. If a default value is declared, when an XML processor encounters an omitted attribute, it is to behave as though the attribute were present with the declared default value.

Validity Constraint: Required Attribute

If the default declaration is the keyword `#REQUIRED`, then the attribute must be specified for all elements of the type in the attribute-list declaration.

Validity Constraint: Attribute Default Legal

The declared default value must meet the lexical constraints of the declared attribute type.

Validity Constraint: Fixed Attribute Default

If an attribute has a default value declared with the `#FIXED` keyword, instances of that attribute must match the default value.

Examples of attribute-list declarations:

```
<!ATTLIST termdef
          id      ID      #REQUIRED
          name    CDATA   #IMPLIED>
<!ATTLIST list
          type    (bullets|ordered|glossary)  "ordered">
<!ATTLIST form
          method  CDATA   #FIXED "POST">
```

3.3.3 Attribute-Value Normalization

Before the value of an attribute is passed to the application or checked for validity, the XML processor must normalize it as follows:

- a character reference is processed by appending the referenced character to the attribute value
- an entity reference is processed by recursively processing the replacement text of the entity
- a whitespace character (#x20, #xD, #xA, #x9) is processed by appending #x20 to the normalized value, except that only a single #x20 is appended for a "#xD#xA" sequence that is part of an external parsed entity or the literal entity value of an internal parsed entity
- other characters are processed by appending them to the normalized value

If the declared value is not CDATA, then the XML processor must further process the normalized attribute value by discarding any leading and trailing space (#x20) characters, and by replacing sequences of space (#x20) characters by a single space (#x20) character.

All attributes for which no declaration has been read should be treated by a non-validating parser as if declared `CDATA`.

3.4 Conditional Sections

Conditional sections are portions of the document type declaration external subset which are included in, or excluded from, the logical structure of the DTD based on the keyword which governs them.

Conditional Section			
[61]	`conditionalSect`	`::=`	`includeSect | ignoreSect`
[62]	`includeSect`	`::=`	`'<![' S? 'INCLUDE' S? '[' extSubsetDecl ']]>'`
[63]	`ignoreSect`	`::=`	`'<![' S? 'IGNORE' S? '[' ignoreSectContents* ']]>'`
[64]	`ignoreSectContents`	`::=`	`Ignore ('<![' ignoreSectContents ']]>' Ignore)*`
[65]	`Ignore`	`::=`	`Char* - (Char* ('<![' | ']]>') Char*)`

Like the internal and external DTD subsets, a conditional section may contain one or more complete declarations, comments, processing instructions, or nested conditional sections, intermingled with white space.

If the keyword of the conditional section is `INCLUDE`, then the contents of the conditional section are part of the DTD. If the keyword of the conditional section is `IGNORE`, then the contents of the conditional section are not logically part of the DTD. Note that for reliable parsing, the contents of even ignored conditional sections must be read in order to detect nested conditional sections and ensure that the end of the outermost (ignored) conditional section is properly detected. If a conditional section with a keyword of `INCLUDE` occurs within a larger conditional section with a keyword of `IGNORE`, both the outer and the inner conditional sections are ignored.

If the keyword of the conditional section is a parameter-entity reference, the parameter entity must be replaced by its content before the processor decides whether to include or ignore the conditional section.

An example:

```
<!ENTITY % draft 'INCLUDE' >
<!ENTITY % final 'IGNORE' >

<![%draft;[
<!ELEMENT book (comments*, title, body, supplements?)>
]]>
<![%final;[
<!ELEMENT book (title, body, supplements?)>
]]>
```

4. Physical Structures

An XML document may consist of one or many storage units. These are called **entities**; they all have **content** and are all (except for the document entity, and the external DTD subset) identified by entity **name**. Each XML document has one entity called the **document entity**, which serves as the starting point for the XML processor and may contain the whole document.

Entities may be either parsed or unparsed. A **parsed entity's** contents are referred to as its replacement text; this text is considered an integral part of the document.

An **unparsed entity** is a resource whose contents may or may not be text, and if text, may not be XML. Each unparsed entity has an associated notation, identified by name. Beyond a requirement that an XML processor make the identifiers for the entity and notation available to the application, XML places no constraints on the contents of unparsed entities.

Parsed entities are invoked by name using entity references; unparsed entities by name, given in the value of `ENTITY` or `ENTITIES` attributes.

General entities are entities for use within the document content. In this specification, general entities are sometimes referred to with the unqualified term *entity* when this leads to no ambiguity. Parameter entities are parsed entities for use within the DTD. These two types of entities use different forms of reference and are recognized in different contexts. Furthermore, they occupy different namespaces; a parameter entity and a general entity with the same name are two distinct entities.

4.1 Character and Entity References

A **character reference** refers to a specific character in the ISO/IEC 10646 character set, for example one not directly accessible from available input devices.

Character Reference			
[66]	`CharRef ::=`	`'&#' [0-9]+ ';'`	
		`| '&#x' [0-9a-fA-F]+ ';'`	`[WFC:` Legal Character `]`

Well-Formedness Constraint: Legal Character

Characters referred to using character references must match the production for Char.

If the character reference begins with "&#x", the digits and letters up to the terminating ; provide a hexadecimal representation of the character's code point in ISO/IEC 10646. If it begins just with "&#", the digits up to the terminating ; provide a decimal representation of the character's code point.

An **entity reference** refers to the content of a named entity. References to parsed general entities use ampersand (&) and semicolon (;) as delimiters. **Parameter-entity references** use percent-sign (%) and semicolon (;) as delimiters.

Entity Reference				
[67]	`Reference`	`::=`	`EntityRef | CharRef`	
[68]	`EntityRef`	`::=`	`'&' Name ';'`	[WFC: Entity Declared] [VC: Entity Declared] [WFC: Parsed Entity] [WFC: No Recursion]
[69]	`PEReference`	`::=`	`'%' Name ';'`	[VC: Entity Declared] [WFC: No Recursion] [WFC: In DTD]

Well-Formedness Constraint: Entity Declared

In a document without any DTD, a document with only an internal DTD subset which contains no parameter entity references, or a document with "standalone='yes'", the Name given in the entity reference must match that in an entity declaration, except that well-formed documents need not declare any of the following entities: amp, lt, gt, apos, quot. The declaration of a parameter entity must precede any reference to it. Similarly, the declaration of a general entity must precede any reference to it which appears in a default value in an attribute-list declaration. Note that if entities are declared in the external subset or in external parameter entities, a non-validating processor is not obligated to read and process their declarations; for such documents, the rule that an entity must be declared is a well-formedness constraint only if standalone='yes'.

Validity Constraint: Entity Declared

In a document with an external subset or external parameter entities with "standalone='no'", the Name given in the entity reference must match that in an entity declaration. For interoperability, valid documents should declare the entities amp, lt, gt, apos, quot, in the form specified in "4.6 Predefined Entities". The declaration of a parameter entity must precede any reference to it. Similarly, the declaration of a general entity must precede any reference to it which appears in a default value in an attribute-list declaration.

Well-Formedness Constraint: Parsed Entity

An entity reference must not contain the name of an unparsed entity. Unparsed entities may be referred to only in attribute values declared to be of type `ENTITY` or `ENTITIES`.

Well-Formedness Constraint: No Recursion

A parsed entity must not contain a recursive reference to itself, either directly or indirectly.

Well-Formedness Constraint: In DTD

Parameter-entity references may only appear in the DTD.

Examples of character and entity references:

```
Type <key>less-than</key> (&#x3C;) to save options.
This document was prepared on &docdate; and
is classified &security-level;.
```

Example of a parameter-entity reference:

```
<!-- declare the parameter entity "ISOLat2"... -->
<!ENTITY % ISOLat2
         SYSTEM "http://www.xml.com/iso/isolat2-xml.entities" >
<!-- ... now reference it. -->
%ISOLat2;
```

4.2 Entity Declarations

Entities are declared thus:

<table>
<tr><th colspan="4">Entity Declaration</th></tr>
<tr><td>[70]</td><td>EntityDecl</td><td>::=</td><td>GEDecl | PEDecl</td></tr>
<tr><td>[71]</td><td>GEDecl</td><td>::=</td><td>'<!ENTITY' S Name S EntityDef S? '>'</td></tr>
<tr><td>[72]</td><td>PEDecl</td><td>::=</td><td>'<!ENTITY' S '%' S Name S PEDef S? '>'</td></tr>
<tr><td>[73]</td><td>EntityDef</td><td>::=</td><td>EntityValue | (ExternalID NDataDecl?)</td></tr>
<tr><td>[74]</td><td>PEDef</td><td>::=</td><td>EntityValue | ExternalID</td></tr>
</table>

The `Name` identifies the entity in an entity reference or, in the case of an unparsed entity, in the value of an `ENTITY` or `ENTITIES` attribute. If the same entity is declared more than once, the first declaration encountered is binding; at user option, an XML processor may issue a warning if entities are declared multiple times.

4.2.1 Internal Entities

If the entity definition is an `EntityValue`, the defined entity is called an **internal entity**. There is no separate physical storage object, and the content of the entity is given in the declaration. Note that some processing of entity and character references in the literal entity value may be required to produce the correct replacement text: see "4.5 Construction of Internal Entity Replacement Text".

An internal entity is a parsed entity.

Example of an internal entity declaration:

```
<!ENTITY Pub-Status "This is a pre-release of the
 specification.">
```

4.2.2 External Entities

If the entity is not internal, it is an **external entity**, declared as follows:

External Entity Declaration				
[75]	ExternalID	::=	'SYSTEM' S SystemLiteral | 'PUBLIC' S PubidLiteral S SystemLiteral	
[76]	NDataDecl	::=	S 'NDATA' S Name	[VC: Notation Declared]

If the NDataDecl is present, this is a general unparsed entity; otherwise it is a parsed entity.

Validity Constraint: Notation Declared

The Name must match the declared name of a notation.

The SystemLiteral is called the entity's **system identifier**. It is a URI, which may be used to retrieve the entity. Note that the hash mark (#) and fragment identifier frequently used with URIs are not, formally, part of the URI itself; an XML processor may signal an error if a fragment identifier is given as part of a system identifier. Unless otherwise provided by information outside the scope of this specification (e.g. a special XML element type defined by a particular DTD, or a processing instruction defined by a particular application specification), relative URIs are relative to the location of the resource within which the entity declaration occurs. A URI might thus be relative to the document entity, to the entity containing the external DTD subset, or to some other external parameter entity.

An XML processor should handle a non-ASCII character in a URI by representing the character in UTF-8 as one or more bytes, and then escaping these bytes with the URI escaping mechanism (i.e., by converting each byte to %HH, where HH is the hexadecimal notation of the byte value).

In addition to a system identifier, an external identifier may include a **public identifier**. An XML processor attempting to retrieve the entity's content may use the public identifier to try to generate an alternative URI. If the processor is unable to do so, it must use the URI specified in the system literal. Before a match is attempted, all strings of white space in the public identifier must be normalized to single space characters (#x20), and leading and trailing white space must be removed.

Examples of external entity declarations:

```
<!ENTITY open-hatch
         SYSTEM "http://www.textuality.com/boilerplate/OpenHatch.xml">
<!ENTITY open-hatch
         PUBLIC "-//Textuality//TEXT Standard open-hatch boilerplate//EN"
         "http://www.textuality.com/boilerplate/OpenHatch.xml">
<!ENTITY hatch-pic
         SYSTEM "../grafix/OpenHatch.gif"
         NDATA gif >
```

4.3 Parsed Entities

4.3.1 The Text Declaration

External parsed entities may each begin with a **text declaration**.

Text Declaration			
[77]	`TextDecl`	`::=`	`'<?xml' VersionInfo? EncodingDecl S? '?>'`

The text declaration must be provided literally, not by reference to a parsed entity. No text declaration may appear at any position other than the beginning of an external parsed entity.

4.3.2 Well-Formed Parsed Entities

The document entity is well-formed if it matches the production labeled `document`. An external general parsed entity is well-formed if it matches the production labeled `extParsedEnt`. An external parameter entity is well-formed if it matches the production labeled `extPE`.

Well-Formed External Parsed Entity			
[78]	`extParsedEnt`	`::=`	`TextDecl? content`
[79]	`extPE`	`::=`	`TextDecl? extSubsetDecl`

An internal general parsed entity is well-formed if its replacement text matches the production labeled `content`. All internal parameter entities are well-formed by definition.

A consequence of well-formedness in entities is that the logical and physical structures in an XML document are properly nested; no start-tag, end-tag, empty-element tag, element, comment, processing instruction, character reference, or entity reference can begin in one entity and end in another.

4.3.3 Character Encoding in Entities

Each external parsed entity in an XML document may use a different encoding for its characters. All XML processors must be able to read entities in either UTF-8 or UTF-16.

Entities encoded in UTF-16 must begin with the Byte Order Mark described by ISO/IEC 10646 Annex E and Unicode Appendix B (the ZERO WIDTH NO-BREAK SPACE character, #xFEFF). This is an encoding signature, not part of either the markup or the character data of the XML document. XML processors must be able to use this character to differentiate between UTF-8 and UTF-16 encoded documents.

Although an XML processor is required to read only entities in the UTF-8 and UTF-16 encodings, it is recognized that other encodings are used around the world, and it may be desired for XML processors to read entities that use them. Parsed entities which are stored in an encoding other than UTF-8 or UTF-16 must begin with a text declaration containing an encoding declaration:

Encoding Declaration				
[80]	`EncodingDecl`	`::=`	`S 'encoding' Eq ('"' EncName '"' | "'" EncName "'" )`	
[81]	`EncName`	`::=`	`[A-Za-z] ([A-Za-z0-9._] | '-')*`	/*Encoding name contains only Latin characters */

In the document entity, the encoding declaration is part of the XML declaration. The `EncName` is the name of the encoding used.

In an encoding declaration, the values "`UTF-8`", "`UTF-16`", "`ISO-10646-UCS-2`", and "`ISO-10646-UCS-4`" should be used for the various encodings and transformations of Unicode / ISO/IEC 10646, the values "`ISO-8859-1`", "`ISO-8859-2`", ... "`ISO-8859-9`" should be used for the parts of ISO 8859, and the values "`ISO-2022-JP`", "`Shift_JIS`", and "`EUC-JP`" should be used for the various encoded forms of JIS X-0208-1997. XML processors may recognize other encodings; it is recommended that character encodings registered (as *charsets*) with the Internet Assigned Numbers Authority [IANA], other than those just listed, should be referred to using their registered names. Note that these registered names are defined to be case-insensitive, so processors wishing to match against them should do so in a case-insensitive way.

In the absence of information provided by an external transport protocol (e.g. HTTP or MIME), it is an error for an entity including an encoding declaration to be presented to the XML processor in an encoding other than that named in the declaration, or for an entity which begins with neither a Byte Order Mark nor an encoding declaration to use an encoding other than UTF-8. Note that since ASCII is a subset of UTF-8, ordinary ASCII entities do not strictly need an encoding declaration.

It is an error for a `TextDecl` to occur other than at the beginning of an external entity.

It is a fatal error when an XML processor encounters an entity with an encoding that it is unable to process.

Examples of encoding declarations:

```
<?xml encoding='UTF-8'?>
<?xml encoding='EUC-JP'?>
```

4.4 XML Processor Treatment of Entities and References

The table below summarizes the contexts in which character references, entity references, and invocations of unparsed entities might appear and the required behavior of an XML processor in each case. The labels in the leftmost column describe the recognition context:

Reference in Content

as a reference anywhere after the start-tag and before the end-tag of an element; corresponds to the nonterminal `content`.

Reference in Attribute Value

as a reference within either the value of an attribute in a start-tag, or a default value in an attribute declaration; corresponds to the nonterminal `AttValue`.

Occurs as Attribute Value

as a `Name`, not a reference, appearing either as the value of an attribute which has been declared as type `ENTITY`, or as one of the space-separated tokens in the value of an attribute which has been declared as type `ENTITIES`.

Reference in Entity Value

as a reference within a parameter or internal entity's literal entity value in the entity's declaration; corresponds to the nonterminal `EntityValue`.

Reference in DTD

as a reference within either the internal or external subsets of the DTD, but outside of an `EntityValue` or `AttValue`.

	Entity Type				Character
	Parameter	Internal General	External Parsed General	Unparsed	
Reference in Content	Not recognized	Included	Included if validating	Forbidden	Included
Reference in Attribute Value	Not recognized	Included in literal	Forbidden	Forbidden	Included
Occurs as Attribute Value	Not recognized	Forbidden	Forbidden	Notify	Not recognized
Reference in EntityValue	Included in literal	Bypassed	Bypassed	Forbidden	Included
Reference in DTD	Included as PE	Forbidden	Forbidden	Forbidden	Forbidden

4.4.1 Not Recognized

Outside the DTD, the `%` character has no special significance; thus, what would be parameter entity references in the DTD are not recognized as markup in `content`. Similarly, the names of unparsed entities are not recognized except when they appear in the value of an appropriately declared attribute.

4.4.2 Included

An entity is **included** when its replacement text is retrieved and processed, in place of the reference itself, as though it were part of the document at the location the reference was recognized. The replacement text may contain both character data and (except for parameter entities) markup, which must be recognized in the usual way, except that the replacement text of entities used to escape markup delimiters (the entities `amp`, `lt`, `gt`, `apos`, `quot`) is always treated as data. (The string "`AT&T;`" expands to "`AT&T;`" and the remaining ampersand is not recognized as an entity-reference delimiter.) A character reference is **included** when the indicated character is processed in place of the reference itself.

4.4.3 Included If Validating

When an XML processor recognizes a reference to a parsed entity, in order to validate the document, the processor must include its replacement text. If the entity is external, and the processor is not attempting to validate the XML document, the processor may, but need not, include the entity's replacement text. If a non-validating parser does not include the replacement text, it must inform the application that it recognized, but did not read, the entity.

This rule is based on the recognition that the automatic inclusion provided by the SGML and XML entity mechanism, primarily designed to support modularity in authoring, is not necessarily appropriate for other applications, in particular document browsing. Browsers, for example, when encountering an external parsed entity reference, might choose to provide a visual indication of the entity's presence and retrieve it for display only on demand.

4.4.4 Forbidden

The following are forbidden, and constitute fatal errors:

- the appearance of a reference to an unparsed entity.
- the appearance of any character or general-entity reference in the DTD except within an `EntityValue` or `AttValue`.
- a reference to an external entity in an attribute value.

4.4.5 Included in Literal

When an entity reference appears in an attribute value, or a parameter entity reference appears in a literal entity value, its replacement text is processed in place of the reference itself as though it were part of the document at the location the reference was recognized, except that a single or double quote character in the replacement text is always treated as a normal data character and will not terminate the literal. For example, this is well-formed:

```
<!ENTITY % YN '"Yes"' >
<!ENTITY WhatHeSaid "He said %YN;" >
```

while this is not:

```
<!ENTITY EndAttr "27'" >
<element attribute='a-&EndAttr;>
```

4.4.6 Notify

When the name of an unparsed entity appears as a token in the value of an attribute of declared type `ENTITY` or `ENTITIES`, a validating processor must inform the application of the system and public (if any) identifiers for both the entity and its associated notation.

4.4.7 Bypassed

When a general entity reference appears in the `EntityValue` in an entity declaration, it is bypassed and left as is.

4.4.8 Included as PE

Just as with external parsed entities, parameter entities need only be included if validating. When a parameter-entity reference is recognized in the DTD and included, its replacement text is enlarged by the attachment of one leading and one following space (#x20) character; the intent is to constrain the replacement text of parameter entities to contain an integral number of grammatical tokens in the DTD.

4.5 Construction of Internal Entity Replacement Text

In discussing the treatment of internal entities, it is useful to distinguish two forms of the entity's value. The **literal entity value** is the quoted string actually present in the entity declaration, corresponding to the non-terminal `EntityValue`. The **replacement text** is the content of the entity, after replacement of character references and parameter-entity references.

The literal entity value as given in an internal entity declaration (`EntityValue`) may contain character, parameter-entity, and general-entity references. Such references must be contained entirely within the literal entity value. The actual replacement text that is included as described above must contain the *replacement text* of any parameter entities referred to, and must contain the character referred to, in place of any character references in the literal entity value; however, general-entity references must be left as-is, unexpanded. For example, given the following declarations:

```
<!ENTITY % pub    "&#xc9;ditions Gallimard" >
<!ENTITY   rights "All rights reserved" >
<!ENTITY   book   "La Peste: Albert Camus,
&#xA9; 1947 %pub;. &rights;" >
```

then the replacement text for the entity "`book`" is:

```
La Peste: Albert Camus,
© 1947 Éditions Gallimard. &rights;
```

The general-entity reference "`&rights;`" would be expanded should the reference "`&book;`" appear in the document's content or an attribute value.

These simple rules may have complex interactions; for a detailed discussion of a difficult example, see "D. Expansion of Entity and Character References".

4.6 Predefined Entities

Entity and character references can both be used to **escape** the left angle bracket, ampersand, and other delimiters. A set of general entities (`amp`, `lt`, `gt`, `apos`, `quot`) is specified for this purpose. Numeric character references may also be used; they are expanded immediately when recognized and must be treated as character data, so the numeric character references "`<`" and "`&`" may be used to escape `<` and `&` when they occur in character data.

All XML processors must recognize these entities whether they are declared or not. For interoperability, valid XML documents should declare these entities, like any others, before using them. If the entities in question are declared, they must be declared as internal entities whose replacement text is the single character being escaped or a character reference to that character, as shown below.

```
<!ENTITY lt     "&#38;#60;">
<!ENTITY gt     "&#62;">
<!ENTITY amp    "&#38;#38;">
<!ENTITY apos   "&#39;">
<!ENTITY quot   "&#34;">
```

Note that the `<` and `&` characters in the declarations of "`lt`" and "`amp`" are doubly escaped to meet the requirement that entity replacement be well-formed.

4.7 Notation Declarations

Notations identify by name the format of unparsed entities, the format of elements which bear a notation attribute, or the application to which a processing instruction is addressed.

Notation declarations provide a name for the notation, for use in entity and attribute-list declarations and in attribute specifications, and an external identifier for the notation which may allow an XML processor or its client application to locate a helper application capable of processing data in the given notation.

Notation Declarations			
[82]	NotationDecl	::=	'<!NOTATION' S Name S (ExternalID | PublicID) S? '>'
[83]	PublicID	::=	'PUBLIC' S PubidLiteral

XML processors must provide applications with the name and external identifier(s) of any notation declared and referred to in an attribute value, attribute definition, or entity declaration. They may additionally resolve the external identifier into the system identifier, file name, or other information needed to allow the application to call a processor for data in the notation described. (It is not an error, however, for XML documents to declare and refer to notations for which notation-specific applications are not available on the system where the XML processor or application is running.)

4.8 Document Entity

The **document entity** serves as the root of the entity tree and a starting-point for an XML processor. This specification does not specify how the document entity is to be located by an XML processor; unlike other entities, the document entity has no name and might well appear on a processor input stream without any identification at all.

5. Conformance

5.1 Validating and Non-Validating Processors

Conforming XML processors fall into two classes: validating and non-validating.

Validating and non-validating processors alike must report violations of this specification's well-formedness constraints in the content of the document entity and any other parsed entities that they read.

Validating processors must report violations of the constraints expressed by the declarations in the DTD, and failures to fulfill the validity constraints given in this specification. To accomplish this, validating XML processors must read and process the entire DTD and all external parsed entities referenced in the document.

Non-validating processors are required to check only the document entity, including the entire internal DTD subset, for well-formedness. While they are not required to check the document for validity, they are required to **process** all the declarations they read in the internal DTD subset and in any parameter entity that they read, up to the first reference to a parameter entity that they do *not* read; that is to say, they must use the information in those declarations to normalize attribute values, include the replacement text of internal entities, and supply default attribute values. They must not process entity declarations or attribute-list declarations encountered after a reference to a parameter entity that is not read, since the entity may have contained overriding declarations.

5.2 Using XML Processors

The behavior of a validating XML processor is highly predictable; it must read every piece of a document and report all well-formedness and validity violations. Less is required of a non-validating processor; it need not read any part of the document other than the document entity. This has two effects that may be important to users of XML processors:

- Certain well-formedness errors, specifically those that require reading external entities, may not be detected by a non-validating processor. Examples include the constraints entitled Entity Declared, Parsed Entity, and No Recursion, as well as some of the cases described as forbidden in "4.4 XML Processor Treatment of Entities and References".
- The information passed from the processor to the application may vary, depending on whether the processor reads parameter and external entities. For example, a non-validating processor may not normalize attribute values, include the replacement text of internal entities, or supply default attribute values, where doing so depends on having read declarations in external or parameter entities.

For maximum reliability in interoperating between different XML processors, applications which use non-validating processors should not rely on any behaviors not required of such processors. Applications which require facilities such as the use of default attributes or internal entities which are declared in external entities should use validating XML processors.

6. Notation

The formal grammar of XML is given in this specification using a simple Extended Backus-Naur Form (EBNF) notation. Each rule in the grammar defines one symbol, in the form

```
symbol ::= expression
```

Symbols are written with an initial capital letter if they are defined by a regular expression, or with an initial lower case letter otherwise. Literal strings are quoted.

Within the expression on the right-hand side of a rule, the following expressions are used to match strings of one or more characters:

`#xN`

where `N` is a hexadecimal integer, the expression matches the character in ISO/IEC 10646 whose canonical (UCS-4) code value, when interpreted as an unsigned binary number, has the value indicated. The number of leading zeros in the `#xN` form is insignificant; the number of leading zeros in the corresponding code value is governed by the character encoding in use and is not significant for XML.

`[a-zA-Z]`, `[#xN-#xN]`

matches any character with a value in the range(s) indicated (inclusive).

`[^a-z]`, `[^#xN-#xN]`

matches any character with a value *outside* the range indicated.

`[^abc]`, `[^#xN#xN#xN]`

matches any character with a value not among the characters given.

`"string"`

matches a literal string matching that given inside the double quotes.

`'string'`

matches a literal string matching that given inside the single quotes.

These symbols may be combined to match more complex patterns as follows, where `A` and `B` represent simple expressions:

`(expression)`

`expression` is treated as a unit and may be combined as described in this list.

`([-'()+,./:=?;!*#@$_%])`

characters matching this list are treated as an `expression`.

`A?`

matches `A` or nothing; optional `A`.

`A B`

matches `A` followed by `B`.

`A | B`

matches `A` or `B` but not both.

`A - B`

matches any string that matches `A` but does not match `B`.

`A+`

matches one or more occurrences of `A`.

`A*`

matches zero or more occurrences of `A`.

Other notations used in the productions are:

`/* ... */`

comment.

`[ wfc: ... ]`

well-formedness constraint; this identifies by name a constraint on well-formed documents associated with a production.

`[ vc: ... ]`

validity constraint; this identifies by name a constraint on valid documents associated with a production.

Appendices

A. References

A.1 Normative References

IANA

(Internet Assigned Numbers Authority) *Official Names for Character Sets*, ed. Keld Simonsen et al. See ftp://ftp.isi.edu/in-notes/iana/assignments/character-sets.

IETF RFC 1766

IETF (Internet Engineering Task Force). *RFC 1766: Tags for the Identification of Languages*, ed. H. Alvestrand. 1995.

ISO 639

(International Organization for Standardization). *ISO 639:1988 (E). Code for the representation of names of languages.* [Geneva]: International Organization for Standardization, 1988.

ISO 3166

(International Organization for Standardization). *ISO 3166-1:1997 (E). Codes for the representation of names of countries and their subdivisions -- Part 1: Country codes* [Geneva]: International Organization for Standardization, 1997.

ISO/IEC 10646

ISO (International Organization for Standardization). *ISO/IEC 10646-1993 (E). Information technology -- Universal Multiple-Octet Coded Character Set (UCS) -- Part 1: Architecture and Basic Multilingual Plane.* [Geneva]: International Organization for Standardization, 1993 (plus amendments AM 1 through AM 7).

Unicode

The Unicode Consortium. *The Unicode Standard, Version 2.0.* Reading, Mass.: Addison-Wesley Developers Press, 1996.

A.2 Other References

Aho/Ullman

Aho, Alfred V., Ravi Sethi, and Jeffrey D. Ullman. *Compilers: Principles, Techniques, and Tools.* Reading: Addison-Wesley, 1986, rpt. corr. 1988.

Berners-Lee et al.

Berners-Lee, T., R. Fielding, and L. Masinter. *Uniform Resource Identifiers (URI): Generic Syntax and Semantics.* 1997. (Work in progress; see updates to RFC1738.)

Brüggemann-Klein

Brüggemann-Klein, Anne. Formal Models in Document Processing. Habilitationsschrift. Faculty of Mathematics at the University of Freiburg, 1993, available at `ftp://ftp.informatik.uni-freiburg.de/documents/papers/brueggem/habil.ps`.

Brüggemann-Klein and D Wood

Brüggemann-Klein, Anne, and Derick Wood. *Deterministic Regular Languages.* Extended abstract in A. Finkel, M. Jantzen, Hrsg., STACS 1992, S. 173-184. Springer-Verlag, Berlin 1992. Lecture Notes in Computer Science 577. Full version titled *One-Unambiguous Regular Languages* in Information and Computation 140 (2): 229-253, February 1998.

Clark

James Clark. Comparison of SGML and XML. See `http://www.w3.org/TR/NOTE-sgml-xml-971215`.

IETF RFC1738

IETF (Internet Engineering Task Force). *RFC 1738: Uniform Resource Locators (URL)*, ed. T. Berners-Lee, L. Masinter, M. McCahill. 1994.

IETF RFC1808

IETF (Internet Engineering Task Force). *RFC 1808: Relative Uniform Resource Locators*, ed. R. Fielding. 1995.

IETF RFC2141

IETF (Internet Engineering Task Force). *RFC 2141: URN Syntax*, ed. R. Moats. 1997.

ISO 8879

ISO (International Organization for Standardization). *ISO 8879:1986(E). Information processing -- Text and Office Systems -- Standard Generalized Markup Language (SGML).* First edition -- 1986-10-15. [Geneva]: International Organization for Standardization, 1986.

ISO/IEC 10744

ISO (International Organization for Standardization). *ISO/IEC 10744-1992 (E). Information technology -- Hypermedia/Time-based Structuring Language (HyTime).* [Geneva]: International Organization for Standardization, 1992. *Extended Facilities Annexe.* [Geneva]: International Organization for Standardization, 1996.

B. Character Classes

Following the characteristics defined in the Unicode standard, characters are classed as base characters (among others, these contain the alphabetic characters of the Latin alphabet, without diacritics), ideographic characters, and combining characters (among others, this class contains most diacritics); these classes combine to form the class of letters. Digits and extenders are also distinguished.

<table>
<tr><th colspan="4">Characters</th></tr>
<tr><td>[84]</td><td>Letter</td><td>::=</td><td>BaseChar | Ideographic</td></tr>
<tr><td>[85]</td><td>BaseChar</td><td>::=</td><td>[#x0041-#x005A] | [#x0061-#x007A]
| [#x00C0-#x00D6] | [#x00D8-#x00F6]
| [#x00F8-#x00FF] | [#x0100-#x0131]
| [#x0134-#x013E] | [#x0141-#x0148]
| [#x014A-#x017E] | [#x0180-#x01C3]
| [#x01CD-#x01F0] | [#x01F4-#x01F5]
| [#x01FA-#x0217] | [#x0250-#x02A8]
| [#x02BB-#x02C1] | #x0386 | [#x0388-
#x038A] | #x038C | [#x038E-#x03A1]
| [#x03A3-#x03CE] | [#x03D0-#x03D6]
| #x03DA | #x03DC | #x03DE | #x03E0
| [#x03E2-#x03F3] | [#x0401-#x040C]
| [#x040E-#x044F] | [#x0451-#x045C]
| [#x045E-#x0481] | [#x0490-#x04C4]
| [#x04C7-#x04C8] | [#x04CB-#x04CC]
| [#x04D0-#x04EB] | [#x04EE-#x04F5]
| [#x04F8-#x04F9] | [#x0531-#x0556]
| #x0559 | [#x0561-#x0586] | [#x05D0-
#x05EA] | [#x05F0-#x05F2] | [#x0621-#x063A]
| [#x0641-#x064A] | [#x0671-#x06B7]
| [#x06BA-#x06BE] | [#x06C0-#x06CE]
| [#x06D0-#x06D3] | #x06D5 | [#x06E5-
#x06E6] | [#x0905-#x0939] | #x093D
| [#x0958-#x0961] | [#x0985-#x098C]
| [#x098F-#x0990] | [#x0993-#x09A8]
| [#x09AA-#x09B0] | #x09B2 | [#x09B6-
#x09B9] | [#x09DC-#x09DD] | [#x09DF-#x09E1]
| [#x09F0-#x09F1] | [#x0A05-#x0A0A]
| [#x0A0F-#x0A10] | [#x0A13-#x0A28]
| [#x0A2A-#x0A30] | [#x0A32-#x0A33]
| [#x0A35-#x0A36] | [#x0A38-#x0A39]
| [#x0A59-#x0A5C] | #x0A5E | [#x0A72-
#x0A74] | [#x0A85-#x0A8B] | #x0A8D
| [#x0A8F-#x0A91] | [#x0A93-#x0AA8]
| [#x0AAA-#x0AB0] | [#x0AB2-#x0AB3]
| [#x0AB5-#x0AB9] | #x0ABD | #x0AE0
| [#x0B05-#x0B0C] | [#x0B0F-#x0B10]
| [#x0B13-#x0B28] | [#x0B2A-#x0B30]
| [#x0B32-#x0B33] | [#x0B36-#x0B39]
| #x0B3D | [#x0B5C-#x0B5D] | [#x0B5F-
#x0B61] | [#x0B85-#x0B8A] | [#x0B8E-#x0B90]
| [#x0B92-#x0B95] | [#x0B99-#x0B9A]
| #x0B9C | [#x0B9E-#x0B9F] | [#x0BA3-
#x0BA4] | [#x0BA8-#x0BAA] | [#x0BAE-#x0BB5]
| [#x0BB7-#x0BB9] | [#x0C05-#x0C0C]
| [#x0C0E-#x0C10] | [#x0C12-#x0C28]
| [#x0C2A-#x0C33] | [#x0C35-#x0C39]
| [#x0C60-#x0C61] | [#x0C85-#x0C8C]
| [#x0C8E-#x0C90] | [#x0C92-#x0CA8]
| [#x0CAA-#x0CB3] | [#x0CB5-#x0CB9]
| #x0CDE | [#x0CE0-#x0CE1] | [#x0D05-
#x0D0C] | [#x0D0E-#x0D10] | [#x0D12-#x0D28]</td></tr>
</table>

			| [#x0D2A-#x0D39] | [#x0D60-#x0D61] | [#x0E01-#x0E2E] | #x0E30 | [#x0E32-#x0E33] | [#x0E40-#x0E45] | [#x0E81-#x0E82] | #x0E84 | [#x0E87-#x0E88] | #x0E8A | #x0E8D | [#x0E94-#x0E97] | [#x0E99-#x0E9F] | [#x0EA1-#x0EA3] | #x0EA5 | #x0EA7 | [#x0EAA-#x0EAB] | [#x0EAD-#x0EAE] | #x0EB0 | [#x0EB2-#x0EB3] | #x0EBD | [#x0EC0-#x0EC4] | [#x0F40-#x0F47] | [#x0F49-#x0F69] | [#x10A0-#x10C5] | [#x10D0-#x10F6] | #x1100 | [#x1102-#x1103] | [#x1105-#x1107] | #x1109 | [#x110B-#x110C] | [#x110E-#x1112] | #x113C | #x113E | #x1140 | #x114C | #x114E | #x1150 | [#x1154-#x1155] | #x1159 | [#x115F-#x1161] | #x1163 | #x1165 | #x1167 | #x1169 | [#x116D-#x116E] | [#x1172-#x1173] | #x1175 | #x119E | #x11A8 | #x11AB | [#x11AE-#x11AF] | [#x11B7-#x11B8] | #x11BA | [#x11BC-#x11C2] | #x11EB | #x11F0 | #x11F9 | [#x1E00-#x1E9B] | [#x1EA0-#x1EF9] | [#x1F00-#x1F15] | [#x1F18-#x1F1D] | [#x1F20-#x1F45] | [#x1F48-#x1F4D] | [#x1F50-#x1F57] | #x1F59 | #x1F5B | #x1F5D | [#x1F5F-#x1F7D] | [#x1F80-#x1FB4] | [#x1FB6-#x1FBC] | #x1FBE | [#x1FC2-#x1FC4] | [#x1FC6-#x1FCC] | [#x1FD0-#x1FD3] | [#x1FD6-#x1FDB] | [#x1FE0-#x1FEC] | [#x1FF2-#x1FF4] | [#x1FF6-#x1FFC] | #x2126 | [#x212A-#x212B] | #x212E | [#x2180-#x2182] | [#x3041-#x3094] | [#x30A1-#x30FA] | [#x3105-#x312C] | [#xAC00-#xD7A3]
[86]	Ideographic	::=	[#x4E00-#x9FA5] | #x3007 | [#x3021-#x3029]
[87]	Combining Char	::=	[#x0300-#x0345] | [#x0360-#x0361] | [#x0483-#x0486] | [#x0591-#x05A1] | [#x05A3-#x05B9] | [#x05BB-#x05BD] | #x05BF | [#x05C1-#x05C2] | #x05C4 | [#x064B-#x0652] | #x0670 | [#x06D6-#x06DC] | [#x06DD-#x06DF] | [#x06E0-#x06E4] | [#x06E7-#x06E8] | [#x06EA-#x06ED] | [#x0901-#x0903] | #x093C | [#x093E-#x094C] | #x094D | [#x0951-#x0954] | [#x0962-#x0963] | [#x0981-#x0983] | #x09BC | #x09BE | #x09BF | [#x09C0-#x09C4] | [#x09C7-#x09C8] | [#x09CB-#x09CD] | #x09D7 | [#x09E2-#x09E3] | #x0A02 | #x0A3C | #x0A3E | #x0A3F | [#x0A40-#x0A42] | [#x0A47-#x0A48] | [#x0A4B-#x0A4D] | [#x0A70-#x0A71] | [#x0A81-#x0A83] | #x0ABC | [#x0ABE-#x0AC5] | [#x0AC7-#x0AC9] | [#x0ACB-#x0ACD] | [#x0B01-#x0B03] | #x0B3C | [#x0B3E-#x0B43] | [#x0B47-#x0B48] | [#x0B4B-#x0B4D] | [#x0B56-#x0B57] | [#x0B82-#x0B83] | [#x0BBE-#x0BC2]

<table>
<tr><td></td><td></td><td></td><td>| [#x0BC6-#x0BC8] | [#x0BCA-#x0BCD]
| #x0BD7 | [#x0C01-#x0C03] | [#x0C3E-
#x0C44] | [#x0C46-#x0C48] | [#x0C4A-#x0C4D]
| [#x0C55-#x0C56] | [#x0C82-#x0C83]
| [#x0CBE-#x0CC4] | [#x0CC6-#x0CC8]
| [#x0CCA-#x0CCD] | [#x0CD5-#x0CD6]
| [#x0D02-#x0D03] | [#x0D3E-#x0D43]
| [#x0D46-#x0D48] | [#x0D4A-#x0D4D]
| #x0D57 | #x0E31 | [#x0E34-#x0E3A]
| [#x0E47-#x0E4E] | #x0EB1 | [#x0EB4-
#x0EB9] | [#x0EBB-#x0EBC] | [#x0EC8-#x0ECD]
| [#x0F18-#x0F19] | #x0F35 | #x0F37
| #x0F39 | #x0F3E | #x0F3F | [#x0F71-
#x0F84] | [#x0F86-#x0F8B] | [#x0F90-#x0F95]
| #x0F97 | [#x0F99-#x0FAD] | [#x0FB1-
#x0FB7] | #x0FB9 | [#x20D0-#x20DC] | #x20E1
| [#x302A-#x302F] | #x3099 | #x309A</td></tr>
<tr><td>[88]</td><td>Digit</td><td>::=</td><td>[#x0030-#x0039] | [#x0660-#x0669]
| [#x06F0-#x06F9] | [#x0966-#x096F]
| [#x09E6-#x09EF] | [#x0A66-#x0A6F]
| [#x0AE6-#x0AEF] | [#x0B66-#x0B6F]
| [#x0BE7-#x0BEF] | [#x0C66-#x0C6F]
| [#x0CE6-#x0CEF] | [#x0D66-#x0D6F]
| [#x0E50-#x0E59] | [#x0ED0-#x0ED9]
| [#x0F20-#x0F29]</td></tr>
<tr><td>[89]</td><td>Extender</td><td>::=</td><td>#x00B7 | #x02D0 | #x02D1 | #x0387 | #x0640
| #x0E46 | #x0EC6 | #x3005 | [#x3031-
#x3035] | [#x309D-#x309E] | [#x30FC-#x30FE]</td></tr>
</table>

The character classes defined here can be derived from the Unicode character database as follows:

- Name start characters must have one of the categories Ll, Lu, Lo, Lt, Nl.
- Name characters other than Name-start characters must have one of the categories Mc, Me, Mn, Lm, or Nd.
- Characters in the compatibility area (i.e. with character code greater than #xF900 and less than #xFFFE) are not allowed in XML names.
- Characters which have a font or compatibility decomposition (i.e. those with a "compatibility formatting tag" in field 5 of the database -- marked by field 5 beginning with a "<") are not allowed.
- The following characters are treated as name-start characters rather than name characters, because the property file classifies them as Alphabetic: [#x02BB-#x02C1], #x0559, #x06E5, #x06E6.
- Characters #x20DD-#x20E0 are excluded (in accordance with Unicode, section 5.14).
- Character #x00B7 is classified as an extender, because the property list so identifies it.

- Character #x0387 is added as a name character, because #x00B7 is its canonical equivalent.
- Characters ':' and '_' are allowed as name-start characters.
- Characters '-' and '.' are allowed as name characters.

C. XML and SGML (Non-Normative)

XML is designed to be a subset of SGML, in that every valid XML document should also be a conformant SGML document. For a detailed comparison of the additional restrictions that XML places on documents beyond those of SGML, see Clark.

D. Expansion of Entity and Character References (Non-Normative)

This appendix contains some examples illustrating the sequence of entity- and character-reference recognition and expansion, as specified in "4.4 XML Processor Treatment of Entities and References".

If the DTD contains the declaration

```
<!ENTITY example "<p>An ampersand (&#38;#38;) may be escaped
numerically (&#38;#38;#38;) or with a general entity
```

then the XML processor will recognize the character references when it parses the entity declaration, and resolve them before storing the following string as the value of the entity "`example`":

```
<p>An ampersand (&#38;) may be escaped
numerically (&#38;#38;) or with a general entity
(&amp;amp;).</p>
```

A reference in the document to "`&example;`" will cause the text to be reparsed, at which time the start- and end-tags of the "`p`" element will be recognized and the three references will be recognized and expanded, resulting in a "`p`" element with the following content (all data, no delimiters or markup):

```
An ampersand (&) may be escaped
numerically (&#38;) or with a general entity
(&amp;).
```

A more complex example will illustrate the rules and their effects fully. In the following example, the line numbers are solely for reference.

```
<?xml version='1.0'?>
<!DOCTYPE test [
<!ELEMENT test (#PCDATA) >
<!ENTITY % xx '&#37;zz;'>
<!ENTITY % zz '&#60;!ENTITY tricky "error-prone" >' >
%xx;
]>
<test>This sample shows a &tricky; method.</test>
```

This produces the following:

- in line 4, the reference to character 37 is expanded immediately, and the parameter entity "xx" is stored in the symbol table with the value "%zz;". Since the replacement text is not rescanned, the reference to parameter entity "zz" is not recognized. (And it would be an error if it were, since "zz" is not yet declared.)
- in line 5, the character reference "<" is expanded immediately and the parameter entity "zz" is stored with the replacement text "<!ENTITY tricky "error-prone" >", which is a well-formed entity declaration.
- in line 6, the reference to "xx" is recognized, and the replacement text of "xx" (namely "%zz;") is parsed. The reference to "zz" is recognized in its turn, and its replacement text ("<!ENTITY tricky "error-prone" >") is parsed. The general entity "tricky" has now been declared, with the replacement text "error-prone".
- in line 8, the reference to the general entity "tricky" is recognized, and it is expanded, so the full content of the "test" element is the self-describing (and ungrammatical) string *This sample shows a error-prone method.*

E. Deterministic Content Models (Non-Normative)

For compatibility, it is required that content models in element type declarations be deterministic. SGML requires deterministic content models (it calls them "unambiguous"); XML processors built using SGML systems may flag non-deterministic content models as errors.

For example, the content model `((b, c) | (b, d))` is non-deterministic, because given an initial `b` the parser cannot know which `b` in the model is being matched without looking ahead to see which element follows the `b`. In this case, the two references to `b` can be collapsed into a single reference, making the model read `(b, (c | d))`. An initial `b` now clearly matches only a single name in the content model. The parser doesn't need to look ahead to see what follows; either `c` or `d` would be accepted.

More formally: a finite state automaton may be constructed from the content model using the standard algorithms, e.g. algorithm 3.5 in section 3.9 of Aho, Sethi, and Ullman [Aho/Ullman]. In many such algorithms, a follow set is constructed for each position in the regular expression (i.e., each leaf node in the syntax tree for the regular expression); if any position has a follow set in which more than one following position is labeled with the same element type name, then the content model is in error and may be reported as an error.

Algorithms exist which allow many but not all non-deterministic content models to be reduced automatically to equivalent deterministic models; see Brüggemann-Klein 1991 [Brüggemann-Klein].

F. Autodetection of Character Encodings (Non-Normative)

The XML encoding declaration functions as an internal label on each entity, indicating which character encoding is in use. Before an XML processor can read the internal label, however, it apparently has to know what character encoding is in use--which is what the internal label is trying to indicate. In the general case, this is a hopeless situation. It is not entirely hopeless in XML, however, because XML limits the general case in two ways: each implementation is assumed to support only a finite set of character encodings, and the XML encoding declaration is restricted in position and content in order to make it feasible to autodetect the character encoding in use in each entity in normal cases. Also, in many cases other sources of information are available in addition to the XML data stream itself. Two cases may be distinguished, depending on whether the XML entity is presented to the processor without, or with, any accompanying (external) information. We consider the first case first.

Because each XML entity not in UTF-8 or UTF-16 format *must* begin with an XML encoding declaration, in which the first characters must be '`<?xml`', any conforming processor can detect, after two to four octets of input, which of the following cases apply. In reading this list, it may help to know that in UCS-4, '<' is "`#x0000003C`" and '?' is "`#x0000003F`", and the Byte Order Mark required of UTF-16 data streams is "`#xFEFF`".

- `00 00 00 3C`: UCS-4, big-endian machine (1234 order)
- `3C 00 00 00`: UCS-4, little-endian machine (4321 order)
- `00 00 3C 00`: UCS-4, unusual octet order (2143)
- `00 3C 00 00`: UCS-4, unusual octet order (3412)
- `FE FF`: UTF-16, big-endian
- `FF FE`: UTF-16, little-endian
- `00 3C 00 3F`: UTF-16, big-endian, no Byte Order Mark (and thus, strictly speaking, in error)
- `3C 00 3F 00`: UTF-16, little-endian, no Byte Order Mark (and thus, strictly speaking, in error)
- `3C 3F 78 6D`: UTF-8, ISO 646, ASCII, some part of ISO 8859, Shift-JIS, EUC, or any other 7-bit, 8-bit, or mixed-width encoding which ensures that the characters of ASCII have their normal positions, width, and values; the actual encoding declaration must be read to detect which of these applies, but since all of these encodings use the same bit patterns for the ASCII characters, the encoding declaration itself may be read reliably
- `4C 6F A7 94`: EBCDIC (in some flavor; the full encoding declaration must be read to tell which code page is in use)
- other: UTF-8 without an encoding declaration, or else the data stream is corrupt, fragmentary, or enclosed in a wrapper of some kind

This level of autodetection is enough to read the XML encoding declaration and parse the character-encoding identifier, which is still necessary to distinguish the individual members of each family of encodings (e.g. to tell UTF-8 from 8859, and the parts of 8859 from each other, or to distinguish the specific EBCDIC code page in use, and so on).

Because the contents of the encoding declaration are restricted to ASCII characters, a processor can reliably read the entire encoding declaration as soon as it has detected which family of encodings is in use. Since in practice, all widely used character encodings fall into one of the categories above, the XML encoding declaration allows reasonably reliable in-band labeling of character encodings, even when external sources of information at the operating-system or transport-protocol level are unreliable.

Once the processor has detected the character encoding in use, it can act appropriately, whether by invoking a separate input routine for each case, or by calling the proper conversion function on each character of input.

Like any self-labeling system, the XML encoding declaration will not work if any software changes the entity's character set or encoding without updating the encoding declaration. Implementors of character-encoding routines should be careful to ensure the accuracy of the internal and external information used to label the entity.

The second possible case occurs when the XML entity is accompanied by encoding information, as in some file systems and some network protocols. When multiple sources of information are available, their relative priority and the preferred method of handling conflict should be specified as part of the higher-level protocol used to deliver XML. Rules for the relative priority of the internal label and the MIME-type label in an external header, for example, should be part of the RFC document defining the text/xml and application/xml MIME types. In the interests of interoperability, however, the following rules are recommended.

- If an XML entity is in a file, the Byte-Order Mark and encoding-declaration PI are used (if present) to determine the character encoding. All other heuristics and sources of information are solely for error recovery.
- If an XML entity is delivered with a MIME type of text/xml, then the `charset` parameter on the MIME type determines the character encoding method; all other heuristics and sources of information are solely for error recovery.
- If an XML entity is delivered with a MIME type of application/xml, then the Byte-Order Mark and encoding-declaration PI are used (if present) to determine the character encoding. All other heuristics and sources of information are solely for error recovery.

This algorithm does not work for UTF-7.

These rules apply only in the absence of protocol-level documentation; in particular, when the MIME types text/xml and application/xml are defined, the recommendations of the relevant RFC will supersede these rules.

G. W3C XML Working Group (Non-Normative)

This specification was prepared and approved for publication by the W3C XML Working Group (WG). WG approval of this specification does not necessarily imply that all WG members voted for its approval. The current and former members of the XML WG are:

Jon Bosak, Sun (Chair); James Clark (Technical Lead); Tim Bray, Textuality and Netscape (XML Co-editor); Jean Paoli, Microsoft (XML Co-editor); C. M. Sperberg-McQueen, U. of Ill. (XML Co-editor); Dan Connolly, W3C (W3C Liaison); Paula Angerstein, Texcel; Steve DeRose, INSO; Dave Hollander, HP; Eliot Kimber, ISOGEN; Eve Maler, ArborText; Tom Magliery, NCSA; Murray Maloney, Muzmo and Grif; Makoto Murata, Fuji Xerox Information Systems; Joel Nava, Adobe; Conleth O'Connell, Vignette; Peter Sharpe, SoftQuad; John Tigue, DataChannel

D

XML Schemas and Data Types

In Appendix E, I have given the status and version of each note, draft, proposed recommendation or recommendation I mention. You can see that the topics we have covered are either full recommendations or working drafts. Schemas, on the other hand, are still at the proposal stage, with several notes that are being considered by a W3C Working Group.

Because of this early stage of the schema work, we haven't used any of these proposals in Centaur. Instead, we will look at the reasons behind the proposals and the proposals themselves here.

In this appendix we will look at:

- the requirements for alternatives to the DTD
- two proposals to replace the DTD
- an implementation of an XML schema

XML Schemas

Given that a schema is simply a way to describe the characteristics of data, we already have the DTD as an XML schema. Why should we want something different? To answer this, we first need to look at the requirements for describing the characteristics of the data in XML documents, then see how the DTD falls short in respect of certain processing needs. People are already aware that the DTD does not meet their needs, and so have made several competing proposals to the World Wide Web Consortium. We will be looking at some of these here. The W3C Working Group currently (March 1999) is working at producing a single integrated specification that combines the best features of all the different proposals.

Schema Requirements

What do people want from an XML schema? The answer is that different types of XML users want different things. We can look at their requirements in two broad categories: those that relate to the power, or functionality of the schema, and those that relate to ease of use. Perhaps we should add a third – compatibility. We must always remember that one of the strengths of XML is that, being based on SGML, there is a wealth of knowledge and tools already out there. And the DTD is an intrinsic part of both XML and SGML. The following requirements are based on my experience, discussions with XML users and opinions gathered from the schema proposals, XML Usenet groups and Internet mailing lists (see Appendix E for references).

Functionality

The electronic commerce community makes it very clear that the DTD does not meet its needs. One of the strengths of traditional EDI is that both the syntax and semantics of messages can be checked, whereas the DTD provides very limited semantic checking of XML. Let me explain.

The syntax of an XML document or message defines the structure of the message. The DTD does a pretty good job of defining this by stating what elements must be present, what attributes they must have and in what order the elements must appear. There have been simplifications from the SGML DTD that limit to some extent the definition of a syntax, but the overall compromise is suitable for most needs. An example of a limitation of XML is that an element with mixed content (a combination of PCDATA and further elements) cannot specify the order of the elements.

The semantics of the document specify the meaning. For example, we know, as human readers, that an element called `departure-date` should contain a date. The XML DTD has no way of validating this. Similarly, if we are accepting orders using XML messages, we might have a minimum order quantity. There is no way of specifying this in a DTD. The DTD has limited semantic checking of attributes by being able to specify allowed values. However, this does not go far enough, and so improved semantic checking is a requirement of any replacement of the DTD.

The DTD also lacks namespace support, and the ability to use sections of another DTD. Earlier in the book I mentioned an example of a simple application to mark up a document with definitions from a dictionary. This dictionary will have a namespace, and use this namespace when adding elements to the source document. This ensures that the resulting document uniquely defines all its elements. However, if the source document used a DTD, adding the additional elements from the dictionary will stop the document from being valid. While I can specify the namespace, I cannot tell the parser that these elements should be validated from a separate DTD. Of course, I could add the elements to the existing DTD, but this is fraught with difficulties. I would have to add my new elements and then ensure that they are allowed inside the elements in which I am placing them. And all this without a standard Application Programming Interface (API) since the Level 1 DOM does not provide support for manipulating the DTD.

Ease of Use

As well as these two main functional requirements of a schema – better semantic checking and better descriptive power for data – there are requirements to make a schema easier to use.

Firstly, good DTDs are not easy to write. By "good" I mean DTDs that are both easy for a human to understand and that maximise the amount of checking undertaken. Why is it necessary for a DTD to be understandable by people? Because it is they who will be writing applications to produce or use XML that matches existing DTDs. If I am writing an application to process a certain type of document, such as a purchase order, it is no use looking at examples of purchase orders since these may have optional fields missing. I must use the DTD as the basis for my application. Also, if a DTD is complex and difficult to understand, that makes updating it to suit new technological requirements difficult.

Other aspects that affect the writing of DTDs are the lack of extensibility and poor version control mechanisms. If I have an application with a DTD and I change the output of the application, I have to add to the DTD. Perhaps I have added a new element. In this case, I will have to make this new element optional if I wish to maintain compatibility with old applications. We have already seen how XSL can be used to provide some form of DTD version control in this instance, but it is far from perfect. There is certainly no mechanism for negotiating DTD versions between applications, so allowing the common functionality to be re-used.

Finally in this area, we should consider the writers of XML parsers. Currently, the writers of parsers have to cope with both the syntax of the XML itself, and a different syntax for the DTD. It would clearly be simpler if the syntax were the same for both. Why should we, as users, care about this? One reason is that competition is generally a good thing, and the simpler the task of writing parsers, the more will be around to choose from. Also, of course, the simpler they are, the fewer bugs there will be in them. However, possibly a more important reason is the size and complexity of the code. This may not be important on your PC, but XML is about communication, and we also use devices such as Personal Digital Assistants (PDAs) and phones to communicate. Shortly, we will want XML parsers that can be built into these, and the smaller the parser, the sooner we will get them.

Lastly, there is the issue of translating one data structure into another, where applications don't have compatible interfaces to XML data. If a schema were written in the same syntax as an ordinary XML document, then it could be manipulated using XSL in a similar way.

Compatibility

Compatibility is the last requirement. The DTD is part of the XML version 1.0 recommendation, and many documents and applications have been written that use DTDs. Any schema needs to co-exist in a world that includes these documents and applications, and their respective data structures.

Alternative Schemas

Here we will look briefly at the DTD in the context of the above, and discuss two alternative proposals and one implementation. You may have heard elsewhere of a proposal known as XML-Data that Microsoft and others made to the World Wide Web Consortium in December 1997. This proposal met many of the requirements outlined above, and formed the basis for the schema implemented in IE5. Following this, Microsoft was involved in a second proposal, Document Content Description, based on XML-Data. Since this effectively replaces the XML-Data proposal, it is the one we will consider here.

Meanwhile, a separate group submitted a proposal for a Schema for Object-oriented XML, or SOX, that we will also look at briefly. It is important to remember that both these are proposals that are being considered by the World Wide Web Consortium, and the final recommendation, assuming there is one, will be different from both.

The DTD

As we went through the requirements for a schema, we discussed some of the weaknesses of the DTD. These can be summed up as follows:

- poor support for semantic checking
- no data typing
- no relational support
- no support for object features such as inheritance
- no ability to use parts of other DTDs
- difficult to write
- no extensibility
- no version control mechanism
- a unique syntax

Since the schema proposals are designed to improve on the DTD, it is natural to concentrate on the weaknesses. Of course, the DTD also has some strengths, such as good syntax checking, that need to be kept.

Document Content Definition (DCD)

DCD uses an XML vocabulary known as the **Resource Description Framework** (RDF) to describe its syntax. RDF is not used at all in Centaur, but I shall provide a brief overview here to help in the description of DCD.

Resource Description Framework

In the body of this book, we discussed the reasons for the development of XML, and one was that it could provide a context to make searches of the web more intelligent. I gave an example of finding a company based on various tag names, but gave no indication of how these tag names would be defined. RDF provides help in this area by providing a model and syntax for describing **metadata**, or data about data. Once we have a common means of describing the meaning of data, we can start to do more useful things with it.

RDF provides a simple model based on sentence construction. Firstly, we have the entity we are describing. This is known as a **resource**, and is represented by a URI. The resource is the **subject** of the sentence. Next we have the **property**, which is the **predicate** of the sentence. So if we take a resource such as `http://www.boynings.co.uk`, we can say that the URI is the resource, and it has property of "manager". We then have the **object**, which in this case would be "Paul Spencer". The object can be either a **literal**, such as in this example, or it can be another resource.

We can draw this simple model as:

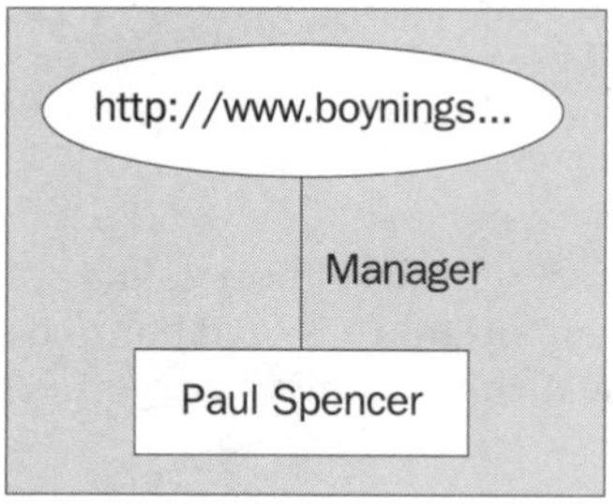

We can read this as "http://www.boynings.co.uk has a manager Paul Spencer". It would be represented in the RDF syntax as:

```
<rdf:RDF>
  <rdf:Description about="http://www.boynings.co.uk">
    <s:Manager>Paul Spencer</s:Manager>
  </rdf:Description>
</rdf:RDF>
```

Somewhere in the file, we would need to reference the `rdf` namespace, and the namespace `s`, which it would be up to me, as the author of the document, to identify.

Why would we want to make the object another resource rather than just a literal? In this case, we might want to describe me as a resource, and give me some additional properties:

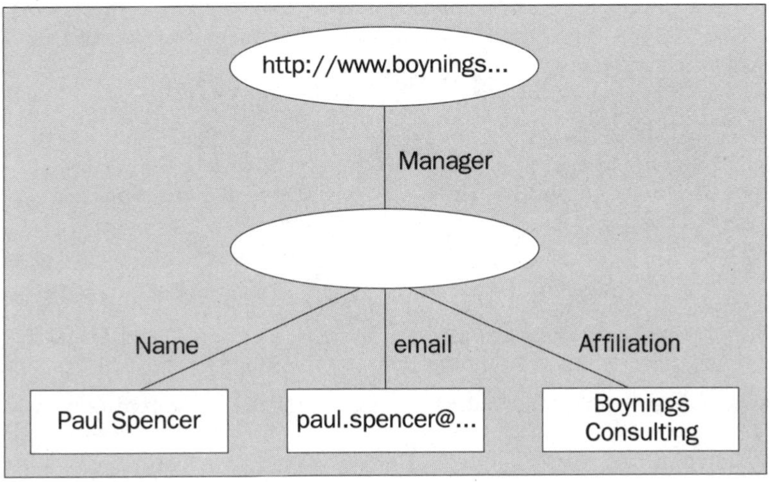

Note that the new resource is anonymous in this model. We could read this as "http://www.boynings.demon.co.uk is managed by something with a name Paul Spencer, an email address paul.spencer@boynings.co.uk and an affiliation Boynings Consulting". Following on from the previous example, we can see that the logical (and correct) syntax for this model is:

```
<rdf:RDF>
  <rdf:Description about=" http://www.boynings.co.uk ">
    <s:Manager>
      <s:Name>Paul Spencer</s:Name>
      <s:email>ps2289@boynings.co.uk</s:email>
      <s:Affiliation>Boynings Consulting</s:Affiliation>
    </s:Manager>
  </rdf:Description>
</rdf:RDF>
```

There is a lot more to RDF than this. However, this is sufficient for our purposes. The full recommendation is available on the W3C web site at `http://www.w3.org/TR/REC-rdf-syntax/`.

DCD Aims

DCD aims to be a superset of the DTD, providing constraints on the structure and contents of XML documents. The design principles reflect the general principles of most XML-related standards in maintaining human readability and consistency with other standards:

- DCD semantics shall be a superset of those provided by XML DTDs.
- The DCD data model and syntax shall be conformant with that of RDF.
- The constraints in a DCD shall be straightforwardly usable by authoring tools and other applications that wish to retrieve information about a document's content and structure.
- DCD shall use mechanisms from other W3C working groups wherever they are appropriate and efficient.
- DCDs should be human-readable and reasonably clear.

The proposal suggests a change to the RDF vocabulary to achieve its principles, whilst stating that, if the change is not made, the DCD syntax will change instead. At the time of writing (March 1999), the latter looks the more likely option.

DCD Elements

There are six high level element types defined in DCD, two of which, the `ElementDef` and the `AttributeDef` contain further structure. In RDF terms, these element types are property types. The full list is as follows:

DCD	ElementDef	InternalEntityDef
Group	AttributeDef	ExternalEntityDef

The `DCD` element itself simply indicates that its contents form the document content definition.

The `ElementDef` and `AttributeDef` elements provide the constraints on elements and attributes in the document that the DCD is describing. These allow us to apply the constraints we could in a DTD, but also all the constraints mentioned earlier in the schema requirements. We shall look at some of these through examples.

The `Group` element is used to group together the descriptions of child elements of an element in the document being described. For example, in the book catalog, a book has several child elements. The descriptions of these would be contained within a `Group`.

The `InternalEntityDef` and `ExternalEntityDef` do exactly as we would expect, allowing us to define substitutions such as:

```
<InternalEntityDef Name="xia" Value="XML Design and Implementation" />
```

or

```
<ExternalEntityDef resource="#copyrightNotice" />
```

Some DCD Examples

Let's look at the ElementDef and AttributeDef elements through some examples. We will start by replacing the DTD in the book catalog. This is the DTD we had before:

```
<?xml version = "1.0"?>
<!DOCTYPE books [
<!ELEMENT books (book)*>
<!ELEMENT book (title, authors, publisher, pages?, isbn, price+)>
<!ELEMENT authors (author+)>
<!ELEMENT title (#PCDATA)>
<!ELEMENT author (#PCDATA)>
<!ELEMENT publisher (#PCDATA)>
<!ELEMENT pages (#PCDATA)>
<!ELEMENT isbn (#PCDATA)>
<!ELEMENT price (#PCDATA)>
<!ATTLIST price currency CDATA #REQUIRED>
]>
```

Let's start by defining the books element:

```
<DCD>
  <ElementDef Type="books" Model="Elements" Content="Closed">
    <Description>A collection of book elements</Description>
    <Group Occurs="ZeroOrMore">
      <Element>book</Element>
    </Group>
  </ElementDef>
...
```

After the DCD opening tag, we start defining the books element by stating that it contains elements, and that it is a Closed model. This means that we cannot have any elements within the books element other than those we specifically allow here. The alternative to this is to have an attribute value of Open. The books element must then follow the content description here as a minimum requirement, but it may have additional elements as well. In my dictionary example earlier, I mentioned that when the application adds elements, the document would cease to be valid according to its DTD. With DCD, I could specify the element within which the additional markup occurs as Open, thereby allowing additional markup within this element. I would also need to allow these new elements to be used without being declared in the DCD. To do this, I would change the DCD element to read:

```
<DCD Content="Open">
```

The DCD proposal allows a plain text Description of the element, which we have used here. Following this, we simply state that the books element contains zero or more book elements with Occurs="ZeroOrMore". Using ZeroOrMore allows us to take into account the possibility that the document might not contain any data as the result of, say, a failed search on a database, without the parser flagging an error and halting the application.

We then need to describe the book in a similar way:

```
<ElementDef Type="book" Model="Element" Content="Closed">
    <Description>Description of a single book in the catalog</Description>
    <Group RDF:Order="Seq">
      <Element>title</Element>
      <Element>authors</Element>
      <Element>publisher</Element>
      <Group Occurs="Optional">
        <Element>pages</Element>
      </Group>
      <Element>isbn</Element>
      <Element>price</Element>
    </Group>
  </ElementDef>
```

Here, we use the fact that the default for the `Occurs` attribute of a `Group` is `Required`. We then use the `Order` attribute to say that the following elements must occur in sequence. The `Order` attribute is qualified with the namespace prefix `RDF` to indicate that it uses the RDF collection ordering facility. We have made the number of pages optional.

We can then go on to define the constraints on these elements. Here it is for the book title:

```
<ElementDef Type="title" Model="Data" Content="Closed" Datatype="string" />
```

In this case, both the `Model` and `Datatype` have taken default values as defined in the proposal, so we could abbreviate this to:

```
<ElementDef Type="title" Content="Closed" />
```

The "`Data`" value of the `Model` attribute specifies that (to quote from the DCD proposal), "Elements of this type contain text, but must not contain any child elements." The range of `datatypes` available matches those typically used in database work. A full list taken from the DCD proposal is given at the end of this appendix.

The `price` element in our catalog contains an attribute:

```
<ElementDef Type="price" Content="Closed">
  <AttributeDef Name="Currency" />
</ElementDef>
```

In the `ElementDef`, we have taken advantage of the defaults to show that this element contains `Data` of type `String`. If we wanted to restrict the currencies, we could use an `enumeration`:

```
<ElementDef Type="price" Content="Closed">
  <AttributeDef Name="Currency" Datatype="enumeration">
    <Values>USD GBP</Values>
  </AttributeDef>
</ElementDef>
```

Note that, unlike most other attribute values, `enumeration` does not use an initial capital letter. This sort of inconsistency will be ironed out as the W3C working group works on its schema recommendation.

A Note on the Syntax

DCD allows elements and attributes to be used interchangeably in many cases. For example, we have defined the price element above using a Type attribute. We could instead use elements:

```
<ElementDef>
  <Type>price</Type>
  <Content>Closed</Content>
  <AttributeDef>
    <Name>Currency</Name>
    <Datatype>enumeration</Datatype>
    <Values>USD GBP</Values>
  </AttributeDef>
</ElementDef>
```

If we want to restrict the syntax, we can specify that the properties `Type`, `Model`, `Occurs`, `RDF:Order`, `Content`, `Root`, `Fixed` and `Datatype` must use the attribute syntax, while all others must use the element syntax. We specify this with a Processing Instruction, which we put after the `DCD` element:

```
<DCD>
  <?DCD syntax="explicit"?>
  <ElementDef ...
```

DCD Summary

I hope that has given you enough of a flavour of DCD. If you would like more detail, refer to the proposal itself at `http://www.w3.org/TR/NOTE-dcd`. Remember it is only a proposal, and no supporting software will ever get beyond a technology preview stage. However it does provide a good indication of the shape of things to come.

We have seen that DCD gives all the power of the DTD as well as providing data typing and other useful features, all within an RDF syntax. As well as the features we have seen here, DCD allows the use of namespaces to allow elements to be selected from other DCDs.

The proposal recognizes that there are missing features in DCD, and points out that, to reach its full potential, some features would need to be added. These are:

- Sub-classing and inheritance to make DCD creation and maintenance take on the modularity of object-oriented software.
- More database-like facilities such as the uniqueness of values, key fields and referential integrity.
- A reflection of the fact that a database is an unordered collection of columns.

Internet Explorer 5 XML Schema

Internet Explorer 5 implements a schema with approximately the functionality of DCD, but with a different syntax based on the earlier XML-Data Schemas proposal. Since it is based, not just on a proposal, but largely on a proposal that has been superceded, it should be treated as a technology preview. Play with it and learn about schemas, but remember that any applications based on this schema syntax will almost certainly not be supported beyond IE5, and it is quite possible that an update to the XML components of IE5, using the Windows Update facility, could significantly alter the implementation in due course.

The element types for the IE5 schema will mostly be familiar from the DCD:

Element	Purpose
`Attribute`	Refers to a declared attribute type that can appear within the scope of the named `ElementType` element.
`AttributeType`	Defines an attribute type for use within the `Schema` element.
`datatype`	Specifies the data type for the `ElementType` or `AttributeType` element.
`description`	Provides documentation about an `ElementType` or `AttributeType` element.
`element`	Refers to a declared element type that can appear within the scope of the named `ElementType` element.
`ElementType`	Defines an element type for use within the `Schema` element.
`group`	Organizes content into a group to specify a sequence.
`Schema`	Identifies the start of a schema definition.

Using the IE5 syntax, we could implement a schema for our book catalog from Chapter 3 as follows:

```
<?xml version = "1.0"?>
<Schema xmlns="urn:schemas-microsoft-com:xml-data"
        xmlns:dt="urn:schemas-microsoft-com:datatypes">
  <ElementType name="title" content="textOnly" />
  <ElementType name="author" content="textOnly" />
  <ElementType name="publisher" content="textOnly" />
  <ElementType name="pages" content="textOnly" />
  <ElementType name="isbn" content="textOnly" />

  <AttributeType name="currency" dt:type="enumeration" dt:values="USD GBP" />
  <ElementType name="price" content="textOnly" dt:type="fixed.14.4">
    <attribute type="currency" required="yes" />
  </ElementType>

  <ElementType name="authors" content="eltOnly" model="closed">
    <element type="author" minOccurs="1" maxOccurs="*" />
  </ElementType>

  <ElementType name="book" content="eltOnly" model="closed">
    <element type="title" />
    <element type="authors" />
    <element type="publisher" />
    <element type="pages" />
    <element type="isbn" />
    <element type="price" />
  </ElementType>

  <ElementType name="books" content="eltOnly" model="closed">
    <element type="book" minOccurs="1" maxOccurs="*"  />
  </ElementType>
</Schema>
```

We can then utilise this schema for all elements of the book catalog by referencing it in the root element:

```
<books xmlns="x-schema:schema.xml">
```

The x-schema part of the URI for the default namespace is a Microsoft proprietary mechanism that makes a call to the Microsoft schema-oriented parser with schema.xml as a parameter. If we now open the catalog with IE5 by accessing the file catalog.xml directly, we will see the structure of the document displayed using IE5's default stylesheet. This shows that the document is valid according to the schema, otherwise the parser would have reported an error:

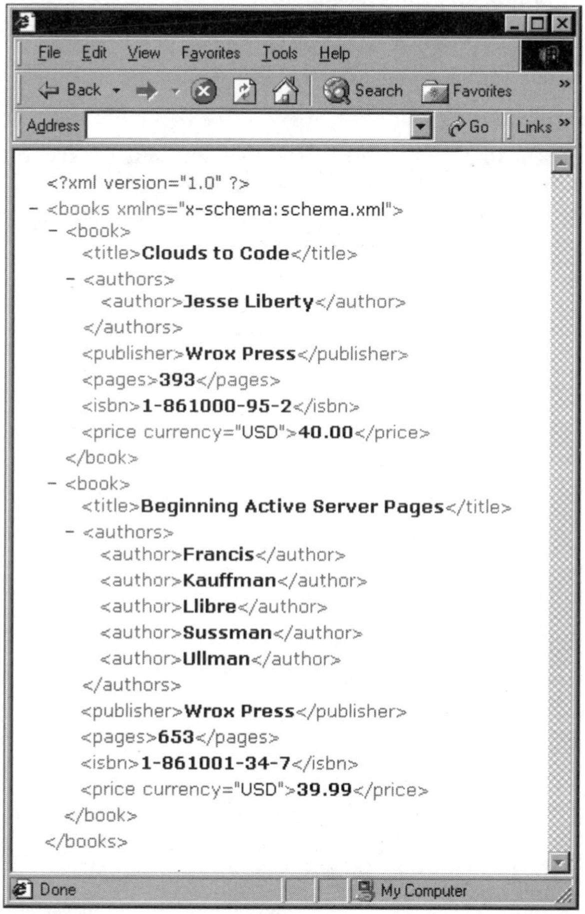
File Edit View Favorites Tools Help
Back
Search
Favorites
Address
Go
Links
<?xml version="1.0" ?>
- <books xmlns="x-schema:schema.xml">
- <book>
<title>Clouds to Code</title>
- <authors>
<author>Jesse Liberty</author>
</authors>
<publisher>Wrox Press</publisher>
<pages>393</pages>
<isbn>1-861000-95-2</isbn>
<price currency="USD">40.00</price>
</book>
- <book>
<title>Beginning Active Server Pages</title>
- <authors>
<author>Francis</author>
<author>Kauffman</author>
<author>Llibre</author>
<author>Sussman</author>
<author>Ullman</author>
</authors>
<publisher>Wrox Press</publisher>
<pages>653</pages>
<isbn>1-861001-34-7</isbn>
<price currency="USD">39.99</price>
</book>
</books>
Done
My Computer

The schema itself is available with the example files for this book as schema.xml. You can see that the schema uses similar concepts to the DCD schema elements we showed before. For example, the equivalent of the Occurs attribute of the DCD are two attributes, minOccurs and maxOccurs.

We are also using two namespaces – a default namespace for the schema itself, and a separate namespace for the data types.

The IE5 schema has the advantage that you can use it now. There is further documentation available on the Microsoft web site at `http://www.microsoft.com/xml`. Just remember the warning – be aware of the consequences of using this for live applications.

Schema for Object-oriented XML (SOX)

SOX has very much the same aims as DCD, on which it is partly based. Like DCD, it has support for data typing and inheritance, and uses an XML syntax. Here, we will briefly look at its aims and features, describe the book catalog using SOX and look at some of the additional features that give SOX its power. Before starting this, I will say that the SOX proposal, written by Matt Fuchs and Alex Milowski of Veo Systems and Murray Maloney of Muzmo Communication, is a wonderful example of writing a specification that is both precise and readable. This attitude is carried forward into the SOX language itself, which contains elements to help make SOX documents themselves easy to understand. Have a look at the proposal at `http://www.w3.org/TR/NOTE-SOX`.

SOX Aims

SOX has two main goals. The first is that it should be useful for modeling markup relationships. The second is that, compared to the DTD, SOX documents should enable more efficient software development and decrease the complexity of supporting interoperation between applications. The proposal notes four specific aims relating to this second goal:

- SOX should enable software mapping from SOX documents into data structures in relational databases, common programming languages, and interface definition languages (such as Java, IDL, COM, C and C++), resulting in usable code.
- SOX should enable reuse at the document design and the application programming levels
- SOX should be able to express domain abstractions and common relationships among them directly and explicitly. (e.g., subtype/supertype, etc.)
- SOX should support the generation of common application components (marshal/unmarshal, programming data structures) directly from SOX documents.

The proposal also notes seven requirements of the language:

- SOX shall use XML syntax and be expressed in valid instances according to a valid XML DTD.
- SOX and SOX documents shall be interoperable with XML software and conventions.
- SOX shall enable a software mapping from SOX documents into an XML DTD, and from an XML DTD into a SOX document without losing the grammatical structure of the original DTD.
- SOX shall provide an extensible datatyping mechanism.
- SOX shall comply with and be compatible with applicable W3C recommendations, IETF RFCs and ISO Standards, and Proposed Standards.
- SOX documents shall provide support for embedded documentation.
- SOX documents shall be human-readable.

These goals and requirements show that SOX is clearly aimed at the database, as well as the document, world. Note that a requirement is for SOX documents to be able to be mapped to DTDs and vice versa. This reflects the requirement stated earlier that a requirement of any schema is that it support existing documents that use a DTD. In fact, SOX can not only be mapped to and from a DTD, but the goal of easing software development is met in part by an ability to generate classes for common programming languages directly from the SOX schema.

A SOX Example

Let's rebuild the book catalog DTD as a SOX schema. Any SOX schema must have `schema` as its root element. This element may optionally reference a namespace:

```
<?xml version="1.0"?>
<schema name="catalog"
        namespace="http://www.boynings.co.uk/namespaces/SOX/catalog"
>
...
```

This is followed by a title for the document:

```
<h1>Book Catalog</h1>
...
```

Of course, you recognize the `h1` element – SOX makes heavy use of HTML markup elements as these are familiar to everyone who is likely to be using the schema. It also means that a schema can be displayed using a relatively simple XSL stylesheet.

I mentioned before that SOX enables schema writers to create schemas that are easy to understand. This is achieved through further HTML markup that is allowed within the schema. Apart from the required `h1` element, `h2` and `h3` elements may be used as children of the schema element. These may themselves have `intro` elements that can have `h4`, `h5` and `h6` and a variety of other HTML elements as children. SOX also has an `explain` element that appears within any definition, and this can have `title`, `synopsis`, `help` and a variety of HTML elements as children.

Let's use some of these features to continue our schema:

```
<h2>Introduction</h2>
<intro>
  <p>This schema describes the catalog of books published by Wrox Press</p>
  <p>The following features of books are described:</p>
  <ul>
    <li>title</li>
    <li>authors</li>
    <li>publisher</li>
    <li>pages (optional)</li>
    <li>isbn</li>
    <li>price (in various currencies)</li>
  </ul>
</intro>

<h3>The "books" root element</h3>
<elementtype name="books">
  <explain>
    <title>Book Catalog</title>
    <synopsis>A simple schema for use in the book XML in Action</synopsis>
    <help>
      <p>If you want to know more about this, go buy the book!</p>
    </help>
  </explain>
  <model>
    <element name="book" occurs="+" />
  </model>
</elementtype>
...
```

Of course, for such as simple schema, much of the commentary would not be included in practice. This example shows that a catalog comprises one or more books. We can then describe a book in a similar way:

```
<h3>The description of the main "book" element</h3>
<elementtype name="book">
  <model>
    <sequence>
      <element name="title" />
      <element name="authors " />
      <element name="publisher " />
      <element name="pages " occurs="?" />
      <element name="isbn " />
      <element name="price " />
    </sequence>
  </model>
</elementtype>
...
```

And then the remaining elements:

```
<elementtype name="title">
  <model><string /></model>
</elementtype>

<elementtype name="authors">
  <model>
    <element name="author" occurs="+" />
  </model>
</elementtype>

<elementtype name="publisher">
  <model><string /></model>
</elementtype>

<elementtype name="pages">
  <model><string datatype="number" /></model>
</elementtype>

<elementtype name="isbn">
  <model>
    <string>
      <mask>#-######-##-#</mask>
    </string>
  </model>
</elementtype>

<elementtype name="price">
  <model>
    <string datatype="number" />
    <attdef name="currency" datatype="string">
      <enumeration>
       <option>USD</option>
       <option>GBP</option>
      </enumeration>
      <required />
    </attdef>
  </model>
</elementtype>
```

```
    <elementtype name="author">
      <model><string /></model>
    </elementtype>
  </schema>
```

There are a few points to note here. The `occurs` attribute can take values such as `*`, `+` and `?` in the same way as a DTD. However, it can also take minimum and maximum values. So `occurs="?"` is the equivalent of `occurs="0,1"`. This can be useful in cases where the minimum and maximum values are not these common values. For example, a software house may restrict the number of elements in a data flow diagram to be between five and nine. If they developed an XML language to describe data flow diagrams, they could build this restriction into a SOX schema.

The `isbn` element uses a mask to ensure the correct format of digits and spaces. Masks can also be used with alphabetic and mixed data. The currency has its attribute as before. This uses the `enumeration` element to restrict the possible values, and the `required` element to force its presence. As you can see, the authors of SOX have continued the similarity to HTML by using a syntax for `enumeration` that is similar to the HTML `select` element syntax. The SOX proposal contains many more examples of more complex uses of the schema.

You can see that it is a lot more verbose than the DTD (although cutting out the inline documentation would reduce this). This disadvantage must be offset against the greater power and ease of use of the schema.

Some More SOX Features

One aspect of the DTD that can be frustrating is the inability to use part of an external DTD or to use one element description as the basis for another. SOX addresses both of these weaknesses. It also addresses extensibility by, for example, providing only a limited range of data types, but providing a facility to add more. In fact, SOX combines the strengths of the DTD, previous work on schemas, object-oriented language constructs and database structures to provide a powerful, yet simple to use, XML schema.

Future Work

As with DCD, the group that developed SOX recognizes that there is more work to do for the schema proposal to reach its full potential.

Like DCD, SOX cannot represent a database as an unordered collection of columns. This is possible in SGML, but not in XML, since allowing this makes parsing a document significantly more complicated.

The SOX developers identified a need to be able to turn validation off for parts of documents. This can provide an alternative allowing better error checking than a `content` model of `Open`.

Consideration was also given to including support for XML Links and XML Pointers. However, the draft recommendations were seen as too immature to include them when the SOX proposal was written.

Summary

In this appendix we have provided an overview of two proposals for XML schemas. We have also looked at the schema implementation in IE5. We looked at each of these in fairly broad terms, since they are not used in the Centaur case study.

During 1999, the W3C will be looking at schemas and working on a recommendation for them.

We have seen:

- that the DTD does not provide all the functionality required in some applications, especially electronic commerce
- the requirements for alternative schemas
- the proposals for DCD and SOX and how they meet these requirements while maintaining a level of compatibility with the DTD
- how IE5 provides support for a schema as a technology preview
- that the W3C is working on a schema recommendation, which will be based on the best features of the various schema proposals

XML-Data & DCD Datatypes

This table is copied from the W3 note at:

`http://www.w3.org/TR/1998/NOTE-XML-data-0105/`

Specific Datatypes

This includes all highly popular types and all the built-in types of popular database and programming languages and systems such as SQL, Visual Basic, C, C++ and Java(tm).

Name	Parse type	Storage type	Examples
`string`	`pcdata`	string (Unicode)	Ομωνυμα λεγαται ων ονομα μον ον κοινον, ο δε κατα τουνομα λ ογοσ της ουσιας ετεροσ, οιον ζυ ον ο τε ανθροπος και το γεγραμμ ενον.
`number`	A number, with no limit on digits, may potentially have a leading sign, fractional digits, and optionally an exponent. Punctuation as in US English.	string	15, 3.14, -123.456E+10

Name	Parse type	Storage type	Examples
`int`	A number, with optional sign, no fractions, no exponent.	32-bit signed binary	1, 58502, -13
`float`	Same as for `number`	64-bit IEEE 488	.314159265358979E+1
`fixed.14.4`	Same as `number` but no more than 14 digits to the left of the decimal point, and no more than 4 to the right.	64-bit signed binary	12.0044
`boolean`	`"1"` or `"0"`	bit	0, 1 (1=="true")
`dateTime.iso8601`	A date in ISO 8601 format, with optional time and no optional zone. Fractional seconds may be as precise as nanoseconds.	Structure or object containing year, month, hour, minute, second, nanosecond.	19941105T08:15:00301
`dateTime.iso8601tz`	A date in ISO 8601 format, with optional time and optional zone. Fractional seconds may be as precise as nanoseconds.	Structure or object containing year, month, hour, minute, second, nanosecond, zone.	19941105T08:15:5+03
`date.iso8601`	A date in ISO 8601 format. (no time)	Structure or object containing year, month, day.	19541022

Table Continued on Following Page

Name	Parse type	Storage type	Examples
`time.iso8601`	A time in ISO 8601 format, with no date and no time zone.	Structure or object exposing day, hour, minute	
`time.iso8601.tz`	A time in ISO 8601 format, with no date but optional time zone.	Structure or object containing day, hour, minute, zonehours, zoneminutes.	08:15-05:00
`i1`	A number, with optional sign, no fractions, no exponent.	8-bit binary	1, 255
`i2`	"	16-bit binary	1, 703, -32768
`i4`	"	32-bit binary	
`i8`	"	64-bit binary	
`ui1`	A number, unsigned, no fractions, no exponent.	8-bit unsigned binary	1, 255
`ui2`	"	16-bit unsigned binary	1, 703, -32768
`ui4`	"	32-bit unsigned binary	
`ui8`	"	64-bit unsigned binary	
`r4`	Same as `number`	IEEE 488 4-byte float	
`r8`	"	IEEE 488 8-byte float	
`float.IEEE.754.32`	"	IEEE 754 4-byte float	

Name	Parse type	Storage type	Examples
`float.IEEE.754.64`	"	IEEE 754 8-byte float	
`uuid`	Hexidecimal digits representing octets, optional embedded hyphens which should be ignored.	128-bytes Unix UUID structure	F04DA480-65B9-11d1-A29F-00AA00C14882

`uri`	Universal Resource Identifier	Per W3C spec	`http://www.ics.uci.edu/pub/ietf/uri/draft-fielding-uri-syntax-00.txt`
			
			`http://www.ics.uci.edu/pub/ietf/uri/`
			
			`http://www.ietf.org/html.charters/urn-charter.html`

`bin.hex`	Hexidecimal digits representing octets	no specified size	
`char`	string	1 Unicode character (16 bits)	
`string.ansi`	string containing only ascii characters <= 0xFF.	Unicode or single-byte string.	This does not look Greek to me.

All of the dates and times above reading "iso8601.." actually use a restricted subset of the formats defined by ISO 8601. Years, if specified, must have four digits. Ordinal dates are not used. Of formats employing week numbers, only those that truncate year and month are allowed (5.2.3.3 d, e and f).

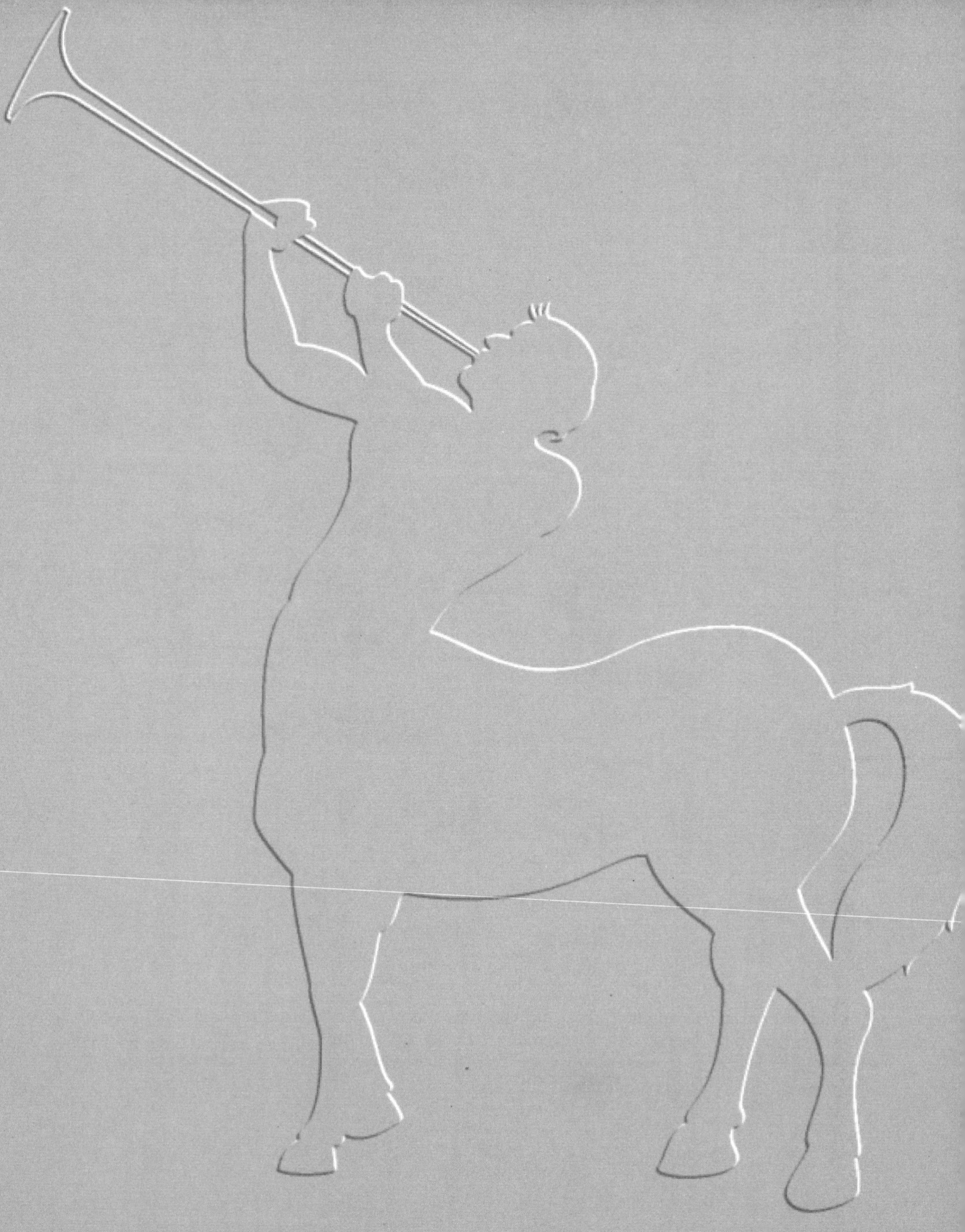

E

XML Resources and References

There are a many useful XML resources available on the Internet. This appendix lists several of them, first are a number of general sites, these are followed by specific chapter references.

The W3C site is the home of all the XML specifications, as well as a number of other useful resources.
`http://www.w3.org`

XML related specifications

Standard	Status	URL
Extensible Markup Language (XML)	W3C Recommendation *10-February-1998*	`http://www.w3.org/TR/REC-xml`
Document Object Model Level 1 (DOM)	W3C Recommendation *1- October-1998*	`http://www.w3.org/TR/REC-DOM-Level-1/`
Document Object Model Level 2	W3C Working Draft *28-December-1998*	`http://www.w3.org/TR/WD-DOM-Level-2/`
Extensible Style Language	W3C Working Draft *16-December-1998*	`http://www.w3.org/TR/WD-xsl`
Cascading Style Sheets, Level 1	W3C Recommendation *17-December 1996*	`http://www.w3.org/TR/REC-CSS1`

Standard	Status	URL
Cascading Style Sheets, Level 2	W3C Recommendation *12-May-1998*	`http://www.w3.org/TR/REC-CSS2/`
Extensible Link Language	W3C Working Draft *3-March-1998*	`http://www.w3.org/TR/WD-xlink`
XML Pointer Language	W3C Working Draft *3-March-1998*	`http://www.w3.org/TR/WD-xptr`
Namespaces in XML	W3C Recommendation *14-January-1999*	`http://www.w3.org/TR/REC-xml-names/`
XML Data	Note *17-December-1997*	`http://www.w3.org/TR/1998/NOTE-XML-data/`
Document Content Description	Note *31-July-1998*	`http://www.w3.org/TR/NOTE-dcd`
Schema for Object-oriented XML	Note *30-September-1998*	`http://www.w3.org/TR/NOTE-SOX/`
Resource Description Framework	W3C Recommendation 22-*February*-1999	`http://www.w3.org/TR/REC-rdf-syntax/`

Microsoft has a rapidly expanding range of XML resources on their SiteBuilder site. You can also download a number of XML parsers from this site.
`http://www.microsoft.com/xml`

Information about Microsoft technologies can be found at:
`http://msdn.microsoft.com/developer/techsite/default.htm`

Tim Bray's site hosts a number of resources and links to useful information. This is where you can download Tim's Lark and Larval parsers.
`http://www.textuality.com/XML/`

Peter Flynn's site maintains an extensive FAQ list at:
`http://www.ucc.ie/xml/`

James Tauber hosts three sites on XML.
`http://www.xmlinfo.com` for general XML information.
`http://www.schema.net` for DTD's and other schemata and
`http://www.xmlsoftware.com` for XML-related software.

ArborText are heavily involved in the production of XML specifications, their site covers XML news, resources and links, and can be found at:
`http://www.arbortext.com/xml.html`

XML.com is an impressive collection of XML resources including a very useful version of the annotated XML spec (created by Tim Bray) at:
`http://www.xml.com/`

Lisa Rein runs a comprehensive site with lots of XML resources including a FAQ, links to several parsers, and other XML resources at:
`http://www.finetuning.com/`

WebDeveloper.Com host The XML Files, with tutorials, links and discussion, they can be found at:
`http://webdeveloper.com/xml/`

Café Con Leche is a large source of XML related news and information it can be found at:
`http://sunsite.unc.edu/xml/`

CommerceNet's XML Exchange is a resource for sharing DTDs and other Schemas. You can find these at:
`http://www.xmlx.com/`

Poet Software maintain a site that has several useful links to papers on XML. See:
`http://www.poet.com/xml/`

Robin Cover has a list of resources on XML at:
`http://www.oasis-open.org/cover/xml.html`

The XML/EDI group promotes EDI as an XML application, their site is hosted at:
`http://www.xmledi.com/`

Boynings Consulting includes information and examples of practical uses of XML at:
`http://www.boynings.co.uk/`

Chapter 1: Introducing the Centaur Case Study

Microsoft Expedia travel site:
`http://expedia.msn.com/daily/home/default.hts`

Chapter 2: XML Overview

HotBot search engine:
`http://www.hotbot.com`

Altavista search engine:
`http://www.altavista.digital.com`

Tim Bray's annotated version of the XML 1.0 recommendation:
`http://www.xml.com/axml/testaxml.htm`

Information about the Unicode character set;
`http://www.unicode.org/unicode/uni2book/u2.html` and
`ftp://ftp.unicode.org/Public/UNIDATA/UnicodeData-Latest.txt`

The Free Online Dictionary of Computing:
http://wombat.doc.ic.ac.uk/foldoc/index.html

The HTML 4.0 specification
http://www.w3.org/TR/REC-html40

Chapter 3: The Document Object Model

The Microsoft-Datachannel parser for Java:
http://www.datachannel.com/xml_resources/developers/parser.shtml

The Simple API for XML for event-based parsing:
http://www.megginson.com/SAX

Chapter 4: Displaying XML

The CSS1 specification can be found at:
http://www.w3.org/TR/REC-CSS1

The CSS2 specification can be found at:
http://www.w3.org/TR/REC-CSS2

Linking an XML document to a style sheet is discussed in a note found at:
http://www.w3.org/TR/PR-xml-stylesheet

Chapter 5: XSL in Theory and Practice

These pages contain the latest news on the XSL front:
http://www.w3.org/Style/XSL/

A list of the requirements for XSL can be found here:
http://www.w3.org/TR/WD-XSLReq

Here is the Working Draft of the XSL specification:
http://www.w3.org/TR/WD-xsl

And a note on the CSS namespace can be found at this site:
http://www.w3.org/TR/NOTE-XSL-and-CSS

Information about the Open Financial Exchange standard:
http://www.ofx.net/ofx/

More information on XSL numbering in IE5 can be found on the Microsoft Web site at:
http://www.microsoft.com/workshop/xml/xsl/reference/xslmethods.asp

The Microsoft documentation for XSL in IE5:
http://www.microsoft.com/workshop/xml/xsl/reference/start.asp

Chapter 6: Further XML Techniques

Cookie using site:
`http://www.doubleclick.com`

Information on the IE5 DHTML behaviours:
`http://www.microsoft.com/workshop/author/behaviors/overview.asp`

Microsoft documentation for the XMLHttpRequest object;
`http://www.microsoft.com/workshop/xml/xmldom/reference/IXMLHttpRequest_interface.asp`

Chapter 7: Under the Hood of Centaur

For more information on the process of database table normalization visit:
`http://www.bsbpa.umkc.edu/sward/mis552/CH05/index.htm` or
`http://www.cba.nau.edu/morgan-j/class/subtop2_3/sld001.htm`

Other Information

The design principles of XLL:
`http://www.w3.org/TR/NOTE-xlink-principles`

The XLink specification:
`http://www.w3.org/TR/WD-xlink`

The XPointer specification:
`http://www.w3.org/TR/WD-xptr`

Robin Cover's XML pages. Links to everywhere.
`http://www.oasis-open.org/cover/`

An interesting 176 slide talk by Eve Mahler, the co-editor of the XLL specification
`http://www.oasis-open.org/cover/xlink9805/index.htm`

How Can the XML Pointer Language (XLink and XPointer) Help Solve the Problem of Broken Links on the Net? – Posting from Eve Maler.
`http://www.oasis-open.org/cover/maler980331.html`

F

IE5 XSL Reference

IE5 broadly supports the **Transformations** section of the working draft of XSL released by W3C on 16th December 1998, though there are some minor differences. It does *not* support the proposals for **Formatting Objects** or **Flow Objects**. This reference section details the XSL support available in the IE5 final release.

XSL defines a set of XML elements that have special meaning within the `xsl` namespace (i.e. each is prefixed with the `xsl` namespace identifier). These elements perform the transformation of the document into a new format. From here, under the W3C proposals, Formatting Objects would be used to define the actual output format for each element transformation. In IE5, we will generally use HTML within the transformations to define the new document format.

Bear in mind that XSL can also be used to transform *any* XML document into another (different) XML document, or into a document in almost any other format. This means, for example, that it can be used to transform an XSL stylesheet document into another XSL stylesheet document, or into some custom format that defines the styling in a way suited to some other application.

The IE5 XSL Elements

XSL in IE5 provides twenty elements that are used to create XSL stylesheets, or style sections within an XML document. The elements are:

Name	Description

`xsl:apply-templates`	Used inside a template to indicate that XSL should look for and apply another specific template to this node. The attributes are:
	
	`order-by="[+|-] xsl-pattern"`
	
	`select="xsl-pattern"`

`xsl:attribute`	Used to create a new `Attribute` node and attach it to the current element. The single attribute is: `name="attribute-name"`
`xsl:cdata`	Used to create a new `CDATASection` at this point in the output. Has no attributes.
`xsl:choose`	Used with the `xsl:when` and `xsl:otherwise` to provide a selection mechanism based on individual conditions for the same or different nodes. Similar to an `If...ElseIf...Else` construct. Has no attributes.
`xsl:comment`	Used to create a new `Comment` node at this point in the output. Has no attributes.
`xsl:copy`	Used to copy the current node in its entirety to the output. Has no attributes.
`xsl:define-template-set`	Used to define a set of templates that have a specific scope in the stylesheet. Has no attributes.
`xsl:element`	Used to create a new `Element` node at this point in the output. The single attribute is: `name="element-name"`
`xsl:entity-ref`	Used to create a new `EntityReference` node at this point in the output. The single attribute is: `name="entity-reference-name"`
`xsl:eval`	Used to evaluate a string expression and insert the result into the output. The string can be a mathematical or logical expression, an XSL function or a custom script function. The single attribute is: `language="language-name"`

Name	Description

`xsl:for-each`	Used to create a loop construct similar to a `For...Next` loop, allowing the same template to be applied to multiple more than one node. The attributes are:
	`order-by="[+|-] xsl-pattern"`
	`select="xsl-pattern"`

`xsl:if`	Used to create conditional branches within a template, in the same way as an `If...Then` construct, to allow a template to provide different output based on a condition. The single attribute is: `test="condition-pattern"`
`xsl:node-name`	Used to insert the name of the current node into the output as a text string. Has no attributes.
`xsl:otherwise`	*see* `xsl:choose` (above). Has no attributes.
`xsl:pi`	Used to create a new `ProcessingInstruction` node at this point in the output. The single attribute is: `name="processing-instruction-name"`
`xsl:script`	Used to define an area of the template that contains global variable declarations and script code functions. The single attribute is: `language="language-name"`

`xsl:stylesheet`	Used to define the 'root' element of an XSL stylesheet, the scripting language used, whether to preserve any white space in the input document when creating the output document, and a namespace declaration for the `xsl` prefix. The attributes are:
	`xmlns:xml="http://www.w3.org/TR/WD-xsl"`
	`language="language-name"`
	`indent-result="[yes|no]"` (default is `"no"`)
	NOTE: The namespace **must** be as shown here for XSL to work in IE5.

`xsl:template`	Used to define a template which containing contains the instructions for transforming the XML input into the output for nodes that match a specific pattern. The attributes are:
	`language="language-name"`
	`match="xsl-pattern"`

Table Continued on Following Page

Name	Description
xsl:value-of	Used to evaluate an XSL pattern in the `select` attribute, and insert into the template as text the value of the matching node and its descendents. The single attribute is: `select="`*`xsl-pattern`*`"`
xsl:when	*see* `xsl:choose` (above). The single attribute is: `test="`*`xsl-pattern`*`"`

XSL Stylesheet Structure

The following shows the more common ways in which the XSL elements are used to construct an XSL style sheet, showing the kinds of structures that can be created. This isn't by any means the only combination, as most of the elements can be nested within most of the other elements. However, in general, each stylesheet will consist of one template that matches the root element in the document, followed by others that apply specific style and formatting to specific elements within the document.

```
<xsl:stylesheet xmlns:xsl="http://www.w3.org/TR/WD-xsl">

   <xsl:template match="...">
      <xsl:value-of select="..." />
      <xsl:eval> ...    </xsl:eval>
      <xsl:if match="..."> ... </xsl:if>
      <xsl:copy />

      <xsl:choose>
         <xsl:when match="..."> ... </xsl:when>
         <xsl:otherwise> ... </xsl:otherwise>
      </xsl:choose>

      <xsl:for-each select="...">
         <xsl:value-of select="..." />
         <xsl:eval> ... </xsl:eval>
         <xsl:if match="..."> ... </xsl:if>
         <xsl:copy />
         <xsl:apply-templates />
      </xsl:for-each>

      <xsl:apply-templates select="..." />
   </xsl:template>

   <xsl:define-template-set>
      <xsl:template match="..."> ... </xsl:template>
      <xsl:template match="..."> ... </xsl:template>
   </xsl:define-template-set>

   <xsl:script> ... </xsl:script>

</xsl:stylesheet>
```

Creating New Nodes in XSL

The XSL elements that create new nodes in the output document are `xsl:attribute`, `xsl:cdata`, `xsl:comment`, `xsl:element`, `xsl:entity-ref` and `xsl:pi`.

To create the XML node `<![CDATA[This is a CDATA section]]>` we could use:

```
<xsl:cdata>This is a CDATA section</xsl:cdata>
```

To create the XML node `<!ENTITY copy "©">` we could use:

```
<xsl:entity-ref name="copy">©</entity-ref>
```

To create the XML node `<!--This is the comment text-->` we could use:

```
<xsl:comment>This is the comment text</xsl:comment>
```

To create the XML node `<?WroxFormat="StartParagraph"?>` we could use:

```
<xsl:pi name="WroxFormat">StartParagraph</xsl:pi>
```

To create the XML element `<title>Instant JavaScript</title>` we could use:

```
<xsl:element name="title">Instant JavaScript</xsl:element>
```

and to add a `print-date` attribute to it we could use:

```
<xsl:attribute name="print_date">1998-02-07</xsl:attribute>
```

This gives us the XML result:

```
<title print_date="1998-02-07">Instant JavaScript</title>
```

XSL Stylesheet Runtime Methods

The `xsl:eval` element can be used to execute a number of built-in methods available in XSL in IE5. The `IXTLRuntime` object provides these methods:

Name	Description
`absoluteChildNumber (this_node)`	Returns the index of a specified node within its parent's `childNodes` list. Values start from `"1"`.
`ancestorChildNumber (node_name, this_node)`	Finds the first ancestor node of a specified node that has the specified name, and returns the index of that node within its parent's `childNodes` list. Values start from `1`. Returns `0` if there is no ancestor.

Table Continued on Following Page

Name	Description
childNumber(this_node)	Returns the index of the specified node within its parent's childNodes list of children with the same name (i.e. its index within the list of the node's identically named siblings) or 0 if not found. Values start from 1.
depth(start_node)	Returns the depth or level within the document tree at which the specified node appears. The XMLDocument or root node is at level 0.
elementIndexList (this_node, node_name)	Returns an array of node index numbers for the specified node and all its ancestors up to and including the document root node, indicating each node's position within their parent's childNodes list. The ordering of the array starts from the root document node. When the node_name parameter is not supplied, the method returns an array of integers that indicates the index of the specified node with respect to all of its siblings, the index of that node's parent with respect to all of its siblings, and so on until the document root is reached. When the node_name parameter is specified, the returned array contains entries only for nodes of the specified name, and the indices are evaluated relative to siblings with the specified name. Zero is supplied for levels in the tree that do not have children with the supplied name. Although this method is included in the Microsoft documentation, it was not supported by IE5 at the time of writing.

Name	Description
`formatDate(date, format, locale)`	Formats the value in the date parameter using the specified formatting options. The following format codes are supported: `m` - Month (1-12) `mm` - Month (01-12) `mmm` - Month (Jan-Dec) `mmmm` - Month (January-December) `mmmmm` - Month as the first letter of the month `d` - Day (1-31) `dd` - Day (01-31) `ddd` - Day (Sun-Sat) `dddd` - Day (Sunday-Saturday) `yy` -Year (00-99) `yyyy` - Year (1900-9999) The locale to use in determining the correct sequence of values in the date. If omitted the sequence month-day-year is used.
`formatIndex(number, format)`	Formats the integer number using the specified numerical system. `1` - Standard numbering system `01` - Standard numbering with leading zeros `A` - Uppercase letter sequence "`A`" to "`Z`" then "`AA`" to"`ZZ`". `a` - Lowercase letter sequence "`a`" to "`z`" then "`aa`" to "`zz`". `I` - Uppercase Roman numerals: "`I`", "`II`", "`III`", "`IV`", etc. `i` - Lowercase Roman numerals: "`i`", "`ii`", "`iii`", "`iv`", etc.

Table Continued on Following Page

Name	Description
`formatNumber (number, format)`	Formats the value number using the specified format. Zero or more of the following values can be present in the format string: # (pound) – Display only significant digits and omit insignificant zeros. 0 (zero) – Display insignificant zeros in these positions. ? (question) – Adds spaces for insignificant zeros on either side of the decimal point, so that decimal points align with a fixed-point font. You can also use this symbol for fractions that have varying numbers of digits. . (period) – Indicates the position of the decimal point. , (comma) – Display a thousands separator or scale a number by a multiple of one thousand. % (percent) – Display number as a percentage. E or e - Display number in scientific (exponential) format. If format contains a zero or # (hash) to the right of an exponent code, display the number in scientific format and inserts an "E" or "e". The number of 0 or # characters to the right determines the number of digits in the exponent. E- or e- Place a minus sign by negative exponents. E+ or e+ Place a minus sign by negative exponents and a plus sign by positive exponents.

Name	Description
`formatTime(time, format, locale)`	Formats the value in the time parameter using the specified formatting options. The following format codes are supported: `h` - Hours (0-23) `hh` - Hours (00-23) `m` - Minutes (0-59) `mm` - Minutes (00-59) `s` - Seconds (0-59) `ss` - Seconds (00-59) `AM/PM` - Add "`AM`" or "`PM`" and display in 12 hour format `am/pm` - Add "`am`" or "`pm`" and display in 12 hour format `A/P` - Add "`A`" or "`P`" and display in 12 hour format `a/p` - Add "`a`" or "`p`" and display in 12 hour format `[h]:mm` – Display elapsed time in hours, i.e. "`25.02`" `[mm]:ss` - Display elapsed time in minutes, i.e. "`63:46`" `[ss]` - Display elapsed time in seconds `ss.00` - Display fractions of a second The locale is used to determine the correct separator characters.
`uniqueID(this_node)`	Returns the unique identifier for the specified node.

As an example, this code transforms a number which is the content of the current element into Roman numerals using the built-in `formatIndex()` method:

```
<xsl:eval>
   intNumber=parseInt(this.text);
   formatIndex(intNumber, "i");
</xsl:eval>
```

Note that the content of the element must first be transformed from string format (which is the default for all XML content, unless we specify otherwise in the XML document's schema using data types).

The IE5 XSL Pattern-Matching Syntax

Using the elements described earlier, XSL can create a stylesheet document that contains one or more XSL `template` elements. These templates are applied to individual elements or sets of elements in the source document to create a particular section of the output document. To define which template applies to which of the source elements or nodes, a **pattern** is used. This pattern has one of two generic forms, and can define the node or nodes that match through:

- The **position** and **hierarchy** of the node or nodes within the source document
- The application of a **filter** that selectively targets one or more nodes

Node Position and Hierarchy

To select or match nodes (i.e. elements) through their position and hierarchy within the source document, we use a series of **path operators** to build up a pattern string. The path operators are:

Operator	Description
`/`	A forward slash is the child path operator. It selects elements that are direct children of the specified node, in much the same way as we use it to specify paths in a URL. For example, we use `book/category` to select all `<category>` elements that are children of `<book>` elements. To indicate the root node, we place this operator at the start of the pattern, for example: `/booklist/book`.
`//`	Two forward slashes indicate the recursive descent path operator. It selects all matching nodes at any depth below the current node, i.e. all descendents, for example: `booklist//title` to select all `<title>` elements that are descendents at any level of the `<booklist>` element. When it appears at the start of the pattern, it indicates recursive descent from the root node, i.e. all elements in the document.
`.`	The period or 'full stop' is the current context path operator. It is used to indicate specifically the current node or 'context', for example: `.//title` to select all `<title>` elements at any level below the current element. The combination `./` always indicates the current context and is usually superfluous–for example `./book/category` is the same as `book/category`.
`@`	The 'at' operator is the attribute path operator. It indicates that this part of the pattern refers to attributes of the current element. For example, `book/@print_date` selects the `print_date` attributes of all `<book>` elements.
`*`	The asterisk is a wildcard path operator, and is used when we want to select all elements or attributes regardless of their name, for example `book/*` to select all child elements of all `book` elements, or `book/@*` to select all the attributes of all `<book>` elements.

Node Index Position

The path operators always return all elements or nodes that match the pattern. The node **index** can be used to specify a particular node within the set (or collection) of matching nodes, and the special XSL `end()` function can be used to specify the last node:

```
/booklist/book[0]      'first <book> element in root <booklist> element
/booklist/book[2]      'third <book> element in root <booklist> element
/booklist/book[end()] 'last <book> element in root <booklist> element
```

Note that the following three examples select different nodes within the same document:

```
book/category[2]       'second <category> element from all <book> elements
book[2]/category[2]    'second <category> element in second <book> element
(book/category)[2]     'second <category> element within the set of all ...
                       '... <category> elements from all <book> elements
```

In the last example, think of it as the pattern within the parentheses being applied first to create the set of all category elements from all book elements, followed by the index operator selecting just the second one.

XSL Filters and Filter Patterns

An **XSL filter** has the generic form `[operator pattern]` where *`operator`* is an optional **filter operator** that defines how the pattern is applied, and *`pattern`* is the required XSL **filter pattern** that selects one or more elements based on a range of criteria. One or more white-space characters separate the filter operator and the filter pattern. The optional *`operator`* part can also consist of more than one filter operator expression if required. If omitted, any or all nodes that match the criteria in the filter pattern will be selected.

Filter Patterns

XSL filter patterns are very powerful, and offer an almost infinite number of pattern combinations. The following is a broad guide to the different kinds of ways that they can be used. The examples cover:

- Selecting by **child node name**
- Selecting by **node value**
- Selecting by **attribute existence**
- Selecting by **attribute value**
- Selecting by a **combination** of these

Selecting by Child Node Name

The position and hierarchy syntax we looked at earlier works by selecting elements based on their name as well as their position within the document. For example, `book/category` selects all `<category>` elements that are child elements of `<book>` elements. This is equivalent to the filter:

```
book[category]/category
```

because the filter book/category is actually a shorthand way of saying we want to select all <book> elements that have a <category> element (equivalent to book[category]), and then select the <category> element. A more useful way of using the longhand technique is when you want to specify a *different* child element to return. For example,

```
book[title]/category
```

means select only the <category> elements of books that have a <title> child element. To find all books that have both a <category> and a <title> child element, we use two filters:

```
book[title][category]
```

Selecting by Node Value

Extending the filter pattern that selects a node by its name, we can also select by value:

```
book[category = 'Scripting']
```

will select all <book> elements that have a <category> element with the value of 'Scripting'. If we want to get the title of books in this category we would use:

```
book[category = 'Scripting']/title
```

To specify a value for the current element, we can include the period path operator. For example:

```
book/title[. = 'Instant JavaScript']
```

selects the title of the book 'Instant JavaScript'.

Selecting by Attribute Existence

The '@' attribute operator can also be used in a filter pattern to specify that the element must have a matching attribute:

```
book[@print_date]
```

selects only book elements that have a print_date attribute.

Selecting by Attribute Value

We can also specify the value that the attribute must have in order to match the pattern:

```
book[@print_date = '1998-05-02']
```

Selecting by a Combination of Methods

And, of course, we can combine all these methods to select exactly the element or node we require. For example:

```
book[@print_date = '1998-05-02']/title[. = 'Instant JavaScript']
```

to find the book titled 'Instant JavaScript' that was printed on 2nd May 1998, or:

```
/booklist//cover_design[issue = "final"]/*[@url = 'images']
```

to select all elements that:

- Have *any* name, but also have an attribute named `url` that has the value 'images' (from the `*[@url = 'images']` part);
- Are child elements of `cover_design` elements that themselves also have a child element named `issue` with the value 'final' (from the of `cover_design[issue = "final"]` part);
- Are descendents of the root `booklist` element (from the `/booklist//` part).

Note that the values of elements and attributes can be enclosed in single or double quotes.

Comparison Operators

The above examples all use the normal equality operator '=' to test if two values are equal. This works for numbers as well as strings. All XML values are strings by default, but IE5 casts them to appropriate data types before carrying out the comparison if possible. The data type chosen is based either on the content of the node value string, or on a **schema** (if one is present) that specifies the data type. This means that a comparison such as `[price = 29.95]` (without quotes around the numeric value) is perfectly valid.

If a schema is present and the content of the node cannot be cast into the type specified in the schema, for example if it contains characters that are illegal for that data type, such as letters in a numeric value, it is omitted from the set of matching nodes.

As well as the equality operator, there is a full set of other comparison operators:

Shortcut	Operator	Description
=	`$eq$`	Case-sensitive equality, for example `[price = 29.95]`
!=	`$ne$`	Case-sensitive inequality, for example `[category != 'Script']`
< *	`$lt$`	Case-sensitive less than, for example `[radius $lt$ 14.73]`
<= *	`$le$`	Case-sensitive less than or equal, for example `[age $le$ 18]`
>	`$gt$`	Case-sensitive greater than, for example `[name > 'H']`
>=	`$ge$`	Case-sensitive greater than or equal, for example `[speed >= 55]`
	`$ieq$`	Case-insensitive equality

Table Continued on Following Page

Shortcut	Operator	Description
	`$ine$`	Case-insensitive inequality
	`$ilt$`	Case-insensitive less than
	`$ile$`	Case-insensitive less than or equal
	`$igt$`	Case-insensitive greater than
	`$ige$`	Case-insensitive greater than or equal

** Note that the '<' and '<=' operators cannot be used un-escaped in XSL attributes, because these have to follow XML standards of well well-formed-ness. Instead, it is better to use the equivalent `$lt$` and `$le$`. Also note that all filter operators* ***names*** *(such as `$eq$`) are case sensitive, i.e. they must be all lower-case.*

The shortcut operators perform exactly the same operation as the longer version, so the following are equivalent:

```
[category = 'Scripting']
[category $eq$ 'Scripting']
```

as are:

```
[category != 'Scripting']
[category $ne$ 'Scripting']
```

The case-insensitive operators have no shortcut operator syntax. They are useful, however, when you need to match irrespective of case. There is no `UCase` or `LCase` function included in XSL (unless you provide your own script function), so it saves having to do multiple tests, i.e.:

```
[category = 'html' $or$ category = 'HTML']
```

Instead, we just use:

```
[category $ieq$ 'html']
```

Logical Filter Operators

As well as single comparison tests, we can use logical operators to combine patterns to build up more complex ones (as seen in the final example in the previous section). The logical operators are:

Shortcut	Operator	Description
`&&`	`$and$`	Logical AND
`||`	`$or$`	Logical OR
	`$not$`	Negation, logical NOT

So, using these we can do things like selecting books that have a <category> element that is either 'Scripting' or 'HTML':

```
book/[category = 'Scripting' $or$ category = 'HTML']
```

or which have the title 'Instant JavaScript' (case-insensitive match), but are not in the category 'Scripting':

```
book/[category $ne$ 'Scripting' $and$ title $ieq$ 'Instant JavaScript']
```

The not operator simply changes the 'truth' of the match, so the following are equivalent, and match <book> elements which have a child <category> element with the value 'Scripting' but no child <category> element with the value 'HTML' (thus excluding <book> elements which have child <category> elements with both values):

```
book/[category = 'Scripting' $and$ category $ne$ 'HTML']
book/[category = 'Scripting' $and$ $not$ category = 'HTML']
```

Filter Set Operators

Remember that all the above examples of filter patterns that use comparison operators rely on the fact that the default filter action, if no operator is specified in the filter, is to return any or all nodes that match the pattern. However, there are ways that we can specify more exactly which of the matching elements we want, in a similar way to using an index to specify the first element. We use the **set** operators, `$any$` and `$all$`:

Operator	Description
`$all$`	Returns `True` only if the specified pattern matches all of the items in the collection.
`$any$`	Returns `True` if the specified pattern matches any of the items in the collection.

The easiest way to appreciate the difference is to think about the way that elements are selected. For an element named <book>, we can specify that we want it to be included in the results if it has a <category> child element with the value 'HTML' by using the pattern:

```
book[category = 'HTML']
```

However, this will only match the <book> element if the *first* <category> element has the value 'HTML'. If it doesn't have this value, even if other (later) child elements do, the <book> element will not be selected. However, if we use the pattern:

```
book[$any$ category = 'HTML']
```

we will get a match for this <book> element, because we specified that we want the <book> elements where *any* of the child elements has the value 'HTML'. If we use the alternative set operator, `$all$`, we are specifying that we only want to select <book> elements where *all* of their category child elements have the value 'HTML', not just the first one or any one or more of them. For the book to be included in the results, they must all have the value 'HTML':

```
book[$all$ category = 'HTML']
```

Of course, if the book only has one <category> child element, with the value 'HTML', all three of these filters will return this book element. The differences only appear when the pattern specifies elements with more than one matching child (or other) element.

XSL Built-In Methods

We saw one of the built-in methods of XSL earlier on when looking at selecting elements by their index. The last node in a collection of matching nodes is returned by the `end()` method:

```
booklist/category[end()]
```

The Information Methods

Other **information** methods are available to help isolate a specific node in a collection:

Name	Description
`end()`	Selects and returns the last node in a collection.
`index()`	Selects and returns the index (number) of the current node within its collection.
`nodeName()`	Selects and returns the tag name of the current node, including any namespace prefix.
`nodeType()`	Selects and returns as a number the type of the node (as used in the DOM).
`date()`	Returns a value in date format.
`text()`	Selects and returns the text content of the current node.
`value()`	Returns a type cast version of the value of the current node.

The `value()` method is the default, so the following are equivalent:

```
book[category!value() = "Script"]
book[category = "Script"]
```

The exclamation mark operator (sometimes called the ***'bang'*** *operator) denotes that* `value()` *is a method of the* <category> *element. The normal use of a period (or 'full stop' character) here is not legal. It would be confused with the* ***current path*** *operator.*

The `index()` method is also optional when we want a specific element:

```
book[index() = 5]
book[5]
```

However, it is useful for selecting several elements, for example the fourth and fifth <book> elements only:

```
book[index() > 3 $and$ index() < 6]
```

The Collection Methods

It's also possible to select elements or other nodes using the **collection** methods supported by XSL in IE5:

Name	Description
`ancestor()`	Selects the ancestor node nearest to the current node that matches the pattern, starting at the parent node and working back up the document hierarchy. Returns a single element or `null` if none match.
`attribute()`	Selects all attribute nodes of the current node, returning them as a collection. The optional parameter can specify the attribute name to match.
`comment()`	Selects and returns as a collection all child comment nodes.
`element()`	Selects all child element nodes of the current node, returning them as a collection. The optional parameter can specify the element name to match.
`node()`	Selects and returns as a collection all child nodes that are not attributes.
`pi()`	Selects and returns as a collection all child processing instruction nodes.
`textnode()`	Selects and returns as a collection all child text nodes.

As an example, we can select all of the comment elements within our <book> elements using:

```
book/comment()
```

The `attribute()` and `element()` methods accept a text parameter that can be used to limit the matching nodes:

```
book/attribute('print_date')
```

Of course, this is equivalent to the '@' operator we saw earlier, so these provide the same result:

```
book/attribute('print_date')
book/@print_date
```

And the `element()` method is equivalent to the earlier syntax as well–these two provide the same result:

```
book/element('category')
book/category
```

The `ancestor()` method also accepts a text parameter containing the pattern to be matched. For example:

```
ancestor(book/category)
```

will match the nearest `<category>` ancestor node which is a child of a `<book>` element. Note that this method cannot occur to the right of a `'/'` or `'//'` in the pattern, and that, unlike the `attribute()` and `element()` methods, the name of the node to be matched should not be placed in quotes.

Important Note

Remember that, of all of the XML-related technologies, XSL is probably the most 'volatile' at the moment, in terms of changes that will come about in the language and syntax. There are subtle differences between the W3C working draft and Microsoft's implementation of XSL in IE5. You may wish to confine your development effort to experimental and induction projects until the future standards are more firmly established.

G

XSL Stylesheets DTD

The DTD below is taken from the World Wide Web Consortium Working Draft of 16-December-1998 posted at `http://www.w3.org/TR/WD-xsl`.

Editors

James Clark (jjc@jclark.com) [Tree Construction]
Stephen Deach, Adobe (sdeach@adobe.com) [Formatting Objects]

Copyright © 1998 W3C (MIT, INRIA, Keio), All Rights Reserved.
`http://www.w3.org/Consortium/Legal/` W3C liability, trademark, document use and software licensing rules apply

DTD for XSL Stylesheets

The following entity can be used to construct a DTD for XSL stylesheets that create instances of a particular result DTD. Before referencing the entity, the stylesheet DTD must define a `result-elements` parameter entity listing the allowed result element types. For example:

```
<!ENTITY % result-elements "
  | fo:inline-sequence
  | fo:block
">
<!ENTITY % instructions "
  | xsl:apply-templates
  | xsl:apply-imports
  | xsl:for-each
  | xsl:value-of
  | xsl:number
  | xsl:counter
  | xsl:counters
  | xsl:counter-increment
```

```
    | xsl:counter-reset
    | xsl:counter-scope
    | xsl:choose
    | xsl:if
    | xsl:contents
    | xsl:invoke
    | xsl:text
    | xsl:pi
    | xsl:comment
    | xsl:element
    | xsl:attribute
    | xsl:use
    | xsl:copy
">

<!ENTITY % template "
 (#PCDATA
  %instructions;
  %result-elements;)*
">

<!ENTITY % space-att "xml:space (default|preserve) #IMPLIED">

<!ELEMENT xsl:stylesheet
 (xsl:import*,
  (xsl:include
    | xsl:id
    | xsl:strip-space
    | xsl:preserve-space
    | xsl:macro
    | xsl:attribute-set
    | xsl:constant
    | xsl:template)*)
>

<!ATTLIST xsl:stylesheet
  result-ns NMTOKEN #IMPLIED
  default-space (preserve|strip) "preserve"
  indent-result (yes|no) "no"
  id ID #IMPLIED
  xmlns:xsl CDATA #FIXED "http://www.w3.org/TR/WD-xsl"
  %space-att;
>

<!-- Used for attribute values that are URIs.-->
<!ENTITY % URI "CDATA">

<!-- Used for attribute values that are patterns.-->
<!ENTITY % pattern "CDATA">

<!-- Used for attribute values that are a priority. -->
<!ENTITY % priority "NMTOKEN">

<!ELEMENT xsl:import EMPTY>
<!ATTLIST xsl:import href %URI; #REQUIRED>

<!ELEMENT xsl:include EMPTY>
<!ATTLIST xsl:include href %URI; #REQUIRED>
```

```
<!ELEMENT xsl:id EMPTY>
<!ATTLIST xsl:id
  attribute NMTOKEN #REQUIRED
  element NMTOKEN #IMPLIED
>

<!ELEMENT xsl:strip-space EMPTY>
<!ATTLIST xsl:strip-space element NMTOKEN #REQUIRED>

<!ELEMENT xsl:preserve-space EMPTY>
<!ATTLIST xsl:preserve-space element NMTOKEN #REQUIRED>

<!ELEMENT xsl:template %template;>
<!ATTLIST xsl:template
  match %pattern; #REQUIRED
  priority %priority; #IMPLIED
  mode NMTOKEN #IMPLIED
  %space-att;
>

<!ELEMENT xsl:value-of EMPTY>
<!ATTLIST xsl:value-of select CDATA #IMPLIED>

<!ENTITY % conversion-atts '
   format CDATA "1"
   xml:lang NMTOKEN #IMPLIED
   letter-value (alphabetic|other) #IMPLIED
   digit-group-sep CDATA #IMPLIED
   n-digits-per-group NMTOKEN #IMPLIED
   sequence-src %URI; #IMPLIED
'>

<!ELEMENT xsl:number EMPTY>
<!ATTLIST xsl:number
   level (single|multi|any) "single"
   count CDATA #IMPLIED
   from CDATA #IMPLIED
   %conversion-atts;
>

<!ELEMENT xsl:counter EMPTY>
<!ATTLIST xsl:counter
  name NMTOKEN #REQUIRED
  %conversion-atts;
>

<!ELEMENT xsl:counters EMPTY>
<!ATTLIST xsl:counters
  name NMTOKEN #REQUIRED
  %conversion-atts;
>

<!ELEMENT xsl:counter-increment EMPTY>
<!ATTLIST xsl:counter-increment
  name NMTOKEN #REQUIRED
  amount NMTOKEN #IMPLIED
>
```

```
<!ELEMENT xsl:counter-reset EMPTY>
<!ATTLIST xsl:counter-reset
  name NMTOKEN #REQUIRED
  value NMTOKEN #IMPLIED
>

<!ELEMENT xsl:counter-scope %template;>
<!ATTLIST xsl:counter-scope %space-att;>

<!ELEMENT xsl:apply-templates (xsl:sort*)>
<!ATTLIST xsl:apply-templates
  select %pattern; #IMPLIED
  mode NMTOKEN #IMPLIED
>

<!ELEMENT xsl:apply-imports EMPTY>

<!-- xsl:sort cannot occur after any other elements or
any non-whitespace character -->

<!ELEMENT xsl:for-each
 (#PCDATA
  %instructions;
  %result-elements;
  | xsl:sort)*
>

<!ATTLIST xsl:for-each
  select %pattern; #REQUIRED
  %space-att;
>

<!ELEMENT xsl:sort EMPTY>
<!ATTLIST xsl:sort
  select %pattern; "."
  lang CDATA #IMPLIED
  data-type (text|number) "text"
  order (ascending|descending) "ascending"
  case-order (upper-first|lower-first) #IMPLIED
>

<!ELEMENT xsl:if %template;>
<!ATTLIST xsl:if
  test %pattern; #REQUIRED
  %space-att;
>

<!ELEMENT xsl:choose (xsl:when+, xsl:otherwise?)>
<!ATTLIST xsl:choose %space-att;>

<!ELEMENT xsl:when %template;>
<!ATTLIST xsl:when
  test %pattern; #REQUIRED
  %space-att;
>

<!ELEMENT xsl:otherwise %template;>
<!ATTLIST xsl:otherwise %space-att;>
```

```
<!ELEMENT xsl:attribute-set (xsl:attribute|xsl:use)*>
<!ATTLIST xsl:attribute-set
  name NMTOKEN #REQUIRED
>

<!ELEMENT xsl:constant EMPTY>
<!ATTLIST xsl:constant
  name NMTOKEN #REQUIRED
  value CDATA #REQUIRED
>

<!-- xsl:macro-arg cannot occur after any other elements or
any non-whitespace character -->

<!ELEMENT xsl:macro
 (#PCDATA
  %instructions;
  %result-elements;
  | xsl:macro-arg)*
>

<!ATTLIST xsl:macro
  name NMTOKEN #REQUIRED
  %space-att;
>

<!ELEMENT xsl:macro-arg EMPTY>
<!ATTLIST xsl:macro-arg
  name NMTOKEN #REQUIRED
  default CDATA #IMPLIED
>

<!-- This is allowed only within xsl:macro -->
<!ELEMENT xsl:contents EMPTY>

<!-- xsl:arg cannot occur after any other elements or
any non-whitespace character -->

<!ELEMENT xsl:invoke
 (#PCDATA
  %instructions;
  %result-elements;
  | xsl:arg)*
>

<!ATTLIST xsl:invoke
  macro NMTOKEN #REQUIRED
  %space-att;
>

<!ELEMENT xsl:arg EMPTY>
<!ATTLIST xsl:arg
  name NMTOKEN #REQUIRED
  value CDATA #REQUIRED
>

<!ELEMENT xsl:text (#PCDATA)>
<!ATTLIST xsl:text %space-att;>
```

```
<!ELEMENT xsl:pi %template;>
<!ATTLIST xsl:pi
  name CDATA #REQUIRED
  %space-att;
>

<!ELEMENT xsl:element %template;>
<!ATTLIST xsl:element
  name CDATA #REQUIRED
  %space-att;
>

<!ELEMENT xsl:attribute %template;>
<!ATTLIST xsl:attribute
  name CDATA #REQUIRED
  %space-att;
>

<!ELEMENT xsl:use EMPTY>
<!ATTRIBUTE xsl:use attribute-set NMTOKEN #REQUIRED>

<!ELEMENT xsl:comment %template;>
<!ATTLIST xsl:comment %space-att;>

<!ELEMENT xsl:copy %template;>
<!ATTLIST xsl:copy %space-att;>
```

H

Links in XML

HTML has powered the web successfully for years with a linking system so simple that some in the SGML fraternity have sneered at it as too simple to be of any use. Well, the good news is that, not only is simple linking like this more than adequate for most needs, but XML supports more powerful linking as well using its own linking language, XLink, and another standard for finding a resource within a document, XPointer. If you think of a link to a point with an HTML document such as

```
<A href = "http://www.boynings.co.uk/index.htm#contact"></A>
```

which finds the contact details on my home page, you have an analogous situation. The URL up to and including `index.htm` would be part of an XLink link in XML, while the final `#contact` would use XPointer. In the page itself, I have the line:

```
<div Class="boynings"><a name="contact">Contact Information</a></div>
```

The `name="contact"` here indicates that this can be the destination of a link.

At the time of writing, the XLink and XPointer specifications were still at working draft stage at the World Wide Web Consortium, so we must apply the usual warnings that they will change before final publication. Neither is directly supported by Internet Explorer 5 at the moment, but, as we look at the recommendations themselves, we will look at how we can render some links for display in Internet Explorer 5.

Although Centaur does not use the XLink and XPointer recommendations (it might have had the standards been firm and Internet Explorer 5 supported them), I have found them sufficiently important in other applications that I will describe them in some detail here.

Some Terminology

I wrote the paragraph above without using much of the terminology associated with linking. However, to get further, it is important to understand the terms used when discussing links and pointers. The quotations included in this section are taken from the XLink working draft (`http://www.w3.org/TR/WD-xlink`). A **link** is an "explicit relationship between two or more data objects or portions of data objects". These data objects are known as **resources**, which might be **source** or **destination** resources. In the example above, the source was clearly the HTML anchor element (`<A href= ...>`) that contained the URL of the destination. The destination was the anchor element named `contact`. Both of these are known as **participating resources**. Following this link is known as **traversal**, which is simply "the action of using a link".

The `href` itself is known as the **locator** since it is used to locate the destination. This is both a **simple** link and an **inline** link: **simple** because it has only one locator, and **inline** because the source acts as one of its own resources. An **extended** link, conversely, "can connect any number of resources, not just one local resource (optionally) and one remote resource".

An extended link can also be **out-of-line** (in fact, a simple link can also be out-of-line, although this is less useful). This means that, "its content does not serve as one of the link's participating resources". That allows, for example, a database of links to be set up that is separate from the documents that act as the sources and destinations of the links. Why do that? We will see in a moment.

What Can I Do With XML Links?

This is a bit of a difficult question to answer, as the draft recommendation only describes the language for describing the links, not what a browser should do with them. However, in many cases, it is fairly clear how a browser could implement a link or a pointer.

The first, and most obvious, is for moving from one point in a document to another point in the same or another document. This is exactly the linking that is provided in HTML, and needs no further explanation. XLink actually provides three ways to do this: to replace the existing document with the new one (as is commonly done with HTML); to open a new window for the new document (also frequently done in HTML using the `target` attribute); or to embed the new document in the old one.

We could also use the capabilities of XLink so that, when we follow a link, we not only replace the source document in the window, but automatically open other windows showing related documents.

We can use XLink to provide a list of links related to a resource. We might, for example, use a technical term, and want to provide multiple references for it – perhaps one to a definition, another to a less formal description and others to related terms. We can do this by using a extended link with multiple locators. A browser could render this as a list of links that pops up when you click on the source resource, as we shall do in a moment.

The XLink draft also allows us to traverse links in either direction. For example, a description of a herb could provide links to recipes that use it. In the recipes, we could equally follow the link the other way to find out more about the herb we are using.

Perhaps most important of all the changes from HTML links in terms of usability of the web is the ability to hold links in a database. We have looked at the meaning of **inline** links. **Out-of-line** links are held separately from the source and destination resources. So, if I decide to move my home page, instead of every page that links to it causing a broken link (and I don't necessarily know who is linking to my home page), I could maintain a link database and just change one entry. If other sites use this database to find my home page, their links will be automatically repaired.

Another useful feature of out-of-line links is that they enable someone to set up links from source documents where they do not have permission to write to the document. Since both the source and destination locators are held in a separate document, this is useful to provide annotations or comments on other people's documents.

Simple Links

Simple links effectively emulate the hypertext linking of HTML, although they are slightly more powerful. All XLinks are identified by including an `xml:link` attribute in an element start tag, with a value indicating whether this is a simple or extended link. A simple link also needs a locator and may have some additional attributes. An example would be:

```
Have a look at my <mylink xml:link="simple"
href="http://www.boynings.co.uk/index.htm">home page</mylink>
```

If we were to define `mylink` in a DTD, we could include the `xml:link="simple"` there, indicating that all instances of `mylink` elements are simple links and save typing every time we use one:

```
<!ELEMENT mylink (#PCDATA)>
<!ATTLIST mylink
     xml:link          CDATA    #FIXED "simple"
     href              CDATA    #REQUIRED
     content-role      CDATA    #IMPLIED
>
```

We could now use the `mylink` element as:

```
Have a look at my <mylink href="http://www.boynings.co.uk/index.htm">home
page</mylink>
```

As well as indicting whether a link is inline or out-of-line, we can define its **role** and **title**. The role indicates to an application the purpose of the resource (both source and destination resources can have roles). A resource could, for example, be tagged as an author's biography, to be displayed when clicking on an author's name. The title is simply a title for the link that a browser can use if it wishes. This could, for example, be implemented as a ToolTip when the mouse is held over the resource.

There are three other optional attributes that can be present in a simple link. I have already mentioned that the result of actuating a link can be to replace the source document, open a new window or embed the target in the source. This behavior is determined by the **show** attribute, which, not suprisingly, can have the values `embed`, `replace` or `new`.

There is an **actuate** attribute, which can take the values `auto` or `user` to indicate whether the link is to be actuated automatically or on some user action (such as clicking on the source resource).

The final attribute is **behavior**. This provides the application with a detailed indication of how it is to treat the link. While `show` and `actuate` are examples of behaviors that are built into the XLink recommendation, this attribute allows more detailed behaviors to be defined.

Extended Links

The power of XLink really shows when we start using extended links. As we saw earlier, an extended link can connect any number of resources, and can be declared as out-of-line. It is these features that allow us to use links in some of the ways we discussed earlier.

Inline Extended Links

An inline extended link could be used to provide several targets from a single source resource. For example, when I mention a book, I may want to provide links relating to the book itself, the author and the publisher. I could even provide a link to Amazon.com or some other source for buying the book. I could do this in HTML or with simple links by including each of these links separately. With an extended link, I can reference each destination resource in a single link.

Since Internet Explorer 5 does not support extended linking, let's see how we can implement an inline extended link using a script:

```
<HTML>
<HEAD>
<STYLE>
  .link
  {
    color = "blue";
    text-decoration = "underline";
    cursor = "hand";
  }
</STYLE>
</HEAD>
<BODY onLoad = "onLoad()">
<DIV Id="tgtResult"></DIV>

<XML Id="Island">
<?xml version="1.0"?>
<para>I have just discovered this great book called<space />
<extended xml:link="extended" inline="true">
  <locator href="http://www.boynings.co.uk" title="Author's home page" />
  <locator href="http://www.wrox.com" title="Publisher's home page" />
  <locator href="http://www.amazon.com" title="Bookshop" />
  XML Design and Implementation
</extended>
. You should go out and buy it.
</para>
</XML>
<SCRIPT>
function onLoad()
{
  var root,i,j,lstNode;
  var strResult = "";

  dom = Island;
  if (dom.parseError != 0)
    alert(dom.parseError.reason);
  root = dom.documentElement;
```

```
  for (i = 0 ; i < root.childNodes.length ; i++)
  {
    node = root.childNodes.item(i);

    // first the text nodes
    if (node.nodeType == 3)
      strResult += node.text;

    // then the extended links
    else if (node.nodeName == "extended")
    {
      strResult += "<SPAN id='list' style='display:none'>";
      strResult += "<SELECT onChange='select(this)'>";
      strResult += "<OPTION selected>Select a link to follow</OPTION>";
      lstNode = node.childNodes;

      // now we have the locators and the text that follows
      for (j = 0 ; j < lstNode.length ; j++)
      {
        // the text element
        if (lstNode.item(j).nodeType == 3)
        {
          strResult += "</SELECT></SPAN>";
          strResult += "<SPAN id='link' class='link' onclick='displayList()'>"
          strResult += lstNode.item(j).text;
          strResult += "</SPAN>";
        }
        else if (lstNode.item(j).nodeName == "locator")
        // the locators
        {
          strResult += "<OPTION value=";
          strResult += "'" + lstNode.item(j).getAttribute("href") + "'";
          strResult += ">";
          strResult += lstNode.item(j).getAttribute("title");
          strResult += "</OPTION>";
        }

        else
          alert("Inline.htm error: The node type=" + lstNode.item(j).nodeType + ",
name=" + lstNode.item(j).nodeName + " is not permitted within a locator element");
      }
    }
    else if (node.nodeName == "space")
      strResult += " ";
    else
      alert("Inline.htm error: This node type is not permitted");
  }
//  alert(strResult);
  tgtResult.innerHTML = strResult;
}

function displayList()
{
  list.style.display = "";
  link.style.display = "none";
}
```

```
function displayText()
{
  list.style.display = "none";
  link.style.display = "";
}

function select(selection)
{
  var idx,dest;

  idx = selection.selectedIndex;
  if (idx != 0)
  {
    dest = selection.options[idx].value;
    window.open(dest,"","resizable=yes");
  }
  displayText();
}
</SCRIPT>
</BODY>
</HTML>
```

When the page is loaded, it looks like this:

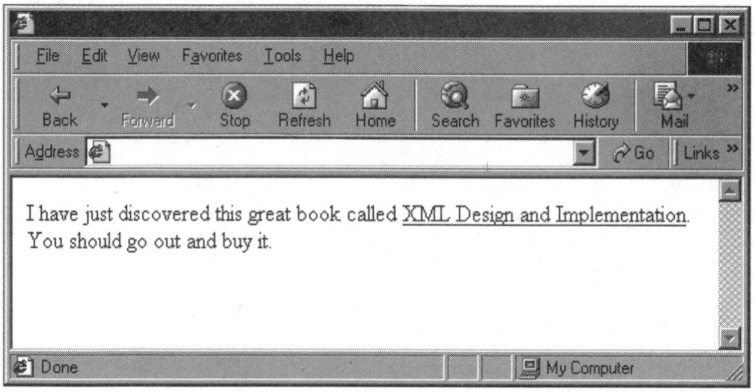

If I now click on the underlined text, I see:

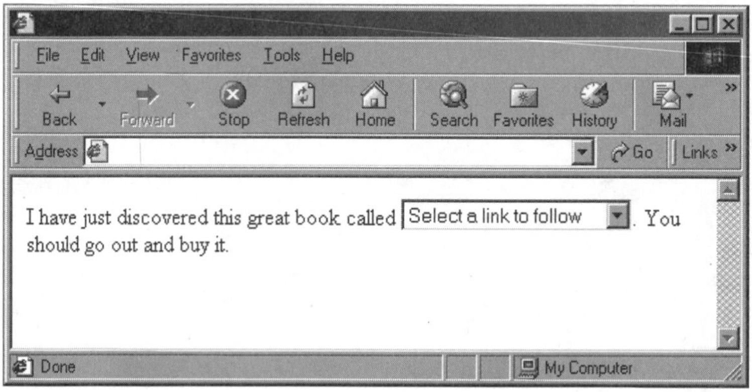

I can then use the drop-down box like on any normal HTML page:

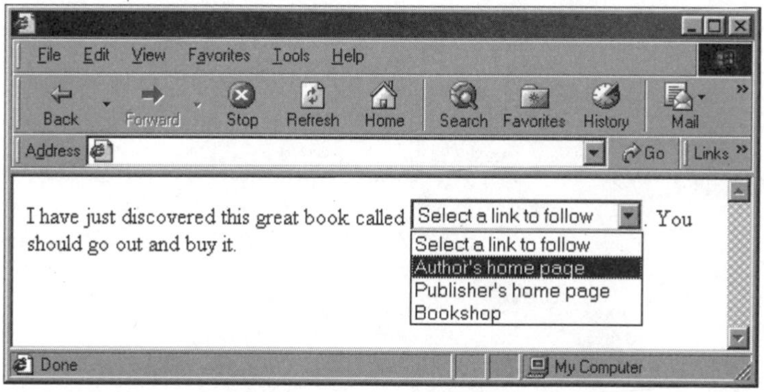

If I select the text Author's home page, the original window is returned to its previous state as shown in the first of the above diagrams and my home page is retrieved in a new window:

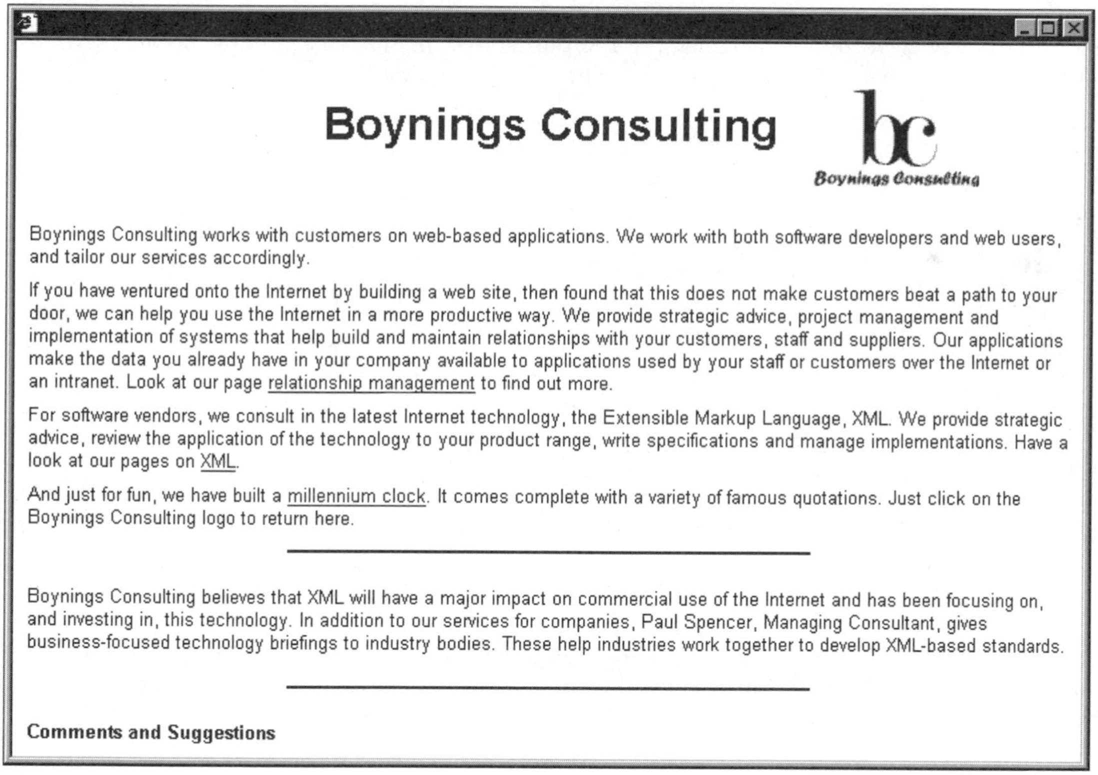

Boynings Consulting
bc
Boynings Consulting
Boynings Consulting works with customers on web-based applications. We work with both software developers and web users, and tailor our services accordingly.
If you have ventured onto the Internet by building a web site, then found that this does not make customers beat a path to your door, we can help you use the Internet in a more productive way. We provide strategic advice, project management and implementation of systems that help build and maintain relationships with your customers, staff and suppliers. Our applications make the data you already have in your company available to applications used by your staff or customers over the Internet or an intranet. Look at our page relationship management to find out more.
For software vendors, we consult in the latest Internet technology, the Extensible Markup Language, XML. We provide strategic advice, review the application of the technology to your product range, write specifications and manage implementations. Have a look at our pages on XML.
And just for fun, we have built a millennium clock. It comes complete with a variety of famous quotations. Just click on the Boynings Consulting logo to return here.
Boynings Consulting believes that XML will have a major impact on commercial use of the Internet and has been focusing on, and investing in, this technology. In addition to our services for companies, Paul Spencer, Managing Consultant, gives business-focused technology briefings to industry bodies. These help industries work together to develop XML-based standards.
Comments and Suggestions

The basic technique of building up an HTML string and using dynamic HTML to insert it into a `DIV` element is familiar by now, so I shall not describe that here.

The XML itself looks like this (`inline.htm`):

```
<XML Id="Island">
<?xml version="1.0"?>
<para>I have just discovered this great book called<space />
<extended xml:link="extended" inline="true">
  <locator href="http://www.boynings..co.uk" title="Author's home page"
  />
  <locator href="http://www.wrox.com" title="Publisher's home page" />
  <locator href="http://www.amazon.com" title="Bookshop" />
  XML Design and Implementation
</extended>
. You should go out and buy it.
</para>
</XML>
```

This is somewhat limited – I can only have a single `para` element since it is my root element. Later, I restrict this to text and the `space` and `extended` elements. It would obviously be simple to change this at the cost of additional code.

In the script, I check for errors reported by the parser and find the root element in the standard way, then loop through each child node taking the appropriate action. Since the children of the `para` element can only be text, spaces, or extended elements, I treat all others as errors:

```
  for (i = 0 ; i < root.childNodes.length ; i++)
  {
    node = root.childNodes.item(i);

    // first the text nodes
    if (node.nodeType == 3)
      ...

    // then the extended links
    else if (node.nodeName == "extended")
      ...

    // then the spaces
    else if (node.nodeName == "space")
      strResult += " ";

    // anything else is an error
    else
      alert("Inline.htm error: This node type is not permitted");
  }
```

Naturally, most of the work is done in the code handling the extended links. In the display, we want to show the text XML Design and Implementation, and only display the drop-down list on demand. Both of these are therefore put in named `SPAN` elements, the `SPAN` for the drop-down list having a style of `hidden`.

The first thing is simply to set up an HTML string for the drop-down list, with the first entry hard-coded and an action when a list entry is selected:

```
    strResult += "<SPAN id='list' style='display:none'>";
    strResult += "<SELECT onChange='select(this)'>";
    strResult += "<OPTION selected>Select a link to follow</OPTION>";
```

Then we can find the child elements of the extended element:

```
lstNode = node.childNodes;
```

These will be the locator elements followed by the text to display. We loop through these, handling the text node first. We set this up as something that looks like an HTML link (using a cascading style sheet on the "link" class):

```
        // the text element
        if (lstNode.item(j).nodeType == 3)
        {
          strResult += "</SELECT></SPAN>";
          strResult += "<SPAN id='link' class='link' onclick='displayList()'>"
          strResult += lstNode.item(j).text;
          strResult += "</SPAN>";
```

Then we handle the locator elements, setting them up as options on the drop down list. We display the title attribute from the element, while setting the value to the href:

```
else if (lstNode.item(j).nodeName == "locator")
        // the locators
        {
          strResult += "<OPTION value=";
          strResult += "'" + lstNode.item(j).getAttribute("href") + "'";
          strResult += ">";
          strResult += lstNode.item(j).getAttribute("title");
          strResult += "</OPTION>";
        }
```

After handling the <space /> element, we treat anything else as an error:

```
        else
          alert("Inline.htm error: The node type=" + lstNode.item(j).nodeType + ",
name=" + lstNode.item(j).nodeName + " is not permitted within a locator element");
```

By uncommenting the alert(strResult); towards the end of the function, we can see the string that is created:

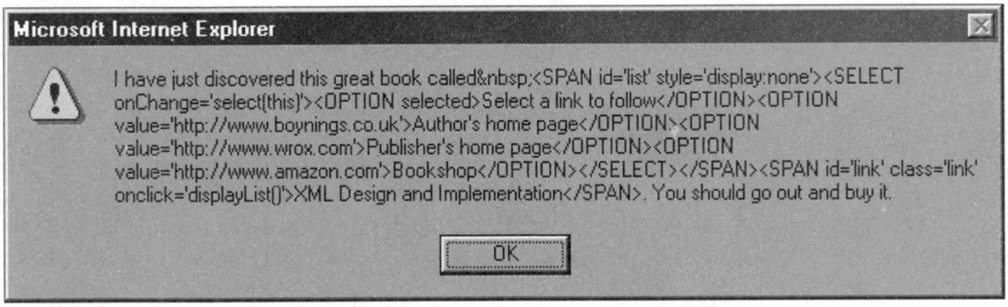

So that just leaves the code that is run when actions are taken:

```
function select(selection)
{
  var idx,dest;

  idx = selection.selectedIndex;
  if (idx != 0)
  {
    dest = selection.options[idx].value;
    window.open(dest,"","resizable=yes");
  }
  displayText();
}
```

When any option other than the first (which is just to show the link again) is selected, a new window is opened and loaded with the page pointed to by the `href`. In all cases, a small function, `displayText()` sets the display style of the text to an empty string (i.e. displayed) and the display style of the drop down list back to "none".

As implemented here, the code is specific to the piece of XML embedded in the XML island at the start of the document. If you want the technique for general use, I suggest writing a function that takes a parameter of the extended link and returns the display HTML as a well-formed HTML node. It is then simple to include the function in documents, pass it the link, and replace the original node with the new one in the document. Once you have done this, you can, if you wish, pass the modified XML source to the parser with an XSL style sheet using the `transformNodes()` method as we have done before. All you need to do in the style sheet is make sure that all the HTML elements are passed to the output using `xsl:copy` as we did with the Scottish play in Chapter 5.

Out-of-Line Extended Links

So far with our links, we have not had to think too much about what we mean by a "link". The concept of clicking on a piece of blue underlined text (even though these days the text is not always blue or underlined) and loading a new page is familiar from the current HTML-based web. However, these links are actually performing two functions – they are declaring a connection between the resources and defining an action.

The XLink simple link separates these by allowing us to define the action within the link element using the `show` attribute. Our example of handling inline extended links merely extended the addressing side of link behavior by providing a drop-down list of addresses to move to. With out-of-line extended links, it is clearer that all we are doing is asserting that there is a connection between resources, without specifying what to do with this connection.

Let's look at how out-of-line extended links could be used in Centaur had they been supported by Internet Explorer 5. We have several (OK then – two) tour operators and a list of vacations. Although these vacations are stored in a database, we have already seen that they could have been stored as documents instead, possibly by extracting the data from the database. Clearly there is a link between the tour operators and the vacations. In fact this link is defined by using the tour operator code as a foreign key field in the database.

We could define this connection as:

```
<panorama xml:link="extended" inline="false" title="Vacations with Panorama">
  <locator xml:link="locator" href="panorama.xml" title="Panorama" />
  <locator xml:link="locator" href="aziza.xml" title="Hotel Aziza" />
  <locator xml:link="locator" href="fourati.xml" title="Hotel Fourati" />
  ...
</panorama>
```

Of course, we could do this equally well defining the sports available at a resort or any other connection between documents.

Having defined these links, we could build an application that uses them in whatever way we like. Although we have no access to the pages describing the tour operators or the pages describing the hotels, we could build a new page that uses the information provided in the links.

Earlier, we looked at some uses for links in XML. The XLink draft mentions four uses for out-of-line extended links:

- Enabling outgoing links from documents that cannot be modified to add an inline link
- Creating links to and from resources in formats with no native support for embedded links (such as most multimedia formats)
- Applying and filtering sets of relevant links on demand
- Enabling other advanced hypermedia capabilities

Extended Link Groups

If you think about how Centaur could have been produced using just sets of XML pages with XLink links between them, you can imagine that the numbers of out-of-line extended links could be fairly large. On a bigger site, they would become unmanageable, and on the whole Internet unimaginable. The XLink draft therefore allows links to be grouped. Thus one document could include the out-of-line link group:

```
<links xml:link="group">
  <doc xml:link="document" href="linkdoc1.xml" />
  <doc xml:link="document" href="linkdoc2.xml" />
</links>
```

where `linkdoc1.xml` and `linkdoc2.xml` identify documents containing further out-of-line links. Of course, these could also be group links and point to other documents containing group links. To stop this getting out of control, the XLink draft provides an optional attribute **steps** that limits how many links are to be traversed. How this is to be implemented is not defined in the working draft.

XPointers

While the XLink language defines links between documents, the XPointer language defines how to point to specific points or areas within a document. As discussed earlier, in HTML terms, this is analogous to the `#contact` part of the HTML link:

```
<A href = "http://www.boynings.co.uk/index.htm#contact"></A>
```

As you would expect, XPointers provide additional functionality that makes them more powerful than this.

It is likely that the only people who will use any but the simplest of XPointers at the moment are those who are writing software to handle them. Therefore, I am not going to go through the XPointer language in detail, but instead show some examples to give you an idea of what will become available.

Let's start with a familiar XML document (`macbeth.xml`), then see what we can do with it. For reasons that will become apparent, I have added some `id` attributes to some elements. The lines containing these are highlighted.

```
<?xml version="1.0"?>
<?xml-stylesheet type="text/css" href="macbethxml.css"?>
<play>
  <title>The Tragedy of Macbeth</title>

  <fm>
    <P>Text placed in the public domain by Moby Lexical Tools, 1992.</P>
    <P>SGML markup by Jon Bosak, 1992-1994.</P>
    <P>XML version by Jon Bosak, 1996-1997.</P>
    <P>This work may be freely copied and distributed worldwide.</P>
  </fm>

  <scndescr>SCENE  Scotland: England.</scndescr>

  <playsubt>MACBETH</playsubt>

  <act id="act1">
    <title>ACT I</title>
    <scene id="scene1">
      <title>SCENE I.  A desert place.</title>

      <stagedir>Thunder and lightning. Enter three Witches</stagedir>
```

A definition before we continue: a **location term** simply specifies a location in the document. It is the combination of location terms that identifies the precise location being referenced. Many locations are identified relative to the current location term, so it is always important to understand what the current location is.

In the XML extract above, an XPointer could reference the first `scene` element of the first `act` element as:

```
root().child(1,act).child(1,scene)
```

If this were being referenced from outside the document, we could specify a link as:

```
<speech xml:link="simple" href="macbeth.xml#root().child(1,act).child(1,scene)">
```

Note that the indexes start from 1, not 0, to access the first element. The `root()` ensures that the reference is from the root element of the document, but is not strictly necessary as this is assumed if no other absolute term is used. Also unnecessary is the second `child` keyword, since this is assumed if no other keyword is used. The XPointer above is therefore equivalent to:

```
<speech xml:link="simple" href="macbeth.xml#child(1,act).(1,scene)">
```

The hash (#) is known as a **connector**, and indicates to the application that the whole document is to be retrieved, then the XPointer processing is to be performed on the client. This is exactly analogous to HTML, where we would expect the complete document to be sent to the browser, but the start of Act 1 Scene 1 to be visible on the screen. There is an alternative connector (|), which does not specify any processing model. Presumably, in most cases, the server will then process the XPointer, sending only the part of the document specified to the client. The use of connectors is actually defined as part of the XLink, rather than the XPointer language.

So what other absolute terms can be used? One is `origin()`, which can be thought of as the current point in the document. Clearly, this only has meaning for links within the same document. If we are at the start of the first speech of scene 1, we could reference the third speech as:

```
origin().fsibling(2,speech)
```

In this case, `fsibling` indicates that we are looking for the second following sibling (i.e. child of the same parent element) from our current point in the document.

As well as following siblings, we can specify preceding siblings (`psibling`), any descendants (`descendant`) and ancestors (`ancestor`) of the current sub-resource, immediate children (`child`) or nodes preceding (`preceding`) or following (`following`) the current sub-resource.

Not surprisingly, we can identify not only element nodes, but also other XML node types, such as processing instructions and comments and can also identify nodes by their attributes.

Finding Nodes by ID

So far, we have found nodes by their position in the document. While Shakespeare plays may not change over time, other documents certainly will. The XPointer draft therefore allows and encourages the use of the `id` attribute to identify the destination of a pointer. This is clearly a more robust mechanism, and could, for example, be used to identify the Chairman's report in a company annual report as having `id="chairmansReport"` rather than by its being, say, the third major section in the document. Returning to our play, we could find Act 1 Scene 1 using the attributes I mentioned that I had added by:

```
<speech xml:link="simple" href="macbeth.xml#act1.scene1">
```

This is clearly not only more robust, but also more obvious to both write and read.

The html Keyword

This keyword is included to allow XPointers to reference parts of HTML documents, that use the anchor (`<A>`) tag to identify a destination. As the working draft puts it:

If an XPointer begins with `html(NAMEVALUE)`, the location source is the first element whose type is `A` and which has an attribute called `NAME` whose value is the same as the supplied `NAMEVALUE`. This is exactly the function performed by the "#" fragment identifier in the context of an HTML document.

Extracting a Section of a Document

Earlier, I mentioned use of the | connector as possibly being used to extract a segment of a document. This could be useful in all sorts of ways. For example, I do not have a permanent connection to the Internet, so I like to download W3C recommendations and other specifications and store them locally for later use. In many cases, this is easy as they are single documents. In others, it is hard as long documents have been divided to save download time for people who are reading extracts on-line. While sometimes there is a Zip file I can download, in others there is not. If these documents were saved as XML files using XPointers, the complete document could be stored in a single file, but people could choose whether to get the complete document or an extract defined by XPointers within the Table of Contents. How would this be done? By using the `span` keyword.

This keyword simply allows you to specify a start and end point for the sub-resource you want. The speeches in the first scene of the first act of our play could be identified as:

```
span(act1.scene1.#element(1,speech),act1.scene1.#element(-1,speech))
```

The use of the `span` keyword is self-explanatory. The other point shown here is that positive integers identify elements counting forwards from the current location, while negative integers count backwards from the last matching element to the first.

Finding Partial Nodes

So far, we have only looked at using XPointers to find sub-resources that are complete nodes. It is possible to find partial nodes by using the `string` keyword. This simply looks for text strings in the document, ignoring all tags. For this reason, we can find partial elements or even text that spans different elements.

I could, for example find the second, third and fourth characters of the second `speech` element as:

```
act1.scene1.(2,speech).string(2,"",,3)
```

The digit `2` indicates that I am looking for the second occurrence of something. The empty string that follows indicates that the "something" is any character, then the `3` indicates that I want to extract three characters. The missing field is a position field that would allow me to specify an offset before I start retrieving characters. Don't ask me why I might want to get the string "irs", but the point is that I can!

I mentioned before that this allows us to span elements. I could instead have used the XPointer:

```
act1.scene1.(2,speech).string(7,"",,15)
```

This would extract the text "WitchWhen shall". Note that there is no space between "Witch" and "When" as there is none in the original text.

Summary

In this appendix we have shown you the core ideas and syntax involved in XLink and XPointer. For more information, read the working drafts at `http://www.w3.org/TR` .

Support and Errata

One of the most irritating things about any programming book can be when you find that bit of code you've just spent an hour typing in simply doesn't work. You check it a hundred times to see if you've set it up correctly and then you notice the spelling mistake in the variable name on the book page. Grrr! Of course, you can blame the authors for not taking enough care and testing the code, the editors for not doing their job properly, or the proofreaders for not being eagle-eyed enough, but this doesn't get around the fact that mistakes do happen.

We try hard to ensure no mistakes sneak out into the real world, but we can't promise that this book is 100% error free. What we can do is offer the next best thing by providing you with immediate support and feedback from experts who have worked on the book and try to ensure that future editions eliminate these gremlins. The following section will take you step by step through the process of posting errata to our web site to get that help. The sections that follow, therefore, are:

- Wrox Developers Membership
- Finding a list of existing errata on the web site
- Adding your own errata to the existing list
- What happens to your erratum once you've posted it (why doesn't it appear immediately?)

There is also a section covering how to e-mail a question for technical support. This comprises:

- What your e-mail should include
- What happens to your e-mail once it has been received by us

So that you only need view information relevant to yourself, we ask that you register as a Wrox Developer Member. This is a quick and easy process, that will save you time in the long-run. If you are already a member, just update your membership to include this book.

Wrox Developer's Membership

To get your FREE Wrox Developer's Membership click on Membership in the navigation bar of our home site

www.wrox.com.

This is shown in the following screen shot:

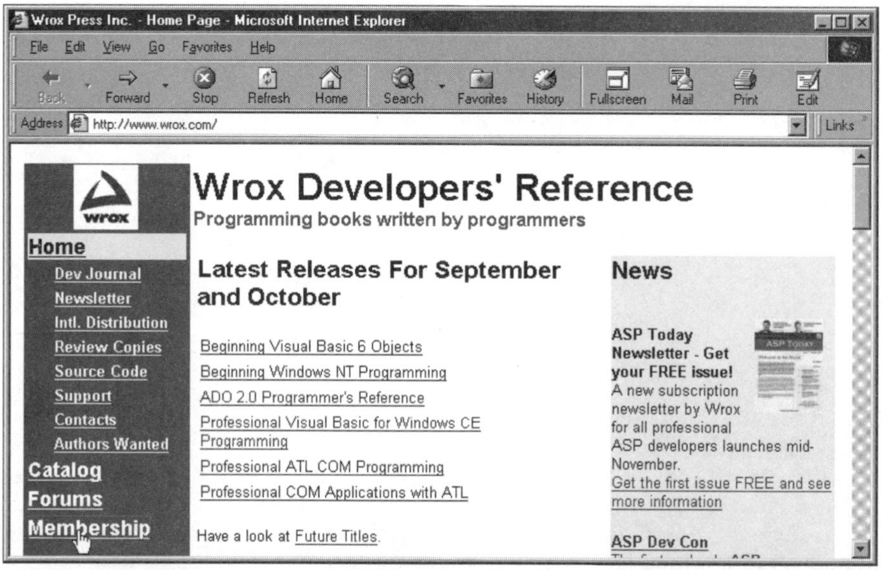

Then, on the next screen (not shown), click on New User. This will display a form. Fill in the details on the form and submit the details using the submit button at the bottom. Before you can say 'The best read books come in Wrox Red' you will get this screen:

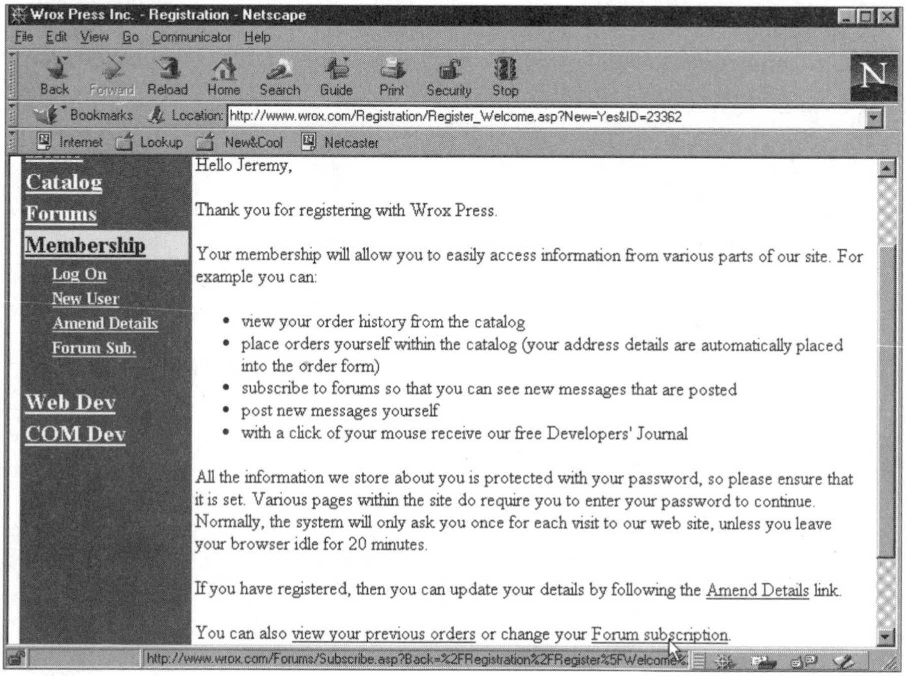

Finding an Errata on the Web Site

Before you send in a query, you might be able to save time by finding the answer to your problem on our web site: **`http:\\www.wrox.com`**.

Each book we publish has its own page and its own errata sheet. You can get to any book's page by clicking on support from the left hand side navigation bar.

From this page you can locate any books errata page on our site. Select your book from the pop-up menu and click on it.

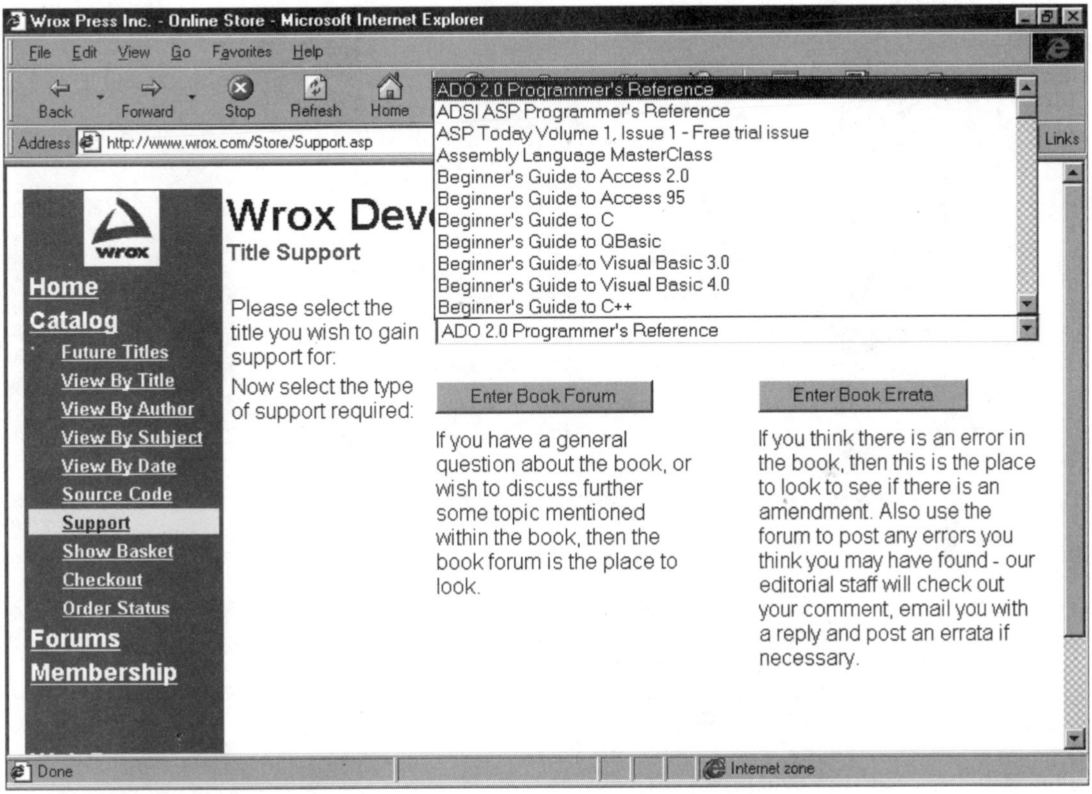

Then click on Enter Book Errata. This will take you to the errata page for the book. Select the criteria by which you want to view the errata, and click the apply criteria button. This will provide you with links to specific errata. For an initial search, you are advised to view the errata by page numbers. If you have looked for an error previously, then you may wish to limit your search using dates. We update these pages daily to ensure that you have the latest information on bugs and errors.

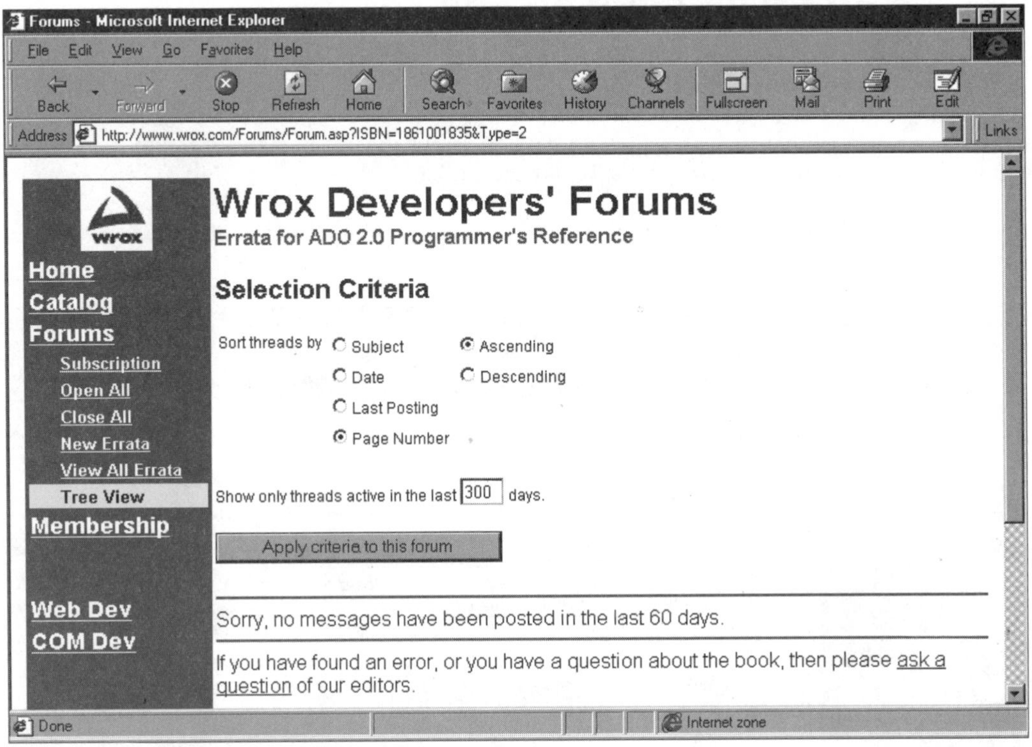

Adding an Errata to the Sheet Yourself

It's always possible that you may find that your error is not listed, in which case you can enter details of the fault yourself. It might be anything from a spelling mistake to a faulty piece of code in the book. Sometimes you'll find useful hints that aren't really errors on the listing. By entering errata you may save another reader hours of frustration, and of course, you will be helping us provide even higher quality information. We're very grateful for this sort of advice and feedback. You can enter errata using the 'ask a question' of our editors link at the bottom of the errata page. Click on this link and you will get a form on which to post your message.

Fill in the subject box, and then type your message in the space provided on the form. Once you have done this, click on the Post Now button at the bottom of the page. The message will be forwarded to our editors. They'll then test your submission and check that the error exists, and that the suggestions you make are valid. Then your submission, together with a solution, is posted on the site for public consumption. Obviously this stage of the process can take a day or two, but we will endeavor to get a fix up sooner than that.

E-mail Support

If you wish to directly query a problem in the book with an expert who knows the book in detail then e-mail `support@wrox.com`, with the title of the book and the last four numbers of the ISBN in the subject field of the e-mail. Your e-mail **MUST** include the title of the book the problem relates to, otherwise we won't be able to help you. The diagram below shows what else your e-mail should include:

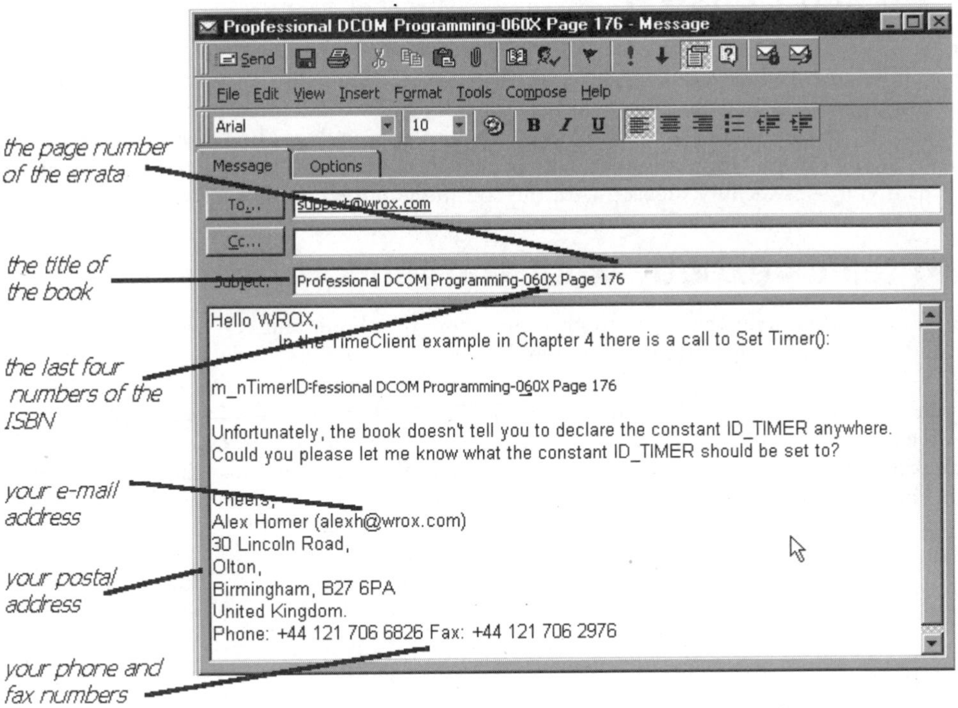

We won't send you junk mail. We need the details to save your time and ours. If we need to replace a disk or CD we'll be able to get it to you straight away. When you send an e-mail it will go through the following chain of support:

Customer Support

Your message is delivered to one of our customer support staff who are the first people to read it. They have files on most frequently asked questions and will answer anything general immediately. They answer general questions about the book and the web site.

Editorial

Deeper queries are forwarded to the technical editor responsible for that book. They have experience with the programming language or particular product and are able to answer detailed technical questions on the subject. Once an issue has been resolved, the editor can post the errata to the web site.

The Authors

Finally, in the unlikely event that the editor can't answer your problem, s/he will forward the request to the author. We try to protect the author from any distractions from writing. However, we are quite happy to forward specific requests to them. All Wrox authors help with the support on their books. They'll mail the customer and the editor with their response, and again all readers should benefit.

What we can't answer

Obviously with an ever growing range of books and an ever-changing technology base, there is an increasing volume of data requiring support. While we endeavor to answer all questions about the book, we can't answer bugs in your own programs that you've adapted from our code. So, while you might have loved the help desk systems in our Active Server Pages book, don't expect too much sympathy if you cripple your company with a live adaptation you customized from Chapter 12. But do tell us if you're especially pleased with the routine you developed with our help.

How to tell us exactly what you think

We understand that errors can destroy the enjoyment of a book and can cause many wasted and frustrated hours, so we seek to minimize the distress that they can cause.

You might just wish to tell us how much you liked or loathed the book in question. Or you might have ideas about how this whole process could be improved. In which case you should e-mail **`feedback@wrox.com`**. You'll always find a sympathetic ear, no matter what the problem is. Above all you should remember that we do care about what you have to say and we will do our utmost to act upon it.

Index

D

O

P

Q

R

S

T

Wrox writes books for you. Any suggestions, or ideas about how you want information given in your ideal book will be studied by our team. Your comments are always valued at Wrox.

Free phone in USA 800-USE-WROX
Fax (312) 893 8001

UK Tel. (0121) 687 4100 Fax (0121) 687 4101

Beginning Access 2000 VBA - Registration Card

Name ______________________

Address ______________________

____

____

____

City ____________ State/Region ____________

Country ____________ Postcode/Zip ____________

E-mail ______________________

Occupation ______________________

How did you hear about this book? ____________

- ☐ Book review (name) ____________
- ☐ Advertisement (name) ____________
- ☐ Recommendation ____________
- ☐ Catalog ____________
- ☐ Other ____________

Where did you buy this book? ____________

- ☐ Bookstore (name) ____________ City ____________
- ☐ Computer Store (name) ____________
- ☐ Mail Order ____________
- ☐ Other ____________

What influenced you in the purchase of this book?

- ☐ Cover Design
- ☐ Contents
- ☐ Other (please specify) ____________

How did you rate the overall contents of this book?

- ☐ Excellent ☐ Good
- ☐ Average ☐ Poor

What did you find most useful about this book? ____________

What did you find least useful about this book? ____________

Please add any additional comments. ____________

What other subjects will you buy a computer book on soon? ____________

What is the best computer book you have used this year?

____

Note: This information will only be used to keep you updated about new Wrox Press titles and will not be used for any other purpose or passed to any other third party.

wrox

PROGRAMMER TO PROGRAMMER™

NB. If you post the bounce back card below in the UK, please send it to:

Wrox Press Ltd., Arden House, 1102 Warwick Road,
Acocks Green, Birmingham B27 6BH, UK.

Computer Book Publishers

NO POSTAGE
NECESSARY
IF MAILED
IN THE
UNITED STATES

BUSINESS REPLY MAIL

FIRST CLASS MAIL PERMIT#64 CHICAGO, IL

POSTAGE WILL BE PAID BY ADDRESSEE

WROX PRESS
1512 NORTH FREMONT
SUITE 103
CHICAGO IL 60622-2567

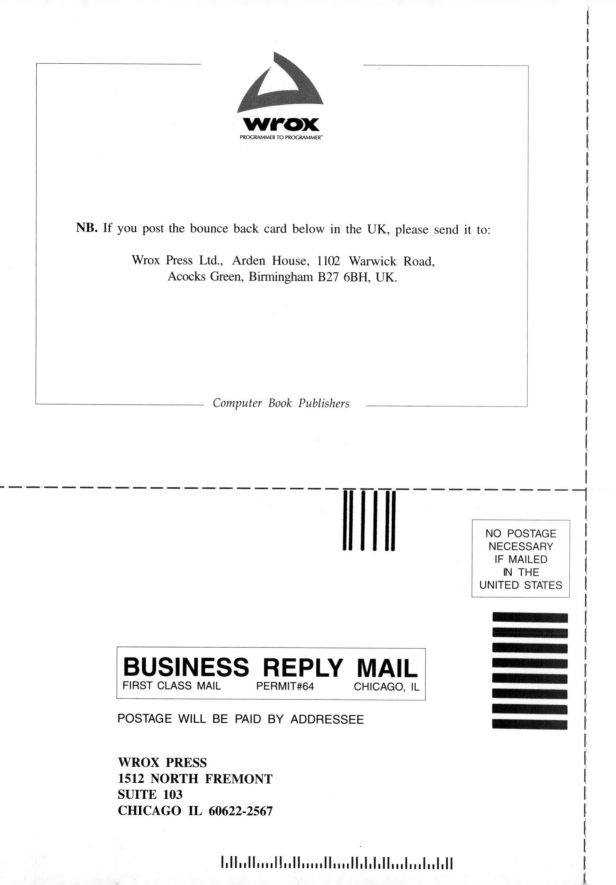